DAY BY DAY THROUGH THE
in a Northamptonshire Mark

The Diary of John Coleman Binder
Grocer, Baker and Town Councillor in Oundle

July 25 1914 to November 12 1918

Published by Oundle Museum Trust
Charity Commission Reg. No.1045378
Transcribed by Alice Thomas
ISBN 978-0-9927232-0-0

Printed By BookPrinting UK Peterborough

These Diaries, kept during the 1914-18 War, by John Coleman Binder. Then living at No 8 Stoke Hill Oundle. And keeping the shop + bakehouse on Binders Row, Benefield Rd. Now burnt down + new cottages built. Were given to me. Percy Charles Edward Clarke. by. Mrs Binder, Johns widow in the year 1938.

I am very grateful to the late Mr. P. C. E. Clarke and his family for allowing me to transcribe the nine volumes of J.C.Binder's Diary.

I thank Oundle Rotary, Mr A. Hayward, Mr D.C. Wills, Peterborough Museum and Oundle Museum for permission to use the photographs.

I have had vital help from my son Mark Stephens with computer problems and Binder family history, and my husband Ioan Thomas has greatly encouraged and assisted me in preparing the Diary for publication.

© Copyright Oundle Museum
Published by Oundle Museum 2013

ISBN 978-0-9927232-0-0

Obtainable by email from
oundle.museum@gmail.com

or by post from
Alice Thomas
3, Seymour Place, Oundle
Peterborough PE8 4QB

The Diary is in nine notebooks:

Volume 1   July 28, 1914 --   November 5, 1914

Volume 2   November 5, 1914 --   March 4, 1915

Volume 3   March 6, 1915 --   June 17,   1915

Volume 4   June 18, 1915 --   November 19, 1915

Volume 5   November 20, 1915 -- March 22, 1916

Volume 6   March 23, 1916 -- December 10, 1916

Volume 7   December 14, 1916 -November 29, 1917

Volume 8   November 30, 1917 --   July 4, 1918

Volume 9   August 4, 1918 --   November 12, 1918

List of Illustrations

Front Cover	Oundle Market Place 1914	Rotary Club of Oundle
page ii	John Coleman Binder and Louisa Clara Binder	E.G. Clarke
iii	Dixon's shop, West Street (formerly Binder's)	Oundle Museum
iii	J.C. Binder's house, 8, Stoke Hill, Oundle	Alice Thomas
iv	The first page of the Diary	E G. Clarke
5	Soldiers leaving Oundle Station	A. Hayward
6	J.H. Smith invitation to a Conference 1914	E. G. Clarke
7	Drawing of £1 note 1914	E. G. Clarke
8	H.L.C. Brassey's notice 1914	E.G. Clarke
70	Markham's Stationers	Rotary Club of Oundle
	Oundle Court House	Rotary Club of Oundle
71	Congregational Church	Rotary Club of Oundle
	Queen Victoria Hall	D.C. Wills
72	Instructions in case of Invasion	E.G. Clarke
141	Postcard sent to Percy Knight	Oundle Museum
264	At Last! 11 November 1918	E. G. Clarke
266	Unveiling of Oundle War Memorial 1920	Rotary Club of Oundle
	Oundle School Memorial Chapel	Alice Thomas
267	List of names of Oundle and Ashton men killed	
268	The nine volumes of the Diary	Alice Thomas
Inside Back Cover	Map of Oundle 1926	Ordnance Survey

Preface

When John Coleman Binder began his Diary at the outbreak of war in August 1914 he was fifty-one years old. He planned to record only local events, but he very soon felt it necessary to write down what was happening further afield. He followed developments in Parliament closely, especially when they affected agriculture and the regulation and supply of food. Like everyone else, he was anxious for the latest news of the war. *"This grim and bloody war is in all our thoughts"*. Although there was no radio, telegrams with the latest news were sent to the Post Office and were displayed in the window there, and there were both morning and evening newspapers.

As an Oundle & Urban District Councillor Mr Binder was involved in the life of the town, and took on further responsibility during the war as a special constable and by serving on the local Tribunal when Conscription began.

As a Grocer, Baker and Corn Dealer he was professionally concerned with the weather, agriculture, the harvest and food supplies, and is highly critical of the Government's actions, though willing to admit to changing his mind when rationing, for example, works better than he expected.

Though he frequently expresses his own feelings and opinions, he tells us only a little about his private life, and his wife is mentioned only once or twice. They had no children, but three nephews were in the forces, and seem to have survived the war.

Like Mr Binder, when I began to transcribe the diary I planned to include only events and comments concerning Oundle and the surrrounding area. But I too found that events further afield could not be left out, because they were what everyone was thinking and talking about. Volumes One and Two contain all the local references, but not all the foreign news. In Volume Three I have summarised (in italics) what was taking place abroad, but eventually found it easier to include everything Mr Binder wrote.

There have been some words and names which have been difficult to decipher, but his spelling is rarely at fault. Curiously, he hardly ever uses a question mark , though he often asks questions. Sometimes small words are ommitted accidentally, and I have added these. Where I have had to guess at a word I have used square brackets. Where Mr Binder has left a blank, intending to fill in the names or numbers later, I have marked these blanks with dashes (- - - .)

Though I have sometimes thought that it might be better to let these terrible events, with the hatred , brutality and suffering on both sides, be forgotten, they were an inescapable part of life for everyone involved, and a part of our history. A first hand account such as this is a valuable and vivid record of how life was for this thoughtful Oundle man in his fifties, in the years between 1914 and 1918.

Alice Thomas 2013

John Coleman Binder, 1863 - 1933, Grocer, Baker and Corn-dealer.

Louisa Clara Binder, née Middleton, 1858 - 1944.

Biographical Note

John Coleman Binder was born in Oundle in 1863, the youngest of nine children. His father, Henry Binder was a Grocer, Baker and Corn-dealer, with a shop and bakehouse on West Street, next to the cottages known as Binder's Row. He is listed there in Kelly's Directory of 1847.

He died when John was only seven. John's mother, Christiana Binder née Coleman, carried on the business.

John's life can be traced through the Census returns. In 1881, at 18, he was boarding with a family in Northampton and working as a shopman for a cabinet maker. At 28 he had returned to Oundle, and was living in the Market Place with his eldest sister Mary and her husband William Coaten,

plumber and painter. John is listed as a grocer, so was probably working at the family shop. Kelly's Directory of 1898 shows that shop as Binder Brothers. In 1901, 38, and still single, John was living at the shop with his brother Charles and his wife. Both Charles and John are listed as employers.

That same year John married Louisa Clara Middleton, five years older than him. Born in Suffolk, she had worked as a draper in Aylesbury.

They had no children. The 1911 Census shows them living at the shop, but later they moved just round the corner to 8, Stoke Hill.

John had considerable responsibilities in Oundle as Urban District Councillor, Trustee for Lathams almshouse, and, during the war, Special Constable and member of the Tribunal to hear appeals against conscription.

He died aged seventy in 1933, and his wife lived on till 1944, when she died aged 88.

This was Binder's Grocery and Baker's shop, 100 West St. (now Benefield Rd.) It was burnt down in 1966.

Mr and Mrs J.C. Binder's house, 8, Stoke Hill.

This Diary was kept by John Coleman Binder of Oundle in the County of Northampton. Grocer Baker and Corn Dealer. during the great European War. which commenced on July 28 1914.

I do not intend to write down so much the history of the war, but only local events but it is necessary to give a short statement of the main facts.

For the last ten or fifteen years. Europe has been one armed camp and it has been obvious to all that preparations have been going on for a vast struggle between the nations

On one side have been ranged. Germany Austria and Italy on the other Russia. France and England

Efforts have been made by many people. and also Public Bodies both in Germany and England to improve the feeling between the two nations and these to some extent had succeeded although at times the tension had been very great. The great cause of

The first page of the Diary.

The Diary of John Coleman Binder, Baker and Grocer, of 8 Stoke Hill Oundle
Volume One

This Diary was kept by John Coleman Binder of Oundle in the County of Northamptonshire Grocer, Baker and Corn Dealer during the great European War which commenced on July 28 1914.

I do not intend to write down so much the history of the war but only local events but it is necessary to give a short statement of the main facts.

For the last ten or fifteen years Europe has been an armed camp and it has been obvious to all that preparations have been going on for a vast struggle between the nations.

On one side have been ranged Germany Austria and Italy on the other Russia France and England.

Efforts have been made by many people and also Public Bodies both in Germany and England to improve the feeling between the two nations and this to some extent had succeeded although at times the tension had been very great. The great cause of offence to England was the fact that Germany had built such an enormous fleet, and this it was thought could only be [used] against us. It was hoped that relations between us had much improved .. during the last year and the nation as a whole did not realize that we were slowly drifting to a war.

The first real warning of the coming storm was given in the newspapers of Friday July 24th which had announcements of 'A Grand Crisis in Europe'.

We in England and Ireland had all been deeply interested in the Home Rule controversy and had not paid that attention to foreign affairs that we should have done.

1914 July 25 The Crisis is deepening and we are all turning our attention to what is going on between Austria and Servia.

July 27 The situation appears to be worse this morning as one can see by the speeches in the House of Commons.

July 28 The War has started and Austria is at war with Servia. To-day we bought German granulated Sugar in Lynn at 14s 10½d per cwt about the usual price. The sellers were Ginner Mortons and Goddard of London.

July 29 Further anxiety as Russia is reported to be mobilising. People here do not seem at present very much concerned as to what is taking place.

July 30 Germany appears to be moving and the Kaiser is evidently [making] preparations.

July 31 A state of War is said to exist in Germany.

August 1 Public interest is much awakened but we do not know in what way it will affect us here in England.

To-day the Boys from the Laxton Grammar School and the Grocers Company School have gone away for their Holidays.

DAY BY DAY THROUGH THE GREAT WAR

In connection with the Grocers School there is an Officers (Army) Training Corps which usually at this time of year goes into Camp with the regular army, but this year they are not to do so as measles have been very prevalent in the School.

Have seen several Millers (local) also men travelling for London and Liverpool people. Prices are rather nervous. We are asked to-day 30/- per sack (20 stone) for ordinary flour. This is considered too much, so we wire to Ranks of Hull, also to Browns of Huntingdon who offer at 28/- and 28/6. We buy some of both.

1914 Sunday August 2 A day of intense anxiety. We do not see any London papers except one called Lloyds.

During the time we were in Church this morning a telegram was received saying that the Russians and Germans had exchanged shots across the frontier. About 7.30 pm another telegram to hand. This says that Germany has sent an Ultimatum to France, so that war is now inevitable. Our hope is that England may not be involved.

Monday August 3 Bank Holiday and a general holiday throughout England, but a most curious holiday. Everyone appears to be holiday making without having the least wish for it. The London daily papers are received here about 8.30 am and there is now a great rush for them each morning. The news this morning is momentous. All naval reservists have been called up and the entire British Fleet is mobilised. Where it is is not generally known, but we know the 1st Battle Squadron put out from Portland last Wednesday night with sealed orders. The Bands were playing and the men cheering. With this squadron is young Hornstein a son of one of the Masters in the School. He is now an officer on the "Bellepheron" and so is in the first fighting line. A naval pensioner named White employed at the Workhouse left to join to-day.

The Papers also contain the news that Germany has invaded Luxembourg. Nothing to do much here. Had some friends staying with us so went on the river in the morning, in the afternoon drove to Kirby Hall.

To-nights papers (local papers published each evening at Northampton and are received here at 7.30) announce that Germany has made war on Belgium. Sent out a notice asking all the Bakers of the town and neighbourhood to meet at our house to-morrow Tuesday evening.

Also wrote to Messrs Hanson & Son of London asking them to quote prices of German granulated sugar.

The Banks are all closed and it is announced to-night that they will continue so until Friday, so that time may be given to put £1 and also 10/- notes into circulation and also to prevent a rush on them and thus create a panic. At present there is no sign of this.

Tuesday August 4 The most tremendous day for England. Mr Asquith said in the House to-day that England had sent a request to Germany to respect the neutrality of Belgium and asking for a satisfactory reply by twelve o'clock to-night.

Of course this means war and so the last hope of peace is gone. About five o'clock the proclamation calling out the reserves was posted in the Post Office Window. The Post Office will remain open all night so that Reserves may receive all instructions.

I am sorry to say that this morning signs of panic began to show themselves. On commencing business people commenced to come in with large orders to buy up food especially flour and sugar. I quickly discerned this and refused to supply any person with more than 14lb of Flour or 14lb Sugar and thus although we continued to be very busy all day we were able to cope with the rush.

I am sorry to say this course was not taken by other shops in the town, so that some people were able to secure an unfair quantity of Provisions.

THE DIARY OF JOHN COLEMAN BINDER

In some of the larger towns to-day extraodinary scenes were witnessed on people trying to buy up food.

The meeting of Bakers was held to-night and it was decided to raise the price of bread to 5½d per 4lb loaf (an increase of ½d per loaf) and to meet again on Thursday.

I received a telegram from Messrs Hanson quoting granulated sugar at 38s 6d per cwt in Lynn and loaf sugar at 44/- per cwt.

The Government to-day have commenced to buy horses for the Army. They have a register of all the horses in the country and now calling on the owners to produce them. They are paying not more than £50 for any horse, and if the owner considers it to be worth more than that he will have to sue the Government in the Courts. Gordon Wilson, Mr Brassey's agent at Apethorpe and Nichols the vet Surgeon are acting in this district..

I should before finishing to-night wish to record some impressions of to-day. One is struck by the fact that all Party distinctions in politics have gone under and although some do not agree with the policy that has brought this war about, now that it has come, we are all united. There is not much brag or bluster but a fixed and great determination to see the war through to the end.

I should have said that yesterday Post Office men were dismantling all wireless telegraphy installations in the town here. There were several of them. The principal one is at the Grocers Co.School and had been used for experimental purposes.

1914 Wednesday August 5 We were awakened at 6 o'clock this morning by a bugle call. One of the reservists had got a bugle and gone round to waken the others up. It is quite a wet morning and so things look a little gloomy. When the newspapers arrived we found that war had been declared at   11 o'clock last night.

The reservists 17 in number whose names are as under   [*not listed*] formed up in the Market Place at 10 o'clock and marched to the Station (Railway) where they were addressed by Mr J.H.Smith, Chairman of the Oundle Urban Council in presence of about 300 people. Each one has gone to join the depot of his own regiment.

We received our consignment of Flour to-day from Browns of Godmanchester and are thus in a better position. Ranks of Hull have to-day cancelled our contract for flour with them. This they were entitled to do on the outbreak of war.

Before closing to-night I will write a few lines respecting our food supply as it appears to me.

Stocks of Wheat and Flour are quite low in the hands of Millers and Bakers as it appeared there would be a good harvest and this certainly will be the case if only we have fine weather to gather it in. Wheat cutting commenced about a week since in this district but the weather has been showery since so that much progress has not been made.

So long as the German fleet is kept in their own ports or the North Sea I think prices will not rise to an alarming extent but should they get into the Atlantic and interrupt our trade routes the position would be serious. To-day the government has decided to allow 80 per cent of the insurance on all cargoes of food coming to this country.

The buying of food by all classes has gone on as briskly to-day.

Thursday August 6 Market day. Millers to-day are asking prohibitive prices. £2 and £2 2/- for ordinary Bakers Flour. I expect that many of them do not wish to sell as they have no stock. Sharps are £8 per ton. Bran £7. Barley Meal 18/- per sack of 14 stone.

We hear nothing of our Fleet. War news comes through very slowly. Everyone to-day is talking of the stand the Belgians are making at Liege, thus holding back the Germans from advancing into France.

DAY BY DAY THROUGH THE GREAT WAR

I hear that they (the government) have taken 10 horses from Mr Brassey's (Hunters) also 21 from the Kennels at Milton Park and all from Mr Stokes at Market Harboro. The number put on rail here up to to-day is about 40.

The Panic in buying still continues. Bread was raised to 6d per loaf to-day.

Friday August 7 This morning came the news of our first loss at sea. One of our Cruisers the "Amphion" was blown up by a mine off Aldeborough about 130 were lost but the remainder 120 and the Captain were saved. The Belgians still hold out at Liege. The Banks are open to-day and business is going on as usual. I tried to obtain a £1 note also a 10/- one but could not do so as they have not reached here yet. As much as 30/- was payed in London for the earliest notes issued.

The old age pensioners and postmen were payed to-day in postal orders instead of coin. People are quieter to-day.

1914 Saturday August 8 A wet day again. The Germans have called for an Armistice for a day at Liege so that they may bury their dead. They admit they have lost 24,000 men. The Belgians say they have lost about 2,000.

The Week closes. One of the most exciting weeks in my life. I remember the Franco-Prussian War of 1870 but of course that did not affect us to the same extent that this is doing. The feeling in England is very bitter against the German Emperor and it is currently reported that he is not quite sane. I do not credit this myself but must admit that sometimes his actions and speeches have shown that he thinks he is almost equal to the Almighty.

Sunday August 9 The First Sunday of the War. We have had quiet dignified Sermons at Chapel to-day from our Minister urging upon all the duty of self restraint.

A report is published to-day that a battle has taken place at Mulhause in Lorraine in which the Germans have lost 30,000 men and the French 15,000.

We shall see what confirmation of this is in tomorrows papers. Ernest Mowbray one of our congregation leaves tomorrow having taken service in the Army Medical Corps.

We do not know where the army is concentrating that is to be sent abroad, but think it must be on the South Coast of England.

The newspapers publish very little news of the preparations that are being made. £250,000 was raised on the first day in response to an appeal from the Prince of Wales to assist the poor and wounded.

The Panic of Food buying in this town had quite subsided yesterday.

A conference of the Oundle Urban & Rural Councils has been called for to-morrow, Monday, to consider what steps shall be taken to minimize any distress arising from the Empire's present critical position. I as a member of the Urban Council shall attend if possible.

I hear rumored to-day that the Boys will not return to the Schools at the usual time.

Captain Watts-Russell of Biggin Hall has joined his old regiment the Guards.

1914 Monday Aug 10 A glorious warm day, giving us hopes of the Harvest.

Not very much War news to-day except that the Germans have occupied the town of Liege. The Forts are still holding out.

The great battle reported yesterday appears to have been reconnaissance in force by the French into Lorraine. There was undoubtedly sharp fighting, but the losses are not so great as first reported.

The French evidently used the Bayonet to clear the Germans out of some of their earthworks. This will be a surprise to many military men, as they have held the opinion that the Bayonet as weapon was obsolete.

THE DIARY OF JOHN COLEMAN BINDER

Soldiers leaving Oundle Station.

DAY BY DAY THROUGH THE GREAT WAR

Cobthorne,

Oundle,

August 7th, 1914.

Dear Sir,

I write to invite you to a CONFERENCE of Members of the Oundle Rural and Urban Councils to be held in the BOARD ROOM of the OUNDLE WORKHOUSE on MONDAY NEXT, 10th inst., at 4.30 p.m., to take into consideration what steps, if any, shall be taken locally for the purpose of minimizing any distress arising from the Empire's present critical position.

Your attendance is earnestly requested.

Yours faithfully,

J. H. SMITH.

Letter from JH Smith

THE DIARY OF JOHN COLEMAN BINDER

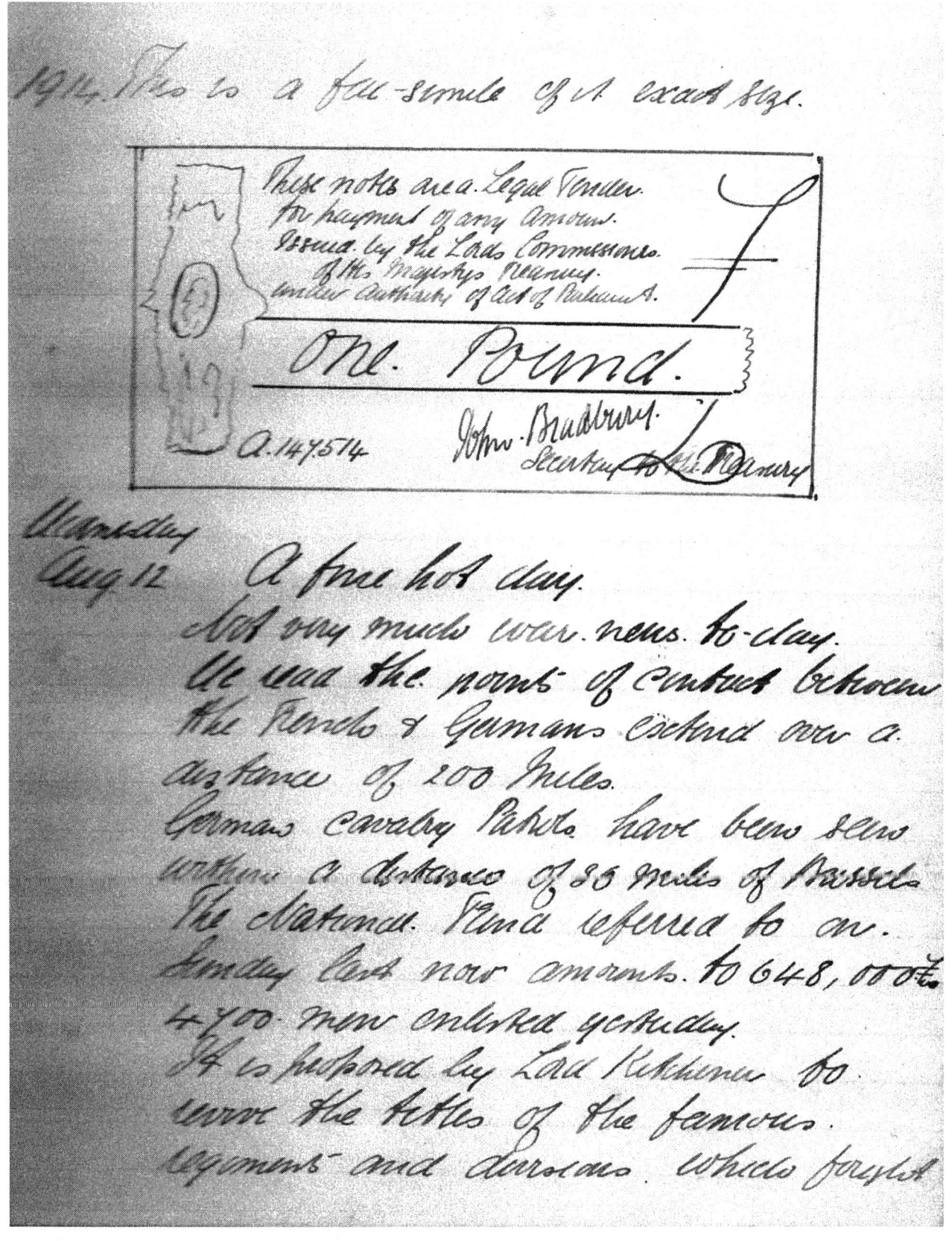

J.C. Binder's drawing of the new £1 note.

DAY BY DAY THROUGH THE GREAT WAR

APETHORPE HALL,
WANSFORD,
NORTHAMPTONSHIRE.
12th August, 1914.

Dear

A large number of men in this neighbourhood—as in other parts of England—are anxious to assist at this critical moment but are in doubt as to what they can do.

To those eligible for service in the Regular Army or the Territorials their duty is clear. But there are large numbers of men between say 35 and 55 who are not eligible for either of these forces. How can they assist?

The suggestion of Sir Arthur Conan Doyle seems to me and to others with whom I have spoken a good one, viz.:—That in different districts Civilian Companies of the National Reserve should be formed.

With this object in view a Meeting will be held at the VICTORIA HALL, OUNDLE, at 6 p.m., on MONDAY, 17th AUGUST, to consider the formation of such a body for Oundle and District. Should such a course be decided on, I am permitted to say that Mr. Sanderson has most kindly promised to do what he can in the way of allowing the use of the Oundle School Rifle Range, lending rifles for practice, and giving other facilities for training.

Believe me,
Yours truly,
H. L. C. BRASSEY.

P.S.—Please bring this to the notice of any who may be interested.

The following are Sir A. Conan Doyle's suggestions.

CIVILIAN NATIONAL RESERVE.

To form a local Company—

1. Call a public meeting, explain that the men are only honour-bound, that they are to drill and learn to shoot and be very earnest to become efficient.
2. Let the first appointments be merely two drill-sergeants. Let gentlemen remain in the ranks. Let the Company later choose its own officers.
3. Let it be clearly understood that no man who can possibly join the Territorials should enrol himself.
4. Let the men be from 17 to 60 so long as they can march 10 miles.
5. Let the class of work they may be asked to undertake be explained. Anything in case of invasion. At other times to form bridge guards, fortress work for limited periods, etc.
6. The County Territorial Association cannot recognise you, but should be kept well informed so that they may know of your existence and strength. In time you will get arms. Meanwhile some simple uniformity of hat and putties can be attempted. There are rifles for practice at the local butts. Above all, do not stand in the way of Territorials, but feed them in every way.

A. CONAN DOYLE.

THE DIARY OF JOHN COLEMAN BINDER

I hear to-day the Northants are to concentrate at Derby. They assembled last Wednesday at P'boro and [? Northampton]. Private letters from the soldiers in 48th (Northampton) Regiment say that they embarked at Plymouth on Friday last for France. I hear also that the Artillery and many other troops are across so that evidently the idea is to move up at the back of the French Army. We hear of no German ships in the Channel.

I omitted to say that last Wednesday a big motor passed through here filled with Police. They were armed with Rifles and ball cartridge and were on their way to guard Seaton Viaduct as it was thought possible an attempt might be made by the enemy's spies to wreck it.

Attended the conference mentioned yesterday. There were about 40 members of both Councils present. Mr J.H.Smith presided. A committee of twelve was formed to deal with various matters affecting relief of distress and other matters. The Committee to consist of 12 Members. Six from the Oundle Urban District viz Messrs J H Smith, J Rippiner, R W Todd, J M Siddons, E P Monckton and myself. Six from the rural parishes viz Messrs Goosey, Copley ...

A letter was read from Mr Brassey the member of Parliament for North Northants saying that it was probable that new regiments would be formed and suggesting that one should be raised in this division with Oundle for its Head Quarters.

The farmers attending the meeting said they had plenty of labour and given fine weather were confident that Harvest would soon be in.

A riot took place at Peterboro on Saturday night caused by the action of a German pork butcher who made insulting remarks about Englishmen. His shop was raided, the meat thrown into the street and other damage done. The Riot Act was read and the squadrons of the Northants Yeomanry who had mobilized at the City were called and helped to quell the disturbance.

A telegram from the Admiralty says that the German Submarine Flotilla attacked our Fleet in the North Sea yesterday but was driven off and one of them sunk. It is thought we shall hear of a big battle between the Germans and French during the next few days.

There is no other topic of conversation except the War. Wherever people meet, at home, in the street, at market, at Church or Chapel, in fact everywhere, the war is the sole topic. Prayers are offered daily in all the Churches and other places for our Country.

My friend Mr John Viccars commenced Harvest to-day. Several of his men have enlisted. All sorts and conditions of men are going. Peers and Peasant, Workmen, Clerks, Artisans and men from all classes of Society. The recruiting offices are besieged and are kept open day and night. There is no dissentient voice heard, all party differences are sunk.

The Appointment of Lord Kitchener as War Secretary has met with great approval. Three or four men stand out supreme at this moment. Mr Asquith, Sir Edward Gray, and Mr Lloyd George. The last named has done a great work as Chancellor of the Exchequer in restoring public credit and confidence in our money system.

Spies abound everywhere and scores are arrested daily. It is estimated there are 60,000 Germans in England.

1914 Tuesday Aug 11 A quiet day to-day. Warm and fine. Harvest being proceeded with in all directions.

Very little war news comes through to-day, except that the French are moving more into Lorraine, but the Austrians are threatening them on their right flank. In consequence of this France has formally declared war on Austria. We read that 400 fishing smacks from Grimsby and Hull are still out in the North Sea, apparently they have not learned that we are at war, so have not run for home. Determined efforts were made yesterday to warn them. Yarmouth trawlers, who dare not put out to sea to fish yesterday volunteered to trawl for the mines laid down by the enemy off our coasts. A very brave thing this, as these mines are still holding out. Nothing is heard from the Fleet except the capture of a big liner in the Cruiser Essex. The National Relief Fund to-day amounts to half a million of money.

DAY BY DAY THROUGH THE GREAT WAR

We expect the first big battle will take place in Belgium or Luxembourg. Very little is heard of the war on the Russian frontier. Russia is a huge country and moves very slowly. New White Wheat is quoted to-day at Mark Lane (London) at 42/- to 46/- per quarter. Red 41/- to 45/-.

Attended a Meeting of the Trustees of Latham's Hospital to-day. All the old ladies there are nearly scared out of their wits by the war.

I have a nephew in Harrods Stores London. He writes to-day that he has been told that each employee will have to stand off one week in each month so long as the war lasts.

Took the first £1 note to-day.

Wednesday August 12 A fine hot day. Not very much war news to-day. We read the points of contact between the French and Germans extend over a distance of 200 Miles.

German cavalry Patrols have been seen within a distance of 30 miles of Brussels.

The National Fund referred to on Sunday last now amounts to £648,000.

4,700 men enlisted yesterday. It is proposed by Lord Kitchener to revive the titles of the famous regiments and divisions which fought under Wellington in the Peninsular and Waterloo campaigns.

We are receiving offers on all sides from the Colonies. Today Alberta (Canada) offers 500,000 bushels of oats to help feed the Army Horses.

Men are hastening home from everywhere to join the army, from the back blocks of Australia, from New Zealand, from India, The Cape, Canada, in fact from all round the world they are coming to help us in this war.

. I did not mention that last week the Government passed a law by which they took over control of all the Railways. So far this has interfered very little with goods traffic, except that goods are a little longer getting through. . . Also a very drastic law [on] Saturday by which they have power to requisition all the food supplies in the country if they like.

Paper money is coming into circulation. If you tender a 2/- piece at the Post Office to pay for 1/- worth of stamps they give you a 1/- postal order for the change and so on with all other business at Government offices. Coin is received readily but only paper paid out.

Railway excursions are being resumed on the South and West coasts but not on the East Coast.

Mr Horsford of Stoke told me to-day that he had bought Oundle Lodge Farm, but not the two meadows down the Herne, which up to this time have always gone with it.

1914 Thursday August 13 Market day but no wheat is on offer to-day as scarcely any has been threshed. Merchants say it is worth 40/- to 41/ per quarter.

We are still waiting for news of the great Battle, which we think is now taking place along the front. The Belgians with the help of the French have evidently checked the advance of the Germans at Liege, and they are entrenching themselves there. It is said that some English Artillery Officers are at Liege, but this is not confirmed.

Sixteen troop trains passed through Oundle station to-day on their way from the Midlands to Diss in Norfolk

THE DIARY OF JOHN COLEMAN BINDER

Officially it is announced to-day they have seized all the savings of the people which are in what answers to our Post Office Savings Bank. . . . .

It is currently reported that [the Germans] are fighting this war with very little heart, that is apart from the Kaiser and the military caste in Germany. Possibly it may yet mean the break-up of the German Empire. The events taking place from day to day are so stupendous that one cannot now measure them.

…. Tyson Baker, son of the late G.F. Baker of Barnwell Mills enlisted yesterday. His youngest brother is in the Yeomanry so of course had gone a week since. . . .Most of the newspapers are about half the usual size.

Friday August 14 Another very hot day. Fruit is ripening fast. Not a very heavy crop. People are not making much jam on account of the high price of sugar. . . . .

We are all very anxiously waiting news from our Fleet, but nothing comes through. Four provision ships crossed the North Sea yesterday to England, so evidently there are not many German War vessels there.

Had a letter and newspaper from Rochdale this morning. Troops are being billeted there on private houses. I hear this is being done in other towns also. Camps are being formed all down the east Coast, so that if invasion should come we shall be quite prepared, but invasion at present is quite impossible.

Saturday August 15 Tonight a large number of trains passed down the line here, carrying troops. I hear they have come across to Holyhead from Ireland and are on their way to Harwich and so to France or Belgium. . . .

Business is quiet. More notes are beginning to appear. The poorer classes do not like the paper money at all; they are afraid of losing it.

Sunday August 16 Official news is now posted in every Post Office window on Sunday mornings. The telegram to-day says there are no British losses. There had been rumours about that our army had joined the Allies and had taken part in the fighting, but evidently they have not done so at present. . . . Although all communication by sea or telegraph or post is cut off with Germany, messages are being sent and received (under military supervision) by the Marconi wireless. It is curious to note how men's opinions differ about the length of this war. Some say it will only last a month or so, others longer, and again others say it will be a year or two. I myself cannot think it will be over quickly.

1914 Monday August 17. There were a great lot of soldiers came down by rail through here yesterday. I hear to-day that earthworks are being formed all down the east coast at such points the Germans might be expected to land, if they got the chance.

Attended a meeting held at the Victoria Hall at 6pm. The Meeting was called by Mr Brassey M.P. for North Northants for the purpose of forming a Town Guard and make men acquainted with the use of the rifle…About 60 men were enrolled and Mr. Sanderson, Head Master of the Schools promised the use of the range belonging to the School and also to lend the rifles belonging to the Officers Training Corps. The Range is on the Elmington Lodge Farm. The magazine belonging to the Officers Training Corps (in connection with the School) and which is situate on the School grounds (near the Pits) is now strictly guarded as indeed almost every Railway Bridge and culvert in the country.

Tuesday August 18 It is officially stated by the War Office that the entire Expeditionary Army numbering 165,000 men together with all necessary supplies is now landed in France, and this without a single casualty. . .Of course it was surmised in England what was being done, but not a single newspaper published any news relating to the movement of troops. As a matter of fact large numbers were moved in the night and the men themselves were not told where they were going,

DAY BY DAY THROUGH THE GREAT WAR

Had to go to Yarwell Mill to-day to see Robinson the miller, and during the time I was there (¾ hour) saw 3 trains carrying troops pass. I counted one and found it consisted of 1 Engine, 23 Coaches and cattle trucks, (many of the troops are being conveyed in these trucks) 5 waggons filled with Artillery and a Brake Van, which altogether made a very long train. I was told that since Saturday last and including to-day 36 such trains had passed.

The other important news is that Japan has ordered Germany to clear out of China and has given her eight days to do so. This may have most momentous consequences. America (the States) do not regard the move with very friendly eyes.

. .The Changes wrought by this war in a single fortnight are so vast that one cannot realize them. It is almost like seeing a Cinematograph moving before your eyes and one wonders what will happen next.

Wheat to-day is quoted at 36/- at Thrapston Market. Nine tenths of the corn I saw to-day is cut and a good deal has been carted.

Wednesday August 19 . . .The War Office have promptly forbidden the formation of the Town Guard mentioned on Monday. Probably the men who gave in the names will be sworn in as Special Constables and be under the control of the civil authorities.

Lord Kitchener's address to the Army has been issued to every soldier in the Expeditionary Force to be kept in his Active Service Book, and is so admirable that I think it well to write it down here. It is as follows:

'You are ordered abroad as a soldier of the King to help our French comrades against the invasion of a common enemy. You have to perform a task which will need your courage, your energy, your patience. Remember that the honour of the British Army depends on your individual conduct. It will be your duty not only to set an example of discipline and perfect steadiness under fire, but also to maintain the most friendly relations with those whom you are helping in the struggle. The operations in which you are engaged will for the most part take place in a friendly country and you can do your country no better service than in showing yourself in France and Belgium in the true character of a British soldier.

Be invariably courteous, considerate and kind. Never do anything likely to injure or destroy property, and always look upon looting as a disgraceful act. You are sure to meet with a welcome and to be trusted: your conduct must justify that welcome and that trust.

Your duty cannot be done unless your health is sound. So keep constantly on your guard against excesses. In this new experience you may find temptations both in wine and women. You must entirely resist both temptations and while treating all women with perfect courtesy you should avoid any intimacy.

Do your duty bravely. Fear God. Honour the King.

Kitchener   Field Marshal

1914 Thursday August 20 . . .   What is known as "A Rose day" took place here today. Young girls went about with trays of Roses asking everybody to buy one or more. The price was not to be less than 2d each but one could pay as much more as you liked. The money so realized amounted to £14 10/- and will be sent to the Prince of Wales Fund which today amounts to £1,315,000. Those who sold the roses were Misses Ramshay, Dolby, Curtis, Wood, Mawdesley, Ashbie (2) and Skeffington.

Friday August 21   . . Usually no trains pass through Oundle during the night, but for the last ten or twelve nights there have been a good number coming through. I find they are food trains carrying food and stores from the depots which are all in the centre of England down to the army on the coast.

THE DIARY OF JOHN COLEMAN BINDER

An enquiry came to the police here to-day as to the number of soldiers we could provide for, so possibly it is the intention to quarter some men here. Some have been at Northampton and Wellingboro but are now leaving, but a much larger number are expected next week.

Sunday August 23 . . .Our soldiers and sailors are not allowed to send anything home except printed postcards which merely say 'I am well' 'I am in hospital' etc. etc. So that [it] is almost impossible to obtain any real news of what they are doing or where they are.

Monday August 24 This has been a day of tense anxiety. This mornings papers brought the news that great fighting was taking place in Belgium and it was reported our own army was engaged at Mons. No details were given but it seems certain that one of the great struggles of the war was in progress. About 3pm came the news that Namur had fallen - in consequence of this the French will have to fall back. It is evident the Germans are making the most desperate efforts to break through and reach the French Frontier. . No official news is given of our own troops except that they are holding their own at Mons.

The losses must have been terrible, we shall see what the morning will bring. I pray God that it may bring better news.

Japan has now actively commenced war against Germany. . Thus the tide of war rolls round the whole world. We have often read of Armageddon and truly it seems to have come in our time.

Tuesday August 25 There was an eager rush for the papers this morning, but they were not able to give us much fresh news as to what had occurred during the great battle of Saturday and Sunday except to confirm the report that Namur had fallen. . . I should like to record how very quietly the English people have taken this reverse as it is generally admitted to be. There has been no panic or despair, but only a deeper determination to fight on. . . Money still continues to flow into the Prince of Wales Fund, which now amounts to £1,650,000. On Sunday we had collections here in the Churches - between £40 and £50 pounds was collected.

I hear that over 100 horses have been sent from Oundle and just round.

Wednesday August 26 We hear from time to time of exploits by the airmen, no doubt they have been of service but I am inclined to think they are not of such use as it was thought they would be. Directly one appears they are greeted with tremendous firing from the opposing forces and frequently brought down. Germany possesses about eleven Air-ships known as 'Zeppelins'. Six of these have already been put out of action, but one sailed over Antwerp yesterday dropping bombs and caused some damage but not much.

Lord Kitchener made his first statement in the House last night as War Minister. A brief soldierly address. Dissociates himself from all party politics and says he is only doing his best for the country. There is a growing impression that the bulk of the people have not yet realized that the very existence of the empire is at stake. I am of opinion that before the war closes we shall see compulsory military service.

Today 30,000 troops who had mobilized at Cambridge moved by train to Southampton on their way to France. Hearing from a good source that socks would be very acceptable to them a collection of socks was made here and in about an hour 300 pairs were collected and conveyed to Cambridge by motor by Mrs Coombs, wife of Mr Gurney Coombs, solicitor of this town. Am glad I was able to help in this.

Attended a meeting of the relief Committee for this town. Such committees have been formed in every parish in this County and are working in conjunction with the Central Committee at Northampton. The duty of these committees is to look after all cases of distress which may arise through the war; also to consider questions of unemployment and other matters. The money for working this will be supplied from the Prince of Wales Fund.

1914 Thursday August 27 . . .Post cards have been received yesterday and to-day from some of the reservists who joined lately. They say they are in France but do not say if they are in the fighting line. These cards were written on Tuesday and received here this morning which proves that the Postal Service is excellent. . .

DAY BY DAY THROUGH THE GREAT WAR

Friday August 28 …German spies continue to abound in this country. The police here yesterday and to-day were on the look-out for one of whom they had been warned. He was riding a motor cycle and was trying to get in touch with sentries at various places. Twelve hundred soldiers are coming to Raunds tomorrow where they will form a camp.

Sunday August 30 … Terrible charges are brought against the German troops by the Belgian government in a paper published by them this week, and these charges are borne out by Belgian refugees who are fleeing to England for safety. Pillage, violation of women and girls, shootings of old men and other things. It seems quite certain these charges are true as the Germans seek to justify themselves by saying it is necessary to strike terror into the inhabitants.

The military authorities have taken possession of Castle Station Northampton to-day and to-morrow and are moving 20,000 men there and billeting them in the town.

Monday August 31. Meetings are being arranged to be held in every town village and hamlet in the kingdom to rouse the entire community to a sense of the danger we are in. The Prime Minister will open the meetings by speaking in London, Edinburgh, Dublin and Cardiff. Party politics are entirely sunk and men of all parties creeds and sects are appearing on the same platforms and urging upon the nation the way to do its duty. On Saturday night a large meeting was held at Peterboro. Addresses were given by Mr Brassey, Tory MP for this division and also by Mr G. Nichols a liberal who fought him at the last election. Another meeting was held at Thrapston of a similar character - about 1000 people were present, and after each of these meetings numbers volunteered (at Thrapston over 40)

Tuesday September 1 A beautiful day for the first of September, such a day that one usually associates with the opening of the shooting season, but I am sure there will be very little shooting or hunting in this country during this autumn and winter. In all directions Masters of Hounds are sending their horses to the front and asking their grooms and kennel-men to enlist. From what I can hear there will be only cubbing this year and in many cases the Master's wife is acting as MFH in his absence at the war. Lady Exeter is doing this with the Burghley Harriers, the Marquess being away as OC the Peterboro Artillery, and the same is being done with the Pytchley Hounds

1914 September 8 A friend of mine today told me that a lady (née Miss Kirby of Glapthorne) who had married a Brazilian naval officer, had really come over from Russia with some of these (Russian) troops and that they were brought over on liners belonging to the Cunard Co.

September 11 Last night the police issued a notice in London asking that the lights at night should be made as low as possible. It seems there is an idea that an airship from Germany might possibly sail over London dropping bombs and they wish all public buildings to be rendered as inconspicuous as possible. An English airship has been hovering over London the last few days.

September 12 The Northants Yeomanry are home on 2 days leave. They say they are going to France next week. A letter from my brother today says that his son Fred Binder has joined the Army. This makes 3 nephews who are now soldiers.

September 14 Forty new recruits from Oundle and neighbourhood were passed and sworn in yesterday morning at the Victoria Hall and most of them have left this morning.

September 15 I hear today that Lieut. Michael Smith, son of Mr J.H. Smith of this town is posted as 'missing'. He was in the Manchester Regiment and it was very much cut up at Mons. Possibly he may turn up later or it is quite possible that he is dead as French had to abandon very many of his wounded during his retreat from Mons to Paris.

THE DIARY OF JOHN COLEMAN BINDER

Wednesday September 16... A Meeting was held here tonight in the Victoria Hall to explain what had been done with regard to some Belgian Refugees. A committee has been formed and they have decided to take entire charge of 10 refugees (2 families if possible). Mr John Clark of St Osyth's Lane has offered the committee the first house in Snowdon Terrace, free of all charge, for so long as it is required. It will have to[be] furnished and the committee are appealing for all things (on loan) necessary to furnish a house of that size. They estimate it will cost £4-10-0 per week to maintain these people and they will be glad of offers of money or food. Of course these poor people are absolutely destitute, and have only just the clothes they have on. Many of them are people in good circumstances but have lost everything. The Mayor of Peterborough (Sir R. Winfrey) is going to London to-day to bring 50 to Peterboro and 10 are to be sent on here.

September 19 .. Definite news was received to-day by Mr J.H.Smith of the death of his son Michael. He died of wounds received at Cambrai during the French retreat from Mons to the Marne. This will be a great grief to his father and mother and also to his sister. He was the only son. The (Belgian) refugees did not arrive today. They arrived at Peterborough yesterday (39 of them) but it was decided to entertain the whole party there. We expect our party will come on Tuesday. Our own government have in hand the whole affair of bringing them across and allotting them to various towns which are willing to entertain them. It is expected that at least 60,000 will come over.

It is estimated that there are 4,500 English prisoners (including soldiers) in Germany. I do not know how many there are in this country, but there are large numbers of them. One huge camp where they are kept is at Dorchester.

September 20 .. Yesterday the Government appealed to the people to send spare blankets for the use of the newly raised army at the various centres. They had <u>purchased</u> all that was possible and now are asking the people to send them. The response has been amazing. Blankets are being sent in by hundreds of thousands

1914 September 21 The great struggle along the banks of the Aisne and to the east still continues. It has now been going on for a week without intermission, and some accounts of it are now coming. I think we can only describe it in one word, and that is, it is Hell.

It is being fought very largely under leaden skies, with driving rain storms in some places the entrenchments are waist- deep in water, and everywhere the air is charged with the fumes of the explosives. The Germans are strongly entrenched but the Allies are slowly, very slowly, gaining ground, and what they do gain they hold, but the sacrifice of human life is awful

September 22 Mr Shelmerdine, relieving officer to the Board of Guardians was last Thursday granted leave to go to the front. His wife will act as deputy during his absence.

September 24 We can see by the casualty lists that the Northants regiment has had some hard fighting. Three officers are posted as missing, and one, Mr Ward Hunt of Wadenhoe is wounded. A private named Afford from here is also among the wounded.

A brilliant feat by our Flying Corps is reported this morning. A squadron have made a dash for Dusseldorf where the Zeppelin Air Ships are located and also made. They succeeded in dropping bombs on some of the sheds and according to a Rotterdam telegram destroyed them, and then got back again quite in safety to the place they started from. Where it was we are not told, but in any case they must have flown nearly 400 miles without stopping.

September 26 The Refugees arrived today. Seven men. Very woe-begone they appeared to be. They were taken to the Workhouse Infirmary at first where they had a good bath, fresh clothing and tea, and were then taken to their house in St Osyth's Lane. I understand there are a few more to arrive on Monday. The narratives of these poor people are horrible in the extreme. Absolutely destitute, many of the relatives and friends murdered by the Germans after being subjected to nameless indignities and tortures. They fled from their villages and towns and followed the Belgian Army, living on such scraps as they could obtain from the soldiers.

DAY BY DAY THROUGH THE GREAT WAR

These barbarities have aroused deep and fierce resentment against the Germans throughout the entire world and will ever remain branded on the German people. The refugees here are Roman Catholics and a Chapel has been arranged for them in Mr Dolby's office in the Market Place next to Amps the Grocers. The Priest will come from Peterborough. (Sugar prices 3 ¾d per lb for granulated 4 ¼d lump and 4d West Indian. These are retail prices. I think this is the dearest article of food we have and I think we should be glad we have such a splendid navy).

Sunday September 27 A telegram in the Post Office window says that desperate efforts were made yesterday by the Germans to re-capture Pernine and also to break through our lines but everywhere they were repulsed with heavy loss. We shall have to wait until tomorrow for more particulars.

September 29 The Belgian refugees have shaken down into their surroundings very well. There are five peasants, one small farmer and one stonemason. They are all from the same place, Malines, which the Germans have again bombarded and fired today. They have been at work for several people in the town today. The money they receive as wages will be placed to their credit in the Post Office Savings Bank. This is by order of our own government (who have made a set of rules for the guidance of people who are looking after these people). It is hoped that the money will enable them to make a start again after the war is over.

Thursday October 1 Two months to-day since war was declared. It seems as if it were two years, so much have we gone through since then. The strain and stress is still as acute as ever, although we have suffered so very, very little, in fact one living in these small country towns can scarcely believe that we are in the midst of such an awful struggle.

Only in Belgium and France, more especially Belgium, has war spent its full terrible force, and the effects, even as <u>we</u> read and hear, are ghastly, but it is obvious we do not know a tithe of what has taken place, as I remarked once before in this journal, it is simply Hell. There is no other word to describe it.

1914 October 3 Four more Belgian refugees arrived here today. A man, his wife and two children so that there are eleven here altogether now.

October 7 The Special Constables mentioned on August 19 are now formed into a company and are drilled on the Cricket Field near the Cross Keys Inn. The drills are held on Wednesdays and the drill sergeant is Leverton who is connected with the School. The Schools are all in working order again. A number of the older boys who are about 19 years old, also a number of the Old Boys, have joined the Army. I hear today that a young fellow named Cullop who was called up as a reservist on August 4 and whose parents live on the Benefield Road here has been killed in action

October 8. The price of food is quite normal except sugar, and this is not very dear, 3¾ d per lb, although this [is] higher than we have [been] used to the last few years. The Government have absolute control of the supply and will only allow of it being retailed at the fixed price. Yesterday they bought £18,000,000 worth of raw sugar from various sources. This they will sell to the refiners and wholesale brokers who in turn supply the grocers. This I believe is really the only article of food for which they have at present assumed direct responsibility.

October 10 [Belgian refugees] continue to arrive daily in this country and are being welcomed with open arms. Hundreds of cities, towns and villages are housing and feeding them. Today a regiment of cavalry (territorials) passed through here at 4pm on their way from Huntingdon to Apethorpe where they are to remain for a week at the invitation of Mr Brassey, M.P. for North Northants. They are Lovat's Scouts and have been raised by Lord Lovat. They are mostly Scotchmen. All were mounted very largely on stout Scotch shooting ponies. They are training at Huntingdon and the King went to inspect them a few days since. Amongst them is a Mr Walter Scott a distant relative of the Duke of Buccleuch. He has been living here for a short time but has now joined the Army. They had some mounted pipes at their head. I did not count them but should think there were about 150 of them. They looked as if they had had a hard week's work.

THE DIARY OF JOHN COLEMAN BINDER

October 11 Some interesting news has been sent the last few days by Colonel Smith, the officer commanding the Northamptons. He says they have been in the thick of the fighting from the time they landed in France. At one place they captured 4 Machine Guns and are hoping to send one home to Northampton. It appears they were one of the first regiments across, having left England on Aug. 12th.

Monday October 12 . . .Another Zeppelin airship has been destroyed by a daring raid of our airmen into Germany on Friday last. No damage was caused or attempted to any building except the hangar where this ship was housed. The Germans are trying to terrorize Paris by bomb dropping and yesterday 17 people were killed and wounded by these tactics. Great pressure is being put on the Allies to retaliate by dropping bombs on to some of the towns but up to the present they have not done so. Lovat's Scouts came through again to-day about 12 o'clock on their way back to Huntingdon.

October 13 Coin is getting scarce. Large quantities of silver coins have been put into circulation but it is not at all plentiful. Last Friday we paid into the Bank £50, but there was not a single coin amongst it. It was all notes, cheques and Post Office orders.

October 15 Captain Russell of Biggin Hall who rejoined his old Regiment at the beginning of the war, and who has been at Windsor, left yesterday for the front with a draft of men. Refugees are still crowding over into Folkestone and Dover from Belgium and are being dealt with as regards food, clothing and housing. Many towns and cities are taking them in large numbers and are making themselves responsible for them by quite voluntary help. Leeds has 500, Birmingham the same and so on.

1914 October 16 The 'Hawk', a cruiser with about 400 men has been torpedoed in the North Sea on Thursday. Only about 45 men and officers were saved and they were landed at Aberdeen this morning. One of the officers of this ship was Arthur Coombs, son of Mr Gurney Coombs of this town. He was well known to everybody here, having lived here all his life and was educated at Oundle School. He did remarkably well in his exams and promised to make his way to a high position in the Navy. His father received a telegram from the Admiralty this afternoon saying that he was missing so that probably he has gone down with the other brave men. Another man on board was Jinks of Morborne who has relations here. He was a gunner and was one of the best marksmen in the service. The Northamptons have lost heavily lately. Besides Cullop other men who have been killed or wounded is Sharp (Ashton) and today a man named Butt, a reservist employed at the School and was called up at the beginning of the war, is posted as missing. This parish has already lost 5 men killed besides wounded a fairly high percentage in view of the fact that a good many men who were called up at the first are still at Weymouth and other depots.

October 19 At tonight's meeting of the Urban Council here it was decided to make a register of all men who are serving with colours from this parish and to embody it in some permanent form and also to keep it revised as men are going from here again in a few days. Colonel Lees who has rented Herne Lodge for the last few years left last week to rejoin his old regiment the Cheshires. He has been a member of the local council for the last two years.

Public feeling is rising very much against the Germans who are in England very much on account of the accounts received from the Belgian refugees. It has been found that German spies have come across with some of these refugees and on account of the difficulty in detecting them all Belgian refugees have been ordered to leave the east coast towns and villages, also Dover and Brighton.

October 21 The second battalion of the Northants Regiment (the old 58th} has now gone to the front. This battalion has been in Egypt and as far as I can learn has been brought home and is now going to France. Some of the men were in Northampton yesterday…..About 2000 men together with horses are quartered at Northampton.

The Officers Training Corps connected with the School here is hard at work drilling etc in their spare time. This is taking the place of games. Last Saturday they had a route march fully equipped by Benefield and Glapthorne. Today they have been at tactical exercises on Bailey Hill.

DAY BY DAY THROUGH THE GREAT WAR

October 22 [Enteric Fever has broken out on the Continent.] The Local Government Board have today sent down a request asking what number of enteric cases can be accommodated here. A meeting is to be held of the Isolation Hospital Committee this afternoon to consider the matter… It was agreed tonight to offer 8 beds for enteric patients at the local hospital.

October 23 Several men of the 2nd Northants (58th) have been home. They landed at Liverpool and were granted 60 hours leave of absence and are going to the front as soon as they get back.

October 26 Captain Wallis (Grenadier Guards) son of Aubrey Wallis of Farming Woods is amongst the killed this morning. We have been able to make a complete and accurate list of all men from this parish who are taking any part in this war. Up to the present it contains 115 names and I hope to keep it complete and revise it as casualties occur.

It is rumored to-day that 70,000 reinforcements are going across to France this week. Amongst them the 2nd Battalion of the Northants and also the Northants Yeomanry. They are being concentrated at Winchester.

I have read today a letter from A.D. Hornstein (or Lowdell as he is called in the Army). He fought at Mons, got separated from his corps and did not pick them up for four days.

1914 October 28 A very bad piece of news comes from South Africa to-day. De Wet a Boer General who was one of our chief enemies during the Boer War of 1900 has headed a rebellion against us. Prompt measures have been taken by General Botha and his government to deal with the situation and it is hoped that they may be effective. As far as one can judge the greater part of the people (including the Dutch and Boers) are quite loyal.

I had to go to Daventry to-day on business and stayed a few hours in Northampton. The town is full of soldiers (a Welsh Artillery division). One meets them everywhere. Their camp takes up practically the whole of the Racecourse and a large number are on the south side of the town also. The horses are picketed out in the open at present but wooden shelters are being built for them, in fact a great many are finished. The men are billeted at private houses. They appear to be a smart well set up body of men. I watched the training for some time at the camp. It has been showery the last week and there is plenty of mud there. A large number of the newly raised Kitcheners Army is there also, but many of them are without uniform at present. Going through Weedon I also saw the barracks full of recruits.

October 30 Colonel Ferguson who commands the 2nd Life Guards and whose home is at Polebrook Hall has been wounded in the leg and is in hospital in Reading.

I also hear today that Edward Bennett whose father is horsekeeper for Mr Baker at Barnwell Mill has died of wounds received in action in France. He was a private in the 1st Battalion Northants.

November 1 The arrangements as regards those [Belgian refugees] already here are working very smoothly. The men are given a very good word by those who employ them and the committee are quite satisfied.

November 2 Captain Watts Russell was invalided home on Saturday suffering from typhoid. His father also died on Saturday. The marching orders for the Yeomanry are countermanded and they are still at Winchester. Mr Brassey of Apethorpe MP for this division has been granted a commission in the regiment.

November 3 Sir Arthur Buck was buried at Benefield today and I am told that some of the officers attending his funeral received urgent telegrams recalling them at once.

November 4 Arrangements have now been made to entertain a further number of Belgian Refugees here. Mrs Hames has kindly lent the house at the bottom of Inkerman Yard on the right hand side and has undertaken to put it into good repair. Furniture will be lent and the Committee think from the promises they have received they will be quite able to make it a success. No rates at all will be levied on the house and no charge made for water.

THE DIARY OF JOHN COLEMAN BINDER

I saw one of the new £1 notes today. It is a great improvement on the first issue, being larger, better printed and better paper with a quite distinct watermark.

November 5 Another Oundle man is reported killed today. His name is Jacobs, a private in the Northants regiment. Two others (both Sharps) are wounded.

END OF VOLUME 1

THE DIARY OF JOHN COLEMAN BINDER

Volume Two

5 November 1914 to 4 March 1915

1914 November 5 continued The brigade which has been concentrating at Winchester left there last night and sailed for Belgium from Southampton at 9pm. In this brigade is included the 2nd Battalion of the Northants Regiment also the Northants Yeomanry. Postcards giving the above particulars were received here from some of the men to-day. I believe the Yeomanry are the first mounted regiment of Territorials to go to the front. …Wheat is gradually getting dearer. It is quoted today in local markets at 42/6d. Bread is still 5 ½d per 4lb loaf here. In some parts it is 6d and 6 ½d

November 6 Friday …The man Jacobs reported dead yesterday is a prisoner. A Post Card was received from him. A card was also received from the man Burt this morning saying that he is a prisoner at Doebritz in Germany.

November 8 Sunday Some discussion has been taking place the last few days with regard to recruiting. Recruits have not joined in such numbers as they did in the first few months of the war, and suggestions have been made that conscription will have to be used. I do not think this is likely at present but it may come before the war is over. My own opinion is that the nation would agree to it, if it can be shown to be necessary.

A considerable number of the new recruits are still under canvas. Huts are being erected as quickly as possible but it looks as if private billeting would have to be resorted to in a much larger degree to solve this difficulty.

Proposals have been made that we should bring over a Japanese Army of say 500,000 to help the Allies on the continent. Personally I think it would be a very wise measure, if it could be done.

The casualty list this last week has been a dreadful one, and a sense of sadness is over all the county. High and low, rich and poor are all concerned in this dreadful war, and all feel the overshadowing sense of grief. In reading the obituary notices in the Times one is struck by the frequency of such announcements as "the only son", "the eldest son", "the only child" of so-and-so, but in spite of all this there is a grim determination to hold on. I should like to write down here as to how this war has welded us together as an Empire and a Nation. Throughout the whole land today there is no discordant voice. … We are all <u>Englishmen</u> to-day fighting for our country. The poor are giving their lives and helping with their labour. The rich are giving their riches and their help in every possible way. All feel that the Government is doing and has done splendidly, backed as it has been by the Conservative Party.

Parliament meets again on Wednesday but it is certain that no great measures will be attempted. All its labours must turn to financing of the war. It is estimated that <u>we</u> are spending something over a million a day. It is evident to all of us that this generation cannot pay this huge debt, we shall do what we can, but some of it must be left to future generations. When I said that we were fighting for our country I should have included other countries as well. There is a fixed and quiet determination that not one inch of territory shall be annexed by Germany. That Belgium must be restored and that France must be compensated.

Monday November 9 …. The Belgians still fight on bravely. Their King and Queen are with the Army and have never left them. The Queen came over here about a month since to bring their children to a place of safety, but only stayed a few hours, and at once returned to the Army.

DAY BY DAY THROUGH THE GREAT WAR

Starvation is upon those who are left in Brussels and the other Belgian cities. Funds are being raised both here and in America to help to feed them this winter.

The official report of the French Government which is issued every day at 3pm and which we down here receive about 6pm shows that the enemy have recommenced their attack on us in Belgium.

1914 Tuesday November 10, The Battle at Ypres is still raging furiously…

Thursday November 12 Parliament met yesterday. It was announced that a loan of 200 millions would probably be issued at an early date.

Friday November 13 …Our losses have been very heavy. Mr Asquith said today that up to the end of October we had lost 57,000 men and it is estimated that up to today our losses are 70,000. So that nearly a third of the original force which went in August has been put out of action. It seems very doubtful if any of those who went first will come back again. Wounded men are beginning to be seen in all places. As soon as they are convalescent they are allowed to come home for a week or two and then have to rejoin the colours.

Sunday November 15 This morning we woke up to find snow, but it quickly disappeared. A very early telegram announces the death of Lord Roberts. One of our great soldiers. A most pathetic incident. He was quite an old man, over 80 years old, and of course had not taken any active part in this war although he was still hale and active. He had gone across to Belgium to see the Indian troops who had come over to help us and by whom he was well known having spent so much of his life in India. He was seized with pneumonia and succumbed. Poor old man. Everybody will be very sorry.

Monday November 16 The topic of conversation today amongst all classes is the death of Lord Roberts. Deep and real sorrow is felt on all sides…. A public funeral was offered in the Abbey but was declined and he will be buried quietly at Ascot.

The Council here tonight decided to keep a "Roll of Honour" of all men who are engaged in the war. A special book will be provided and as far as can be ascertained a short record kept of each man. A list of all men serving is now posted in each place of Worship in the Parish.

Very sensational rumours have been current throughout the country today respecting the attempt the Germans may make to raid the East Coast. One does not know whether to credit these rumours, but this much is quite certain, large bodies of troops have been constantly on the move in this county the last few days, also all trains travelling at night have been compelled to keep the carriage blinds down to obscure the light. We were warned last week from Holland that there was unusual activity in the Kiel Canal where the German fleet has been in hiding since war was declared.

Tuesday November 17 …Great preparations have and are being made for a winter campaign. Ever since war was declared, the women of this empire have been engaged in preparing articles of warm clothing for our sailors and soldiers and it is quite certain they will be wanted. A fund has been started and is nearing completion by which every man will have a plum pudding at Christmas. This will cost about £5,000. The Prince of Wales Fund is now close upon 4 millions.

The telegrams this evening give accounts of the sitting of the House of Commons this afternoon. The Chancellor introduced his amended budget and proposes the following taxation, 1d per pint extra on beer, 3d per lb extra on tea, making it 8 per lb duty, and the income tax is doubled making it 1/6d on earned income and 2/6d on unearned. This is indeed heavy taxation, but it will be met with bravery by the nation. Last night the Prime Minister said in the House that the war was costing us a million a day or £2 /10/- every time a watch ticks.

THE DIARY OF JOHN COLEMAN BINDER

Part of the money will be raised by loan to be issued at 95 bearing interest at 3½per cent. It is also decided to raise another million men and in the middle of next year we shall have nearly 3 millions of men under arms, exclusive of the navy…..The Russians and Germans are at terrible grips on the Russian and German Frontiers. It is stated that Germany has 2 ½ Millions of men engaged there and Russia 3 ½ Millions. We are told these things but it is impossible to grasp them. They are too vast.

Wednesday November 18 The sole topic of conversation today is the new taxation. On the whole it has been received very well indeed. Of course there are criticisms but everybody knew that the taxes would be much increased. I think the net might have been thrown a bit wider. For instance a man who does not drink beer and whose income does not exceed £160 will escape the new taxation altogether, except the tea duty and this is a very small thing. It now remains to be seen what response there will be to the new loan, but we are told that over 100 millions have already been applied for. Certainly it is not a bad investment….

Lord Roberts will be buried in St Paul's tomorrow at 12 o'clock. The feeling was so strong that he should be buried there that his family consented. His body will be drawn to its last resting place on the gun carriage which his son lost his life in saving at the battle of Colenso, South Africa in 1901 and which was presented to Lord Roberts by the War Office.

1914 Thursday November 19 A bitterly cold day. Rain and sleet. All our thoughts are turned to the hardships of our soldiers at the front. The fighting the last two days is not quite so violent as the weather in Flanders is as bad as here. Everything that can be done will be done to lessen the sufferings of the men. The War Minister said today in the House that 300,000 fur-lined coats were being sent out for them….

There is one fact in connection with the woollen and other trades in this county that is worth recording. These trades were in danger of being brought to a standstill owing to their being unable to procure aniline dyes. These dyes were almost exclusively made in Germany and imported into this country. Of course, war put a stop to this but the Government has taken the matter up. A company has been formed amongst the manufacturers for the purpose of making these dyes, and it will be largely financed and subsidised by the Government.

Bread is advanced to 6d per 4lb loaf today. Flour 2/2d per 14lbs

Friday November 20   …Five recruits went from Benefield yesterday.

Saturday November 21   …Reports today say that considering all things our men are as well as can be expected. The trenches are to some extent quite a comfort to them as being below the ground level they are a shelter from the biting wind…... The second battalion of the Northants regiment has evidently been in action as I see from the casualty list this morning that their Colonel is wounded.

Sunday November 22… Notice was given yesterday by the Government that the entrances to all ports are mined and that no vessel must attempt to enter or leave these ports except they have a mine pilot on board.

Monday November 23   …An appeal for recruits is being sent by post to every house in England from a committee belonging to all political parties. It is being sent from London. A start was first made in this district and the response so far is said to be good.. There is no compulsion but the head of each house is asked to put down the name of any man residing in the house(between 19 and 35) who would be willing to enlist. A register of these will be kept and they will be called up as wanted. The new War Loan of £350,000,000 has been a success and it is said that it has been over subscribed,…

DAY BY DAY THROUGH THE GREAT WAR

Tuesday November 24   A number of recruits are leaving here for Northampton tomorrow. They are chiefly for the Territorials, and are nearly all boys about 17. I do not think very much of them and if we are to depend on such lads as these in case of invasion it will be a bad day for us. I think it would be very much better if we cannot get different men to these that we should have compulsory service in some form, as it is quite certain that there are plenty of men from 26 to 30 who might go. I am inclined to think that even now the great mass of the people do not realize our danger, we live so securely and quietly guarded by our fleet that life goes on about as usual. I for one should not be at all sorry if the Germans would raid this country for a few hours - it would wake the people up.

Our airmen made a very daring raid into Germany on Monday to the Zeppelins factory at Friedrichshafen on Lake Constance. Three of them went in three machines and they positively affirm that they did much damage by bomb dropping although the Germans deny this. One of them was shot down and captured but the other two reached French territory again safely. They flew about 300 miles without stopping. These aeroplanes are playing a very great part in this war and have almost entirely changed it. They are able so clearly to locate the enemy and to give such accurate information to the commanders that a surprise attack is almost impossible.

Friday November 27   Lord Kitchener made a statement as to the war in the House last night. He was quite optimistic and said that the Germans had received the worst defeat they have known during this war. Referring to our own position he made the interesting statement that 30,000 recruits per week were still joining the army but there was still room for all who would come and that every man would be needed. He also said the appeal for recruits which I mentioned on Nov 23 had been quite a success.

A number of recruits are leaving here on Monday, mostly boys from 17 to 20. In many trades this recruiting is making labour very scarce.

Quietness in Flanders still continues, and some of the officers have been allowed about 3 days leave. Captain Riddell who married one of the Miss Smiths at the Rectory, is now home but will have to rejoin on Monday. He has been in the firing line from the first and being in the Artillery this has been awful.

1914 Sunday November 28   Today 30 special constables are being sworn in here. They are all farmers and come one from each village in the Petty Sessional Division. This is being done throughout all the country. These men will not be drilled but will act under the police in case of invasion, removing stock, requisitioning transport and duties of that kind. It will be seen by this that although invasion is not probable arrangements are being made to meet it should it come.

A large force of civilians has also been enrolled consisting of men who cannot join the army on account of age or because of some other good and sufficient reason. These are called "Citizens Corps" and now number about 1,000,000. They will be armed with rifles, but will not wear any uniform, only a badge.

We do not fear invasion very much, but it is suggested that the enemy may try to raid us in the early spring when a large number of our men have gone abroad.

The Northants Yeomanry are up in the fighting line but no casualties are reported at present.

Tuesday December 1   Quite a surprise is announced this morning. The King has gone over to France to see the Army. Not since George the Second fought at Dettingen has a British King gone abroad in war time.

THE DIARY OF JOHN COLEMAN BINDER

Thursday December 3 ...Very little today from Flanders. Arrangements have been made for billeting 5000 soldiers in Peterboro', Stamford and the adjacent villages.

No more refugees have arrived at present. The rush from Belgium has stopped and not so many are coming across so that it is possible we shall not get any more here.

Our Territorial soldiers are being sent across. Quite a number of Yeomanry regiments are there, but at present they have not seen much fighting.

[Thursday] December 10   All lights will be put out in the Channel. Much discussion is going on as to the amount paid by the War Office for billeting troops. I believe it works out at about 21/- or 22/- per week. This is certainly excessive and I should think it is quite possible that it could be for 14/- or 15/-. Some trades are enormously busy just now, especially those who provide for the army. Khaki cloth is manufactured by the million yards That this is quite possible may be gathered from these facts:

We have already a million men in Khaki. Another million are waiting for their uniforms. Each man at the front requires a new outfit every month. It takes 3 yards to make a suit and 2 yards an overcoat. Boot manufacturers are working very hard. The War Office discourage the enlisting of shoe operatives as they are so much needed to fulfil the army needs.

Cloth mills are working 24 hours a day and all day on Sundays.

Saturday December 5   No news from Russia or Poland today. We have had great storms and gales especially the last few days and telegraphic communication with that country is 30 hours behind. Not much from Flanders. The King is still there and it is said he may remain for some time. Recruiting still goes on at a normal rate. A number of recruits are leaving here again on Monday.

Sunday December 6 A typical December day, dull foggy and cold. Our thoughts go across to the brave men in the field and also to our sailors.   No official news today.

Colonel Edmund Smith, son of Mrs Smith of the Rectory, is home from India and has gone to the front. Captain Watts Russell I saw today. He rejoins the Grenadiers in a few days.   People are about used to the paper money. Gold is very scarce, but new silver is very much used.

1914 Monday December, A slight forward movement of the Allies is reported from Flanders this morning, but progress is very slow. Around Ypres the flooding of the country has made the movement of troops very difficult...I wish I could write that we could see some sign of breaking in this terrible time of strain and stress but I cannot do so.

Peace is quite out of the question at present and our only hope seems to be in wearing Germany down, and this decision is inflexible. How long they will be able to bear the strain no-one can say.   There is some impression that the end will come all at once and unexpectedly. This is not my own view. We can only live from day to day and it is of very little use speculating on the future.

Tuesday December 8... Officers are being allowed 5 days leave of absence. A day to come, three clear days at home, and a day for return. Today Lieut. Hornstein (Lowdell) of the A.S.C. whom I mentioned as being one of the earliest to cross to France has come home for the 3 days. He is well and fit and so far has come through without a scratch. I think we can judge from this leave of absence that no great operations are likely to be undertaken at the present....

DAY BY DAY THROUGH THE GREAT WAR

The King came back on Monday. He has been everywhere (except in the trenches) and seen everything. His visit has cheered the men, especially the Indians on one of whom he personally conferred the V.C. [Victoria Cross] This is the first V.C. to be granted to an Indian and has greatly pleased them….

Army boots are being purchased by the Government at 18/6 per pair. The French Government have bought a million pairs in Northampton. It is scarcely possible to buy civilian boots in Northampton now. Manufacturers are working on Army work almost entirely.

Wednesday December 9 …A telegram tonight reports that General Beyers one of the chief rebel leaders at the Cape has been drownded. He was rounded up on the banks of a river and in trying to escape was shot and drownded. This about completes the collapse of this rebellion and I do not think much further trouble will occur in that quarter.

Thursday December 10 …Today many of the recruits who left here on Sept.6 and have been training at Shoreham and Aldershot have come home on 8 days furlough. They are dressed in dark blue (this is undress) Khaki is full dress. They talk about going to India but I do not think they will go abroad at present. They look remarkably well and have all much improved in physique. They say they are well fed (4 meals a day) Of course things were a bit rough at first as everything was so unprepared but everything is shaking down and although we have not got perfection in this army affair I have no doubt we shall pull through.

The Kaiser is reported very unwell today. Nervous prostration and bronchial catarrh. He returned to Berlin in the middle of Tuesday night and has been in bed since. Evidently the strain is telling on him.

Friday December 11 …I had a long talk with an Oundle soldier today named Bennett. He is a driver in the R.F. Artillery and came back with his battery about three weeks since from India. He tells me that when they left Bombay they had 75,000 troops on board about 40 transports and these were guarded by warships. The whole convoy stretched for nearly 50 miles and coming across the Indian Ocean presented a most splendid spectacle. Part of the troops went to the Persian Gulf, another part to British East Africa. The native Indian contingent was landed at Marseilles and hurried up into the fighting line and [the] rest came on to England and are now waiting orders to go to the front. Those landed here numbered 40,000 and are some of the finest regiments in our Army, so that it will be seen we are not quite played out yet.

The Kaiser is reported better today. The Germans are said to have tried to raid Dover harbour yesterday morning with submarines. Anyway there was a good deal of firing going on there.

1914 Sunday December 13 A very wet day. We have had very little real winter at present here. No snow and scarcely any frost.

…The record taxation imposed on beer has affected that trade very much especially in these smaller towns and villages. People decline to pay 4d per pint for beer and it must have made a considerable difference to the brewers. Smith here have only brewed once during the last fortnight instead of twice a week.

THE DIARY OF JOHN COLEMAN BINDER

Monday December 14 The Germans are again making fierce attacks on us at Ypres but without the last success, in fact they are slowly being driven back, but it is only yard by yard that this is being done… It is curious to note how old methods of war are being revived in this time. Hand Grenades are being freely used by both the Allies and the Germans in trench fighting. Another method of throwing missiles by a kind of catapult is being practised by the Austrians….

Bearing upon my note of yesterday re the effect of taxation on beer, Mr Phipps of Northampton (the brewer) said today at a public meeting that it was estimated the consumption of beer in most places had decreased 50 per cent and that even in a town like Northampton where the staple trade was exceptionally good the decrease was at least 30 per cent.

Wednesday December 16 [Defeat of Austrian troops in Servia reported]….

According to this mornings news the Germans have again been fought to a standstill in Poland and Russia is again moving forward. The great drawback to Russia is her want of railways. Germany is admirably supplied with these, and most of them have been planned with a view to military needs. Great use is being made of them, and a whole army is frequently moved in a few days.

The above was written early today. Since writing it we have received most important news. About 11.30 this morning the Press Bureau issued this announcement which was received here about 1 pm and it caused very great excitement. These are the actual words

"German movements of some importance are taking place this morning in the North Sea.

Scarborough and Hartlepool have been shelled. Our flotillas have at various points been engaged".

Later the War Office issued the following statement: "The Fortress commander at West Hartlepool reports that German war vessels engaged that fortress between 8 and 9 o'clock this morning but were driven off. A small German war vessel opened fire on Scarborough and Whitby". This is all the official news we have up to 10 pm tonight.

Private telegrams say that about 40 shells were fired on Scarborough, one house caught fire and the Balmoral Hotel was struck. A woman was also killed in a shop. Some loss of life is known to have taken place at Hartlepool.

I have quite expected that these raids would occur, and I have no doubt that they will take place again. During the long dark hours of these winter nights it is not very difficult for the enemy to creep in and to open fire as soon as day breaks. They are not very likely to do this during the night as ever since the wars commenced every light facing the sea down the whole of the East Coast has been ordered out. These raids will cause scares but of course are of no serious importance. Far more important is the battle which has opened in the North Sea and we are waiting news of this most eagerly.

Thursday December 17 The German Naval Raid is the sole topic of conversation today. The affair is more serious than was reported yesterday. That is as regards loss of life. It is estimated that nearly 50 persons were killed and 150 wounded in the three towns of Whitby, Hartlepool and Scarborough…..

Friday December 18 The raid on the North East coast still engages public attention and we now know the full extent. Up to this morning the total death roll is 97 and 150 wounded. It is probable that there will be some more deaths as many of the wounded are very badly hurt….

I had a letter today from my sister in Darlington. She heard very plainly the sound of the guns at Hartlepool.

DAY BY DAY THROUGH THE GREAT WAR

1914 Saturday December 19 A good piece of news is announced today. The British Government has deposed the Khedive of Egypt, as he has been siding with our enemies. They have proclaimed a Protectorate and have appointed a new Ruler. We hear of no fighting at all there….

We know that the Northants Yeomanry are in the trenches. Of course there is no use for cavalry just now. Their day will come later on. Several of these men have been wounded. …

Sunday December 20 Big movement of troops are taking place today in this country, but what they are for is known to the military authorities only.

From a certain point of view the railways are very much disorganised. They are nearly 20 per cent short of labour and the war requirements are tremendous. They are under the entire control of the Government. I foresee that delays in all branches will be very great this Christmas time.

There is very little heart in Christmas this year with all this dreadful war. Nobody seems to care very much about it and what preparations are being made are being done in quite a half-hearted way.

There is a certain amount of hunting being done, but the fields are very small and I think it is more for the sake of keeping the packs in order than from any desire for Sport. Shooting is very slack. In many cases the game is being sent to the Hospitals.

Recruits are still coming forward in quite good numbers. Quite as fast as the Authorities can deal with them. Since the raid on Wednesday recruiting has gone up by leaps and bounds. …

Monday December 21 Not much news today. Nothing of any importance from Belgium except we learn that the Belgian Army is back again in the fighting line. They have had a rest, been re-clothed and had new boots and are now once more ready to meet the enemy. They are much diminished in numbers but they are as brave as ever. They are quite unbroken in spirit and fight as well as ever.

Belgium itself is in a terrible condition and has moved the pity and compassion of all civilised countries. Efforts are being made to meet the hunger and wretchedness of the poor people. America is taking a good part in this work. Large funds have also been raised in this country to help.

Germany seems to have at last realized that there is no sympathy for her in any country except Turkey. She has made great efforts to secure support in America, but during the last few weeks public opinion there has definitely gone against her, more especially since the attack on Scarborough and Whitby…..

The whole of the Welsh Division of troops who had been in Northampton since Aug 31 were moved yesterday. I have not learned where they have gone to as the destination of troops is never mentioned in the papers. A fresh division is expected before long.

Saturday December 26 Owing to business I am sorry to say I have been unable to write this Diary since Monday last. We have now passed Christmas Day. Probably no such Christmas has ever been in England. To some little extent the war has been forgotten, but not for long, and how could one be very lively when we think of the terrible battle and fighting that is going on so close to us, and even if it were possible to try to forget it we have been sharply reminded by the enemy that we are at War.

On Thursday a German Aeroplane flew over Dover and dropped a bomb. It fell into a garden and very little damage was done. Yesterday, Christmas Day, another flew up the Thames Estuary about 11 o'clock. It was sighted at once by the look out men and chased and also fired upon, but escaped. These raids have been made possible by the weather we have had the last two days. Very cold and calm with slight fogs. Today has been terribly cold and for an hour or two sleet fell heavily this morning. One's heart aches for the poor fellows out in the trenches.

…..Christmas festivities are very small indeed this year. No Balls, Concerts, or anything of the kind are taking place. Some trades such as florists, sellers of Christmas Cards, Jewellers and that kind of thing have felt the depression very [much] and all articles of luxury have been very much at a discount.

THE DIARY OF JOHN COLEMAN BINDER

Wheat is getting dearer and today is worth about 49/- per qtr. It is probable that Bread in London will be raised to 7d early next week. The cause of this dearness is the lack of shipping to bring wheat over. The demand for vessels is without precedent and owners are making a lot of money. This is partly caused by the huge demand for war purposes and also to the fact that German shipping has been swept from off the seas.

1914 Sunday December 27 Yesterday the Government announced they would compensate all owners for damage done during the Raid on the North East Coast. One estimate puts it as high as 250,000, but assessors will be appointed whose duty it will be to make a report to the Government.

Today is the 146th day of the war and I cannot see that the end is at all in sight. Advices from Germany report that they are as determined as ever and most certainly this is the same with us and our Allies.

A good many soldiers are home on furlough this Christmas, and everywhere one goes you see Khaki. The new recruits are fast developing into useful soldiers and probably by March we shall be able to put another half million men into Belgium, with the certainty that as time goes on we shall be able to increase that number.

The new recruits and indeed all soldiers are having a hard time of it this winter. We have not had much snow, but alternate wet and frost, and this has made the whole country <u>Mud.</u> Mud everywhere and in all places. We are hoping now that we have turned Christmas that we may get drier weather so that training may take place under better conditions.

The Belgian Refugees are still here and a Catholic Chapel has been fitted up for their use in the house in West Street lately occupied by the York family, but has now been recently purchased by the County Council as a site for a School, and at present is not being occupied. The Refugees at Thrapston are brought over to Service here by Lord Lilford's Motor Car.

December 28 A remarkable piece of news is published this morning. On Christmas Day seven of our aeroplanes and hydroplanes made a surprise attack on the German naval base at Cuxhaven. They were accompanied by two swift warships and several submarines so that all the most recent innovations in naval war were brought into play in this battle….

Tuesday December 29 ….No news comes from Russia this morning as communication is much interrupted owing to the storms of the last few days. Yesterday was very bad. Rain hail snow and last night a perfect deluge of rain which turned to snow during the night. An immense quantity of wet fell and today the floods are rapidly rising. Berlin is much upset by the raid on Cuxhaven and threatens to attack our grain ships with submarines. This they will find rather difficult.

December 30 The storm and gale which I mentioned yesterday was general and was especially violent over the South of England, the Channel and Flanders. All warships and war craft of every description had to run for shelter, and all operations in Belgium were at a standstill…..

Campaigning this winter is awful work. Apart from the fighting, many of the men are suffering from rheumatism and frostbite. This can [be] quite understood when we know that in many instances the men are knee deep in water and liquid mud in the trenches.

December 31 Thursday Today the last day of 1914 and what a year it has been. Very few if any could have thought how it would end. Probably to some of the Germans it was known that War would break out this year. Some few in England and France dreaded that it might come, but to almost every one this war which is now being waged had been so long predicted that we had grown quite careless as [to] its coming.

Today sees 9 nations engaged in the most horrible and deadly strife that one can imagine. The horrors and ravages are impossible to describe and indeed are unknown except to those who are taking part in it, and then the area is so vast that they can only say what they have seen in their small way…..We now living cannot judge or realize in what a stupendous way History is being made from day to day. It will be for those who come after us to try if possible to learn some of the lessons of this war. As far as one can dimly discern there are two quite opposite views of it in this country, and I can clearly see that when Peace has come the divisions will be very sharp and distinct. On one hand we have a party declaring that this war will be the end of all war, and on the other a party saying that this war must naturally lead to conscription and a greater readiness for future wars. Time can only prove which is right, but of this I am firmly convinced, that Germany (even if she is beaten) will not give up war.

The love of war and the idea that 'Might is Right' is so deeply sunk into the German (or rather the Prussian) people that until this is got rid of there can be no permanent peace in the world....

The price of wheat is steadily advancing. Today it is worth 50/- per qtr and ordinary Bakers Flour is 40/- per 20st. sack It is generally thought in the trade that should [the war] be prolonged after next year's harvest, we shall see wheat much dearer. Farmers in this country have been urged to plant a larger acreage of wheat, but as far as can be judged at present they do not appear to have done so. Possibly this may [be] done in the Spring if the weather is favourable.

THE DIARY OF JOHN COLEMAN BINDER

1915 Friday Jan 1st The Year has opened badly for us.

This afternoon a telegram announces that the battleship 'Formidable', a vessel of 15,000 tons, has been sunk in the Channel. The survivors are only 70 so that probably about 700 brave sailors have gone down. The cause is not given, probably it was either a mine or a submarine. ….The ship we can replace, but it is the loss of the men that grieves one so much.

In other directions the news is good today. The French are making some progress in Alsace and are gradually driving the Germans back, but it is only a few hundred yards at a time.

Letters which have been received from the front seem to say there was an informal truce along the lines at Christmas. In many places the men left the trenches to talk to each other and in one place went so far as to play a game of football, but fighting was grimly renewed at night.

Saturday Jan 2nd. A dearth of news today… The weather conditions are fearful. Continued rain. December was the wettest month on record and this is all against army movements… Tonight a telegram says that a total of 100 men were saved from the 'Formidable' and that they were brought into Torbay.

Sunday Jan 3. The first Sunday of the New Year.

Today is being observed as a day of Intercession throughout the British Empire, also in America, France, Belgium and Russia. Special services are being held in every place of Worship and collections are being taken on behalf of the Red Cross Fund.

It is not called a Day of Humiliation but a day of Intercession and Thanksgiving and assuredly we in these Islands have deep cause for thankfulness. It is true we are helping to bear the strain and stress, but at present not one hostile soldier or sailor has set foot on these shores…

Monday Jan 4 ….I hear today on good authority that one reason we are not moving much is that we are waiting for new heavy artillery. I think the delay is all to our advantage as it allows a longer training for the new Armies. Time is without doubt on our side.

The composition of our new Armies is announced today. There are to be six of [them] but we are not told how many divisions each will consist of. Each will be under the command of a well-known General, all of whom have held high command under Sir John French.

The wet still continues and the rain is almost incessant not only here but also on the Continent. This of course is also greatly against all fighting.

Bread today is advanced to 6 ½ d per 4lb loaf.

Tuesday Jan 5…..A few more men have gone from here, but the supply of eligible men here is pretty well exhausted.

The recruiting papers which I mentioned as being sent to every house by post are now being tabulated and up to the present about 250,000 promises to enlist have been received. These are being called up as accommodation is provided for them. It will be about 4 months from now before the total result of this appeal is known.

1915 Wednesday Jan 6 We have today a day without rain. I do not think this has occurred for the [past] 5 or 6 weeks. The Floods are very high, more especially in the Thames valley and the West country. The nave of Salisbury Cathedral is flooded, a thing which has not taken place for 70 years…..

Thursday Jan7 News of Turkish defeats in the Caucasus.

Rumours are circulating today to the effect that the Government will shortly take over the whole of the railways for about a week and only let through traffic that is very urgent as they intend to move about 750,000 men to the front. The working of the railways is causing very much inconvenience and delay to traders. Every line is very much blocked and there is a great shortage of labour. Goods coming from London are sometimes a week on the way. In ordinary times they only take a day to get through.

DAY BY DAY THROUGH THE GREAT WAR

Jan 8 Friday ….A statement was made in the House of Lords last night regarding the sinking of the 'Formidable'. It was stated that the Admiralty were quite of opinion that she was torpedoed by a submarine. This evidently was the opinion of her Captain (a Northants man) for the last signal he hoisted was a warning for the other ships to sheer off as he was afraid they might share his fate.

Jan 9 Saturday Slow advance of French in Alsace.

Amongst the wounded today are the names of Lieut Tryon and Lieut Benyon. The former was a junior master at the School here and was given a commission in the K R Rifles in September, Benyon in the Northants Yeomanry and is a son of Col. Benyon of Islip. He was educated here.

Sunday Jan 10 A sharp frost this morning followed by a cold wet day. The floods are running down very quickly.

Report of French commission of enquiry into charges brought against German troops is published. Break-up of Austro- Hungarian Empire expected, with Italy and Rumania likely to join in..

Jan 11 Monday. …Nothing is more striking than the bearing of the French, both the Army and the Nation. To one who can remember the conflict of 1870 - 71 the change is marvellous. Then they were all excitement shouting "À Berlin". Today they seem as cool and quiet as ourselves, but underneath this one can see the grim determination to see this through. The shouting has all been in Germany this time. Their cry has been "First to Paris, then to London", but signs are not wanting that this is not an easy task to accomplish. The way their Army and People is fooled is almost incredible. An officer (English) writing home on Christmas Day says that during the informal truce on that day a German Officer had asked him "how many troops (German) it had required to capture London" as they had been told that London was taken and that Paris would soon share the same fate. This is only a sample of what is going on. In the Belgian territory now held by the Germans it is a penal offence to be found in possession of an English newspaper, but sooner or later they must learn the real truth.

Concern that America is smuggling copper, hidden in bales of cotton, to Germany, which is desperate for supplies to make ammunition.

Quite a fleet of German aeroplanes were over Dunkirk yesterday afternoon and it was thought they were heading for Dover and London, but the Belgian and French aviators fought them and headed them off. They dropped a lot of bombs on Dunkirk. Five people were killed and a good deal of damage done. News of this raid was sent on to London and the special constables were called up at some points but their services were not required. I quite think they will try the bomb dropping business in England.

Tuesday January 12 ……Wheat continues to advance and today is quoted at 54/- in local markets. The chief causes for this seem to be, violent speculation in America and Canada, bad harvest weather in Argentina, the total absence of Russian and want of ships. This last cause has been worked by ship-owners for all it is worth and they have combined to raise freights to an enormous extent. Freight from Argentina in normal times is about 12/- to 14/- per ton. Today it is 60/-. I hope the government will step in and break up this ring.

1915 Wednesday Jan 13 Amongst the killed in action in today's papers appears the name of Capt F. C. Norbury of the ---------------------- He came to Oundle School when very young, was educated here, and after going to Cambridge came back as a master. He was a Lieutenant in the Officers Training Corps and at once received a commission in the Army when war was declared. He was killed in action at ------. This is the tenth old boy belonging to the School who has been killed or wounded…..

The King and Lord Kitchener yesterday reviewed a splendid division of 20,000 men which has been concentrated at Winchester. They are crossing to France tomorrow. It consists principally of old seasoned soldiers, most of whom have been brought home from India. Colonel Smith of Oundle is in command of one of the Artillery Brigades in this division.

THE DIARY OF JOHN COLEMAN BINDER

Vague rumours are current again today as to the intention of the Turks to invade Egypt. The idea is to draw off pressure from Flanders, but it is very doubtful if they will do much harm. A very remarkable fact of the present situation is the steady loyalty of all the Mussulman people throughout the Empire. The Germans had hoped for great things in this respect, but have been very much disappointed. It was thought that the Sultan of Turkey as the head of the Mohammedan Church would be able to incite a Holy War, but it has fallen quite flat, and all natives are giving us all the help and support they can. This incident reveals one great drawback in the German character. They seem quite unable to take into account the 'Human Factor'. They are so drilled disciplined and dragooned themselves, that they seem quite unable to grasp the fact that there is such a thing as individuality.

Contributions still continue to come in in great numbers from all classes in the Empire to the Red Cross Fund, quite casually I note today a gift of $1000 dollars from a tribe of North American Indians.

The Prince of Wales Fund now exceeds 4 millions and the Red Cross a million. The total amount received from Churches and Chapels on the day of Intercession is not yet announced but it must be very large as long lists are published each day.

There are over 200,000 Indians fighting at the present time for the Empire.

The circumstances under which Captain Norbury was killed I have today heard are quite pathetic. He and several of his men were asleep in the trenches when a shell fired from one of our guns fell short and dropped into the trench, killing three of them instantly and wounding several others.

Thursday Jan 14   Severe fighting near Soissons- French driven back

.Friday Jan 15   Further report of French reverse....   The subscription[s] from this parish to the National Relief Fund up to the present amount to £271. This is exclusive of money contributed to the Red Cross. This drain of money in these rural districts is having an adverse effect on trade. It is [very] difficult to get payment of Ac[counts] and this combined with the high price of almost every article makes trading difficult.

We are almost threatened with a glass famine especially in ordinary window and plate glass. Belgium has had almost a monopoly in these and as they were manufactured in the Liege district the supply to this country has ceased altogether.

The wives and mothers of soldiers in this parish were entertained last night at the National School. There were 70 present.

Sunday Jan 17 A fine clear day today but very cold. ... The price of all corn has been risen very much during the last week, and in consequence Bread has been advanced. The price of the 4lb loaf today in London Is 7 1/2 and 8d.

We are still selling it here at 6 ½d but it will certainly be raised to 7d this week. Flour today is quoted at 43/- and 44/- for ordinary bakers, a rise of 18/- since July.

Various reasons combine to force up the price. The principal one being the shortage of shipping. Of course all German and Austrian ships are driven off the seas, consequently the greater part of the world's carrying falls on the English. The Government have also taken a huge number of ships for all kinds of purposes and this has increased the shortage. Labour is also very scarce at all the Ports and there are delays of two to three weeks in unloading ships. I am told today that there are at least 30 ships in the Mersey awaiting unloading.

I think this is the principal cause, and of course it gives the American speculator a chance to exploit us of which he is not slow to avail himself.

There is a good deal of anger rising against this state of things, and the feeling is that our Government ought to step in to put a stop to it. Complaints are deep and frequent that Parliament is not sitting (they do not meet again until February) as then the question could be raised and possibly some action taken.

DAY BY DAY THROUGH THE GREAT WAR

The second battalion of the Yeomanry which is in training at Towcester, is now full up. 528. They are getting quite efficient an[d] were highly complimented at their inspection this week.

1915 Monday Jan 18 The Russians are routing the Turks in the Caucasus. The Turks are said to be advancing through Syria towards Egypt, where British, Indian and Australian troops are waiting for them..

Tuesday Jan 19 The Russians seem to have gained control of the Black Sea...

Some people here criticise our own Navy and ask what it is doing. If they would only consider a few minutes they could easily see. Their watch and guard is vigilant and unceasing. Our food supplies although dearer are adequate, our shores are guarded to a very large extent, and our communication with the Army in France goes on without the least interruption. The wounded from the front are brought straight home to be nursed and cared for. Many of these within 30 hours of their being injured are in hospital in this country. (many of them are covered with Flanders mud). So these things are quite sufficient proof [of] our Navy's work, and the debt we all owe to them cannot be told.

A very drastic notice is issued by the Treasury today. No new public issues of Capital may be made without their approval as the Government feel that all private considerations [? must] be subordinated to the necessity of husbanding the resources of the country with a view to the successful issue of this war. New issues for undertakings outside the United Kingdom will not be allowed at all.

Wednesday Jan 20 Last night about 8.15 an aircraft flew over Yarmouth and dropped some bombs. 4 persons were killed and a good deal of damage done to buildings. It (or they) then flew along the Norfolk Coast and bombs were dropped at Kings Lynn and also close to Sandringham. The King and Queen had only left for London a few hours before. It is not know[n] whether this aircraft or crafts were Zeppelins or aeroplanes as they were not seen, but the noise of the engines was heard and a flash light was also seen.

The weather has been favourable for these flights the last few days as there has been hardly any wind.

Thursday Jan 21 Berlin jubilant over raid. We know that these attacks on unfortified places and on civilians are quite contrary to all recognised rules of war...

News coming in of naval battle off the Falkland Islands.

Friday Jan 22 Not much news of importance today except that the German Chief of Staff has been dismissed or has resigned. He is the second Chief to go since the war began. These men do not seem very happy with the Kaiser.

Newspapers of neutral countries (especially America) had some scathing comments on the Yarmouth and Lynn raid today. Germany is bluntly told that it will be long before the stain of this wanton act of savagery is wiped out and that she will realize what these raids cost when the time comes to discuss the terms of peace.

Saturday Jan 23 An important piece of news comes to hand this morning. The heir to the Austrian throne together with the new Foreign Minister have gone to Berlin, it is said with the object of getting the Kaiser to allow Austria to conclude a separate peace, but I can hardly think he will agree to this. Nevertheless it shows that Austria is sick of the war as she may well be.

Two Zeppelins were over Lynn and Hunstanton again last night. They were clearly seen and shots were fired at them but they did not drop any bombs. Some of the bombs dropped at various places on Tuesday made holes 10 or 12 feet in diameter and 6 feet deep.

Fierce fighting in the Argonne. A very heavy snow over London and the east of England yesterday. We had very little of it here.

THE DIARY OF JOHN COLEMAN BINDER

1915 Sunday Jan 24 A dull cheerless day to-day. but without rain . An aeroplane passed over here this morning about 10.15. These craft are very active just now and one is always on the look-out, as it is felt that the Germans may try another raid at any time.

Warnings have been issued in all the towns and places on the east coast, telling the people to at once get into cellars or places underground should an airship appear.

Notices have also been issued (there is one in yesterday's Peterboro Advertiser) that immediately any aircraft are seen, all lights are to be put out and that the supply of gas and electricity will be shut off from the works.

A big business has also been done in insurance against damage done by bombs. A good many daily papers are taking it up and any person ordering a regular delivery of a certain paper will be insured to the amount of £250.

Grain prices have steadied somewhat during this week, and although possibly 1/- higher on the week there has been no sensational rise as there was last week.

The Government are putting on some of the captured ships to carry coal to London from the northern ports as the railways are fairly congested. Passenger traffic is about normal but the goods is very bad. Goods which left Liverpool a fortnight since are still on the way.

The total death roll at Hartlepool and Sunderland is over 200.

Monday Jan 25 Splendid news this morning. It is so good that I cannot do better than write down the announcement as issued by the Admiralty last night.

Admiralty, Sunday , 7.50 p.m. Early this morning a British patrolling Squadron of battle cruisers and light cruisers under Vice-Admiral Sir David Beatty with a destroyer flotilla under Commander Tyrwhitt sighted four German battle cruisers and a number of Destroyers steering westward and apparently making for the English Coast.

The Flight and Pursuit The enemy at once made for home at high speed. They were at once pursued and at about 9.10 a.m. action was joined between our battle cruisers Lion, Tiger, Princess Royal, New Zealand and Indomitable on the one hand and the Derflinger, Seydlitz, Molhte and Blucher on the other. A well contested running fight ensued. Shortly after one o'clock the Blucher which had previously fallen out of the line capsized and sank.

Chase checked by Minefields. Admiral Beatty reports that two other battle-cruisers were seriously damaged. They were however able to continue their flight and reached an area where dangers from German submarines and mines prevented further pursuit.

No British ships have been lost and our casualties in personnel, as at present reported, are slight, the Lion which led the line have only eleven wounded and no killed.

A hundred and twenty-three survivors have been rescued from the Blucher's crew of 835 and it is possible that others have been saved by some of our Destroyers.

Light Cruiser Action No reports of any light cruiser action have yet been received by the Admiralty though some has apparently taken place.

Their Lordships have expressed their satisfaction to the Vice-Admiral Sir David Beatty.

The foregoing dispatch tells its own tale, but a few words may be added. It is pretty well known that this raid was expected, and that a very keen look-out was being kept. As I said of the former naval raid they would come once too often, and this has proved to be true.

Apparently they intended a much bigger thing this time, as their fleet consisted of battle cruisers as well as light cruisers, but thank God they have been frustrated. All the Empire is rejoicing to-day at this success………Up to writing this at 4 p.m. no further news of the light cruiser action has been received.

….Things have also been very lively in other directions this week-end. Fierce fighting in Alsace and the Argonne. A German Air raid on Dunkirk which was checked by our (English) airmen, assisted by French and Belgian aviators. The enemy dropped 65 bombs11 Civilians ere killed. The German aeroplane was knocked to pieces and the Pilot and airman (who were wearing British uniforms) were captured.

Our airmen have also been to Zeebrugge again, and dropped some bombs on a German submarine and also on their big guns. All this activity is accounted for by the improved weather. We quite expect that when spring does come, the fighting will be desperate.

The French War Minister was over in this country on Friday and Saturday and was much cheered and astonished by the preparations we are making for the next campaign.

A letter was received to-day from the Oundle man (Butt) who is a prisoner in Germany. He says he is well treated, and has received money and eatables that have been sent to him.

1915 Tuesday Jan 26 ……It is announced to-day that a committee of Cabinet is considering the rise in price of all foodstuffs, with a view to seeking a remedy, more especially as regards bread. I fail to see what they can do in [that] respect to-day, except that possibly something may be done about freight. We are entirely in the hands of America as regards prices just now and the world's wheat market is not at the Baltic as it usually is but in Chicago and New York.

Wednesday Jan 27 The most significant news this morning is that the German Government have seized all the grain in Germany and that no private dealings in it will be allowed after to-day. It would be quite easy to exaggerate the importance of this step. But at the same time it clearly shows that the pressure is being felt in Germany. They have always said they had quite sufficient wheat to carry them well over next harvest, but this seems to be very doubtful. We in this country shall watch with much curiosity the result of this experiment. I do not think the same thing could be done here as conditions in the corn trade are so very different, but there is some talk of it being attempted. …..`

Thursday Jan 28 The Turkish troops who have been crossing the desert to invade Egypt yesterday came into contact with our Patrols. A little skirmishing at long range ensued, but with very little loss. No alarm is felt in this country about this invasion as it is felt that the force we have in Egypt is quite capable of dealing with the Turks.

A significant announcement is made to-day. The Bank of England has lent Roumania 5 millions of money. This looks as if they intended war. ….

Friday Jan 29 A big battle is expected in the Carpathian Mts between Austria and the Russians.

Saturday Jan 30 …The line of contact between Russia and the enemy now stretches for 530 miles, from the Baltic down to Transylvania in [the] South. It is indeed marvellous how these tremendous armies are kept going. Of course, there is not fighting all along the line, but at the same time all points are adequately guarded and should pressure be put on any one place reinforcements are at once hurried up.

So ends the last week of six months of war…..It seems almost useless to try to read the future, but I cannot but think that the Germans will make tremendous efforts to achieve something decisive during the next two months, that is before the Allies can exert their full fighting strength…..We think Austria to be the weak point in her armour, and it [is] probable the first efforts towards peace will be made there; but all talk of peace is at present quite premature. The end is not yet

THE DIARY OF JOHN COLEMAN BINDER

Sunday Jan 31 A quiet winter Sunday. One wonders what news we shall hear to night or in the morning. Sunday during this war has always been a favourite day for German and Austrian attacks. The weather has improved during the last few days and farmers are beginning to think about seeding again. They are being urged to sow a larger area of wheat and I think that tempted by the high prices now ruling they will do so. They are looking forward with some misgiving to the labour questions during next summer. The drain of recruits from every village and hamlet has made labour scarce, and I think the position of the farmer will be rather difficult.

1915 February 1 The chief news to-day is that German submarines have appeared in the Irish Sea off the Mersey during Saturday and yesterday and have blown up at least three of our merchant vessels. They have been threatening to do this for some weeks past and have now put their threat into practice. They also attacked the Irish mail Boat from Fleetwood but the Captain cleverly evaded capture. The crews of the ships were given ten minutes to clear off. A bomb was then taken aboard and exploded causing the ships to sink at once……

Parliament meets to-morrow and the Labour Party to-day issue a manifesto calling upon the Government to purchase and control all grain supplies, and also to regulate the price of coal.

It is a fact beyond dispute that England is the cheapest place in the world for Bread. And I quite believe that more harm than good will be done if the Government attempt to fix prices.

Sixteen recruits left Oundle and the neighbourhood to-day.

Thursday Feb 2 …The sinking of the merchant ships has caused some uneasiness in shipping circles and insurance rates soared up rapidly yesterday.

Yesterday notice was given in Berlin that only ½ lb of Bread would be allowed to each person per day, and this would be 'War Bread' that is a mixture of Potatoes Rye and wheat. The feeding of pigs with grain is also absolutely forbidden. All house refuse is to be collected and sold to pig keepers. One may detest these Germans and their doings, but at the same time, it is impossible not to admire their organising abilities.

Wednesday Feb 3 News of battle in Poland.   Wheat trading has been very excited to-day and yesterday both here and in America. Prices advanced fully 2/6 per quarter and to-day wheat is worth £3 per qr. Delivered to the mill. Millers are asking 46/- per sack for ordinary flour, an advance of 20/- per sack since war began.

Thursday Feb 4 Signs are not wanting that we are entering upon a new era in this awful war. Germany is openly preaching war in its most ruthless forms. To-day she put these into practice by trying to torpedo a hospital ship flying the red cross flag and lying off the French coast. Fortunately the attack did not succeed.

She is also saying they will destroy all merchant vessels without warning and all that kind of thing, but public opinion in this country is quite unmoved and we shall keep on our way to the bitter end. The taking over of all food supplies by the German Government has raised very difficult questions regarding contraband. It is quite probable we shall retaliate by declaring all food consigned to Germany to be contraband. This would be quite without precedent, but the situations caused by this war are so novel and complicated that they can only be dealt with as they arise…..*Battle escalating in Poland.*

Friday Feb 5 The Turks attempted yesterday to cross the Suez Canal but were repulsed by our Troops (Lancastrian Territorials and the Australians). Their equipment was captured, and they were defeated with heavy loss. One of our warships was in the Canal and took part in the action and had ten men wounded…..There was a scare at Peterborough and along the East Coast last week. It was thought the Germans might attempt another Zeppelin raid on the Kaiser's birthday. Troops were hurried into Peterboro (only territorials recruits are quartered there). The lights were put out, all roads leading into the city were barricaded by vehicles being drawn across them and sentries were posted, every one coming in being required to give an account of himself.

DAY BY DAY THROUGH THE GREAT WAR

This was to prevent the airships being guided by motor cars with big headlights. It is practically certain that when they raided Yarmouth and Lynn they were guided by a motor displaying these lights and no doubt driven by spies. It was seen by many persons who thought its movements were suspicious. Nothing occurred at Peterborough and no airships came over at all. This kind of thing is not reported in the papers and I only heard of it yesterday. It was told to me by a man who was held up by the sentries and questioned.

1915 Saturday Feb 6 News of great importance to-day. The battle in Central Poland has and is developing and bids fair to be one of the greatest battles of this great war......

Other equally serious news to-day is the remarkable outburst from neutral nations against Germany's actions with regard to ships. Yesterday they gave notice that they would sink any ships (ours or belonging to neutrals) which they found in certain areas in the Channel or off the coast of France -   I am now speaking of merchant vessels - and would send the crews to the bottom. This is against all international law, and has made public opinion in America furious.

They are told in American papers this morning that they are playing with fire and that the first American ship that is touched will raise most serious questions and may lead to the States joining the Allies.

The pretext assigned by the Germans for this action is that they allege we are using neutral flags to protect our shipping. This is not true....

Feb 7 Sunday....I hear a very surprising piece of news to-day. It is to effect that the Government have forbidden the Railways to accept any more grain for removal at present. What their object is I cannot understand and we shall only learn later on. To say the least of it this must cause grave inconvenience

The food question is growing more serious. Prices are steadily rising and may yet cause many difficulties. To-day I paid 11d per lb. For best joint of Beef. This may not seem dear when compared with larger towns, but it is very high for us. Cheese is 11d and 1/- per lb. Pork is at present fairly cheap i.e. wholesale. As so many pigs are being slaughtered on account of the high price of feeding stuffs. Little pigs 8 weeks old are to be bought at 6/- or 7/- each. The high price of food is due partly to the enormous purchases made [by] our own and foreign governments for the troops. It is quite certain that never before have soldiers on active service been so well fed. They get their meals quite regularly and the food is of excellent quality. The meat question has been made much easier by using chilled meat. This is much easier for transport and the armies do not have to be followed by huge droves of cattle as has been the custom in war. The men all say they are well fed, and certainly they have that appearance.

Monday Feb 8 Good news from Poland to-day for so far the German attacks have not succeeded and the Russians have assumed the offensive.... The Military critic in The Times to-day regards it as Von Hindenberg's last and supreme effort and that if he fails now he will have to fall back....the German position in Poland has become untenable owing to their distance from their base and to the Polish winter......

Fighting still goes on all along the line in France and Belgium. It is assuming a more violent character as the casualty list to-day shows. This contains the names of nearly 50 killed and wounded in the Northamptons.

Tuesday Feb 9 Events are very quiet in the Western area....

Feb 10 Wednesday No news to-day of any importance except that the German government has commandeered all metals and will only allow them to be used as they direct. They are feeling the want of copper very much (it is largely used in making ammunition) so much so that they have closed down many of the public electrical works in the smaller towns and have confiscated the copper fittings. They are using acetylene gas instead. The silent pressure of our navy is slowly but surely throttling Germany in many directions.

THE DIARY OF JOHN COLEMAN BINDER

Feb 11 Thursday Battle in the Carpathian mountains…Germans and Austrians defeated by Russians…… Arrangements have been made to billet 3000 soldiers in Wellingbro next Monday. I have not learned at present what they are. It is quite possible that we shall have some billeted here shortly.

1915 Feb 12 Friday The German submarine U 12 yesterday attempted to hold up one of our merchant ships but she defied them and refused to stop. They then attempted to torpedo her but missed, and after a chase of one hour she escaped into a Dutch port.

The Government in the House last night said they did not intend to fix prices in food stuffs, as they were quite of opinion that matters would right themselves before long. I quite think this is much the best course to take, and it is the opinion of the corn trade (also millers) generally.

We are gradually learning the system that Germany is trying to work with regard to bread supply, and I will write it down in a few days.

Feb 13 Saturday ….Not much is being done ….in Flanders and France. Artillery work still continues and we here know that men are quietly being sent to France in large numbers but it is quite impossible owing to the weather conditions to expect any big movement at present.

Reports sent by neutral persons who have been to Belgium reveal a pitiable state of affairs. The people are groaning under German tyranny and extortions. All work has ceased, in many districts the people are being fed by Americans and helped by money raised in this country but every one who has been there agrees that the Belgian spirit is as brave as ever, and all that the people ask is When will the *English and French come?* …..

Feb 14 Sunday A wet cold winter's day. Yesterday snow fell heavily for some hours but disappeared very quickly. This continued wet is retarding wheat sowing in this county to some extent. Markets are quieter the last few days and prices of wheat have receded about 1/- per qtr. It is now worth about 58/-. The food question is causing much difficulty to Germany. Their new system of bread distribution commences to-morrow, and we shall be very curious to see how it works. The following is a rough sketch of it: The Government have commandeered all grain at a fixed price. Any attempt to try to conceal it is visited by heavy penalties, and the grain may be taken without payment at all if it is concealed. This grain is controlled by local committees under the supervision of a central one. The grain is issued by the committee to the local millers in limited quantities. The Flour is issued to the Bakers on requisitions signed by the Committee, and finally the Bread is issued to the consumers (at the rate of ½ lb per head per day). The head of each household receives a book containing a given number of coupons for which he pays, and these can be exchanged for Bread. At restaurants etc. if a person wishes to eat Bread he has to produce his coupon for that day.

It will be seen by these regulations the system is very complex, and I should say is open to evasion.

A great air raid was made on the enemy's lines at Ostend and other places on Friday by a fleet of 34 aeroplanes and hydroplanes, which left their base at Dover and flew across, did a good deal of damage and returned safely. This is the largest fleet of aircraft that has ever been in action. People living at Dover say they looked like a covey of huge birds. They travelled at about 60 miles an hour so that it would take them about 25 minutes to cross.

Feb 15 Monday The tension between America and Germany over the shipping question is increasing, and it looks as if it may be a very difficult thing to adjust if Germany persists in her threat to torpedo neutral vessels. Public opinion in America is very excited, and their Government is being urged to take action at once.

Tonight the Chancellor said in the House the cost of the war to the Allies up to Dec.31 would be £2,000 Millions. It looks as if this must eventually lead to bankruptcy.

Feb 16 Tuesday. A great night in the House of Commons last night. The Chancellor of the Exchequer and the First lord of the Admiralty both made very important speeches dealing with the war. Reading between the lines of the Chancellor's speech one can see that there are other nations who are waiting to join in this war, and that the Allies are prepared to finance them…..

DAY BY DAY THROUGH THE GREAT WAR

The First Lord speaking of Germany's threat to sink our merchantmen with their crews denounced it as piracy and murder and said that we should retaliate by using the full force of our navy against her. This I take to mean that we shall declare all food contraband. Germany seems to be terribly alarmed by what we have done and without doubt the pressure is growing severe on her.

The outlook between Germany and America is as black as possible. Americans are now leaving in considerable numbers and are coming to Denmark and England. In many instances they have been insulted in the streets of Berlin and other large cities.

…….The Germans are determined if possible to reach a decisive result on their Eastern Frontier before the campaign really opens in France and Belgium.

1915 Feb 17 Wednesday Sir John French's dispatch bringing the war up to Jan 31 is published to-day. It discloses many things we have not known before, especially with regard to the fighting of Dec 17-20. The fighting was very severe and the enemy almost succeeded in forcing our lines. The Indians were nearly broken and it was only by bringing up the 1st Division under Sir Douglas Haig that the rush was stopped. This division is earning for itself a fame that equal[s] the fame of Crawfurd's division in the Peninsular War…..

The first exchange of prisoners has taken place to-day. These are men who are quite maimed for life and so will be incapable of fighting. Our men bring back reports of very indifferent treatment they have received in Germany. All of them confirm the report that English prisoners are treated the worst of all the Allies. The food especially is bad, and is only such as would be thrown away in this country. If complaint is made the Germans reply "England is trying to starve us and you must die first". I quite believe this food question is the most serious one for the enemy. To-morrow is the day on which Germany has announced she will sink without warning *all* shipping coming to this country. So far this threat has had very little effect here as it is generally thought that is "Bluff".

Thursday Feb 18 …..The names of officers and men mentioned in General French's dispatch for distinguished conduct are published to-day. Amongst them are the names of Colonel Wickham (Cotterstock Hall) commanding the Northants Yeomanry, and Major Riddell of the Artillery who married one of the Miss Smiths of the Rectory. Colonel Wickham is the only Yeomanry officer mentioned.

Rumours are current this afternoon that 5 Argentine Wheat Ships have been sunk in the Atlantic, but up to to-night this is not confirmed. Private letters from Portsmouth say that a big lot of soldiers are continually crossing to France, especially this week. It is said 90,000 are going within the next few days. It is almost certain the enemy will try to sink some of them, but I do not think they can do much. The precaution taken is so stringent.

Feb 19 Yesterday passed without anything happening on the sea to our merchantmen or to those of neutrals…..and as far as can be ascertained not a single ship stayed in port.

Another Zeppelin airship was wrecked off the coast. This makes the second that has come to grief this week, and another is reported this morning as having been obliged to come down on neutral territory, in Denmark, and if she cannot get away within 24 hours she will be interned until the end of the war. So far these airships have not played a very successful part in this war. Ever since they were invented we have been told of the great things they would do, but all this boasting proves false like many other tales mad[e] in Germany…..

The food question in Germany is evidently becoming serious. We learn from Copenhagen to-day that rioting occurred yesterday in Berlin when food was being served out at the Municipal Bread Shops.

Feb 20 Saturday The 201st day of the war which we are told is really now commencing and it seems as if this is true.

Hard fighting on our front near Ypres is told to-day and no doubt many of our brave men have gone under. The Casualty list of Jan 1 which is published to-day contains 900 names, amongst them those of 42 Northamptons killed. Our own county regiment has suffered severely during this war, and I cannot think there are many of the 1st Battalion (the 48th) who went out in August that have escaped death or wounds.

I had a talk with the wife of one of them to-day, a man named Fox, she heard from him yesterday and although he has been through all the fighting, up to the present he has not received a scratch. When he wrote he was out of the trenches learning hand grenade throwing. There is a lot of this done on both sides……Notice is given in many papers to-day that Railway traffic next week will be much curtailed, This is taken to mean that large bodies of troops will be moved across to France. Recruiting still goes on briskly. To-day it is reported that up to the present 86,000 men in Ireland have joined the colours. This does not look like rebellion as the Kaiser hoped and believed.

1915 Feb 21 Sunday We have heard no news to-day. It is a beautiful bright spring day and probably it is the same in Belgium. The "Times " Fund to-day for the Red Cross Work reaches a million of money, and the Prince of Wales fund 4,7000,000. This fund has done useful work, but there is very little distress and want. All labour is fully employed and the difficulty is really to find the men to do the work.

The relations between America and Germany still continue very strained. So far the only result of the threatened blockade by the submarines which began last Thursday has been the torpedoing of a Norwegian oil ship off Dover yesterday morning. She did not sink but was towed into the Downs. Great care is being taken to guard the passage of our troops across to France and it is a fact that although a million of men have been carried to and from that country and other countries not a single life has been lost. This will convey some idea of the impotence of the German Navy. Wheat and other prices have remained fairly steady this week. There was a little set back early in the week, but this has been made up again, and the price is now about equal to the highest viz 58/- to 59/- per qtr. Flour is about 47/- to 48/- per sack (wholesale) . Bread here was advanced to 7 ½ d per loaf last Wednesday.

Monday Feb 22 A entirely new move in the war is disclosed this morning. On Saturday the combined English and French Fleets bombarded the forts on the Dardanelles, but they do not know if much damage was done. The object of this move is quite plain, but as to its success I am doubtful. The object is to open a passage to Russia which at the present moment is quite cut off from us. She has a big quantity of corn to export and we should be very glad to get it. Russia is badly in want of arms ammunition and war material of all kinds. Archangel is closed by ice, and of course the Baltic is also barred.

I do not think it will be much use trying to force the Dardanelles, they are too closely guarded by forts and mines.

Hostile aeroplanes were over Essex last night and a bomb was dropped at Coggeshall. No damage except broken windows.

A merchantman carrying copper was sunk off the Welsh coast on Saturday by a submarine. Four of her crew were drownded.

The food business in Germany is getting serious. Every effort is being made to eke out their supplies to the very last, but without doubt they are slowly drifting to starvation. Germany the last 10 years has become a nation which imports large quantities of food and cannot grow enough to support her people. This was pointed out by one of her leading men a few years since. She was prepared for a war lasting six months, but not for one lasting longer than that, consequently she made tremendous efforts to strike quickly and crush her foes at once. Possibly she would have succeeded if we had not come in, and this is the cause of her bitter hatred of us. Starvation may end this war, but not in the way we want it ended. Unless Germany is well beaten in fighting I am quite sure that as soon as she has made preparations and provisioned herself she will be wanting to fight again.

Tuesday Feb 23 No more news concerning the Dardanelles up to to-night. This is thought to be a serious attempt to strike a blow at Turkey and Germany also to help Servia, and to induce Roumania to come in on our side. One can only hope that it has been carefully and well thought out and planned or it may end in disaster. Considering the time the Turks assisted by German officers have had to strengthen the defences it will be a pretty hard nut to crack…..

DAY BY DAY THROUGH THE GREAT WAR

Wednesday Feb 24 Two more merchantmen were sunk in the Channel yesterday. One a Norwegian and the other British. The Boulogne -Calais mail steamer also had a very narrow escape. A submarine fired a torpedo at her and only missed by about 30 yards. She had 92 passengers on board and of course was unarmed. Such acts as these are sheer piracy….

1915 Thursday Feb 25 The Russians have quite resumed the offensive towards the North Polish battle fields again. Once the Germans get out of touch with their railways they are done, and it is quite so now. They cannot get their troops and material over the snowy wastes. The Russians being used to winter conditions are much better served in this respect. The great want of Russia is arms and equipment. She has enormous reserves of men, but cannot bring them into the field as they are not equipped.

   Our armies are getting well off as regards this. Nearly all of them have received their clothes and kit, but rifles are still required in large numbers….

Friday Feb 26 The raids of submarines continue. A week has now elapsed since they put their threat into practice. Sixteen vessels English and neutrals have been sunk in that time, but the damage done is really very small, when compared with the number of ships entering and leaving the ports in this country. These amount to between 12,000 and 13,000 according to official figures….

Saturday Feb 27…..The Allied Fleets have destroyed the forts at the entrance to the Dardanelles…Vessels are also mine sweeping…. Various theories are brought forward as to what is intended by this move in the east….what is really intended is known only to a few people…….I am afraid relations with America do not improve. This question of contraband may yet cause us much trouble.

Sunday Feb 28 This morning it [is] announced that further movements are being made in the Dardanelles. This bombardment has caused a good deal of excitement in the wheat trade the last few days and yesterday prices dropped quite 2/6 per qtr in New York, Chicago and Winnipeg. If the Straits can be forced Russia will be able to send 20,000,000 bushels of wheat besides other corn, and this will tend to reduce prices very considerably here. I think that some speculators may yet burn their fingers. Wheat to-day sold at 56 to 57/-. I know that a lot has been bought at 62/- and 63/-.

   Labour troubles amongst the ship workers and engineers is causing some uneasiness just now. Things seem drifting to a big strike, but yesterday the Government [gave] a sharp warning to all concerned. Practically told them to stop their fooling and to resume work to-morrow morning. It is quite certain the country will not stand any nonsense of this kind when we are fighting for our very life. Yesterday there was issued to every house in the County a circular signed by Earl Spencer Lord Lieutenant giving instructions as to what is to be done in case of invasion. It is too long to quote here but a copy will be found at the end of this book.

   Personally I do not think there is any danger of invasion and have always been f that opinion. The last time the Germans came raiding they got such a mauling that quieted them down and we hear very little of their boasting as to what they intend to do with their fleet.

Monday March 1st. The Admiralty say that warships have gone 15 miles up the Dardanelles Straits, having destroyed the forts at the entrance, and the mine-sweepers having cleared a path. They are now about to attack the forts at the Narrows. …Included in the fleet is the 'Queen Elizabeth', one of the very latest Super Dreadnoughts, carrying 15" guns which are capable of throwing a shell weighing a ton to a distance of 28 miles. This is the heaviest gun mounted on ships in the world……..The battleship 'Queen Elizabeth' mentioned to-day is the first warship that is entirely driven by oil. She does not carry coal (except for minor purposes). Within six months we shall have five more of these ships ready for sea.

   The Prime Minister made a momentous speech in the House this afternoon. He said that we had decided to retaliate on Germany for her piratical submarine policy by stopping her imports of every kind. All shipping going there would be liable to seizure, and if it was found the cargo was destined for Germany either through neutral countries or direct to her own ports it would be brought here and carried into the Prize Courts for decision.

THE DIARY OF JOHN COLEMAN BINDER

Tuesday March 2   …..There has again been some talk of peace but [the Prime Minister] dismissed this idea with scorn and said it was absolutely futile to talk of peace in the midst of all this tumult and uproar. No peace could be thought of until Belgium had been restored to her own, France freed from the incubus of Germany, and the military power of Germany crippled. He said the war was costing us close on two millions a day…and asked for a vote of credit for £362,000,000. This is the largest vote that has ever been asked for. It will carry us on for 100 days…..

1915 Wednesday March 3   Reports are to hand this morning of the feeling in neutral countries respecting the…..holding up of German supplies. Taken altogether they are not so very unfavourable, but the situation with respect to America will require very careful handling or some very unpleasant complications may arise. The German element is very strong in the States and it takes the American Government all its time to steer a course that is acceptable to all parties there……

Thursday March 4   The Dardanelles business is still being continued, but progress is very slow, and of necessity must be so. To-day we learn the ships are attacking the forts at the 'narrows', which is thought to be the most difficult part of the business. Every one in the corn and milling trades is very interested in this affair. Even if [it] should be carried through, it will be between three and four months before we can get any grain here.

A German submarine was sunk by one of our merchantmen yesterday off Beachy Head. The submarine fired a torpedo at the merchantman, which she avoided and she turned round and rammed the submarine and sent her to the bottom with all her crew. This piracy business is being checkmated by our Admiralty. We have heard very little of it the last few days. We are not told what means they are taking to capture them, but it is quite evident they are getting the upper hand of them.

END OF VOLUME TWO

THE DIARY OF JOHN COLEMAN BINDER

Volume Three

6 March 1915 to 17 June 1915

1915 Saturday March 6   Today's news is good. Another submarine was sunk yesterday making the third this week. This will thin them down a little…….

Sunday March 7   A fine bright March day with drying winds. Such days as these are much needed in this country as well as on the Continent as all agricultural work is very backward. The weather has been so very wet that not much could be done.

Looking back over the past week one can see that the feeling of optimism and confidence in the final result of the war has decidedly increased. We do not hide from ourselves that there is still much hard work and hard fighting to be done, but there is a feeling abroad that we are making progress in most directions. It is rumoured that the opinion in high military circles is that the war will be over by September, and it is certain that long odds are being betted on the Stock Exchange that this will be the case.

……One cannot but admire the genius that conceived this stroke in the Dardanelles, and evidence is given that it has been carefully planned. It opens up such immense possibilities. It will probably mean the end of the Turkish Empire in Europe, but as to what will be done with Constantinople is a ticklish question…….It will almost certainly give Russia a port which she will be able to use all the year round, and it will open up a most fertile district in Asia Minor.

Russia has done marvels this winter…….

……I think [Britain] is getting more to realize the tremendous struggle in which we are engaged. There is less disposition for public amusements and things of that kind. Everyone feels that we should all do our level best to end it and a most common question is "When will the war end?" Horse racing goes on but it is very much condemned by a large section - I think I may say by the large majority of the people. Probably there will be very little cricket this year, and football receives very little public attention.

The price of wheat is downwards this week. It shows a drop of about 3/- per qr. Flour is about 1/- lower than the highest point. Wheat holders in America are getting a little nervous about the Dardanelle business and are much more inclined to realize, but even when and if the Dardanelles are forced it must be two or three months before any quantity of Russian wheat is landed here. I know of one man who has bought wheat at 63/- per qr for May delivery - I think he will burn his fingers.

Tuesday March 9   ….This war is well organized on our side without doubt. To-day we learn quite casually that Grimsby fishermen are out in the Dardanelles acting as mine trawlers. It is a most significant fact as to how little invasion is probable that this huge fleet should be out there, but it has got together without weak[en]ing by one ship the "Grand Fleet" as it is called which is guarding the North Sea.

A most drastic measure was introduced in the Commons this afternoon. The Government already have the power to take over any works or factories which are engaged on Government work and this bill increases that power so they may "commandeer" any place they like which is suitable for making war material. They say that they are not getting this fast enough, and they are determined to remedy it. There is no question that these powers will be given to them. At the same time it is a most revolutionary step and shows the seriousness of the crisis through which we are passing.

1915 Wednesday March 10   Three merchantmen are announced to have been submarined yesterday afternoon and evening, entailing a loss of 37 lives. I expect some of these raiders will be caught before long.

Very little fresh war news to-day. The smaller powers in the East are all watching very closely the course of events in the Dardanelles. Greece is most anxious to come in on our side but the King, whose wife is the Kaiser's sister, is holding back. His ministers have resigned and he finds difficulty in securing another set. Italy, Bulgaria, Roumania are all on the *qui vive*. One thing is quite certain and that is if they do not fight now neither will they have any voice in the settling up of affairs

Quite a dramatic stroke is announced to-night. A German submarine was rammed and sunk off (not stated) during last night. The crew were captured. These submarine crews are being more severely treated than other prisoners and it is possible they may [be] tried in the courts as pirates.

Thursday March 11   ….We gained a distinct advantage in Belgium yesterday. Our troops moved forward, captured a village and 1000 prisoners, and inflicted heavy loss on the enemy. Our casualties are not reported at present.

…… Much news reaches us from Berlin as to the shortage of potatoes. It is quite expected that the Government will commandeer the whole supply.

The German daily rations of oats for their army horses is today reduced from 5lbs to 3lbs. A very poor allowance this. Some of their horses are very big (especially the Pomeranians) and must require a great deal more than this to keep them going.

Friday March 12 Wednesday's action in Belgium was a considerable one. The village captured was Neuve Chapelle, and marks a new move in this conflict. Four British Army Corps were engaged. It is thought that this [may be] the beginning of our real move forwards. I do not think so. Probably it is only a feeler to make the enemy show his hand. Our airmen also did excellent work, dropping bombs and destroying the railway leading to Lille.

The Turks are said to be moving their guns from Constantinople, so that it may not be classed as a fortified place, and as such liable to bombardment by the Allies.

Saturday March 13   A further small success is told to-day by Sir J. French. Another village has been captured in Belgium. Some of the wounded in the fight at Neuve Chapelle are back in hospital in England. They arrived during the night on Thursday. This will show how well organised things are, and how perfect communication is with the Army. Amongst them is an Oundle man C.Fox of the Northamptons. He has had his arm broken and a wound in the back. He has been out since October and has had a full share of the fighting.

…………..   No news from the Dardanelles.

Sunday March 14   ……It is …said the French have sent 22 transports with soldiers to the Dardanelles. People are beginning to speculate as to what will be done with Constantinople.

Russia would like it, Greece covets it and Italy would also like it. It will be a difficult question to settle when the war is over. Probably it will end by making it 'A Free City' under the protection of all the powers. It seems to be fairly well agreed that the Turks will be cleared out of Europe, and that a determined attempt will be made to settle the Eastern Question which for the last 80 or 100 years has been such a source of disturbance in Europe.

Some of the male Belgian Refugees from here have gone back to Belgium but it is probable that others will come in their places. They thought they would like to go and try what they could do but I think they will wish themselves back again.

It is estimated there are 180,000 Belgian refugees in this country also 80,000 wounded Belgian soldiers. There is a feeling of confidence and optimism in this country with regard to the final issue of the war. I think it is a bit overdone. People seem to think that Germany is already beaten and that the end is in sight. I am afraid that I do not share these views at present. Germany has been making preparations for 40 years for this war, and has done all it was possible to do (except with regards to food). The Allies certainly were not prepared consequently we have a long arrear to make up and it will take time to do it.

THE DIARY OF JOHN COLEMAN BINDER

Food prices continue about the same. Cheese is extremely dear. Canadian Cheese is quoted at 98/- per cwt in Liverpool. English Cheddar is --- per cwt. Bread continues about the same price, 7 ½d to 8d per 4lb loaf. Wheat is a shilling dearer in the week @ 57/- into the mill. Meat is very dear. I payed 1/- per lb for loin of Mutton this week. Pork is quoted at 13/6 per score at Birmingham, about 12/- to 12/6 in local markets here. Coal is about a shilling cheaper in the lower qualities. Eggs are very dear - retail price 2/- per score. Usually at this time of the year they are about 1/4d to 1/6d. Great quantities are being bought for the wounded and the Russian supply is stopped. Fruit is fairly cheap especially oranges as they cannot be sent to Germany.

1915 Monday March 15   7 merchant vessels sunk out of 1500 entering and leaving our ports last week. Extremely violent fighting in Belgium with intent to capture Lille.

Tuesday March 16   Lord Kitchener spoke in the House last night. He expressed himself well satisfied as to the actual war operations, but uttered a grave warning as to the supply of arms and munitions. He said they were not getting the quantity they expected and had a right to expect and appealed to the workmen to do their utmost to increase the output. I do not think he spoke without cause. There has been much slackness amongst the men in this country, and they do not appear to think that victory is made quite as much in the workshops as on the field of battle. The Government said they intended to take over and work a number of armament factories.

…..Fifty officers are in the casualty list to-day, amongst them Lt Wartnaby of Market Harboro (Northants Yeomanry) A private letter also announces that Gordon Wilson of Apethorpe (Mrs Brassey's agent) is killed. He was engaged in horse-buying at the time the mobilizations took place, but later on joined the Yeomanry (Norths).

The Admiralty announce this morning that on Monday the German cruiser 'Dresden' which escaped in the battle off the Falkland Islands was caught up and sunk off the coast of Chile. She only fought five minutes, and then hoisted the white flag. The crew were taken off before she sank. There is only one German warship now sailing the seas.

Wednesday March 17   The casualty lists this morning contain the names of 80 officers killed and wounded. The lists of men killed during the past week have not been published at present, but private letters inform us that the losses have been very heavy. The Northants Yeomanry and Northants regiment have been in the thick of the fighting and have lost heavily, but not many details are to hand at present. Several Wellingborough men are amongst the Yeomanry killed. Sir John French estimates the German losses up to Monday at about 18,000, and this is only the first real move in this spring campaign. Everybody looks forward with sadness to the inevitable losses which must occur in the near future but there is not the least sign of giving way.

……..Lord Kitchener's appeal on Monday last has met with a good response by both employers and men, and also by trade union officials and on all hands it is declared that the utmost efforts will be made to meet his demands. Incidentally I might mention what a splendid field gun [the French] have, their 75cm. It is acknowledged to be the finest gun of its kind in the world and the French are immensely proud of it. Its accuracy is marvellous.

Thursday March 18   Lieut. Lees, son of Col.Lees is to-day reported as killed in action, also a man named Ellis of North Road. Ellis was shot through the heart. He was a rural postman here.

The casualty lists of the last three days contain the names of 205 officers killed and wounded. These occurred on Wednesday and the following days last week including Sunday. The fight at Neuve Chapelle was a much bigger affair than we thought and the enemy on Thursday, Friday and Saturday brought up huge reinforcements to regain their positions but without any success. Our casualties are not reported up to to-night but it is predicted that we have lost more men than Wellington did at Waterloo…..

A curious fact is noted in the "Times" to-day. A considerable quantity of English sovereigns have come to London from Scandinavia in payment of goods supplied. These coins are part of the indemnity payed by

DAY BY DAY THROUGH THE GREAT WAR

France to Germany in 1871 and 2 and have been hoarded by Germany until now in the fortress of Spandau. Some of the bags were marked with the original labels. This shows that Germany has had to draw on her reserve of gold.

1915 Friday March 19 …..Three more Oundle men, Cottingham, Phillipson and Loakes, are reported to-day as being wounded. Writing home Loakes says that some letters in his pockets saved him, the shrapnel also grazed his face.

Saturday March 20 Unfavourable news from the Dardanelles is published by the Admiralty this morning. On Wednesday a combined attack was made by the allied Fleet. What damage was done to the forts is not disclosed but two of our ships (the Irresistible, 15,000 tons, and the Ocean ---tons) were sunk by floating mines. The French ship Admiral Bouvet was also sunk, and nearly all her crew- 650 men- with her. The crews of our ships were saved. Warships are already on their way, in fact were at once ordered out to supply these losses, and they are now going through the Mediterranean. This setback is quite in accord with [what] I had expected. A good portion of the general public seemed to think that we were simply going to walk or sail through the Dardanelles without any trouble or loss, but I am sure it will [be] a costly business, both on men and ships. The land forces are landed and are co-operating with the war vessels. A rumour to-night says the Russians Black Sea Fleet is close to Constantinople.

Some irritation is felt that the losses amongst the men at Neuve Chapelle and the 4 following days have not been published. Our total loss in officers is given at 510 killed and wounded. The Northamptons are again hard hit having 9 killed and 8 wounded, so that they must have been in the thick of the battles. We all expect that their loss in men must have been very severe, and names are constantly being [reported] of men in their ranks who have either been killed or wounded. To-day another Oundle man is reported as wounded - this is John Fox, (a brother of the C.Fox mentioned the other day). He had been wounded once before and had only just rejoined his regiment. ….

Sunday March 21 A glorious bright spring day. The last week since Wednesday has been very wintery. We had a veritable blizzard on Thursday evening and again early on Friday morning. The snow drifted very much and in some places in this locality the roads were impassable but it went very quickly although some of it is still lying about. No news to-day from the various war operations, but one speculates as to what is being done.

This last fight at Neuve Chapelle has I think revealed something of what we may expect during this coming summer. It will be a terrible one I quite believe, and one can hardly dare to think or speculate about it.

The preparations are being made in all sorts of ways in readiness. Chief amongst these is the determined efforts being made by the Government to rouse the workers and all labour leaders in the country to the urgent necessity of increasing the output of war material. A conference of all parties has been sitting in London this week, and complete agreement has been reached, and it is now hoped that we shall see a much better outlook in this direction.

Hospitals are also being increased in all directions and arrangements are being made for larger numbers of the wounded.

A conference was held at Wellingboro' yesterday of all the Poor Law Guardians in the County and it was resolved to relieve the Kettering and Wellingboro' guardians of their inmates in their Unions by taking them to other Unions in the County, and by so doing to provide accommodation for a large number of wounded.

Monday March 22 ….Zeppelin airships raided Paris during the night on Saturday and dropped incendiary bombs. About a dozen persons were injured but no great damage was done.

A welcome piece of news was published this afternoon about 3 o'clock. The Austrian fortress of Przemysl in Galicia has surrendered to the Russians. This fortress has been besieged ever since last August and the Russians have had to keep a large army there. This will now be liberated and be available for service elsewhere, besides this the town of Premysl is the centre of important railways and should be a distinct help to the Russians.

THE DIARY OF JOHN COLEMAN BINDER

Private accounts still continue to come through of the fighting at Neuve Chapelle. It was a most fiercely fought battle or battles, for in reality it appears to have lasted four days. The carnage was frightful on both sides and it is difficult to estimate what our losses were. Various estimates are put forward and it is generally thought they must be about 10,000 to 12,000. The military authorities do not seem to be at all inclined to let us know what they really were.

1915 Tuesday March 23 The fall of Przemysl has caused a great sensation and it may have very important consequences. Conditions had got very bad there and it was no longer possible for the Austrians to hold out. The civil population were practically starving.

Some uneasiness is caused by the spread of a disease commonly called 'Spotted Fever' - the technical name 'cerebro-spinal meningitis'. It is a very obscure complaint and at present Doctors do not seem to know how to treat it. It frequently comes from long and severe exposure, and is quickly fatal. A good many cases have occurred amongst the troops. Last Saturday one of the Yeomanry stationed at Towcester died from it and a case has also occurred at Kettering. It is very contagious.

Wednesday March 24 The Russians made a huge coup at Przemysl. They captured 9 Generals, 540 officers, 130,000 soldiers and 2400 Guns. The Austrians also lost 40,000 in killed and wounded during the siege, so by the figures it may be judged what effect it will have. The Austrians are quite dismayed, and it now remains to be seen what is the next move [for] the Russians whether they will advance on Buda Pesth and Vienna or whether they will make for Cracow and Silesia.

There has been another scrap in Egypt. Quite a small affair, but still enough to show the Turks are still about…..

Thursday March 25 A very quiet day. Scarcely any news at least from France and Belgium, but we know that our troops are still crossing over in large numbers. The South Midland brigade of Territorials (in which is a nephew of mine F. C. Binder) were crossing last night. They have been at Colchester since they were embodied in September. It is principally Territorials who are going now. Kitchener's army is still in reserve and training.   ……

Friday March 26 "The Admiralty have good reason to believe that the submarine U 29 has been sunk with all hands". This is the brief notice which announces the end of a famous German raider. She has been responsible for sending three of our warships under viz the 'Cressy', 'Hogue' and 'Formidable', but has now paid the penalty. No further particulars are given as to how and when she was destroyed. Probably we shall not know until the war is over.

Saturday March 27 Affairs still continue very quiet in Belgium and France, and scarcely any news is coming through. Indeed to-day Sir John French says that 'He has nothing to report' but we are well aware that this is only the calm before the storm and one really looks forward with dread to that storm.

Accounts are coming through slowly about Neuve Chapelle. It is freely said that the 'Northamptons' lost 1000 killed, wounded and missing out of their total of 1100. [?] So this will give some idea of the ghastly nature of the fighting. Only a very few were taken prisoners.

No further move has been made since this battle, and one wonders what was the real object of it and if it was the success that was claimed for it. These questions I suppose will some day be answered, but at present we are quite in the dark.   ……

March 28 Sunday Letters have been received from the Oundle man, Butt, who was taken prisoner early on in the war and is now at Doebritz. He complains very bitterly about the lack of food, and asks his people to send him a loaf of Bread and other things. We receive such varied reports from Germany as to this food business that it makes one doubt as to whether they are really short of food. As letters from all prisoners are censored before they are sent, one wonders if there is not some scheme behind all this. An attempt maybe to throw dust in our eyes.

During the last few days the French Government have been issuing reports as to the state and efficiency of their Armies. They announce that they have now 2 ½ Millions of men at the front   and 1½ Millions in reserve. Their munitions are ample, and the spirit of the men excellent. Since last August a great number of their leading Generals have been removed and replaced by younger men who have shown their ability during this campaign, so that we shall see some big movements in the near future.

Mine sweeping is still in progress in the Dardanelles under the cover of warships, but up to the present no further news is to hand.

The German Fleet in the Baltic is reported to be getting ready to attack the Russian coasts, but as to their North Sea Fleet [it] might as well not exist for nothing has been heard about it since our men chased them into harbour last January.

1915 March 29 Monday No fresh news of great importance this morning. ...

March 30 Tuesday There are two outstanding features in to-days news. The first is concerning the drink traffic in this country. Yesterday a deputation of all the principal manufacturers of guns, ships and ammunition waited on the Chancellor of the Exchequer and placed a statement before him with regard to this question. They proved without question that since the war commenced the output of these things has decreased owing to the increased drinking that has taken place, and this at a time of grave national peril, when the constant cry of our men and officers at the front is for guns and ammunition, Ammunition and Guns. In fact General French Lord Kitchener and all the leading men have declared it is impossible to carry this war to successful conclusion unless they can get these things. It was shown that some of the men were only working 36 to 40 hours per week, and that the public house receipts in the neighbourhood of large works had increased 20 to 40 per cent. The remedy suggested was a total closing of all public houses in this country. This certainly would be a drastic measure but I am convinced that it would meet with the support of the nation. The Chancellor's reply was that he would give these proposals every consideration and he clearly foreshadowed some extreme action on the part of the Government. I may add that it was stated there was not a single teetotaller in the deputation, so this movement has not been engineered by them.

Our Allies France, Russia and Belgium have adopted this course of checking the drink traffic by closing all their public houses ever since the war began, and if it can be done there it is quite possible to do the same in this country.

The other piece of news is the sinking of a passenger ship "The Falaba", of the Elder Dempster line, off the mouth of the Bristol Channel on Sunday afternoon by a German submarine. Over 100 passengers were drownded as they only gave them about 15 minutes to leave the vessel, and then torpedoed her. It is declared that the crew of the submarine were jeering and laughing during the time these poor people were going under.

A great wave of anger has been aroused by this and all sorts of reprisals are suggested.

March 31 Wednesday No particular news to-day.

April 1 Thursday ...Referring to the Drink question public opinion seems to be averse I think to total prohibition, but at present the Government have not announced what they intend to do.

To-day a letter from the King appears in which he says if [it] is thought desirable he will prohibit the use of [intoxicating drinks in his household during this war. Lord Kitchener also expresses himself in a like sense.

Lord Rothschild died yesterday. He has been a great help in financial matters during this war, and also as President of the Red Cross Society has done a great amount of work.

Friday April 2 Good Friday. Several more ships have been sunk during the last few days. Yesterday one was sunk off Beachy Head without the least warning. Nineteen out of the crew of 21 were drownded.

Our airmen made another raid on the enemy's submarine dockyards at Hoboken and Zeebrugge yesterday and did a lot of damage. ....

1915 April 3 Saturday .....This Easter is a very quiet holiday. Not many people are travelling about as the Railway Companies have withdrawn all facilities for cheap travel. This is partly owing to the lack of labour and also to the railways being so much needed for war purposes. The passenger railway service is much restricted generally. There are fewer trains running, especially long distance ones. It is stated that over 130,000 miners have enlisted since war was declared.

April 6 Tuesday The King today writes a letter saying that from to-day he has absolutely forbidden the use of alcohol in his household. It is hoped this will have a good effect, and that it will [be] largely followed.

What the Government intend to do is not yet known, but it is thought they will limit very much the time public houses shall be open and also quite forbid the sale of spirits.

Submarines continue to sink, our own and also neutral vessels, but the damage is relatively small when compared with the amount of shipping entering and leaving our ports. The last air raid which our aviators made on the German works at Hoboken on --- was very successful. Three submarines were destroyed by bombs, another damaged. 60 workmen were killed and 50 injured.

April 7 Wednesday ..... Numbers of wounded continue to arrive daily in this county. Last night 70 came to Northampton. Some of them had been wounded at Neuve Chapelle. ...

Crime has diminished very much during the war. Various reasons are given for it. I think the principal one is that a great number of men of loose habits are now under military control.

April 8 Thursday The chief news to-day again comes from Russia or rather the Carpathian mountains where the Russians are fighting with great determination. They have captured nearly all the passes and are now ready to descend into the plains of Hungary. These battles are having a most important effect on this (the Belgian and French side) as the Germans are compelled to reinforce their Austrian allies and are thus prevented from sending more troops to the west. Altogether just now there is more cause for hope. From all sources we learn that Germany feels that she cannot win, but still hopes to make a draw of it. This is not sufficient for us. Germany will have to acknowledge defeat before a lasting peace can be made, and we all know that she is a long way yet from confessing herself beaten.

The first instalment of the official casualty list of the Neuve Chapelle fighting is published to-day. Evidently it is far from complete, but so far the Northamptons appear to have suffered the most.

April 9 Friday Sir John French says to-day "I have nothing to report". Another long list of casualties from Neuve Chapelle, bringing the official list up to ---- killed and ---- wounded.

C. Fox of Oundle who had his elbow joint shattered by a bullet will probably be a cripple for life.

A deputation of Brewers, Distillers and Licence Holders waited on the Chancellor to-day. They evidently expect the Government to take some forward step in this drink traffic, and urged that it should be not prohibition of spirits but a much higher duty on them, lighter beer, and restriction of hours.

April 10 Saturday The forward move of the Russians continues and this in connection with the French forward move is said to indicate the opening of the spring campaign. If this is so the advantage is clearly on our side.

Three German spies have been arrested the last few days and are to be tried in the civil courts.

A Government paper published to-day gives details of the bad treatment of English prisoners in Germany. Indeed so bad has it been that some of them have begged to be shot rather than to be treated so badly. They are kept short of food, beaten and insulted continually. Sir Edward Grey has vigorously protested against this.

April 11 Sunday I saw to-day a Northants Yeoman named Fox. He is home for 48 hours as he is one of a draft of 70 men of that regiment who are leaving Towcester next week for the front. He is the only Oundle man going with this draft. All the other Yeomen from just round are quite all right up to the present. Their friends are continually sending them luxuries over. The most useful thing to send these in is a quite light tin box. Some tens of thousands of these parcels are sent every day from all over the country. It is not that the men are not well fed. Their food is ample and excellent but they do not get many luxuries.

DAY BY DAY THROUGH THE GREAT WAR

Yesterday General Joffre issued an order prohibiting altogether the use of strong drink in the army in the field. Any one supplying the soldiers with it in any way will be court- martialled.

1915 April 12 Monday   There have been persistent reports the last two days that a naval action has been fought off the coast of Norway. If this is so, it has probably been brought about by German warships attempting to get out into the Atlantic for the purpose of raiding but up to to-night the Admiralty have not issued any announcement. Two German officers escaped from a detention camp in Wales last week but after being at liberty a few days they were recaptured yesterday on the Welsh coast. . . . .

The great need of our Army now is said to be ammunition, and huge stocks of this are being accumulated in readiness for the next big move. All ordnance works are working day and night Sundays and week days. It is quite realized that the army which is going to win in the coming campaign is the one that is best provided with guns and ammunition. The cavalry as a fighting force are quite out of it at present. The horses are at the base camps and the men are taking their turn in the trenches with the infantry.

April 13 Tuesday   There is no confirmation of the rumours as to a naval battle in the North Sea. Probably they arose from the fact the Fleet was at target practice.

Again a long list of casualties at Neuve Chapelle, bringing up the total to date [to] 7,500 killed and wounded. I do not think it is yet complete. . . .

April 14 Wednesday   The Government to-day announce they are going to control the whole output of ammunition in this country. A committee has been appointed with the Chancellor of the Exchequer as Chairman and the committee will work through local committees and systematically work the whole business. The War Office have been attempting to take this matter in hand but it is certain they have not proved themselves equal to the task. It would have been much better if this step had been taken when the war commenced. It was done in France and Russia.

Fighting still continuing in the Carpathians between the Austrians and Russians in very bad weather conditions.

Food prices continue to advance. Bread is raised to-day to 8 ½ d in London. This particularly on account of the cost of labour, also increased cost of fuel, yeast and salt.

Meat is excessively dear, especially mutton, which is costing the butcher from 1/1d to 1/2d in the wool. Farmers without doubt have had the time of their lives during the last 8 months. It does not matter what they have to sell it is high in price. Wheat 58/- to 59/- Barley 34/- Oats 34/- to 36/-

Hay [?] £5/5/- per ton. Beef 10/6, Mutton 1/1, Pork 10/6 per stone. The new clip of wool is expected to reach from 50/- to 55/- per tod. From these prices it will be seen who is reaping benefit from the war. Grass keeping is also let at very high prices. The tenant at Oundle Lodge Farm (J.P.Smith) who is leaving at Michaelmas let his keeping by auction last week. It realized 50/- per acre from now up to Michaelmas next. He does not pay more than a £1 per acre for it. Some let at Titchmarsh made 87/6.

April 15 Thursday   A Zeppelin airship made a raid over Newcastle and Blyth last night about 8 o'clock. Eight bombs were dropped but very little damage was done.

Sir J. French's dispatch dealing with Neuve Chapelle is published to-day. It was a costly and bloody battle. 12,881 in killed wounded and missing, and as he candidly admits not altogether the success he had hoped for. The operations were under the control of Sir Douglas Haig. All went well for the first 3 hours. Neuve Chapelle was captured, and then owing to his orders not being carried out reserves were not at hand, consequently no further advance could be made and the enemy had time to pull themselves together. Sir J. French still asks for more munitions and says that only by the use of these can the war be brought to a conclusion.

Municipal bodies all over the country are being asked to release some of their employees to help in the manufacture of munitions and to-day the Northampton Corporation decided to allow 200 of their tram and other men to go. Probably engineering works at Northampton will be adapted for this purpose.

THE DIARY OF JOHN COLEMAN BINDER

1915 April 16 Monday Very little fresh news to-day from the war areas.

Last evening a German submarine torpedoed another Dutch vessel in broad daylight. This has caused great anger in Holland, as indeed it may well do. I think myself these things are a deliberate attempt on the part of Germany to drive Holland into war.

Early this morning between twelve and one a Zeppelin appeared over Lowestoft and dropped some bombs. Some little damage was done. A timber yard set on fire, but only one man had his hand slightly wounded.

Between one and two this afternoon a German aeroplane appeared off the Essex coast and threw some bombs, but again no damage was [done]. One cannot quite think what they are doing. The bombs dropped during these last raids are not very explosive, but seem to be highly inflammable.

April 17 Saturday. Sir John French says to-day "I have nothing to report".

Operations in the Carpathians are much hindered by the melting snow and rains, but in spite of these the fighting still continues.

April 18 Sunday. Events move slowly in all the war areas. We cannot know what the reasons for delay are, but no doubt the Commander - in - chief has good ones for still remaining practically on the defensive. I conjecture myself that a good deal of it is owing to lack of ammunition. Strenuous efforts are being made to supply this in great quantities and steps are being taken to organise almost every part of the trade.

. . It is quite certain there has been great delay through these drinking habits of a certain section of the workmen and another factor is the continuous labour Sunday and weekday. It has been conclusively proved that this does not increase production in the ratio that was expected. Men get 'stale' and are unable to work always at extreme pressure. The Woolwich Arsenal men were granted two days holiday at Easter and it was noted that the great majority spent that holiday in bed. They had been working overtime ever since last August.

The delay in stating what is to be done with regard to the drink traffic is causing farmers some inconvenience. It is quite seen that if lighter beers and no spirits are to be brewed less barley will be wanted. In consequence of this many farmers have sown oats and spring wheat in the place of barley.

I believe farm labour will be very scarce this hay time and harvest. Great numbers of the young men have gone and only the old ones are left. The age at which boys may leave school has been temporarily reduced to 12 from 13 by some county Education Authorities. Women are also returning to farm work but only in limited numbers. The introduction of machinery has helped to displace much farm labour, and it is quite certain it will be more used than ever during the coming summer. I note that farmers although they as a class are reaping the most benefit from this war are very loath to raise wages. It is quite certain that no agricultural labourer can to-day live on 15/- to 16/- per week and pay his way, especially if he has children.

April 19 Monday. A most graphic description of Neuve Chapelle is published to-day from an independent source. It was probably written by an officer, and clearly reveals the terrible battle that it was. It is much too long to quote here but I hope to preserve a copy of the narrative.

No special news from the front to-day, except the French report says that our men captured some trenches.

A frontier fight took place between the Italians and the Austrians, but I [am] still doubtful as to whether Italy will come in to this fight. She is a poor country and the expense of this war is awful. I believe the same cause is keeping some of the other smaller nations (Holland, Bulgaria, Greece and Roumania) from joining us against the Germans.

1915 April 20 Tuesday. A letter has been received to-day from Butt the Oundle man, who is a prisoner at Doebritz. He does not say much about the treatment they receive, but says they are very short of food, and also says he has not received the food which has been sent to him from here lately. It is quite certain these prisoners are receiving very hard treatment in Germany, especially the English. No news has been published about the operations in the Dardanelles for some time. We have received a decided check there, and different methods will have to be [followed] if these operations are to be successful. I do not think that many of our people realize how many campaigns we have on hand to-day. There is the campaign in France, also the Dardanelles, Persian Gulf, Egypt, South West Africa, South East Africa, and Persia, so that it will [be] seen what resources are required to carry on these different campaigns. Garrison duty at other places Gibraltar Malta India etc. is being done by Territorials. Australians and Territorials with a few regulars are in Egypt. Some sort of Kitchener's Army have gone there this week. My nephew C Wright is amongst them. Two other nephews are in France, and a niece is going to Servia as nurse. I can truly say I believe there is scarcely a family in this country which is not affected by the war. In some cases there are 6, 7 or even 8 in the army.

The fight reported by the French yesterday turns out to have been a bigger affair than we thought at first. Sir John French says to-day it was quite successful but that our losses are 'very heavy'.

April 21 Wednesday. The Prime Minister went down to Newcastle last night to speak to the Tyneside workers to ask them to do their utmost to increase the output of ammunition and ships. He had a splendid reception and the meeting in reply to his appeal promised 'To deliver the goods' This phrase which I have just written is likely to become historic. It was the answer sent about [a]week since by some workmen to whom the Government had appealed to complete some work at once. Their reply was ' Tell Lord Kitchener we will deliver the goods'

The House of Commons made a great blunder last night. The question of prohibiting the sale of drink in the House was raised and the House instead of following the example of the King and many others in the country shelved the question. This will tell very heavily against any proposals which may be made for limiting the drink traffic. The ordinary man will say 'You are going to compel us to do that which you will not do yourselves'.

April 22 Thursday. We have to-day Sir J French's report of the fighting on Saturday and Sunday last. It will [be] known as the capture of Hill 60. This hill is about 2 miles to the South West of Ypres. It had been held by the Germans since last October and afforded a fine site for their artillery. Our men had mined up to it and then exploded their mine about 6 o'clock last Saturday. The infantry rushed in and a hand to hand fight with the bayonet ensued. The enemy were driven out and during the night our men entrenched themselves as well as they could, although the enemy's fire was very hot. During Sunday and Monday the Germans brought up heavy re-inforcements and made desperate attempts to recapture the hill, but to-night's latest report says that it is still in our possession.

Some remarkable figures were given in the House to-day regarding our army in France. There are nearly 800,000 men there. 140,000 have been put out of action, but these have all been replaced. We are producing 20 times as much ammunition as we did in September last, and this is being daily increased, but it was shown we shall want every bit we can get. It was stated that during the 10 days or 12 days fighting around Neuve Chapelle the artillery used as much ammunition as was used during the whole of the Boer war (22 years).

Friday April 23. To-day's report is that we are still holding Hill 60 but desperate fighting is going on all round it. The Germans appear to be directing very heavy artillery fire on it.

A notice in to-day's papers says that all traffic between this country and Holland is suspended. One can only guess what this is for, but probably some sea operations are about to take place.

1915 Saturday April 24 Not very good news this morning. In a despatch published late last night Sir J French says that on Thursday the enemy made a determined attack on the French lines north of Ypres using shells with deadly gas in them. This caused the French to retire about three miles, consequently our line had to give way also. A wireless from Berlin claims that the Germans captured four of our heavy guns, but this is not confirmed by Sir J French.

Operations have again begun in the Dardanelles . . . . Sir Ian Hamilton is commanding the land forces. . . . . . Today 2 companies of the 2/4 Northants Territorials who with other troops are quartered at Peterboro

THE DIARY OF JOHN COLEMAN BINDER

marched into here with their band. They are on a recruiting march through the county and on Monday will leave for Thrapston and march through the whole county.

Arrangements had been made by the police to billet them on private persons and in no case were they sent to public houses. This is quite a new feature in this war. Years ago when we had a troop or two of cavalry staying here for a night or two they were always billeted on the Publicans, but this has been changed in order if possible to keep men away from the drink.

These men are a smart looking set of men, and look in first rate health. To-night a smoking concert for their entertainment is taking place in the Victoria Hall from 7 to 10

April 25 Sunday. The soldiers quartered here last night this morning attended the Parish Church and afterwards marched through the town.

It is rumoured that we may shortly have 1000 men quartered here, but I learn from the Superintendent of Police that nothing is definitely settled at present. It is certain if they come that everybody will have to take them in - that is unless they go under canvas.

April 26 Monday. The attack which was reported on Saturday has developed into a terrible battle, which was still raging yesterday. The Germans hurled 80,000 men against the French line where they joined up with our men. The Times correspondent to-day says that it may develop into the biggest battle of the war. All eyes are anxiously turned to this affair, but we think that our people will be able to cope with it. It is a repetition of what took place last Autumn, that is an attempt to reach the French coast.

The soldiers left this morning going to Thrapston via Stoke, Aldwinckle, Thorpe etc. They managed to secure a number of recruits here. Colonel Willoughby was in command.

To-night's telegrams say that the German rush has been stemmed and that some of the lost ground has been regained. A short telegram also says that the Army for Turkey has been landed at Gallipoli, and that all the warships are again in action. We await to-morrow's news anxiously. To-day's casualty lists include 97 officers killed and wounded.

Wheat is steadily advancing in price, and made from 63/- to 65/- in country markets on Saturday.

April 27 Tuesday. Not much fresh news is disclosed by this morning's papers, except that Sir J French says that the German onslaught has been held up and that our losses have been very heavy. Our troops commenced to land at Gallipoli before daybreak on Sunday morning, and fierce fighting ensued. This is only a beginning and we do not conceal from ourselves that this is likely to be a stubborn business in the Dardanelles.

It is quite possible that the German attack in Flanders was a retort to this landing and that it was undertaken to influence the neutral countries who are still 'sitting on the fence' and want to be on the winning side. Rumour says Sir J French was quite aware this attack was coming, and that his capture of Hill 60 was to make the position more secure. At any rate, the holding of this hill has caused much loss to the Germans the last few days.

The Canadians lost very heavily both officers and men. On regaining the ground they had lost they discovered that the enemy had bayoneted all the wounded Canadians which had been temporarily left behind. After this no quarter was given, and only 2 Germans were taken prisoners. These battles have had a most stimulating effect on recruiting both in this country and in Canada and men are joining the colours in large numbers. . . .

Very little has been done by submarines lately, and the merchant navy is carrying on practically as if there was no war. Berlin has been crowing the last few days that their Fleet has been in the North Sea. Possibly it has, but at any rate they were very careful not to come anywhere within range of our guns.

Italy still hangs fire, and I almost doubt if she will take any part in this conflict.

1915 April 28 Wednesday. Yesterday fighting was still in progress along the Yser. . . For the first time for many months the cavalry are reported to be in action, (that is mounted). During the winter they have been taking their turn in the trenches with the infantry. This new move is very welcome to them.

Last night the question of the treatment of our prisoners in Germany was debated in both Houses of Parliament. The way these poor fellows have been treated by the Germans is horrible. They have been stripped beaten and in many instances shot. They have marched through the streets for the cowards to gloat over and their captors have spat upon them. The French, Russians and Belgians have been fairly well treated, but this cowardly treatment has been reserved for the English. I think nothing has aroused such anger and passion against Germany as this, and it must leave a legacy of hate towards them that certainly will endure as long as the present generation lasts.

The Prime Minister said that it was a most difficult matter to deal with, but that when peace was discussed, no peace would be concluded until the persons who are responsible for these things had been brought to justice. Personally I believe the Kaiser is directly to blame. It is quite certain he must know, and a few words from him would alter it. Lord Kitchener declared that they (the Germans) were worse in their treatment of our prisoners than the dervishes of the Sudan.

April 29 Thursday. The French cruiser Leon Gambetta was torpedoed by an Austrian submarine yesterday off the coast of Italy and sunk with a loss of 600 men and officers.

The War Office on Sunday last sent an expert to enquire into the nature of the poisonous gas used by the Germans. His report was issued last night, and he says it is _____ and practically produces acute bronchitis.

Yesterday an appeal was issued by the War Office for respirators for the use of the soldiers in France. Half - a -million were asked for, and the authorities were soon overwhelmed by offers. One person alone guaranteeing to contribute 5000 a day. Of course all these will be given. They are easily made and are quite effectual.

To-day 4 motors full of wounded accompanied by nurses passed through here on their way from Northampton to Milton Park, (which has been turned into a nursing home). Amongst them were some who had asphyxiated. They arrived in Northampton last night from Belgium.

April 30 Friday. [*Little news. Sir John French pays tribute to the Canadians.*]

A curious rumour was circulated through London and the country this afternoon. It was said that the German Fleet was out and was bombarding Dunkirk. It turned out to be that the Germans were dropping bombs from their big guns a long way off. The rumour caused some excitement as it was hoped that the German Fleet had at last come out and that there might be a chance of fighting and beating them.

A Zeppelin was over Ipswich and Bury St Edmunds very early this morning. Some little damage was done by bombs, but no person was injured.

During this morning the Police received a telephone message from Peterboro asking them to find billets for a 1000 soldiers. Who and What they are is not known here, neither was said when they might be expected to arrive. Most probably it will be next week. They must be billeted within two miles of the Market Place so this will allow for some of them going to Ashton Polebrook Glapthorn and Stoke. Of course it is now compulsory to take them.

The Government proposals with regard to drink were introduced last night. The duty on spirits, wine and strong beer is raised very much. Light beer is untouched. Provision is also made for stricter control of public houses where troops are quartered and also where munitions are being made.

There were only three fat beast in Oundle Market yesterday and these averaged nearly £40 each. Butchers said this was well over 1/- per lb - a record price.

1915 May 1 Saturday. A despatch dealing with the Dardanelles was issued early this morning. It is the first official despatch we have had since operations were resumed last Sunday and discloses a story of great bravery and hard fighting on the part of our soldiers and sailors. Included in the Army which was landed at three different points are the Australians and New Zealanders, who up to the present have been in Egypt.

THE DIARY OF JOHN COLEMAN BINDER

This landing of troops in the face of an enemy is probably the most difficult thing in war, but it was done well and quickly. Some progress towards clearing the peninsula has been made but we do not conceal from ourselves that some hard fighting will have to be done before Constantinople is ours. Personally I think it is worth trying, as the capture of it would create a profound impression and would be the death blow to all German hopes and intrigue in the Near East.

May 2 Sunday. A beautiful May day to-day after a night of rain which was much needed. Absolutely no news has come through up to this evening.

May 3 Monday. Some account is given to-day of the bombardment of Dunkirk which I mentioned on Friday. The Germans had erected a huge gun or guns, which have a range of about 22 or 23 miles. It fired some 50 or 60 shots and since then has been silent. It is supposed that it has worn itself out or has been destroyed by our aviators.

[Report from Petrograd of a German raid towards Riga.]

May 3 continued. The Budget will be introduced tomorrow and it is surmised that the Chancellor will budget for a continuance of the war for another 12 months. Personally I believe it will continue as long as that and possibly longer. I believe we are a long way from the end, and I believe most people are realizing this. It is a tremendous conflict this, and one that the generations coming after will be in much better position to estimate than we are who are now in the excitement and burden of it.

May 4 Tuesday. *[Germany claims Russians were badly defeated - no news of this from Petrograd.]*

The Germans are again making desperate efforts to recapture 'Hill 60' in Flanders but without any success. The fighting there on Sunday and yesterday was very hot, but in spite of the use of poisonous gas, our men have quite held their own. The response to the appeal of the War Office for respirators was so overwhelming that it had to be withdrawn 12 hours after it was issued and now every man at the front is equipped with one.

The Germans torpedoed a second American ship off the Scillies on Saturday causing some loss of life. She was a tank oil steamer. This affair has caused a good deal of tall talk in America. But I doubt if much will come of it. The Americans have plenty of what we know just now as 'Swank' but it seems to me they are not at all prepared to put their words into deeds.

Bread to-day is advanced to 8d per 4lb loaf. I am now 52 and this is the highest price that I have ever known it to be. War Bread as it is known in Germany which is much inferior, is 10½ to 11d. Curiously enough it is only 7½ d in Paris. It is quite possible these prices may go higher before the next harvest is reaped.

May 5 Wednesday. As if there was [not] enough fighting in the world, to-day two more new areas are added. The Turks assisted by German officers and German gold had fomented a rebellion in Tripoli against the Italians. Severe fighting has taken place and the affair has caused much excitement in Italy. Great events are pending in Italy and it looks as if her decision either to join us or the enemy cannot [be] delayed many hours. It is rumoured this morning that it will [be] decided to-day. Whether this is so or not great preparations have been made for some weeks past.

The other outbreak of war which seems almost certain is between China and Japan. Japan has sent an ultimatum to China demanding certain things which are too long to write down here, and it seems most likely it will end in war. If this is so America can scarcely stand aloof as she has a great aversion to seeing Japan become predominant in the Pacific.

So the tide of war rolls round the whole world. God alone knows when it will cease.*

. . . The Germans are badly in need just now of a great and decisive victory in order to impress and influence neutral countries. There was the usual flag-waving and shouting in Berlin on Sunday. Travellers in Germany report that this displaying of flags is quite made to order. If the police order [it] to be done it has to be done. If they forbid it nothing takes place.

DAY BY DAY THROUGH THE GREAT WAR

1915 May 6 I cannot say that the news this morning is satisfactory. No great change has taken place but for the moment the trend of events seems to be against us

Russia still denies that she has been defeated in the Galicia. Possibly it is not serious, but it is evident there has been a set back.

In Belgium the Germans have been again attacking 'Hill 60' and by the help of poisonous gas had gained a lodgement on the lower slope. I note here a gradual but sure growing of resentment (hate I cannot say it is) or hardening of heart against Germans and Germany during the last two or three weeks. This is due, I think, to two or three causes principally. The first is their brutal treatment of our prisoners. Their sinking of all ships where possible, and now the use of this poisonous gas and to this is added this morning that in the South African campaign they are poisoning the wells. They acknowledge they have done this.

These methods seem to show that we have gone back 1000 years and relapsed into barbarism of the Middle Ages. It is quite certain that no war has been fought with more brutal ferocity than the present one. One cannot realize the horrors of it and men returning from the front are very reluctant to speak about it.

To-day an Agricultural Jumble Sale and sale of Farm Produce has been held in the Cattle Market here, in aid of the Farmers effort to raise funds for the Red Cross. Large quantities of stuff has been sent including 2 Fat Beast from Mr Rothschild Ashton, 1 from Mr Goosey Herne Lodge. An ordinary jumble sale is also being held in the Victoria Hall this afternoon in conjunction with the above. Both these are largely helped by Oundle also. It is hoped to realize from £300 to £400 by this effort. Similar sales are being held all over the country.

On clearing up to-night in connection with this sale it is found that nearly £850 has been realized. This far exceeded all expectations. Young girls (mostly farmers' daughters) collected £19 during the day with Red Cross boxes.

I omitted to mention the Budget, which was introduced on Tuesday. It was really a financial statement more than a Budget. No alteration takes place in taxation at present but the real Budget dealing with fresh taxations will be brought in in November. The Chancellor said really very little as to this but hinted there would be some very heavy taxes imposed then. He gave some stupendous figures as to the cost we are all incurring and said that we had already added 500 millions to the National Debt. It is well known that the savings of the people of this country have been about 400 millions per year for several years past and it is most likely from this source that some fresh taxes will be drawn. I paid 1/2d per lb to-day for a small piece of the Chine of Beef.

I am sorry to say that news has been received to-day of the death of Colonel Smith of the Artillery. He was kill[ed] in action in the Dardanelles. He was a son of the late J W Smith of the Rectory and brother of Mr J H Smith. Mrs Smith his mother an old lady of about 80 is still living at the Rectory with 2 unmarried daughters.

May 7 Friday. Not much fresh news this morning except a ghastly account of the terrible suffering caused by the poisonous gas. The respirators sent out are not altogether a success and further experiments are taking place with [them]. Doctors who have seen and attended the men say it is pitiful to see them. They simply lie gasping for breath and nothing can be done for them. The world stands aghast at these atrocities.

Italy still stands on the brink of war, and it seems almost impossible now for her to avoid it. Everything points to her joining the Allies, but up to to-day she has made no real move.

We have no official news from the Dardanelles, but the Prime Minister said last Night that the operations were going on most successfully but did not give any details.

Later. A telegram posted up to-night just says 'The "Lusitania" torpedoed and sunk'. This vessel is one of the finest vessels in the world. She belongs to the Cunard Line and runs between Liverpool and New York. She is 40,000 tons burthen and I should say must have nearly 2000 people on board. The Germans have threatened to sink her and a notice was circulated in America to that effect but the Americans did not take much notice of it. She must have had hundreds of Americans on board and the first thought that occurs to one is 'What will America do now?'

There is a theory going about that Germany is deliberately trying to provoke America to attack her in order that she may say "I cannot fight all the world so will ask for peace".

I do not give much [credit] to this myself and only give it as an indication of the times.

I can only say that if America quietly acquiesces in this latest outrage, she deserves all she gets. She has been repeatedly warned that if <u>we</u> are beaten (which God forbid) it will be their country which Germany will attack next.

No details are available of this awful outrage at this late hour so we shall have to await tomorrow. Later news says she was sunk off the Irish Coast about 2.15 this afternoon. She was on her way from New York to Liverpool.

1915 May 8 Saturday. This mornings papers only too truly confirm yesterdays telegrams about the Lusitania, and news this afternoon says 1400 people have gone down, a good proportion of them Americans. It is too early to estimate the effect of this. The Press in this country is very restrained in its speech towards America. Does not lecture her or tell her what to do but simply says that she is quite capable of looking after her own interests. . . .

May 9 Sunday. There is nothing to add to yesterday's news. We shall see to-morrow what effect the sinking of the Lusitania has had on all countries. . . .

May 10 Monday. There is nothing new to add this morning concerning the Lusitania except the fact that this outrage seems to have moved the world more than anything else that has taken place since war was declared. America says little about it at present, but it is quite certain there will [be] no war between America and Germany about it. It has caused great anger in America and possibly may lead to the breaking off of diplomatic relations but I think that is as far as it will go.

I do not think that America can help us much, that is directly. Her army does not number more than 50,000 men, and her navy we do not want. The supply of ammunition to us is a great thing in which she helps us much. Of course we all know that she would be equally glad to supply the Germans, if our navy were not strong enough to prevent it. Resentment here in this country is such that no words can describe it. Everybody now looks upon these Germans as utter savages.

A Zeppelin was over Southend about 5 o'clock this morning and dropped about 50 bombs. One woman was killed and a number wounded, and several fires occurred.

General French according to his report to-day has again been attacking the enemy north of La Bassée and says that he had considerable success. Very little news from the Dardanelles except rumours from Athens and other places, but there is no official news. The casualty lists show that some heavy fighting has been going on there the last few days.

May 11. According to both our own and also French reports furious fighting has been going on in Flanders since Sunday morning. It commenced late on Saturday night with great artillery fire, and early on Sunday we attacked the enemy I conjunction with the French who claim to have captured 3000 prisoners, 50 machine guns and 10 Guns up to three o'clock yesterday.

The Artillery fighting is probably the heaviest that has taken place during the war. We are getting a much better supply of ammunition and we shall require every shell we can get.

Reports are now coming through of the landing in the Dardanelles. It was a murderous business. The Turks assisted by German officers had endeavoured to make a landing impossible, and it was only by the most indomitable courage that our men and the Australians and New Zealanders were successful. One of [the] great things used to-day is barbed wire fences or entanglements. All soldiers are supplied with cutters to get this away, but it is quite impossible to do this under heavy fire, so it has to [be] literally blown to bits by Artillery before the troops can advance. It was thought this had been done before one of the landings took place but it was not so consequently the casualties were very heavy. The Russians are hammering

DAY BY DAY THROUGH THE GREAT WAR

away at the other end of the Bosphorus. Our men landed at five different points.

Italy still maintains her neutral position. The Germans alternately threaten and cajole her. All Germans and Austrians have left Italy, and it looks as if a decision cannot long be delayed.

Fierce anger is rising against the German people the last few days. Shops owned by Germans have been wrecked in Liverpool and other places and the authorities have been obliged to intern many Germans to protect them from the violence of the people. This is deplorable, but it is only natural, for the beastly and brutal way in which the Germans are behaving has put them beyond the pale of civilised people.

May 12 Wednesday. The fighting in Flanders is still continuing. The enemy attacked us yesterday and Monday under cover of poisonous gas, and endeavoured to rush us, but our men were ready this time. They came on in their usual close formation, and Sir J French who is not given to exaggeration says 'they were literally mown down'. The precautions taken against this gas seem to be a little more effective. The French also made marked progress yesterday north of Arras and came within sight of Lens. . . .

Rioting and pillaging of German shops took place last night in London and several other places. There is a growing demand that all alien enemies of whatever position shall be interned for the duration of the war. A deputation of 200 members of the Stock Exchange marched down to the House last night and succeeded in getting one of the members to raise this question when the House rose. It was openly stated that in case of Zeppelin attacks on London many of these aliens have duties assigned to them to help the enemy.

The Government promised to announce what [they] intend to do to-night. In many places notices have appeared in the last few days "No dealings with Germans".

The storm also seems to be gathering in America and indeed through every country. The world is beginning to see that this is not merely a fight against Germany, but that it is a fight to see whether civilisation as we know it is to continue to exist or whether we are to relapse into barbarism.

May 13 Thursday. [Heavy losses on both sides in the fighting in Flanders and France.] Rioting was very bad in many places yesterday. I can say that never have I seen the nation roused as it is to-day. The anger against Germany on account of its barbarities is intense, and it is not safe for a German to show himself in a good many towns. This rioting is very foolish and does not help us one bit but at the same time it is only natural. I hope the Government will take strong measures to repress it.

All alien enemies of military age for their own safety will have to be interned, and all other deported.

Later. To-night we received bad news from the Dardanelles. The Battle Ship Goliath

(700 men) has been sunk by a torpedo. 20 officers and 250 men saved, the rest perished. This Dardanelles business is a costly and terrible one.

The Prime Minister announced in the House to-night that all alien enemies over military age are to be interned.

May 14 Friday. [Some success in France]. The policy of interning the Germans meets with general approval. At the present moment there are 19,000 aliens interned in camps and 40,000 (24,000 men and 16,000 women) are still at liberty. It is estimated that of the 24,000 men about 15,000 are of military age i.e. from 18 to 55. So a great number of camps will have to be prepared for them. There is a considerable number of Germans now living in this country who did not respond to the call to join their own army when war was declared and who if they returned now would most likely be shot as deserters. These will welcome the new regulations as they know they will be quite safe.

[The Government publishes a report on the Belgian Atrocities]. It proves beyond the shadow of a doubt how these things were carefully organised and planned by those in high authority in Germany.

A notice such as has not been issued since 1622 is published in the Court Chronicle to-day. It is an order degrading the Kaiser, the Emperor and six other smaller people from the Order of the Garter. Their banners are to be removed from St. George's Windsor to-day.

THE DIARY OF JOHN COLEMAN BINDER

1915 May 15 Saturday. . . . The Italian Cabinet which is in favour of intervention on the side of the Allies has resigned, owing it is said to German intrigue. Up to a late hour last night the King had not accepted the resignation, but it appears to be quite a toss up as to which way things will go. Many street demonstrations in favour of intervention are taking place and public opinion is very excited.

An unconfirmed rumour was in circulation last night that Captain Ward Hunt of Wadenhoe had been killed in action. To-day he is returned as unofficially killed, so that it is most probably correct. He is mentioned in this diary as having been wounded. He came home and recovered and had rejoined his regiment the 1st Northants. This regiment has again suffered terribly. Out of -- -- men they lost -- -- last Sunday May 9th. They were ordered into action about 5 pm and had several hours hard fighting. . . .

May 16 Sunday It is good to be able to sit down to-day and to try to estimate the events in their right perspective. I think this last week has been almost the most trying one we have had since war commenced, except the time when the Allied armies were retreating from Mons last August.

The sinking of the 'Lusitania' . . . and the callous way he Germans are rejoicing over it. . . is very horrible and has touched the imagination of every one even those whom all this war seemed to leave quite untouched, but I must say that the use of the poisonous gas has moved me in a much higher degree.. . A more hellish devilish act has never been recorded in warfare. The death is not quick and soon over as in many other ways, but the agony which is terrible endures for days and even if death does not mercifully put an end to the torture it leaves the victims so shattered that their lives are a burden to them.. . . Of the end of the war there is not the least sign, unless these acts of Germany are like the writhing of a wounded beast. God only knows we must wait and help in every way we can.. . . A hint of conscription was given by Lord Haldane in the House one night this week and it has been accepted without much comment by the whole people. At present I do not think it is probable as recruits have joined in great numbers the last month, and especially this week, but it is possible it may come if the war is carried on for a year or two.

The internment of Germans has had a quieting effect on the people. Their continued liberty might have had a terrible ending. It is well known that the Germans have threatened to bombard London by Zeppelins during the early summer and it is strongly suspected that some of these alien Germans were ready to help them, and have had duties assigned to them in connection with this promised raid. They might have helped I am quite prepared to admit, and might have caused a panic but I am quite certain the majority of them would have been instantly massacred. So much do they know this that they are eagerly welcoming the order for their arrest. In fact hundreds have given themselves up at once.

The protest of America against the sinking of the Lusitania and other ships was sent to Berlin yesterday. It was strong, vigorous and does not leave Germany any room for evasion. I am curious to know what the reply will be. There will [be], I quite think, no war, at any rate at present.

Captain Seymour son of Admiral Seymour of Wadenhoe is amongst those who have fallen this week, also a man named Peacock of this town.

May 17 Monday Again to-day comes the report of hard fighting. The 1st Army (there are two in Flanders now) attacked the Germans at dusk on Saturday and drove them back two miles, and renewed the attack again early yesterday morning. This is all that is said at present.

Italian events seem to be moving much more in favour of the Allies. The King would not accept the resignation of the Ministry as he found that only a cabinet in favour of war was possible. It is confidently said that Italy will join us in a short time. She has an army of a million men and a powerful navy. A Zeppelin raid on Ramsgate this morning.

1915 May 18 Tuesday. [Many prisoners taken in Saturday and Sunday's attack, and some gunned down by their own side to prevent them surrendering.]

The Zeppelin did a good deal of damage at Ramsgate yesterday morning about 1.30 but no lives were lost. It was discovered and a most exciting encounter ensued between it and our own airmen. They flew over around and beneath it, and attacked it with bombs and guns. It is not yet certain if it managed to escape, but that one or another one was destroyed off the French coast a few hours later.

The Russians are struggling in the Carpathians and are hampered in their fight with the Austrians by lack of railways and ammunition.

It is quite certain that we have a very heavy task in the Dardanelles. It will be a long business I think. The natural land defences are so formidable that they can only be captured yard by yard, and until they are taken it will [be] impossible for our ships to pass the "Narrows".

Tonight the Prime Minister said that preparations were being made for 'a long war' and Lord Kitchener said that he wanted 300,000 more recruits. I believe events are moving in the direction of conscription.

May 19 Wednesday The interest to-day is centred more in home politics rather than in the Armies abroad. (Rain and mists have prevented much movement since Sunday). Rumours have been current for some little time that a Coalition Ministry might be formed. These have taken a more definite shape to-day and [it] is almost certain that, should they obtain the approval of their rank and file, certain of the Tory leaders will join the Cabinet taking the places of about 5 or 6 Liberal men who would retire. From the day the war was declared there has been to a large extent a party truce which the Tory leaders have honourably kept, but certain of their rank and file and their newspapers have not done so. Added to this some friction has arisen at the Admiralty between Mr Churchill and Lord Fisher, and it is thought that Lord Kitchener should not be bothered about the supply of munitions but should devote himself entirely to the Army. Of course the Tory leaders have been informed of all that was being done, and Mr Balfour being a member of the Defence Committee has taken a leading place in all work relating to that Committee. He has had room at the Admiralty and has been most assiduous in his attendance there. Mr Asquith said this afternoon certain arrangements were being made which would be announced shortly. I hope these new moves will be for the best interests of the nation. I have my doubts. It will to some extent stifle criticism, which is good for all leaders, and Coalitions in the past have not been a brilliant success, but the times in which we are now living are without precedent in the history of the Nation, and we all hope that this Coalition will prove an exception to the rule.

Lord Kitchener reviewed the war in a speech in the House last night. He [is] optimistic with regard to the operations in the Dardanelles….He also said that the Allies had decided to use Gas against the enemy. I am very sorry they have been driven to do this, and can only hope that the gas we use will not cause the intense agony and suffering that is caused by the Gas the enemy use. From reports that reach us indirectly it seems that this gas business has caused much anger and to a limited extent panic amongst the men, and that the leaders feel themselves bound to do something to restore confidence, so that the men may feel themselves able to meet the enemy on an equality.

May 20 Thursday ... The events which have led up to the formation of the Coalition Ministry are to some extent made public to-day. 1st A Quarrel which has developed at the Admiralty between Mr Churchill and Lord Fisher. Both men of great will power. 2nd A difference between Lord Kitchener and the Army Chiefs in France with regard to ammunition. They complain they have been asking for high explosives and that the greater part which they have received has been shrapnel, also one or two other minor causes. I cannot say that men are very enthusiastic about this business. Ministers may have made some errors, they would not be human if they had not done so, but I am convinced they have done exceedingly well so far. They had to meet a state of affairs without precedent. They were not above asking for outside help and this together with what they were able to do has so far brought us through this terrible war without serious losses. The prompt measures they took respecting Banking Finance and the safety of the Country have been very effectual and have received the support of all Parties. We shall see if the Coalition can do better. I doubt it. I can see that it is a move in the direction of Conscription. The Country may agree to this but it will have to [be] clearly shown that it is necessary. . . .

The Government has at last decided to prohibit Horse Racing (except one meeting at Newmarket). They ought to have done this before. It is a scandal that railways over worked as they are now should be obliged to carry all these racing betting men and touts by special trains, and thus very often hold up troop and other trains. I sincerely hope they will also prohibit professional football during next winter if the war continues. This is no time for these sorts of things.

May 21 Friday [No decision from Italy.] America is also getting uneasy and has warned Americans living in Germany that it would [be] wise for them to leave that country if they can possibly do so. *[Scant reports from the front].*

The political situation is unchanged. The leaders of the two parties met in conference yesterday, but what they did has not been made public at present.

There have been 3 Germans under arrest in this country for some weeks charged as being spies. The trial of one of them Ruphiect[?] began at the Central Criminal Court on Tuesday. He was charged with being a spy and sending information to the Germans in invisible ink. . .it was stated that he was under observation from the first day that he landed in Liverpool from America. His letters were opened and it was found on tests being applied he had secret intelligence between the lines of an ordinary letter in invisible ink. The case was fairly proved against him but the trial had not finished and when it came on yesterday morning it was announced that he had committed suicide by hanging himself in his cell. He left a written message on a slate saying that he had received a fair trial and it was also clear from what he had written that he was a German officer of fairly high rank. He would have been shot there is no doubt. The trial of the other two now under arrest is fixed for June 1.

May 22 Saturday. . . . The casualty lists of the past weeks reveal how severe the fighting of the last fortnight has been. The lists each day usually contain the names of 50, 60 or 70 officers. *[Heavy fighting in Galicia between the Austrians and the Russians with enormous loss of life on both sides].*

Up to to-night Italy has not made a formal declaration of war, but every preparation is being made for it . . It is thought it has been delayed to allow Italians an opportunity of escaping from Austria and Hungary and Germany. Great activity also prevails in America where it is estimated there are 800,000 Italians who are liable to serve. These are to a great extent hastening back and all ships coming eastward are crowded. A terrible railway collision occurred this morning at - - - - on the Scottish border. A troop train ran into another train and a fire ensued, and into all this horror an express dashed. 250 persons were killed and 200 injured.

May 22 Sunday. Whit Sunday. A beautiful May day warm and brilliant sunshine. A typical day for holidays, but that seems to be the last thought with people to-day. There is the usual relaxation from business, but there are scarcely any amusements and no facilities for cheap railway travel such as has been quite the usual thing for many years.

One cannot look back on the events of the past week with much satisfaction or encouragement. That is on political events that have occurred in this country. The Coalition Ministry is in process of formation, and the more the general public consider, the less I believe do they welcome it. The average man considers that the Government we have had since the war began may have made mistakes, but that on the whole it has done supremely well, and that its downfall has been brought about by intrigue and the petty spitefulness of certain Tory newspapers, viz 'The Times', the 'Daily Mail' and one or two others. These are all owned by one man, and all over the country there is a very strong outcry against them They were insistent at the beginning of the war that Lord Kitchener should be made War Minister and now they are ready to consign him to [the] lowest pit. This is simply because Kitchener, who is a man of iron will, will not do as they wish him to do. A curious scene was witnessed on the London Exchanges on Friday. These (the Stock, London Baltic etc.) cannot be said to be the least favourable to any Liberal Ministry, but in all these places copies of the newspapers were burned in bonfires, cheers were given for Kitchener, and groans were given for this man Northcliffe. They have also made an effort the last few days to prevent Lloyd George from remaining Chancellor of the Exchequer, but this created so much alarm in the City that they have desisted. Representations came from all sections of merchant bankers and financiers to Mr Asquith recognizing the excellent work which the Chancellor had done and pointing out that [it] would be nothing short of a national disaster if he did not continue to hold that office.

DAY BY DAY THROUGH THE GREAT WAR

I think myself that the newspapers I have mentioned should be dealt with under the Defence of the Realm Act. There are many men who have been fined or imprisoned under that act since war began who have not done one hundredth of the mischief these papers have done the last fortnight. Men of all parties and creeds are disgusted and amazed at this shameful exhibition and other nations may well point at us in scorn.

The number of our officers killed, wounded and missing during the last three weeks is 2900. This will give some little idea of the terrible nature of this war. This is English officers and does not include any French, Belgian or Russian.

The death of Captain G.C. Hunt of Wadenhoe is now confirmed. It has caused great sorrow at Wadenhoe where he was most popular with both rich and poor.

Colonel Ferguson of Polebrook commanding the 1st Life Guards is again home wounded (not seriously). This is the second time.

Most of the cavalry regiments of the regular army have been in action the last week or two. In the trenches I imagine, as it has never been reported that they are doing much mounted work.

A Telegram late to-night says it is rumoured that Italy declared war this afternoon.

May 24 Whit Monday. Italy has at last come into the war. This is the outstanding fact to-day. She formally declared it yesterday, to commence at midnight last night.

It is a momentous decision, and of such vast import that we cannot judge of it clearly to-day, but when one considers that this Triple Alliance, Germany, Austria and Italy, has been the chief factor in European politics for the last 30 years and is now at an end, it may be judged that events such as this generation or our fathers have never seen are likely to occur. . . .

May 25 Tuesday. . . . News reached here yesterday of the death of another Oundle man. His name is Roughton. His parents live in Havelock Cottages. This up to the present makes - - men killed belonging to this place.

The price of meat continues to steadily advance. The best joints of English Beef are being retailed at 1/9 per lb in London. We have not reached these extreme prices in country places at present. The principal reasons of these very high prices are I think as follows: First, The Government have commandeered all the meat coming from foreign countries, that is Australia, America, the Argentine etc. They take what they want for the troops and the rest is disposed of in the ordinary markets. A secondary cause is that we have a late spring consequently there has not been much grass to bring stock on and feeding stuffs being so high in price farmers have hesitated to buy much. It may be possible that we shall see some little drop in these prices in a month or two, but not much I am afraid. It might be thought that no more meat would be consumed by the soldiers now they are in the army than in the ordinary way in civilian life. The answer to that is they are being fed so much better than they are in civil life. Cheese is also used in enormous quantities by the troops and is very dear.

These high prices of meat are hitting the Butchers very hard. It is quite a common thing to see in the larger towns the notice 'Closed until the war is over' affixed to a butcher's shop. In many places they are only open three days a week.

May 26 Wednesday. The Italians yesterday crossed the frontier and occupied a strong position in Austrian territory. The Austrians so far have retired, taking with them the principal people of the towns the Italians have occupied. . . .

The Coalition Cabinet is now complete. It contains 22 Members and it is too large. Twelve men would have carried this business far better than 22. I do not like Mr Balfour at the Admiralty. He is now nearly seventy years old. I think a younger man should have been placed there. I take it there will be an inner ring in this Cabinet who will control affairs to a large extent. This was so in the last Government.

It is freely rumoured that the Prime Minister Mr Asquith was the chief person who induced Italy to come in on the side of the Allies.

THE DIARY OF JOHN COLEMAN BINDER

1915 May 27 Thursday. Another battleship 'The Triumph' was torpedoed in the Dardanelles on Tuesday. The Admiralty say that most of the officers and men were rescued. This Dardanelles business is a terribly costly one. It is reported (unofficially) that we lost 26,000 men there in the first weeks fighting.

The usual news comes from Flanders to-day. Hammering away but no real progress.

[The fighting in Galicia between the Austro-German Army and the Russians continues].

Two Zeppelins were again over Southend during last night. One hundred bombs were dropped. One woman was killed and a woman and child injured. Some damage to property, but not much.

May 28 Friday. [*Another ship sunk in the Dardanelles.*] A vessel under repair at Sheerness was also blown up yesterday with a loss of 270 lives. It is thought by many people that the explosions on ships in harbour are caused by German spies. I only give the rumour for what it is worth. . . . .

May 29 Saturday. The war news this morning is somewhat more cheerful. The French have given the Germans a severe set-back near Lens and are moving forward to that city. It is a most important railway junction and should it come again into French hands it will be of great service to them. . . . . *[Much misgiving about the Dardanelles expedition.]* .

May 30 Sunday No fresh news up to mid-day to-day.

I should like to note here the tendency which is growing in some quarters towards conscription. It is very difficult to get at the real truth in this matter, but great pressure will be brought to bear upon the Coalition Government to adopt some form of compulsory military service I quite think.

Whether this is necessary can only be decided by the Government as they alone know the number of men that are under arms and what number may be required. At present there are 8,000,000 men in the nation between the ages of 19 and 40. If this thing is really proved to be necessary the people will accept it but it will have to be clearly shown that it is.

The manufacture of war munitions is being organised in all directions and almost every firm who has plant capable of this kind of work will be brought under supervision. Some of the boys at the Schools here are helping to turn parts of shells. Their Carpentry shop has been cleared and new machinery installed at a cost of £600 (it is said the Headmaster bore the expense of this) and here 40 boys are working for several hours daily on this manufacture of shells.

May 31 Monday. I omitted to say that last Thursday a squadron of 16 French Airmen made a raid on the German Poison Factory at Mannheim and did much damage by bomb dropping. Three separate fires were seen also an explosion occurred. . . .

To-night's news says that proceedings were commenced to-day against the Times for publishing news which may be of use to the enemy. These proceedings are taken under the Defence of the Realm Act.

June 1 Tuesday. The threatened air raid on London has come off. The following curious notice appeared in some of the London daily papers this morning. I think it is worth setting down in full. It was issued by the Press Bureau. "The Press are specially reminded that no statement whatever must be published dealing with the places in the neighbourhood of London reached by aircraft or the course supposed to be taken by them, or any statement or diagrams which might indicate the ground or route covered by them.

The Admiralty communiqué gives all the news which can be properly published. These instructions are given in order to secure the public safety, and the present intimation may itself be published by the Press as explaining the absence of more detailed reports." The appearance of the above, which was sent to the newspaper offices very early this morning probably between 3 and 4 o'clock made one suspect that something had at last occurred and confirmation was received by a private telegram which reached here about 10.30. No details were given except that several fires were caused. Probably we shall receive more detailed reports this afternoon.. . . .

The German reply to America with regard to the Lusitania and other vessels was received in New York last night, and this has roused the Americans at last. It is most evasive and irritating and has much increased the tension already existing between the two countries. Indeed it is said in America that the Germans are distinctly trying to cause civil war in the States. That is between the German Americans and American citizens proper. There are said to be 10 million German Americans in the States, and of course they sympathise with the Germans. . . .

1915 June 2 Wednesday. Italy slowly advances into the Trentino meeting with very little resistance. Every effort is being made to induce Roumania and Bulgaria to come in on the side of the Allies, and [it] seems possible that these efforts will succeed.

Very little fresh news is issued about the London Air raid, but it took place about 11 pm on Monday night over the east end. No details are given as to the number of enemy craft or any thing about them. Four people were killed and an inquest was held to-day. Evidence stated that the bombs gave off a heat of 5000 degrees Fahrenheit.

[Still a few ships being sunk by German submarines] . .

June 3 Thursday A most effective reply is given to the attacks on Lord Kitchener to-day. The King has made him a K.G. This meets with the hearty approval of all decent people in the kingdom.

There is quite a distinct fall in the price of wheat the last week. It has dropped about 2/6 per qr. This has been brought about by various causes. France, Belgium and other countries have secured enough to carry them on to harvest. Reaping has commenced in the Southern United States and there is every prospect of a bumper crop in North America and Canada. Corn is backward in this country. There is no wheat in ear in this district at present, but I think the prospect taken altogether is quite favourable. We shall want it all I think. As far as one can see, this war is likely to last for another twelve months and even longer than that possibly. Parliament meets again to-day and the Coalition Government is complete.

[Germany may have recaptured Premysl which would deter Roumania and Bulgaria from joining Allies.]

The new Chancellor of the Exchequer accompanied by the Governor of the Bank of England has gone to Milan to-day to confer with the Italian Minister of Finance. As usual England is the paymaster.

The question of finance will have a great deal to do with regard to conscription in this country. It must be quite evident to anyone who thinks a few minutes that if we are to find the money it will be quite necessary to keep the trade of this country going, and if all men are to be made soldiers trade will be heavily hit. The people in this country who are shouting for Conscription do not seem to realize this.

June 4 Friday. [Recapture of Premysl confirmed and attributed by Lloyd George to Russia's shortage of ammunition] .

[Lloyd George] then went on to declare that every private interest in the engineering trades must be subordinated to the manufacturers of arms and ammunition and he also hinted that if this could not be done without compulsion, compulsion would be used. This was referring to workshops. With regard to recruits for the army he said these were coming in as fast as they could be dealt with, but if the necessity arose for conscription the Government would not hesitate to ask for it, and he was confident that the nation would accept it. . . . .

June 5 Saturday. Some strong fighting is reported to-day from our front, but of no great import. The Prime Minister has been across on a visit to the Army this week and returned yesterday.

[Orderly Russian retreat from Premysl and fighting goes on].

A Zeppelin raid took place very late last night over the east and S.E. Coast.

1915 June 6 Sunday. A hot June day. We are wanting rain. It seems strange that after all the rain we had during the spring and winter that it should be required.

[60 injured in the London raid].   Barnwell Castle has been turned into a convalescent home for wounded soldiers by its owner Mr Czarnokow. Ten wounded arrived there this week.

June 7 Monday. No damage worth recording was done in Saturday morning's raid. We are getting quite accustomed to them now.

THE DIARY OF JOHN COLEMAN BINDER

The submarines have been very active the last few days. Their principal victims have been fishing smacks. Of these they have sunk twelve since Thursday. Glorious warfare this on the part of a mighty nation, to attack and sink unarmed fishing smacks. . . .

The other two German spies who were captured in the country were tried last Friday. One was ordered to be shot and was handed over to the military. The other was sentenced to 7 years penal servitude. Another one was arrested yesterday just as he was leaving England.

Wheat fell in local markets on Saturday from 3/- to 4/- per qr.

Hard fighting has been resumed in the Dardanelles last Friday. Some progress was made, but it is a tough business. The author of it Mr Winston Churchill (late first Lord of the Admiralty) vigorously defended the sending of this expedition in a speech at Dundee on Saturday. He said we were little way from a great victory there and that the consequences of this victory would be incalculable. We shall see. There is many a slip betwixt the cup and the lip.

The casualty list to-day is a terrible one. It contains 5,500 names of killed, wounded and missing. During the last fortnight upwards of 20,000 names have been published in these lists.

. . . .A Zeppelin raid took place last night over the East Coast again. It is not said the places which were visited, but I understand Kings Lynn was amongst them. Six people were killed and 40 injured, and some fires were also caused. In connection with this it is also announced that a Zeppelin was brought down and destroyed in Belgium about three o'clock this morning by our own airmen. Probably this was one that was returning from the raid mentioned.

Tuesday June 8 To-day all England is ringing with the wonderful exploit of Lieut. Warneford, the aviator. The raid mentioned last night was principally at Hull. We have not been told officially but it [is] surmised that our aviators in Belgium were warned that the Zeppelins were over here and would probably return to their base in Belgium. At any rate this young fellow (23 years old) was waiting for them between Ghent and Liege and this time by rising to a height of 6000 feet was able to drop 6 bombs on one of them. His aim was true and the whole thing crashed down to the earth and caught fire. All its crew (28) were burned or dashed to pieces, and unfortunately it fell on some buildings and killed three people. The force of the exploding bombs caused Warneford's monoplane to capsize, but he was able to right himself, but had to come to ground in the enemy's lines. His coolness did not desert him, for he managed to re-start his engines and came safely back to his base within our lines. A marvellous deed this, and one that will cause every Brutish to rejoice that we have such brave men amongst us.

A definite promise was given last night that compulsory service either in the army or in workshops would not be introduced except with the direct consent of Parliament. This is as it should be. An attempt has been made in some newspapers and in certain classes of people to induce the Government to do this by indirect means. This has caused much opposition as the people of this country will not consent to be governed by newspapers even if they (the newspapers) have the Times to lead them. . . . .

Two of our aviators also attacked the Zeppelin base in Belgium yesterday morning and claim that they were able to destroy it, at any rate they set it on fire.

1915 *June 9 Wednesday.* *[Italy is nominally only at war with Austria, but is expected to declare war against Germany soon].*

Thrust and counter thrust is still [going on] along our front and the French front in Belgium and on the whole the advantage is on our side. The German trenches are in many cases most elaborate affairs, made of concrete etc and strengthened in every possible way so that they take a great deal of driving out. We have been repeatedly warned that we must not expect any great events in this area at present.

Lieut. Warneford the aviator whose deeds I wrote of yesterday is to-day given the V.C. and he well deserves it.

I am told that the damage done in London by the last raid was very great, although nothing of it appears in the daily papers. It has also unnerved the people living in that part and many do not go to bed until daylight begins to appear about 2 am. These Zeppelins lie off the coast (out of sight) during the evening and then come inland as soon as it is quite dark.

'Hooters' have been fixed in most towns to give warning of their appearance. One has been fixed at Smiths Brewery here.

Mr Asquith said in the House this afternoon that our total losses up to the present had been 250,000.

June 10 Thursday. *[Unconfirmed rumour that the Dardanelles passage has been forced].* The chief news to-day is from America. A reply has been sent to Germany which re-iterates the demands made in the previous note. It is believed that Germany will refuse these demands, if she does grave consequences may ensue between the two nations From what one can judge American public opinion is very firm in this matter and no further delay will be tolerated.

Private reports which reach me from Hull say that the loss of life during the raid on Sunday night was very heavy probably somewhere about 80 or 90 persons were killed and quite a number injured. Damage to property was also very heavy.

I am told to-day quite confidentially that a Zeppelin might be about this neighbourhood. The police have been warned. A armoured motor car went through about 12.30 to-day.

The Agricultural Jumble Sale funds have now been made up and the amount realized has exceeded £1000 which has been forwarded to the Red Cross Fund.

There is also a depot here for the collection of fresh eggs, which are forwarded weekly to the wounded soldiers in hospitals. The number collected averages about 1200 per week and putting these at the market price of 2/- per score means a contribution of £6 per week.

June 11 No confirmation of the Dardanelles rumours, I was afraid they were too good to be true.

Two of our torpedo boats were sunk in the North Sea yesterday by submarines. Thirty men were lost and 41 saved out of the crews. This submarine warfare is very active just now, principally against our trawlers. Quite a number have been lost lately. I think they knowing the risk they incur are very unwise to go out fishing. Fish is a thing that we can do without, especially if it is to be caught at the cost of men's lives.

June 12 Saturday. *[Russians having more success in the Carpathians. The French having some minor successes in Flanders].*

June 13 Sunday. A quiet June day. We are still without rain, but everything looks well in the country. Hay harvest is just commencing, but I do not think the crop will be heavy. In some districts there is a shortage of labour and the Army authorities have agreed to release a number of men for a definite period. No man will be released for this work for more than 14 days consecutively and this only on the definite understanding that he shall be employed in the hayfield. The farmer will also be obliged to pay him 24/- per week of 6 days if he finds no food, but if he finds him certain food he will have to pay 15/- per week. I do not gather this class of labour will be much used in this district.

A good many local wool sales have been held this last week. Roughly the advance in price is about 10/- or 12/- per tod. The top price realized is about 46/6 to 47/- per tod, and the average about 45/-. So here the farmer will benefit again.

There has been a very sharp decline in grain prices this week. Wheat which was selling a month since at 65/- per qr has had the biggest fall, and by last night's reports I see that merchants would not give more than 50/- to 52/- per qr. This will mean heavy losses to some merchants and millers. Mr Sampson of Water Newton Mills told me on Thursday that even in his comparatively small way of business his stock had depreciated £300. Confidence seems quite lost in the Markets at present as no one can see how far the drop in prices will continue. Various causes are suggested as to why this has occurred. I believe the one most generally thought to be true is the fact that harvest prospects are very good all over the American continent and speculators there realize that they will not be able to manipulate the grain. Something is also due to the Dardanelles campaign for it is certain that if this is successful huge quantities of grain will be shipped from Odessa and all Black Sea ports to this country. It does not do to prophesy unless you know, but it looks at present as if we should have grain prices a deal lower next winter than we have had during the last months.

All kind of meat continues high in price, although a fall in the beef is predicted at an early date. I bought 9 pigs on March 3 at 27/- each. These are now fat and [I] have sold them for £5 each, equal to 10/- per stone of 14lb.

June 14 Monday. [The Germans have suffered a defeat and heavy losses in the battle with the Russians, but not decisive].

Great strides have been made in this country in organising the whole of the engineering shops for the supply of ammunition. Practically everything else is subordinated to this and other war material. Very little private work is being done. Huge quantities of machinery for manufacturing this have been imported from America.

It is announced to-day that the French Government have acquired one of the largest steel works in America for the making of shells etc. This is the Bethlehem Steel Works.

Private reports from Hull say that 160 persons wee killed. There is no official confirmation of this.

June 15 [Greek elections have resulted in a government favourable to joining the Allies]. Another Oundle man, Dickinson, is reported killed to-day.

Colonel Wickham commanding the Yeomanry has been home on leave the last week. He returned to the front on Monday.

June 16 Wednesday. I think we have seen the end of compulsion or conscription for the present. The Prime Minister in the House last night declared against it most definitely. He as speaking on a Vote of Credit for [£] 250,000,000 and said the Government were satisfied "with the organised and willing service rendered by all classes." He did not say in what way this money is to be raised but we are all anxiously looking for some announcement with regard to this. Certainly some of it will be raised by loan again, but taxation in some form must be very heavy. Judging from all appearances this will be accepted without much demur, as every one recognizes that it is inevitable. Our expenditure in war was over 2 ½ million a day it was stated last night. He also gave the principal reason for the forming of the Coalition. He said it was chiefly to reassure our Allies that this was done.

An air raid occurred on our North East Coast late last night (it is not said where) 15 people were killed and numbers wounded. The French also raided Karlsruhe yesterday in conjunction with our men. A fleet of 27 airmen were employed and it is said much damage was done.

1915 June 17 Thursday. Our army made a strong attack on two sections of [the enemy's] lines near Ypres and Festubert yesterday. They were successful at Ypres but at Festubert after gaining some ground were obliged to evacuate it again owing to a strong counter attack by the enemy.

A remarkable meeting in aid of the Red Cross was held at the Mansion House London last night. Over £ 87,000 was raised at this meeting. Some hundreds of thousand pounds have been raised previous to this since last August.

In the House of Commons last night drastic taxation on profits made through the war was foreshadowed. It is said that ⅔ of these profits will be taken and that enormous additions will be made on ordinary income tax. Farmers who hitherto have generally escaped this tax will also be assessed now.

The Northants Yeomanry is quite up to its full strength and no more recruits are wanted at present.

Wool touched 50/- per tod at Northampton to-day.

END OF VOLUME THREE

Markham's Stationers. War news was posted here.

Oundle Court House and Police Station.

Congregational Church, West Street.

Queen Victoria Hall.

NORTHAMPTONSHIRE.

THE FOLLOWING INSTRUCTIONS are published by the Lord Lieutenant, with the approval of H.M. Government, for the information and Guidance of the Civil Population of the County in case of an actual or imminent hostile landing.

1.—These instructions are not issued owing to an apprehension of an immediate attempt by the enemy to land troops in this Country—such a contingency is no more likely to occur now than it was in the earlier stages of the War. However improbable it may appear, it cannot be ignored, and it is necessary that preparatory arrangements should be made to meet it.

2.—The objects of the scheme which is outlined herein are:—

(1) To prevent the operation of His Majesty's Forces being hampered or interfered with;

(2) To render the County as inhospitable as possible to the enemy, by the removal from his reach of what might be useful to him for food, transit, &c.

(3) To warn the inhabitants of the County how they must act, and how assist in the working of the scheme.

INSTRUCTIONS.

3.—To meet these requirements a Central Organising Committee has been formed for the County, and an Emergency Committee in each Petty Sessional Division—the latter being composed of two Civil members and one Military member. The Civil members and Parish assistants have been enrolled as Special Constables.

4.—The policy of the Government is to encourage every man to take his part in the present struggle:—

If he is of the proper age and physique, and not excluded from enlistment by employment in armament works or Government contract work, railways, &c., he should enlist;

If he is not of the proper age or physique he should join the nearest Volunteer Corps which is affiliated to the Central Association of Volunteer Training Corps.

Anyone who has not enlisted, or not joined an affiliated Corps must on no account take part as a combatant:—

If he does it is certain he will bring evil consequences upon himself and others;

He must further be prepared to surrender any arms and ammunition he may possess; and to perform all non-combatant duties such as digging trenches, burying the dead, &c.

5.—No one should flee from home or cease to follow his usual occupation till advised or required to do so by Military or Police Authority.

When ordered to leave home it must be done without hesitation and by the roads or paths indicated by the Police.

THE DIARY OF JOHN COLEMAN BINDER

INSTRUCTIONS.

It is of the utmost importance that His Majesty's Forces and War material should have the free use of certain roads.

If troops should be met, civilians must immediately leave the roads and pass into fields.

6.—Owners of stock, motors, bicycles, horses, harness, carts and other vehicles must be prepared to remove them with the least possible delay if and as directed by order of the Military, by members of Emergency Committees, Police or Special Constables. It is very necessary that these movements should be made by the routes ordered.

Any stock, vehicles, &c., which cannot be moved in time may have to be destroyed by order given by the Military, either direct or through the Police.

The Government will give reasonable compensation for property destroyed by authority.

So far as circumstances permit, orders for the destruction of property will be made in writing—of which a copy should be kept.

If an order to remove or destroy stock or any other property is not obeyed and destruction follows, no compensation will be paid.

Animals destroyed should be shot. If the carcasses are unbled and the entrails are not removed, the flesh becomes practically uneatable in an hour or two. But in any case the animals should be shot, not knifed, so that the blood may be left in them.

A pistol firing a soft lead bullet with a low-velocity explosive is the best weapon.

7.—The Military Authorities may at their discretion order the destruction of flour mills, wholesale stores of provisions, granaries, &c.

INSTRUCTIONS.

Retail and private supplies may be left untouched.

Unless special directions are given by Military order unthreshed cereals should not be destroyed.

8.—No attempt, except under Military orders, must be made to injure or destroy

    Bridges
    Electric light or power stations
    Telegraph or telephone wires
    Wireless stations
    Waterworks
    Sluices or locks
    Piers, jetties or ferries

Prompt assistance, however, should be given to carry out any of these operations.

9.—All tools, pick axes, spades, shovels, barbed wire, and other such articles or equipment should be placed unreservedly at the disposal of Local Emergency Committees and the Military Authorities.

SPENCER,

H.M. Lieutenant for Northamptonshire.

ALTHORP,
    FEBRUARY, 1915.

J. Stevenson Holt, Printer, 20, Newland, Northampton.

THE DIARY OF JOHN COLEMAN BINDER
Volume Four
18 June 1915 to 19 November 1915

1915 Friday June 18   The fighting still continues in all quarters. In some much more than in others. . . . The French have the last two days resumed the offensive in Lorraine and have secured some useful advantages.

A straw will show which way the wind blows. A Parliamentary Committee was appointed yesterday to consider the food supply of this country in case the war is not ended before the harvest of 1916 ! ! This needs no comment, but it discloses to some extent what those people who know think about the duration of this war.

June 19 Saturday   . . . Russia still continues to be the chief centre of interest. A long communication from Petrograd to-day does not disclose any great reasons for pessimism. They say that they are confident that they can hold their own. The Russians have now taken a strong position at [Gorlice] not far from Lemberg (which the Austro- Germans are trying to re-capture.) This struggle is being watched here with the keenest interest as it is evident the result will influence the war for some time, but even if the Russians fail it will not be decisive, as it is estimated that Russia has still six millions of men to bring into the fighting line.

Lieut. Warneford the aviator who distinguished himself about a fortnight since by destroying the Zeppelin was killed on Thursday in Paris whilst trying a new aeroplane.

A very sharp frost this morning doing much damage to all garden crops.

June 20 Sunday. A day of brilliant sunshine. We have had no rain of any consequence for nearly 6 weeks and as may be imagined everything is very much in want of moisture. The hay crop is being rapidly secured, but I am afraid that it is very light. Rain also is much needed for the grain crops, especially Barley, Oats and Peas, also the roots.

The price of all corn is still falling and business is virtually at a standstill. The few farmers who have any wheat left are very unwilling to accept to-day's price for it (about 49/- to 50/- per qr) as they are still thinking that it will leap up again. I believe they are altogether mistaken and it is confidently predicted in the Corn Trade [that] unless anything very unexpected happens we shall have values lower still.

Bread is reduced here to-morrow to 7 ½ d per 4lb loaf.

The stock trade is not so good either as the want of keep is causing some farmers to realize.

Wool continues very high and in some instances 50/- per tod was paid at Northampton Wool Fair this week. This is the highest price since 1873.

DAY BY DAY THROUGH THE GREAT WAR

The following notice has been issued by the Headmaster (Mr Sanderson) of the Schools here:

Oundle School

If any farmer of our neighbourhood is hard-pressed in time of hay-making and cannot get sufficient labour the boys of Laxton School and the younger boys of Oundle School (the older boys are occupied in war-work) will be glad to give them what help they can. We can send boys out in sets. Each boy can give one whole day per week, and the regular work of the School will be provided for at other times or in other ways. Should any farmer think that we can thus be of service, I shall be glad if he will apply to me or see me.

F.W. Sanderson

We only want to do this where assistance is absolutely needed and do not wish to displace local or other labour.

I do not think the above offer will be much taken advantage of, as I believe the farmers will be quite able to secure the hay crop especially as it is so light.

1915 June 21 Monday The longest day and the 322nd day of the war, and a day of unclouded sunshine.

The news this morning is both bad and good. The bad first. Russia appears to be having a bad time, and the Germans are within measurable distance of Lemburg, and although the position is not hopeless it is certainly getting critical.

On the other hand the Italians are moving firmly and steadily into Austrian territory on their way to Trieste... The French appear to be in sight of a real victory in the battle which has been in progress since May 9, the object of which is to capture Lens and Arras. The struggle has been a terrible one, and in spite of desperate German resistance aided by 100,000 fresh troops the French have practically accomplished their design. They are also doing well in Alsace Lorraine.

June 22 Tuesday. The event of most interest to-day is the issuing by the Government of a New War Loan, which will bear interest @ 4 ½ per cent and the amount is unlimited. It will appeal to all classes as money bearing this interest and backed by the security of the British Government must be an investment without equal in the world. It can be subscribed for in amounts of 5/- to £10 at any Post Office and above that amount at the Bank of England.

It is most far and wide reaching as it also deals with the redemption of Consols which can be exchanged for stock or bonds (both will be issued) in the new loans. The price of Consols to-day is nominally 66 ½ but this [is] a purely fictitious value, and I do not think that more than 55 could be obtained for them.

1915 June 23 Wednesday . . . . The new war loan continues to engage public attention very much. . . . It is I think one of the most far reaching events of this war, as it is bound to affect the value of almost every security in this country. In fact many securities have been marked down on Change to-day.

June 24 Thursday. The Austro-German Army has captured Lemburg the capital of Galicia. They admit they have suffered very heavy losses, that they have captured but few prisoners and no war material. They also admit that the Russians retired in good order. This is satisfactory to some degree but it cannot be denied that this is a heavy loss to the Allies as it will greatly influence the Balkans (Bulgaria, Roumania etc.) whom we had hoped would soon have come in on our side, but we must still hope for the best. It can be safely said that these defeats of the Russians have been solely due to lack of ammunition and guns, and if we could only force the passage of the Dardanelles we could give them considerable help, but at present we do not receive very encouraging reports from that quarter.

It is coming to be recognized that this question of ammunition is <u>the</u> question of the war, and this country is at last being organised for the production of it. The Germans foresaw that it would be the most important thing and made provision accordingly, but we were quite unprepared in this respect, and consequently have suffered very heavily.

Speaking last night in the House Mr Lloyd George, who is now Minister of Munitions, said we required

THE DIARY OF JOHN COLEMAN BINDER

8 million shells per month, and he introduced a Bill both for the organising of labour and plant. It is very far reaching but much too long to write down here. One provision of it gives the Trades Unions the opportunity to enlist or provide the skilled labour required within 7 days. If they fail to do so then the Government will use compulsion. This is right. No man or union of men can be allowed to stand in the way now. It is vital to the successful issue of this war that when the public interest demands it all private interests must give way.

I am coming more and more to think and see that we shall have no decisive result of the war during this year, and that not until next year at least can we hope to see anything like the end in sight. I hope I may be wrong, but so it appears to me to-day.

June 25 Friday. The spy Muller was shot yesterday morning in the Tower.

. . . . . Recruiting offices were opened yesterday all over the country for the skilled labour required in the making of ammunition. The response was excellent, many hundreds of men being enrolled. These men will be entirely under Government orders and may be shifted from one district to another if it is found necessary.

The Government announced last night that they intended to introduce a measure into the House next week for the compulsory registration of all men probably between the ages of 18 and 55. Various particulars as to occupation etc will have to be furnished on the return which each householder will be obliged to make.

June 26 Saturday. . . . . In France and Belgium there are few reports to-day, but still the long lists of casualties continue to come through. Every day these lists contain between three and four thousand names so it will be seen what a drain there is on our resources.

June 27 Sunday. . . . Last night reports speak of the excellent results as to enlisting the skilled men to manufacture ammunition. They are joining in hundreds and thousands and are of the best kind, that is skilled turners and fitters, so that we shall hope to regain lost ground in this respect. Having once been aroused and told what is required I do not think there is much need to fear the result. It is quite obvious that when the affair is organised and practically the whole attention of the engineering trade is turned in this direction the output must be enormous.

Yesterday we had a most welcome rain, and already the country has much benefited by it. Practically we have [had] no rain since May 6, and things were beginning to look really serious. Wheat I think has reached its lowest for the present. . Nominally it is quoted at 50/- but there are few sellers at that figure. Farmers have the idea that it is going back to its old figure and even higher. I do not think so.

I think at last the nation is beginning to realize the measure and extent of this war, and has made up its mind that it will be a long, costly and bloody affair. There is a sober earnestness in the great bulk of the people and although there is not much pessimism the nation as a whole is very sober and self restrained. There is a certain despondence, but this is chiefly amongst a section of the Public and Press which should know better. It is confined to the Times and some other newspapers which are all under the direction of one clique and which I think has certain definite political aims to serve. None of us object to criticism in reason, but generally these allied papers are quite unreasonable, and in certain quarters their carping remarks have caused much despondency. We, as a nation, are continually being taunted by them for having done or doing so little in this war. This is absolutely untrue. When one considers our position to-day and what we have done since last August 4 it is marvellous. Our obligation to our Allies was to keep the sea clear and to place an army of 170,000 men in France. Now consider what is our position to-day. Our fleet has cleared every German war ship off the seas in both hemispheres and with exception of the German submarines there is not an enemy ship which dares to venture out of port.

We have raised an army of three millions of men, of which nearly a million are already in France, and we are backing our Allies with the whole of our financial resources. Of course it is quite patent to all men who consider it that we are really fighting our own battles as much in France as if they were fought on English soil, and the Germans are quite aware of this too.

Our strength has not reached its maximum yet and it may be quite another twelve months before it does,

DAY BY DAY THROUGH THE GREAT WAR

but I cannot help thinking and believing that there can only be one end to this war, and that is the defeat and disaster of the Germans. In fact the situation is this - either we have to decisively beat the enemy or life here in England will not be worth living. The difference between the Germans and ourselves is this. <u>We</u> are quite willing they should live and exist and have an equal share with us in all the world's commerce. They <u>hate</u> us from the bottom of their hearts and I really and truly believe that if their Kaiser and his advisers could wipe us all off the face of the earth to-day by some simple act (such as touching a button) they would do it without the least compunction. This is the real reason we are fighting and intend to either win or die.

June 28 Monday. . . . . Rumours are prevalent that Bulgaria is mobilising. If this is so, it can only be with one object that is to come in on our side so that she may have her share in the Turkish Empire. Reports from Constantinople yesterday and to-day say that things are going from bad to worse there, and it is quite possible the end cannot be long delayed.

We have had some delightful rains here yesterday and to-day and the country has much improved.

I saw 2 car loads of wounded soldiers go through here to-day. They were convalescents who are being nursed at Barnwell Castle. It is quite an ordinary sight to see these cars of wounded soldiers on any country road to-day. Very many country houses have been turned into convalescent homes and the soldiers are taken out for drives by the owners of the houses.

June 29 Tuesday. The Russian retreat still continues and they withdraw from the Dniester. It is quite orderly and strong rear guard actions continually occur. What the Germans intend to do is quite obscure as it is certain the more they penetrate into Russia the worse their communications will be, possibly they intend to make another bid for Warsaw.

1915 June 30 Wednesday. There is quite a lull in the fighting the last few days both in France, Italy and the Dardanelles.

At home here all attention is being turned to organising the whole nation, especially with regard to ammunition. The National Register Bill was introduced into the House last night. It will be compulsory for every man and woman between the ages of 15 and 65 to be indexed, saying how they are employed, and whether they would be willing to work in other occupations. The work of doing this will be carried out by the Local Authorities. This thing may be required but personally I see very little use in it.

July 1 Excellent news is published to-day as to the Dardanelles. A heavy attack has been made and our men have gained ¾ mile of trenches. It appears to have been well planned and executed with great precision. . . .

The National Register Bill is being vigorously debated in the Country. Great exception is taken to some of the provisions especially the one making [it] compulsory to register any change of address. I think some change will be made before it actually comes into force.

July 2 Friday. An American liner was sunk by the Germans yesterday and 15 Americans were drownded. Again America sits quiet.

July 3 Saturday. . . . Persistent rumours are afloat that the Germans are about to make a strong move in France. All frontiers have been closed during the last few days, and indeed Berlin already claims they have won an important success in the Argonne. The German Crown Prince is in command here and, since he received a decisive set-back last Autumn, has been very quiet. This man even according to German reports is a very bad lot. He is a thief, robber and also given to drink, and is at the head of the extreme war party in Germany.

. . . . The New War Loan still engages a large share of public interest and a huge campaign is being organised to bring it within the notice of all classes. Subscriptions to it come from all classes. The largest single subscription just announced is for one of 5 millions from the Prudential Assurance Company, and the subscriptions range from this down to shillings. It is quite certain it will bring out a large quantity of gold that has been hoarded up.

THE DIARY OF JOHN COLEMAN BINDER

It is being advertised and written up by every newspaper in the country and thousands of employers are taking active steps to induce their workmen and women to put their savings into it, and to benefit themselves and their country at the same time.

I am glad to see during the last few weeks a clearer appreciation by the bulk of the people of the danger and crisis in which this country now is. I note a deeper sense of earnestness and responsibility and also clearer vision as to what we shall have to do to carry us through. With the exception of a few optimists I think everybody is now convinced that we shall be engaged in a long and bloody war, and one that will tax our resources to the utmost, huge as they are.

There are scarcely any festivities or amusements this summer. No Flower Shows or anything of that kind. People have not the heart for anything like this, and what is being done is generally in aid of some charitable fund connected with the War.

A few Agricultural Shows are being held but this is more from a business than a pleasure point of view.

July 4 Sunday   No news to-day. We are looking rather anxiously for to-morrow's papers as we feel that some renewed attack may have been made in France or Flanders.

We have had most beautiful rains this last week and the country now looks again at its best. Hay making has been slow on account of the showers but the crops are not heavy and given fine weather would soon be gathered in.

The Army people still continue to buy large quantities of forage in this district. The Cavalry Horses at the front must be getting quite fat. Practically they have not had much to do since last October.

There is a little upward move in the price of wheat which to-day is worth about 52 to 53/- but stocks in farmers' hands are now very small.

The congestion of the Railways does not improve, and I think the last fortnight has been the worst time since war began. This is said to have been caused by the large movement of troops.

Yesterday was the Speech Day at the Oundle School, but it was a very tame affair compared with what it generally is. The Grocers' Company did not come down and very little was done.

1915 July 5 Monday   A furious battle has been raging in the Argonne during Friday and Saturday. The Germans made a desperate attempt under the direction of the Crown Prince to pierce the French Lines but up to midnight last night had not succeeded at all. The French admit their own losses are heavy but declare that the Germans have suffered much more severely.

[A naval battle between the German and Russian Fleets in the Baltic on Friday morning].

I received a letter to-day from one of my nephews who is at the front in Flanders in the Oxfordshire Light Infantry, but it contains no real news. He says that a most stringent order has been issued that no further letters from soldiers on active service are to be published in the newspapers here and that if this occurs the writers will be held responsible. He says that the utmost secrecy is observed out there and men of one regiment even if they meet another regiment are not allowed to ask them questions as to where they have been or where they are going.

It is rather absurd the lengths to which this business is carried. For instance to-day an air raid is reported to have taken place at Harwich, but curiously enough, this information comes by wireless from Berlin!!!

July 6 Tuesday   Paris advices early this morning say that the German thrust in the Argonne is practically a failure - they only succeeded in capturing about 400 yards of trenches and are still held up. . . . A report published in to-day's papers says the Kaiser has been speaking in Berlin and saying that there would not be another winter campaign as the war would be over in October. Query: I quite believe they would like it to end before winter but it will not be ended when they like, the Allies will have more to say in this matter.

To show how reliable Official reports from Berlin are I will refer again to the air raid which they reported yesterday as having taken place on Saturday at Harwich. The real truth is that 2 aeroplanes came over, flying very high, and on being chased dropped some bombs into the sea. And this they called a great raid.

DAY BY DAY THROUGH THE GREAT WAR

July 7 Wednesday   A communication is published to-day from Sir John French. He says no material change has taken place during the last 14 days. Trench warfare still continues and is likely to do so. Rumours say that the Germans are about to resume the offensive and to try to reach Calais.

Soldiers continue to arrive home from the front on a few days furlough. Last Saturday a man named Pridmore came home here all covered with mud and dust. He had been in trenches 24 hours before and had come straight away home.

A War Balloon passed over here about 6 o'clock last night. It came down at Bulwick. It belonged to the Naval Flying Corps and only had 1 man in it.

Sir Ian Hamilton's official despatch describing the landing at the Dardanelles is published to-day, and it is safe to say that it is one of the most thrilling despatches that was ever written.   At the same time it reveals the difficulties that have been met with, and which I believe could never have been surmounted by any other soldiers in the world except British.

One is sure that troops with such bravery and endurance will carry the thing through to a successful end, but it is a terrible and bloody struggle. Too much time was given to the enemy to entrench and fortify after the first attempt was made. If troops had been at hand ready to land it is quite possible the whole thing might have been carried through quickly. At any rate it is certain that thousands of lives would have been saved.

1915 July 8 Thursday   Bloody battles in all quarters except on our own front. In France, in the Dardanelles, in Galicia (or Poland) in the Tyrol, in all these places furious fighting is reported   to-day and really without any decisive result.

The Germans have again been using liquid fire at St Michel. . . .

Applications for the new War Loan stock closes on Saturday, and I think it will be a decided success. To-day being market day here I have been talking to many country people and it is quite evident they have grasped the advantage of this new loan, and are investing in it. It has brought out much money that has been lying idle and this is all to the good. One often hears this remark made: We cannot all go to fight but most of us can help a little in this loan.

1915 July 9   A curious piece of news comes to-day from Petrograd. They say that the German Cruiser which was sunk in the naval battle in the Baltic was torpedoed by an English submarine. This comes almost as a surprise to us in England as we were not really sure that any of our fleet were in the Baltic, although it was rumoured as long ago as last October that they had been there.

[The Germans said to be rushing troops to the front in France].

A most cheering telegram was issued this afternoon. It says that the entire German Forces in S.W. Africa have surrendered. This will be a nasty jar for the Kaiser, as it is well known that one of his greatest ambitions has been to found a German colony or Empire in S.W. Africa and to oust us from the Cape Colony altogether. The greatest credit is due to General Botha for the splendid way in which he has managed affairs at the Cape. Confronted by Treason, Rebellion and the enemy's forces he has overcome the lot and now to-day he proposes to raise a contingent to come to help us in Europe. Thus the policy of granting South Africa home rule is entirely justified. Fifteen years ago we were fighting the Boers and the Dutch there. To-day they are helping us for all they are worth.

Another of the Kaiser's mistakes. He quite calculated they would rush to join his army. He is living in a fool's paradise.

July 10 Saturday   A remarkable meeting took place at the Guildhall London yesterday. Lord Kitchener went there incidentally to address this meeting but really to speak to the whole Empire. His journey through the crowded city streets was a perfect triumph and was the nation's reply to the recent dastardly attacks made on him by the "Times" and other papers belonging to the Northcliffe gang.

"The Times", by the way, is to-day lauding him to the skies, but I have no doubt he will be able to estimate such praise at its proper value.

THE DIARY OF JOHN COLEMAN BINDER

He asked for men, and still more men, defended the National Register on the ground that it would completely show the number of men between 19 and 40 who were still available for military service, said that his first contention made last September that the war would be a long one was being fulfilled, and that he had no reason to withdraw that opinion. He refused distinctly to answer the question as to how many men had enlisted or what was the number now in the Army, as this was just what the enemy wished to know ("The Times" has been clamouring for these figures for weeks) and gave the cheering information that we are now able to equip and arm all recruits as soon as they join.

Altogether a most remarkable speech worthy of the man, the occasion, and to the Nation to which it was addressed, and one that will meet with the approval of every Englishman. This man Lord Kitchener is a man to whom we owe the deepest debt of gratitude, a man whom we can trust, and a man who is above fear or favour. It is well known that he has always been most averse to promotion by influence (especially the influence of women), which has been the curse of the Army, and that as far as any man could he has broken this influence.

The news of the German surrender in S.W.Africa has been received everywhere with the greatest satisfaction, not that I think the country is of great value as a colony, but the blow at German prestige is considerable.

To-day all the men who enlisted at the beginning of the war in what was known as Kitchener's Army are home again on furlough until Wednesday next. They mostly joined the 6th Northants and their training is now complete and they are going on active service in about a fortnight. They have not been told where, but think it is the Dardanelles.

Eight motor car loads of wounded convalescent soldiers came through here to-day on their way to Deene to spend the day. A sort of impromptu meeting was held in the Market Place and a welcome was given to them. Some had obviously been badly wounded.

July 11 Sunday An order was issued yesterday by the General commanding this district forbidding any publican to serve a soldier except between 1 pm and 9 pm, also forbidding the serving of any wounded or convalescent soldiers with any kind of drink at all.

The National Register Bill is now law and will be shortly put into force by all Local Authorities. Arrangements are being made to carry out the work in this town.

The National War Loan closed last night at twelve o'clock, so far as the Bank of England is concerned, but applications for up to £100 will still be received for some little time through the Post Office. The applications have been enormous. I think the largest private one was from Lord Mickleham who applied for 1,150,000 pounds worth.

I am glad to say that I was able to add my mite to all these big ones and to invest a few hundreds in it. The Chancellor will make a statement about it in the House to-morrow.

July 12 Monday The chief news of to-day is a long official despatch from Sir J. French giving details of the fighting from April 5 to June 15. It throws much light on some of the things we could not understand at the time they occurred and also discloses how critical the situation has been on one or two occasions, more especially the first time the Germans used gas. He casually mentions means have been taken to render this form of gas quite innocuous.

America and Germany are still squabbling about the sinking of their ships and sending what may be described as childish notes to each other. How long this will continue goodness only knows.

July 13 Tuesday The German navy as far as Cruisers and Battleships is now quite cleared off the sea. The last cruiser, the "Konigsberg" was chased into one of the East African rivers about 2 months since. Our warships could not get up after her, so they sank an old collier at the mouth of the river to prevent her escaping and on Sunday two light monitors, heavily armed but drawing little water arrived on the scene and quickly finished her off.

Very heavy fighting has been going on all along the lines since Sunday, it seems as if the enemy were really trying to make good their threat of breaking through, but so far they are powerless although they drove the French out of the cemetery at Souchez again yesterday. This place has changed hands several times. The last time the French captured it, they set fire [to] it to burn all they could as it was in such an awful state.

1915 July14 Wednesday   A rumour is circulated this morning that Turkey has sent delegates to sue for a separate peace with the Allies. Whether this is true or not, it is certain that events are moving in the Balkans. Turkey is getting short of ammunition and Germany is using every device to send it through across Roumania (such as huge barrels labelled 'Munich Beer'). Now Roumania has stopped all this and in consequence is very much threatened by Germany. This Dardanelles business is the key of the situation and great events are likely to come from it.

The amount subscribed for the New War Loan is £575,000,000, the subscriptions through the Post Office remain open yet - it is quite thought it will reach £600,000,000. The best feature about it is, that it is not confined to any one class, but that all have helped. Up to the present nearly a million people have invested in it and it is quite thought this number will be increased to two millions.

Labour troubles are occurring in South Wales amongst the miners, who are threatening to strike over a few miserable pence in their wages, and so by their action to endanger the safety of the whole Empire, for it is from this district that most of the coal for the Fleets is obtained.

Yesterday the Government issued a proclamation forbidding them to strike, and making it a punishable offence to do so. They have power to do this under an Act recently passed. It now remains to be seen what the result will be. Public opinion will support the Government in any measures they may take. It is intolerable that these men or indeed any men should so defy the public interest in this way.

Hard fighting still continues in France, especially in the Uverre where the Germans are hurling their men under the Crown Prince against the French lines. In no case have they met with any success. Yesterday a squadron of 37 French airmen bombed their railway communications and did a lot of damage.

July 15 Thursday. . . .Up to last night 95,000 skilled ammunition workers had been enlisted and in many cases it is now quite impossible to get private work done.

To-day the Canadian Prime Minister (Sir R. Borden) was present at a meeting of the English Cabinet. This is a precedent and eventually may lead to great consequences.

July 16 Friday. A serious situation has arisen in South Wales. Yesterday 200,000 miners stopped work. This is the most dastardly blow we have had during this war. Treachery without any redeeming feature. Some of the leaders of these men ought to be in Germany. They would [be] set up against a wall and shot without any compunction.

The offensive of the Crown Prince has ceased and the result has been practically nothing. All his attacks have been held up and the cost must have been very heavy.

July 17 Saturday. The situation in South Wales has not improved. The Admiralty have prohibited the export of all coal so that our own navy may be kept supplied.

August 15th has been fixed for the day of National Registration.

The Germans are again resuming he offensive all along the Russian lines (which extend from Riga in the North to the Bukovna.

July 18 Sunday. A beautiful July day. We had a lot of rain for the last few days which has hindered hay making but the country looks really charming to-day. I think we shall have harvest about the end of August. Corn values are nominal as there is very little corn in farmers' hands. Stock of all kinds still makes extreme prices.

There is no news of importance to-day except that Roumania still holds to her determination to prohibit the passage of supplies to Turkey. I think this Dardanelles business is likely to prove the key to the whole war, and it is evident that our authorities at home attach great importance to it from the preparations that are being made. . . . There have been rumours of peace in circulation this week, but I do not attach any importance to them. It is said that Germany has been putting out feelers through financial people in this country. Possibly this may be the case. She can never be in a better position to negotiate than she is to-day, and it is quite certain that she has reached the top of her efforts. On the other hand it is equally certain that the efforts of the Allies will increase and they would not listen to peace proposals for one minute.

1915 July 19 Monday The mornings news shows that a critical time is approaching in Russia. The Germans are making two distinct and separate moves to capture Warsaw, and fierce battles are raging all along the lines. What the outcome will be no one can foretell, but we should all be more hopeful if we knew that our ally had an adequate supply of ammunition. Man for man the Russians are superior to the Germans, but are handicapped by this want of guns and shells.

[The Germans are gaining no ground in France or Belgium despite incessant attacks, with heavy losses on both sides].

Another Cunard Liner narrowly escaped being torpedoed about a week ago. She reported this on arriving at New York yesterday, and it was only owing to the skilful seamanship of the Captain that she escaped.

Men of the 5th Battalion of the Northants are home on leave since Saturday, rejoining again to-night. They are under orders for the Dardanelles or Egypt.

Tuesday July 20 All eyes are anxiously turned to Russia. But very little news comes through to-day either from Petrograd or Berlin. A reassuring report was sent by the Times correspondent on Sunday who has just visited the whole 6 Armies of the Russians. Austria reports that the Russians are fighting stubbornly and this is all we know to-day

I think the recent threats of Germany to make a desperate attempt to capture Calais and their reports as to the big movements of troops was all 'bluff' and was designed to cover their movements in Russia.

Telegrams late to-night say that the strike of colliers in South Wales has been settled and that the men will start work again to-morrow. This is good so far as it goes but the stoppage never ought to have occurred, meaning as it has done the loss of a whole week at a time when every ounce of coal that can be got is required.

July 21 Wednesday Russia is slowly retreating still fighting stubborn rear guard actions but nevertheless retreating, and it looks most probable that they will shortly abandon Warsaw. This retreat is most unfortunate as it must of necessity prolong the war, but so long as the Russian Armies are intact or do not suffer an overwhelming disaster it is not decisive. Events along the lines in France and Belgium are quiet the last few days.

Italy after a fortnight's manoeuvring gained a most brilliant victory. She has many and great difficulties to contend with in the mountains where the principal fighting is going on. She has had 2 Cruisers torpedoed by the Austrians in the Adriatic Sea during the last fortnight.

A speech of great importance was made in the House last night by the Prime Minister. He was proposing a fresh Vote of Credit and asked the House to allow the Government to have a free hand in one direction. He said that expenditure was increasing and would probably increase still more with the adherence to our cause of States which did not [take] part in the War in its earlier [months]. He could not say more than this and he did not think the House would ask him to do so. He evidently meant that it is quite probable that Roumania, Bulgaria and Greece will come in on our side and it also hinted in some quarters that Holland may eventually be obliged to fight.

A curious case as to Prize Vessels is now going on in the Courts. The Americans have been sending enormous quantities of Lard to neutral countries from whence it reaches Germany. The Authorities here contend this is contraband as the Germans have discovered a way of making glycerine from lard, and thus it is in reality 'a munition of war'. The verdict is not yet known, but on the decision will rest the fate of over thirty cargoes of this lard.

1915 July 22 Thursday The news from Russia this morning is very vague, in fact all that comes through is from Berlin and this does not look very hopeful.

DAY BY DAY THROUGH THE GREAT WAR

July 23 Friday The news from Russia received late last night is very disquieting. It is almost certain that Warsaw will be abandoned, if it has not already been done. The Russians are fighting bravely but owing to lack of ammunition are not able to hold the Austro- German armies back. The hard fighting in Italy still continues and the Italians are doing well. Relations between Italy and Turkey are getting very strained, and it seems probable they will be at war before long. Nominally Italy is only at war with Austria, but really she is helping against all our enemies.

July 24 Saturday   The news from Russia this morning is distinctly better and more re-assuring. Warsaw has not fallen and the Germans are being held up although they have gained some local successes. The position is still one of much gravity as it is apparent to us all that it is on this line that for the present the enemy is making the great effort of this year. Should he fail or even be held up it is certain that it will be the beginning of the end.

We on our part here are doing much. Immense movements of troops have and are taking place during this week. They are going both to France and Egypt. The latter place being the place for operations at the Dardanelles.

I am more convinced day by day that the Dardanelles will vitally affect this war. The struggle there has developed into a bloody campaign; it may be long and costly but I do not think the result is doubtful, and when it comes it must exercise a profound influence on the whole field of operations, exclusive of the political importance that will also be exercised by its fall.

The submarine warfare has been at a very low ebb this week. We are not told what measures have been taken to cope with the enemy's craft, but they must be very effective for not a single ship has been lost.

Air raids and Zeppelin expeditions have also quite ceased, and we have heard nothing about them lately, but police and military precautions are as strict as ever, and vigorous steps are being taken with Aliens. Every day reports appear in the papers of these being summoned and fined for some breach of the regulations, such as failing to report themselves, residing in a forbidden area etc.

As for the German Fleet we hear nothing at all about it. We know that it is locked up in the Kiel Canal, and occasionally exercises in the Bight of Heligoland, but otherwise it might as well not exist.

With regard to our own Fleet, the sense of security is such that I am afraid we have almost forgotten its existence, but when we only think a moment we recognise that it is really the main factor in this war. It is only due to its ceaseless vigilance that either we or our Allies are in our present position. Our command of the sea is almost absolute. Not a single troopship has been sunk, and we and our Allies have been able to carry millions of men across the seas. Our food supplies are regular, and indeed there is very little in this direction to indicate that we are at war at all. All this is due to the Grand Fleet which is still 'somewhere in the North Sea', usually, I believe, it is cruising between the Outer Hebrides and Norway.

1915 July 25 Sunday.   No news from Russia to-day, and events all along our lines are quiet so far as we know. Private letters received here from the Northants Yeomanry men say that there [is] nothing much doing, but that the state of the country where they are (near Ypres and Ypres itself) is dreadful. The stench from half buried bodies is also very bad, but the health of the Army is excellent.

We have had very broken weather lately. Much rain and thunder. The hay crop is about 2/3rds secured. I saw a field of winter Oats cut last Wednesday, but harvest will not be general for another month.

July 26 Monday. Fairly good news comes from Russia this morning ......Warsaw is still in their hands and we all hope they will be able to retain it. . . . . .

The chief interest to-day lies in the latest reply of America to Germany, which was handed in at Berlin on Saturday. It is not very long, but is clear and decisive. It puts aside all subterfuges and tells Germany that submarine warfare, so far as Americans or American ships are concerned, must cease. If it does not there will be trouble. In America it is regarded by all sections of the Press as an Ultimatum. Public opinion in Germany according to advices from Amsterdam (from whence we get most of our German news) is furious. America is between the Devil and the deep sea. She is being hammered by Germany, and yet she

THE DIARY OF JOHN COLEMAN BINDER

has so many German Americans in her own borders that she can only go very cautiously. At the same time she is making distinct preparations both as regards her Army and Navy.

The Cape people having smashed the Germans in South Africa are now coming over to help us. A contingent has already been formed and will shortly sail for either France or the Dardanelles.

July 27 Tuesday. Advices to-day say that the Germans are within 12 miles of Warsaw, but that these 12 miles are most difficult country. . . . .

The Boys of Oundle School have broken up to-day but about 65 are remaining behind to continue the manufacture of Ammunition. They will remain 14 days, and then be replaced by another contingent. Boys from other Public Schools will also come to work here during the holidays. At present these boys are engaged in making parts of Bombs or Mines and are controlled by Messrs Brotherhood of Peterboro who are responsible in this area for all Government Munitions Work.

July 28 Wednesday. The Great Battles in Poland still go on, and although the Germans are doing their utmost, the results are still very uncertain. This battle or series of battles is certainly the greatest we have had since this war commenced or I think during any war and the result be it victory or defeat must greatly influence the future of this terrible struggle in which we are all now engaged. . . . .

Figures are published to-night disclosing that up to the present we (the British) have lost 60,000 killed and 280,000 wounded and missing. The officers killed number 4,000.

Thursday July 29. Very important speeches were made in the House last night by the Premier and the Minister of Munitions. The former said that they (the Government) were quite satisfied with the progress of Operations in the Dardanelles and also paid a well deserved tribute to the Russians from whom I am glad to say re-assuring reports are to hand this morning.

The Minister of Munitions made a fairly satisfactory report. Many thousands of men who had enlisted are being released in order that they may go back to their trades of engineering etc. but the most significant announcement was that the Government have arranged to build and equip 10 new Arsenals (in addition to 16 already under their control) for the supply of Guns and ammunition. This perhaps may convey some idea of the magnitude of the task this nation is now engaged upon. He did not say so, but it is quite certain that we hope to be in a position to supply Russia and our other Allies with these things. On all hands preparations are being made for a prolonged war and evidently it is going to [be] a fight to the bitter end.

The Boys on ammunition works are working in two shifts of 5 and 6 hours each day.

To-day I saw Colonel Ferguson of the 1st Life Guards who has been twice wounded in the leg. He is now home on leave. He looks much older and still walks lame. It is doubtful if he will return to the front.

1915 July 30 Friday It is evident that Warsaw has been evacuated by the Russians. This is not officially stated so but reading to-day's report I am driven to the conclusion that this is a fact. There is still continual news of great and bloody fighting going on there, but probably it is only rear-guard actions to cover the withdrawal of the main army.

July 31 Saturday The fall of Warsaw is confirmed to-day. When it actually occurred is not clear but telegrams were received in London at 1am this morning which had been despatched from Warsaw last Sunday and had been held up no doubt by the Russian Censor.

It would be folly not to recognise that this is a severe blow and disappointment to us and all the Allies, not that it is decisive but it is quite clear that it must tend to prolong the war. We had hoped Russia would have been able to stem the attack and so to hold up the enemy. It is well known that the cause of her defeat has been lack of guns and ammunition, at the same time we are all grateful to her for the splendid way in which she has fought and the skilful way her armies have been handled. Her armies are intact and she only retires deeper into her own huge territory. It is confidently asserted that she never intended to defend Warsaw but only did so in deference to French wishes. . . . . .

August 1 Sunday Twelve months to-day the first shots were fired on the Russo-German frontier and 12

85

months to-night Germany threw 100,000 men into Luxembourg to begin the invasion of France.

How far we have travelled since then. It seems almost like a new world that we are living in to-day and although things have not changed much outwardly one is sensible of a real and deep change and none the less real because it is not seen so much in outward things.

To-day is one of the National Bank Holidays and as such is usually given up to amusements of all kinds (that is on the Monday) but what do we see to-day. It is true there will be a certain relaxation from work, but so far as I know there will not be a single fête or public entertainment of any kind. The public feeling is so pronounced against every thing of this kind during this conflict. It is quite unthinkable that we here in England should be merry-making while so many of our men are fighting for us on the sea and in the trenches. In looking over England I see to-day a nation that has passed through (is now passing) deep and terrible times. We know that we are engaged in a struggle for our very existence as an Empire, and we mean with God's help to fight our way to a victorious issue. Indeed there can be no other alternative. I would rather see the whole of the people in this country dead than they should be under the heel of the German Emperor, and I firmly believe this is the spirit and feeling of 95% of my fellow countrymen and women. Indeed the women are more bitter against the Germans than the men are.

In entering on the second year of the war I regret to say that I cannot see the faintest hope of peace. The horizon is as black as ever. We have learned to place a proper value upon what is told to us about Germany being exhausted and all that kind of thing. We know that she is fighting for her life, and that she will fight to the end, and that we shall only win by sheer doggedness and gut. We see Germany to-day in a formidable position. During the last 9 months she has not relaxed her hold on Belgium or France and has gained considerable advance in Poland. But at the same time we are quite aware that (in spite of her protestations) she is being bled terribly both as regards her finances and her men. She has passed the limit of her strength and we have not at present reached our limit. Slowly but surely the whole nation is being organized for war, and at war we shall be until we reach some decisive event.

We have made mistakes without doubt. Our lack of ammunition to wit, and other similar things. Our continual labour disputes and things of this kind, all of which are so liable to be misrepresented abroad and so to encourage the Germans, but I contend the Germans have made far greater mistakes than ourselves. They calculated there would be civil war in Ireland. False. They calculated (and encouraged) S. Africa to rebel. This came true to a limited extent but the result was that Germany has been ousted from that continent. They calculated that our Colonies would fall away. On the contrary they have rallied to us and to-day the Empire is more firmly knit together than ever it was. Thousands and tens of thousands of men from our remotest borders are fighting for England and her empire.

In addition to all this they have lost their Ally Italy, who has not remained a Neutral but is actually fighting against them and they have gained Turkey!!! The most rotten corrupt and effete nation under the sun. These colossal mistakes of theirs have mostly been made because they are such bad judges of human nature. They want to dragoon, drill and force all men into a particular mould and that is trying to do the impossible.

Taking a wide survey to-day I do not see any cause for pessimism, but only for a steady determination to look all facts in the face, and to win our way through with God's help.

We can truly say we have fought with clean hands and have done nothing in warfare of which we are ashamed. Can Germany say this? Only this morning a message was received at 1 o'clock from Sir J. French saying that the enemy had attacked with "Flame Projectors". These things actually roast those with whom they come in contact and then their hellish device of poisonous gas. There are men actually now at Barnwell Castle who are suffering terrible agonies from this gas and even if they live they are likely to suffer all their lives.

Spies are continually being caught in this country. Two were shot in the Tower of London on Friday morning and others are awaiting trial.

1915 Monday August 2 The Russians are still in possession of Warsaw although they may abandon it any day. . . . There has been some talk of burning Warsaw to prevent it falling into German hands but I am glad to say the Russian Commander -in - Chief has vetoed this. It is said that the Germans will be in a similar plight to that of Napoleon in 1812. I do not think the analogy holds good. In 1812 there were no railways and Napoleon's base was much more remote than the German base to-day. Time can only decide these things. It is conjectured the Kaiser is hoping to make a triumphal entry into Warsaw but he has not been able to do so at present.

Aug 3 Tuesday . . . A German warship (a destroyer) was sunk off the German coast on Friday by one of our submarines.

Aug 4 Wednesday Twelve months to-day England formally declared war on Germany. Services of Intercession are being held throughout the Empire and in most places meetings are being held to express the resolve of the nation to fight to a finish and also to re-affirm the justice of our cause. . . .

The casualty lists continue day by day. I should [think] our own average about 1200 men and 30 to 40 officers. About 60 per cent of officers and men return to duty eventually. This is a very high percentage. It is not so good in other countries. . . .

Aug 5 Thursday . . . A piece of news of some importance to-day is that Italy is about to join in the attack on the Dardanelles. Things move very slowly there, and the difficulties are very great. The Turks are good fighters behind earthworks and I am afraid it will be a long and costly business there. Great numbers of troops are continually being sent out to Egypt which is the base of operations.

The first wheat in this neighbourhood was cut to-day at Tansor. The weather is very showery. A good deal of hay is still out, some of it not cut.

1915 Aug 6 Friday The Russians have evacuated Warsaw. Their retreat was quite orderly and they destroyed the bridge across the Vistula before leaving, in fact they removed everything that was of much value. Great numbers of the people also left and it was an almost empty shell that the Germans found. . . .

Aug 7 Saturday . . . This effort of Warsaw is regarded by many critics as Germany's supreme effort and that she has now reached the zenith of her offensive. Signs are not wanting that she would now like to negotiate for peace. A letter has been issued by the Pope calling for Peace, and this is believed to have been inspired by German influence. It is said on good authority they dread another winter campaign and would be glad to fix up a peace on the ' status quo ante bellum' but to us this is clearly impossible. It would mean the triumph of German militarism and as such would make life not worth living either in this country or on the Continent.

I can state it as an absolute reliable fact that the people in this country who want peace to-day do not number five per cent of the population. I believe we all should like peace but we see that under present conditions it is clearly impossible. There are faint signs from Germany that the better informed of her people [know] that their position is untenable, and if they had a free press these opinions would be more openly expressed. Much of the tenacity of Germany is due to the fact that their newspapers, which are all controlled by their Government, have all along preached to them that we and our Allies have long planned this war and that they are fighting to save themselves from destruction. This is absolutely untrue. Evidence accumulates from day to day showing that this bloody war has long been planned and desired by Germany and that the time was carefully chosen by her leaders to commence. There is a story in circulation which says that when the Kaiser had signed the declaration of war he threw down his pen and said to the men standing round him "Gentlemen, you will live to rue this day." I quite believe this prophecy will come true.

August 8 Sunday A dull wet day. Some anxiety is being caused for the harvest in this county by the continual wet we have had the last six weeks. The hay harvest is not yet finished, and a considerable quantity has been got in very bad condition. We have one consolation in this bad weather. Canada has a magnificent harvest and if well got will be quite able to supply all our wants during the next twelve months. The enemy try in vain to prevent these supplies from reaching our shores. It is true they sink some odd ships but they are a few when compared with the vast numbers which reach our ports from day to day. The tonnage entering our ports was greater during the last six months than it was during the preceding six months. So much for the German boastings. They are told by their papers that we in England are in dread of [losing]our naval supremacy. We simply laugh at this, so long as we know that our grim sentinels are lying like watch dogs in the North Sea, we know and feel that we are safe. I wonder what the German people think of their fleet . . . .The latest thing Germany has done is this week to take a census of all her cotton goods everywhere in every house shop and factory. Cotton is much used in making explosives and supplies are only dribbling into Germany now, so that to some extent they are getting a bit anxious. Every cotton garment has to be registered [and] every bit of cotton.

August 9 Monday It is again asserted to-day that the Kaiser approached the Czar with offers of peace last week, but these were contemptuously rejected. Russia replied that she had no desire for peace and moreover she was bound to her Allies, and that her treaties were not "Scraps of Paper".

1915 August 10 Tuesday . . . A beginning was made yesterday in taking the National Register. 25,000,000 forms are being distributed this week and will be collected on the first three days of next week, the actual day (or night) of registration being Sunday August 15th. It is being done almost entirely by volunteer workers.

This town has been divided into eight districts and the work of it has been undertaken by eight members of the Urban Council. I am glad to say I have taken my share in this work, the other Enumerators being Messrs J Rippiner, W B Wood, J Hayes, J M Siddons, A Townsend, R W Ford[?] and J W North. I will make further reference to this Register in a few days.

A Zeppelin Raid took place early this morning on the East Coast. Thirteen people were killed, and 24 injured. To-night's report does not say where it was or how many airships were engaged in it. One of them at any rate was brought down and destroyed.

P.S. This raid was at Hull, Lowestoft etc. This has been a day of terrific thunderstorms in many parts of the country. We escaped them here.

Aug 11 Wednesday There is good news from the Dardanelles this morning. Another landing has been made higher up the country and it is hoped to turn the flank of the Turkish forces. It also appears as if an agreement was in sight between the Balkan States, so that could adjust all their differences and come in on our side. These various Powers (Greece, Bulgaria, Roumania, Servia) are extremely jealous of each other, and are very difficult to manage. . .

Aug 12 Thursday [*Fighting continuing in the Dardanelles   The Germans are pressing on towards Petrograd*].

Aug 13 Friday . . . Bulgaria has thrown her cards on the table and openly declared what she requires as the price of her alliance with the Allies. Her demand is that Servia shall give her back Servian Macedonia which was torn from her at the end of the 1910 war. It remains to be seen whether these claims can be met. If they can and the whole of the Balkans divided up on a racial basis it may bring all these Balkan States in on our side. This would mean a speedy end to the Dardanelles business also a set off to the Warsaw business and would materially shorten the war.

The Admiralty announce to-night that another air raid took place last night between 8.30 and 11.45. Six people were killed and 24 injured. The localities of these air raids are not now published in the papers, we only hear of where they took place from private sources.

Aug 14 Saturday [*The German offensive in Russia seems to have spent itself and there are rumours that she will transfer forces to the western front, but JC Binder doubts this.*] The addition of a few hundred thousand could not increase her striking power very much. Moreover she is well aware that our army in France has been re-inforced immensely during the last few weeks. How large it is, is known only to a few people here, but great numbers of troops have been sent across.

Telegrams to-night say that German [and] Austrian troops are gathering on the Roumanian frontier and it looks as if a decision cannot long be delayed in that quarter, Germany is much amazed because Roumania forbids the transport of munitions to Turkey and as she will not yield to cajolery is now openly threatening her with force.

THE DIARY OF JOHN COLEMAN BINDER

I still look upon the Dardanelles operations as of immense importance in this war and believe that ultimately it will prove the beginning of the end. There can be no drawing back from it now. Our credit in East and West alike is staked on it.

Peace rumours have been in constant circulation this week, all coming from Germany. It is certain that she would like peace now that she has reached her high water mark, but there is a decisive 'NO' from all the Allies. Russia and France have suffered much and have done magnificently, and although they are still suffering they will not listen to any peace proposals. In this country the answer is equally, if not more emphatic.

1915 Aug 15 Sunday To-day is the day when all National Register Forms have to be filled up, and we shall begin to collect them tomorrow, and if possible complete the work by Wednesday.

I will keep two of the Forms and place them with other papers as a memento of this work.

What is the ultimate intention of the Government with regard to this Register has not been openly declared at present.

All the names of men between the ages of 18 and 40 will be copied by the Local Authorities on to a form coloured pink, and this pink form will be at the disposal of the recruiting Officer for the district to which it relates. I presume that in the first place all unmarried men of this age   18-40 will be approached with a view to getting them to enlist. If this is not successful possibly Conscription may be enforced, or attempted to be enforced, but [it] is certain it will meet with very great opposition among the Labour people. This Register will also settle the question about which there is much controversy as to how many men there are still available, and what proportion of them are married and unmarried. I find in delivering my papers that there is much feeling that so many married men should have enlisted (often leaving 4 and 5 children) whilst there are numbers of young unmarried men who could well have gone. The cost of keeping the wives and children of these men is a very heavy drain upon the resources of the county and as pensions will be allowed to their wives (if the men are killed) and also allowances to each child until they reach the age of 15 it will [be] seen this is a most serious question.

The showery thundery weather still continues, and we are getting very anxious about the harvest. Wheat cutting is well commenced.

August 18 Wednesday I am sorry that I have been unable to write up this diary the last two days as all my spare time has been taken up in collecting the forms of the National Register. I have now finished and shall hand them over to the Clerk of the District Council who will issue a ticket to every person upon the register. These tickets will have to [be] retained until the person removes permanently to another town when he or she will have [to] get a fresh certificate and be registered in that town. I am of opinion that this may last for the period of the war but do not think it will continue after.

The Russians are still retreating and things do not look at all hopeful.

An air raid took place on Leyton early this morning --- persons were killed and --- injured.

Disastrous news came to hand yesterday. A transport 'The Royal George' on the way to the Dardanelles with 1400 troops and 220 sailors on board was torpedoed in the Aegean Sea. .   600 were saved and the remainder lost. This is the first transport we have lost and considering the hundreds of thousands of men who have been moved across the seas in all directions it speaks volumes for the efficiency of the navy.

August 19 Thursday Bad news from Russia this morning . . . There is no concealing the fact that the war in this quarter is going badly for the Allies, but at present it is impossible to send aid to the Russians, that is so long as the Dardanelles are closed. Turkey is being hardly pressed and rumours say that Germany will send her assistance at any cost through the Balkan States. If this is attempted Bulgaria, Roumania and Greece will certainly resist. . . .

The White Star Liner 'Arabic' was torpedoed off Queenstown at 9.30 this morning without any warning. 375 passengers were saved. 43 of the crew and 6 passengers were drowned. She only floated 11 minutes after being struck, so that perfect order prevailed or so many would not have been saved. We received this news at 5.30 to-night. The despatch does not say if there were any Americans on board; if there were a most critical situation must now arise between Germany and America as they have been plainly warned that should further loss of American citizens ensue war would follow.

1915 August 20 Friday There has been very heavy fighting at the Dardanelles the last two days. A fresh landing was made and the enemy made great efforts to prevent it, but without success. This was at Suvla Bay.

All the Australian and New Zealand troops are at the Dardanelles, also a big force of our men and I take it the South Africans will go there also.

There does not seem to have been any Americans amongst the passengers drownded in the "Arabic". Only 5 passengers were lost.

August 21 Saturday . . . There were two American passengers amongst those lost in the "Arabic" after all. This has again brought American opinion to a high state of excitement but I am doubtful as to whether they will take any action. They have <u>said</u> so many times what they would do but so far have <u>done</u> nothing. Personally I think that Germans and German interests are so strong in the United States that the Government there will go to any length rather than declare war as it is quite possible that a rising of these people might be attempted.

One new sample of wheat at Northampton to-day for which 5/- was asked.

August 22 [Sunday] A telegram this morning announces that the Allies have declared cotton Contraband of War. This has been a most debated question in this country and America for the last six or eight months. Huge quantities of cotton are required for explosives and it is held that to deprive Germany of this will materially tend to shorten the war. We shall see.

Looking back on the past week one can only say that it has not been a very bright one for us. Our brave Allies the Russians have suffered much and are still suffering and at present we seem powerless to help them.

Again I am compelled to re-iterate that I believe the Dardanelles to be the supreme interest in this war. Once we force the passage I am convinced that we should see a great change. We are constantly assured that we shall force this passage and that before long. At any rate great efforts are being made and great losses incurred as the casualty lists of each day show. There seems to be some idea a broad that next month will show great changes and that a supreme effort will be made to conclude the war before winter. I hope this may be so but I am very doubtful. The bulk of our Armies are now in France and are working hard there, as letters from the front show, and we can only leave it to those in supreme command to decide as [to] when an effort shall be made to move forward. Ammunition and guns of all kinds are now being manufactured in enormous quantities in this country and also on our behalf in America. I believe that this will go on until it is known that practically the supply is unlimited, and then, and not until then, will any attempt be made to end the deadlock on the Western front.

We have had a most welcome change in the weather this week. Hay time is finished and harvest is in full swing. Wheat I believe will be the best crop but I am afraid the condition will not be good. Wheat prospects are good all the world over, so that if our Navy still holds control of the Seas, we may reasonably expect cheaper bread next winter. Labour is not exceptionally scarce, and I think will prove sufficient for all requirements. Mr Brassey has at work on the Apethorpe Estate a traction engine (17 HP) drawing two self binding reaping machines. These cut 26 acres in one morning last week. This cannot be done in many instances as the crops are badly laid.

The naval war is developing in the Baltic. A sharp naval action was fought off Riga on Friday, in which the Germans claim to have had the advantage. Petrograd has not reported it up to last night. One of our submarines was lost on its way to the Baltic last Friday.

1915 August 23 Monday . . . . The submarine which I mentioned yesterday as being lost ran ashore on a Dutch island of Saltholm. This was of course neutral territory and as such the Dutch gave them 24 hours to clear off if possible. However a German torpedo boat came up and launched a torpedo against her, she sank immediately and whilst our helpless men were struggling in the water they opened fire on them and only desisted when the Dutch interposed their boats to shield them. . . . .Italy has formally declared war on Turkey yesterday.

August 24 Tuesday Germany is absolutely silent to-day as to the naval action in Riga Bay. Some doubts exist as to what the Battleship was that has gone down. Whatever it was the work was accomplished by the British Submarine.

August 25 Wednesday . . . .The conscription controversy has again broken out in this country. A group of Newspapers headed by the Times is endeavouring to rush the country to adopt this system, but I do not think they will succeed. The argument of all sane men is this "When the Government say that conscription is needed, then we will consider it, but at present they have not said so and we decline to be ruled by newspapers especially by the group controlled by one man".

August 26 Thursday Details of the recent fierce battles are published this morning. Some progress has been made, but the losses are very heavy. In to-day's list alone there are the names of 40 New Zealand officers who have been killed and this does not include Australian or British, so it may be judged how desperate the fighting is and has been. . . .

We have had a really fine warm week and harvest work is being rapidly pushed on. Wheat shows a downward tendency and is to-day quoted about 45 or 46/- on rail. Barley is scarce and dear and unless we get through the Dardanelles I quite expect it will continue so.

August 27 A most encouraging message is published this morning from the Czar. He says that in spite of the Russian retreat their power is unshaken, that their will is unconquered and that they will fight on to the end. There has also been a remarkable demonstration in Paris yesterday. Some criticism has been going on by opponents of the Government and a strenuous debate was expected in the Chamber but after a speech by the Premier confidence was voted in the Administration by 539 to 1. Such things as these show that the solidarity and confidence of the Allies is unshaken. Germany just now is using all her influence (backed by much expenditure of money) to detach the Allies from each other and to conclude a separate peace with one or more of them, but so far her efforts have met with no success.

Yesterday one of our airmen attacked a German submarine off Ostend and sank it. This was a really fine feat. The Admiralty have taken the opportunity to say that many of these submarines have been sunk but they do not think it wise to [say] when or where.

August 28 Saturday It is rumoured to-day that Germany has promised America (as a way out of their dispute) that no more vessels shall be sunk without warning. This is possibly true, but it looks as if they know that as a means of effective blockade this submarine business is a farce. It certainly comes most opportunely on the sinking of some of them. (It is said the one that sunk the "Arabic" never got back to Germany again.) I quite expect America will be satisfied with this and that it will be the last we shall hear of the incident.

[Russians still slowly retreating.]

August 29 Sunday News came to hand that the 1/4th Northamptons had been seriously engaged at Gallipoli during the recent fighting and that Major Henson of Wellingborough had been killed. There are a number of Oundle lads in this battalion.

This fighting in the Dardanelles is as severe and desperate as any during this war. Our losses there continue to be very heavy.

I wish and hope that we may be able to induce the Balkan States and Greece to adjust their differences and make common cause with us. This would render our task easier and I am almost certain would be the beginning of the end of the war. The feeling is growing every day that we are committed to another winter campaign with all its horrors and misery, but again I can only write there is not the least sign of weakness on our part.

DAY BY DAY THROUGH THE GREAT WAR

We are not told officially how many troops we have at the front, but it must be patent to us all that we have huge numbers there, as the garrisons in all these inland towns are much thinner than they have been for some time. The 7th Northants are leaving for the front this week. The 8th are nearly full up.

1915 August 30 Monday Trouble is again threatened in the South Wales Collieries. The [causes] of the dispute are very difficult for an outsider to judge, but it is criminal folly to raise wage disputes in the face of the enemy.

A huge casualty list to-day 3,440 men and 154 officers, most of these in the Dardanelles. This alone will show how terrible the fighting has been there.

August 31 Tuesday . . . Along the French lines there have been some fierce attacks the last two days. On our own front events are very quiet and Sir John French says that he has nothing to report.

September 1 Wednesday Russia is hitting back at her enemy the last few days and on Monday captured 2,000 prisoners and 25 machine guns besides other war material.

Wheat continues to fall and is now worth about 42/-. Bread to-day is reduced to 7d per 4lb loaf.

September 2 Thursday Germany announces to-day a decided change in her mode of submarine warfare. She has promised America that no more vessels shall be sunk without warning. This is diplomatic victory for America, at the same time Germany is making a virtue of necessity. . . . About a fortnight since our people and the French raided Zeebrugge on the Belgian coast which the Germans use as a base for their submarines and played havoc with them. It is also currently surmised that they are trapped with steel nets. I do not vouch for the accuracy of this. The Admiralty keep their affairs as secret as possible and sailors now on leave here absolutely decline to tell even their own people, where they have been or what they have been doing.

September 4 Saturday . . . From reports received from Germany it seems as if doubts are arising there as to the value of this Russian campaign and it is admitted that it has failed in its main object. It does not seem that it can be made a success in what now remains of the summer. In another month the Autumn rains will commence, to be very quickly followed up by the winter. There are some who predict a great disaster for the Germans if they attempt to remain in Russia during the winter. The strain upon their resources will be very very great, and it is well known that they dread another winter campaign, but I do not think that an overwhelming disaster similar to Napoleon's in 1812 will overtake them.

Fuller details of the latest fighting in the Dardanelles up to August 26 are now to hand. . .   At one time during the attacks on August 6 and 7th the men actually gained the summit and were able to look down on the 'Narrows' but they were unable to hold the ground they had won, and practically the position is the same as it was three weeks ago. The country is a series of natural fortresses and lends itself most readily to defensive tactics and the Turks are adepts at this kind of war.

September 5 Sunday A glorious autumn day after a sharp frost this morning. It does not look possible that looking across the peaceful landscape that within 150 miles from us this terrible war is being carried on, and yet there is a sense of absolute security which I am afraid in a good many cases arises from indifference and want of knowledge, but to any who thinks it is patent that this arises from our Fleet and sea power. . . . Peace talk is again being engineered by Germany, both in America and in this country. That she would like peace is patent to everybody. She has reached her greatest strength and is now going to experience the difficulty of retaining what she has captured. The Prime Minister Mr Asquith summarily disposed of all these rumours here by stating one day this week that no basis of peace could be found so long as one German remained on Belgian, French or Russian soil. This is plain speaking but not plainer than the situation demands, and it is certain that this feeling is endorsed by 90% of the people of this Empire.

1915 September 6 Monday Comment has come quick and sharp on my note of yesterday re the German promise not to torpedo ships without warning. News arrived late last night that the Allan Liner Hesperion carrying 300 passengers and 215 crew outward bound to the States was torpedoed off the south of Ireland during Saturday night, and this without any warning. She did not sink at once, so fortunately no lives were lost but no thanks are due to the enemy for this. (A telegram this morning says that she has gone down) . . . There were no American passengers on board.

THE DIARY OF JOHN COLEMAN BINDER

Advices from Russia say that their retreating Armies have practically made a waste of the country. They have burned many towns and villages and the Germans only find desolation. This does not look very promising for the winter. . . . .

September 7 Tuesday Very little news to-day from any source. America as usual protesting etc etc about the [Hibernian] but that is all.

Some sensation has been occasioned yesterday and to-day by the exposure of a plot organised by the Austrian and German Ambassadors in America to stir up labour troubles and so prevent the manufacture of munitions. A pro-German war correspondent was arrested at Plymouth. His papers were seized and revealed full details of this plot. He was allowed to go on, but full accounts were cabled to America and have tended to strain the relations still more.

September 8 Wednesday News from Russia says that the Grand Duke has retired from the supreme command of the Armies and that the Czar has assumed control.. . . .

News at midday say that three Zeppelins raided the Eastern Counties last night. 56 persons were killed and injured. Reports late to-night say that Zeppelins have again been sighted off the East Coast, and warnings have been issued.

September 9 Thursday The zeppelins rumoured last night evidently made their way inland as a communication issued by the Press Bureau at 2 am says that another raid took place and it is now generally known it was on London. It is said that a good deal of damage has been done.

[Telegrams give news of a substantial Russian victory].

To-night I saw Mr and Mrs Ashworth of Oundle School who had just returned from London. They had been there for a short holiday but had been so terrified by the bombs from the Zeppelins that they came home at once. The airships raided London both last night and the night before. Their objective was evidently Woolwich Arsenal close to which Mr and Mrs A. were staying. No bombs were dropped on the Arsenal although one was only about 40 yards away. Bomb dropping and firing from our own guns was going on for some two hours and although searchlights were much used no Zeppelins could be seen. These ships ride at such a great height that it is almost impossible to see them at night and they can only be located by the noise of their engines. Much damage was done in other parts of London but no panic was caused. These airships came over Wisbech, March etc on their way to London, but at present I have not heard if any damage has been done at these places.

The Bank of England had a narrow escape as also did St Paul's Cathedral. Broad Street Station was much damaged and is closed to-day. Three Zeppelins were concerned in this raid.

1915 September 10 Friday Twenty people were killed, 19 seriously wounded and 72 slightly wounded in the raid. One bomb dropped close to a tram car killing 8 people and wounding several more. Another spy was shot in London this morning.

September 11 Saturday *[More news of Russian successes against the Germans, with munitions probably being supplied by Japan].*

Some terrible fighting has occurred on the French Front the last week. This was brought about by the Germans attacking and although they used much gas and liquid fire they only gained a temporary success and were speedily ejected from the trenches they had won.

September 12 Sunday A very hot September day. Harvest is about ⅔ completed in this district and if the fine weather continues will be quite safe by the end of the week. We have had 10 days hot dry weather and the corn has been stacked in excellent condition. Prices continue about the same: 44/- to 45/- for wheat, 42/- to 43/- barley. Oats 27/- to 28/-.

Meat of all kinds is still very dear, especially Pork, the market price of which is now about 10/6 to 10/9 per 14lb. I sold yesterday 11 fat pigs for £90.

Parliament meets again this week and it is evident that there are two questions which will command immediate attention. One is finance and the other the raising of men.

What will be done in the way of taxation can only be conjectured, but yesterday the Authorities issued a notice forbidding anyone to withdraw extra quantities of Tea, Spirits, Wines or Tobacco from the Customs warehouses. This I think points to extra taxation on these articles. I think income tax will be increased and the present limit of £160 at which taxation now commences much reduced. It is possible that workmen's wages may be taxed, that is by the employer deducting a percentage and handing it over to the State. Many men, (especially in munitions factories) are now receiving very high wages and could well afford this. There are also proposals that the State should assume control of the Railways and coal mines and (after compensating the owners) work them for the benefit of the State.

I think it is hopeless to expect anything much from Germany even when she is beaten. It is patent to all the world that she is practically bankrupt and in many ways is adopting the methods a bankrupt man does by plunging from bad to worse.

The other question of conscription or compulsory service will need most careful treatment or it will divide this empire into two hostile camps. The pink registration forms containing the names of men between 18 and 40 have now been placed at the disposal of the army authorities for each district.

There are a great many Belgians still in this county (some of them still in Oundle) although all men of military age have been called to the colours in their own country.

The Americans have to-day demanded that the Austrian Ambassador about whom I wrote a few days since shall be cleared out and it is probable they will take the same course with the German Ambassador. I think in spite of all America's efforts things are slowly drifting to a rupture. America does not want this we all know. For one thing she is making too much out of this war to want to fight.

September 13 Monday ... A Zeppelin raid took place on Saturday at Grimsby but no damage was done nor were any lives lost. It is claimed that one of the three Zeppelins which were over here on Wednesday just managed to reach her moorings and then collapsed. She had been damaged in the fight   Count Zeppelin [was] the inventor of these airships.

1915 September 14 Tuesday   Parliament met to-day and the Prime Minister said this afternoon   in the House that our casualties in killed wounded and missing amounted to 381,000. This is terrible but comparing it with the enemies' loss it is very small. Their losses are estimated between 4 and 5 Millions

The Prime Minister also rebuked those M.Ps who are also officers in the Army coming back to the House and claiming to speak on behalf of the Army. He told them they were as representatives of the people and not of the Army. This rebuke I think is well deserved. We have had too much of this kind of thing lately. We cannot afford to be ruled by the Army people.

September 15 Wednesday ... Lord Kitchener reviewed the war in a speech in the House to-night and said amongst other things that 'The Germans had almost shot their last bolt in Russia'. Referring to recruiting he said the results had been marvellous. We had close on 3 millions of men under arms. Recruiting had been slow the last few weeks but steps had been taken to remedy this. He spoke neither for nor against conscription. Mr Asquith in the Commons said much the same but added that Conscription had been under Cabinet consideration and their <u>conclusions</u> would soon be laid before the <u>House</u>, <u>Conclusions</u>, <u>not proposals</u>.

September 16 Thursday   A sensational story is current to-day re the recent Russian reverses. It is said that the great Russian Arsenal (practically they have only one) was blown up and destroyed some two months since as the result of secret German plottings, and this just at the moment the Germans were beginning to make their great drive. The Russians consequently were obliged to fall back as practically they had no munitions. Her allies England and Russia [sic] have been sending her vast quantities via Archangel, and this has so depleted their resources that they have not been able to assume the offensive on their own front as was intended. This is the story - I give it for what it is worth.

The war is now costing us 3½ millions a day. The Budget next Tuesday when we may expect very heavy taxation.

THE DIARY OF JOHN COLEMAN BINDER

September 17 Friday ... The fighting all along the lines in France and Flanders is chiefly artillery work, and this has been incessant for now nearly three weeks. I believe there has been very little hand-to-hand fighting, although many casualties have occurred.

September 18 Saturday. A recruiting station has been opened here for men of the Northants regiments especially 1st battalion of the 3rd which is badly in want of men as it feeds the 1st and 2nd, the old 48th and 58th which are still in the first ranks of the fighting in Flanders. There are very very few of the men left in these regiments who went out with the 1st Army in Aug 1914. They have been filled up from time to time with fresh men and have always been in the front fighting line. Their most terrible day was at Aubers Ridge on Sunday May 9th. Practically the whole regiment was annihilated. They had to charge over some open ground up to wire entanglements which were supposed to have been smashed by our artillery fire but were still intact. When they reached these they came under a terrific fire and suffered the most awful loss. It has been said on good authority that the Germans were ordered that day to take no prisoners and it is probably true, for none of the men belonging to our county regiment are posted as missing on that day.

The Russian news to-day is not so good. They are being thrust back.

September 18 Sunday A quiet peaceful Sunday. So quiet it seems after the turmoil of all this week, which has been a very very trying one, and one which gives pause to every thinking man in this country.

The chief centre of interest has for a little time come back to this country and that interest is the question of compulsory service or conscription. This question now Parliament has met seems to dwarf all others and has reached a most anxious and indeed menacing aspect and threatens to split the country from top to bottom even if it does not lead to more disastrous effects.

There is a party in Parliament which is determined to force this question to an issue, and has even gone so far during this week as to threaten a General Election on this question and this alone. It seems incredible that any number of men should be willing to play into the hands of the enemy in this manner, for there can be no question that conscription if pressed must lead parties, to revolution or civil war. There can be no hope of coercing the labour of this country without we have the distinct and explicit announcement that without conscription [it will be impossible] to save the country from defeat and disaster, then possibly it might be accepted by a majority of the people, but there would still be a considerable minority who would not accept it at any price. These are chiefly Trades Unionists and the Labour Party, and as such are very powerful. One of their leaders said in the House on Wednesday that if compulsory service was enforced the Railways and mines would at once cease working. He bluntly told the Conscriptionists in the House that their real object was to get rid of the Prime Minister and Lord Kitchener. This I believe to be true, and if the Government, which is composed of the most able men of all parties, is overthrown, who shall we put in their place? It is a difficulty I have always seen threatening. Some of these people who advocate conscription I believe to be quite honest and think that it would be the best way to end the war and secure the triumph of the Allies, but a good number of them I am quite certain desire conscription as a political force. This is by no means a party question. It is dividing all parties, but personally I am quite content to trust the Government, as they, and they alone, have such information as can enable us to come to a right decision. If they say that conscription is necessary, and absolutely necessary, then I shall be prepared to accept it and not otherwise.

The burden laid upon this empire is already stupendous, and cannot be added to without the gravest reasons. We are helping clear the seas. We have an army of 3 millions of men fighting on two fronts. We are keeping our trade going (under conditions which are intolerable) in order to finance ourselves and our Allies, and we have practically turned all our steel and iron works of every description into munition factories in order to supply their wants and our own. If we withdraw our men compulsorily from these labours it seems to me the result will be collapse. I am neither an Optimist nor a Pessimist but simply a plain citizen who tries to look at these events in the light of reason. We are told the Voluntary System has proved a failure, that we are 'a nation of slackers' etc., etc. This is mere rubbish. No nation that supplies and equips an army of 3 millions in a year ought to be condemned in this way. We have made mistakes without doubt, but have our enemies not done the same. The future to me to-day seems more dark and menacing than ever it has done before, and I am quite sure that it is only by the steady adherence to our cause, by absolute unity and by the greatest endurance and economy that we shall be able to win our way to a successful end.

September 20 Monday   The Russian situation looks more menacing. They have again had to retreat and it looks now as if the enemy might make a dash on Petrograd. I hear a report late to-night that the Germans have attacked Serbia and have crossed the Danube. I can scarcely believe this. It is well known the Turks are in desperate straits and this is the reason the Germans may try to force a passage to them at all costs.

September 21 Tuesday . . . Another spy was sentenced to be shot to-day. A woman who acted under his influence is to [be] imprisoned for 10 years. More rigorous measures are being taken against these people and it is quite time this was done. They are a perfect pest and curse in this country.

The Budget was introduced this afternoon about four o'clock. Too late to get a full report here, but a condensed account says the income tax is increased by 40 per cent and the minimum lowered to £130 (£160 previously) and abatements to £120 (£160 previously). . . .

1915 September 22 Wednesday   The one topic to-day is the Budget. It is a very wide [one] in its scope and will affect every member of the community. The farmer will now have to pay income tax. Before this if his rent did not reach £480 he was exempt. He will now have to be assessed like a tradesman. They can quite afford this as they have had an extraordinary time the last 18 months.

The Sugar duty is raised from 1/10 to 9/10 but the price to be charged by the Government (who since the war commenced have had all sugar under their control) is to be lowered by 2/6 per cwt, so that the real price will be raised 1/2d per lb making it 4d per lb for the sugar which is in general use. An extra 4d per lb on tea making it 1/- per lb duty.

Duty on	Tobacco	raised from	4s 1d	to	6s 1d	
on	Cocoa	from	1d	to	1½d	
on	Coffee		2d	to	3d	
on	Patent Medicines	from	1 1/2d			
	dried fruits		7/- per cwt	to	10/6	to 3d in the shilling
	Motor Spirit	an increase of	3d per gallon			

On <u>Imported</u> motor cars motor cycles or parts thereof, Cinema Films, clocks, watches, musical instruments, plate glass and <u>hats</u> (both men's and women's) a tax of 33⅓ is levied.

All half-penny postage is abolished. (I well remember this being introduced). We have had millions of cards sent for ½ d each. Nothing under a 1d now. Only 1 oz in weight can now be sent for 1d instead of 4 oz as before.

No telegram under 9d now - these have been sent before for 6d (12 words) and many other changes in the Postal Service.

This raising of the postal rates is quite justified as for many years the Post Office has not paid its way.

These are the main provisions of the budget. Every wage earner of over £2 -10 -0 per week will now have to pay direct taxes. The new taxes will yield 100 millions in a full year and the Chancellor hinted that further taxation would be imposed and that he [was] only prevented from doing it now owing to the difficulty of collection.

On the whole the new taxes meet with general approval. It is known we shall have to pay and the inevitable will be accepted with good grace. Personally I think it would have been much better had this new taxation been imposed 12 months earlier.

We have one consolation in this matter, the German Finance Minister said last week that he was not able to impose further taxes (or dare not). Germany is now taxed to her utmost limit. This is certainly not the case here. If it is absolutely necessary further taxation could be borne, although it would possibly be resented.

September 23 Thursday A most dramatic turn has been given to affairs in the Balkans. Bulgaria has suddenly mobilised her army, and it is quite a matter of speculation as to which side (if any) she intends to help. . . . I think myself that she intends to help Germany. If this is so Greece and almost certainly Roumania will come in on our side. . .

1915 September 24 Friday Greece has promptly taken up the Bulgarian challenge and to-day is mobilising so that now the whole of the Balkans are under arms. At present no movement has been made but the whole affair is like a barrel of gunpowder and any moment may see the sparks fall which will cause a terrible explosion there [and] so widen the borders of this terrible war. . .

Saturday September 25 . . . . A large number of troops are coming to Northampton (25,000) for the winter it is said. Not many have been there during the summer. I think the inhabitants will not be so keen to receive them as they were last winter when they were paid in many instances 21/- to 25/- per week. The allowance now is 17/6 and this on account of the increased cost of food leaves very little room for profit. There are no troops at Peterborough now.

The recruiting party here have enlisted about 6 or 8 men this week.

September 26 Sunday . . . I wish I could give a picture of the social life of this country since the war, especially during the last few months. The changes are great, and general, but they have come almost without notice.

A great change has taken place in the life of the big country houses. Many are quite closed as their owners are with the Army, and if not closed they have no guests for there are no shooting parties. Shooting goes on but it is decidedly as a business affair, to keep under the game, and in no sense a sporting business.

The same thing applies to hunting. The hunting men now at the front are continually writing home urging that the hunts should be kept going and I think it is more out of loyalty to them than from any sense of pleasure that this will be done. The Woodland Pytchley will meet four days a week for the sole purpose of keeping under the foxes.

Crime is almost absent especially in these country districts. It is certain that if the Army has enlisted some of our best men it has also got the rougher element too.

I think the Budget of this week has touched everybody and everything, and has done more than any other thing to bring home to the people the seriousness of this war. Not that there is much complaining as I am convinced that on the whole it will be borne without much grumbling, but it is realized on all sides that economy must be the order of the day. Both Public bodies and private individuals are trying to put this into force, and are being urged to do so by the Government.

Here in Oundle the Council has decided to light only 22 lamps at night instead of 79 as before: this will result in a saving of at least £120 for the ensuing 12 months and many similar instances might be quoted. Altogether I think I see to-day a somewhat soberer, less frivolous and more responsible England than that of 18 months ago and if this terrible war has done nothing else it has compelled us to pause and think and I hope to try to restrain some of the almost intolerable evils of drink and gambling and other vices which seemed almost to be our masters. The absurd way in which money had dominated this country has I hope received a check and it [is] now possible that as taxation is so drastic the value of money may be reduced to its proper proportions.

Labour I think has also been made to understand that this country does not consist of the Trades Unions alone, and that there are other people in the country as well as the man who works with his hands.

Monday September 27 News of exceptional importance came through from our lines in Flanders to London yesterday afternoon but we did not hear of it here until this morning. Sir John French reports that on Saturday an attack was made along the whole of the 700 mile line, but the real object was [to] pierce the German lines at given points. This was done. We drove back the enemy about 2 to 2½ miles and are only about 1 mile from Lens. . . .The fighting was continued yesterday and the latest telegrams say that 20,000 prisoners have been captured and 54 Machine Guns. No details are given, but evidently the fighting has been very severe. . . .

1915 September 28 Tuesday The good news from the front is fully confirmed and continued to-day. The Allies have captured 300 officers and 20,000 unwounded men and have fully maintained up to to-night all the ground they have won. . .No estimate has been given of the losses of the Allies, but they must have been very heavy. A train load of wounded from the fighting line arrived in Northampton last night.

September 29 Wednesday . . .Some of the wounded who are back here in England say that a terrific thunderstorm was raging during Friday night when the final phase of the bombardment took place, and that when the big guns joined in early on Saturday morning the din and racket was indescribable. The men could not hear the whistles (which are now used by the officers) ordering the advance and it was only by watching they could tell what was to be done.

In the French section in Champagne the soil is chalk, and Paris telegrams to-day say their wounded are coming into Paris plastered from head to foot with a thick coating of white chalk, so that evidently the same weather conditions occurred there.

The first contingent of 300 prisoners arrived at Southampton last night [and] were at once sent inland to the various prison camps. They are said to be men of good physique and are well clad. Some of them are quite young and others are men of 50 or more. They are said to have the appearance of Slavs and might easily pass for Russians. They do not appear to have had much stomach for the fight and were not at all sorry to be out of the racket.

Russia . . . reports that since Saturday the pressure on her front is somewhat relaxed. It appears by this that the enemy are trying to bring men to the Western front again from Russia. . . . *September 30 Thursday* . . . The French state this morning that the total loss of the enemy amount to 120,000 men.

This victory has greatly upset the Germans. The Kaiser has come rushing back from the Eastern frontier to the West. Generals have been dismissed, fresh ones appointed and all sorts of dodges adopted to explain the defeat, but nothing can explain it <u>away.</u>

Friday October 1 . . . It is rumoured that the 7th Northants Regiment was heavily engaged in the Great Battle at the beginning of the week, but so far no details have come through.

We are told to-day that the Northants battery of Artillery will be route marching through this end of the county next week and are likely to be quartered here next Friday.

A very grave warning to Bulgaria was issued to-night by Sir Edward Grey. It says the Allies understand that German and Austrian Officers are taking the place of Bulgarians in their Army. This will not be tolerated as the Allies do not intend to have a second Turkey on their hands.

October 2 Saturday News from most of the Oundle men who are in the 7th Northants has been received to-day. They are all safe, but had some very hard fighting. They were not in the first attack but were ordered up as supports and got caught in the melee. The fighting in our own lines last Sunday and Saturday and Monday will be known I think as the Battle of Hulloch. Although the attack is not so violent the last few days it is still proceeding. To-day it is reported that our airmen destroyed 16 German aeroplanes the last few days and wrecked 6 trains.

At Eastcote against Towcester there have been interned since the beginning of the war a large number of German <u>Merchant</u> seamen, who have been captured either from neutral vessels coming to ports in this country or on the high seas. Their numbers have increased from time to time until there were nearly 4,000 there. Last Sunday a sudden order was issued and within an hour and a half all of them guarded by a detachment of the Guards were moved to the Alexandra Palace, London where there is a huge concentration camp. It is said Eastcote is to be used as Prison Camp for captured German soldiers.

1915 Sunday October 3 . . . I should like to add one thing to my notes of last Sunday as to the Social life here during the war, and that is that the reduction of lighting has engendered the habit of going earlier to bed.

THE DIARY OF JOHN COLEMAN BINDER

In most places the hour of closing has been 7.30 or 8 but now owing to the absence of light and the drive for economy it will generally be 7 o'clock. The Post Office hours will also be reduced by an hour morning and evening and instead of being from 8 am to 8pm will only be from 9am to 7 pm. This is principally owing to the shortage of labour.

The recruiting is still causing some anxiety. The Labour Party this week have started a big campaign to rally men to the colours, in hopes that any form of conscription may be avoided.

Wheat maintains its value at about 45/- to 46/- Barley is worth 43/- to 46/- so that it is worth more per stone than wheat, a thing I have never known before. This is due to the entire absence of Barley from Russia and the Balkans.

It is announced this week that we have a million men in France and that another 500,000 will be added to them before Christmas.

The Turks have been signally defeated this week in the Persian Gulf campaign and put in full retreat to Bag[h]dad. The fighting is going on still.

October 5 Tuesday . . . Fierce fighting is going on in France and the Germans have recaptured our trench which we took last week. From all the accounts we have received it is certain that the New Army (which was heavily engaged) behaved with much courage. The 7th Northants (whose Colonel was killed) came into the fighting against the Prussia Guards. I thought that all the Oundle Boys in this regiment were safe, but at present no tidings have been received from two or three of them

October 6 Wednesday . . . A most sensational and dramatic turn was given to affairs in the Balkans by the announcement this afternoon that the Greek Premier (a man who is entirely on the Allies side) had resigned this morning as the Greek King had refused to sanction his policy. This is German intrigue again as the Greek Queen is the Kaiser's sister. It is a most tangled and extraordinary situation and the end of which no one can foresee. It is said ' lookers on see most of the game' but to all of us in this country it is perfectly bewildering. Russia has moved her fleet in the Black Sea up to the Bulgarian Port of Varna.

October 7 No additional news from Greece this morning except that some of the Allies troops have left Salonica for Serbia.

The French made another vigorous assault on the 3rd German lines in Champagne yesterday and gained a good foothold capturing a thousand prisoners.

The 7th Northants were very badly mauled at the Battle of Hulloch as can be now seen from the casualty lists which are being published. I think all the Oundle men are safe except one. A young man Percy North son of Mr JW North (Butcher). No tidings have been received from him. I believe all the others have written although some of them are wounded.

Friday October 8 . . . One of the greatest tragedies the world has ever seen has been taking place in this God forsaken kingdom of Turkey during the last 5 or 6 weeks. This is the deliberate massacre of the Armenian race of people. Turkey has long waited for this opportunity and now pushed on by Germany has practically accomplished her object. It is estimated that 800,000 Armenians have been butchered in Asia Minor and other parts and these massacres have been accompanied by every fiendish torture the mind can conceive. The load of guilt of Belgium and these Armenians must indeed be heavy on Germany and must be laid at her door alone.

To-day the Northants Battery of Artillery marched in here from Kettering. Major Walker (son of Dr Walker of Peterborough) being in command. They are a battery that was formed as Territorials about 2 ½ years since, and were at once called up when war was declared and have been in training ever since, and are now keenly anxious to go to the front. They are a fine sturdy lot of men, smart in appearance, and of good physique. The battery is well horsed, most of the horses are black with a few bays, and they are all in first class condition. In fact they would be a credit to any Army.

They arrived about 3 pm having watered their horses and baited at Thrapston. After they had cleaned up the men were entertained to a tea and concert in the Victoria Hall at 6 pm. The men (except those on duty)

also slept in the Hall. The Guns and horses were picketed in the field next to Bradley Cottage on the South Backway. They left again at 9.30 on Saturday morning en route for Stilton and thence to Huntingdon. Nearly all the men in this Battery come from this end of the County.

1915 October 9 Saturday . . . The French . . objective for the moment is a railway which runs just at the back of the German lines in Champagne, and at one point they are now only 1 ½ miles from it.

These are bloody battles day after day. The new German troops in Champagne are most young recruits. They fought bravely but attacked in the absurd German close formation and were mown down literally in thousands. The Germans still cling to this method of attack. It is terribly costly. The Allies have abandoned it long since.

The trenches captured from the Germans recently were found to be in many instances 25 to 30 feet deep. This is [the] reason so many prisoners were taken. Our men rushed up quickly and they were unable to scramble out.

Sunday October 10 . . . The Navy people are recruiting strongly in the County the last few weeks. Although we have lost no really big naval battle we have lost 20,000 men on the sea and they are anxious to keep up and increase the Navy to its full strength.

All the big steamships carrying passengers are having quite an exciting time. All passengers during the voyage are required to undergo 'Boat Drill'. A certain number including women and children are told off to each boat and if the enemy should attack they would each know which boat to go to. This manoeuvre is frequently practised especially during the night (when they are aroused by the Ship's siren)

Passengers coming to England are never quite sure as to what port they may land at, as they are often ordered when off the coast to change their place of disembarkation. This of course is done by wireless telegraphy.

October 11 Monday . . . The Austro- Germans have captured Belgrade after a very gallant stand by the Serbians. Bulgaria has not made any attack at present. This incursion of Germany and the events in the Balkans have I think caused more anxiety in this country than any other event since the battle of Mons. It may mean that they will reach Constantinople in which case I can foresee the campaign in the Dardanelles would have to be abandoned. This would be a heavy blow at the Allies after having thrown away so many lives there, beside which it would mean a great loss of prestige. With the new development it means that 14 nations or peoples are involved in this war and that war is being carried on over more than half the world.

October 12 Tuesday . . . the situation in the Balkans absorbs the attention of everyone. A rumour is going round to-day that the Allied troops will not leave Salonika. This Balkans business is the worst for us of the whole war and may have the most tremendous consequences. It is quite possible the Germans may attempt to reach Egypt. From all we hear they are dreaming the same dreams Napoleon did 100 years ago and are hoping to found an Eastern Empire. History is being made fast during these days, and almost every morning brings some new phase in this world-wide conflict. The end no man can see.

Opposition to the abolition of the ½d post has grown so strong that to-day the Government announce they have decided to retain it.

1915 October 1 Wednesday The Bulgarians joined in the war yesterday by attacking the Serbians. A most dastardly business and one that ultimately must recoil on themselves. Greece still hangs fire, although by treaty she is bound to help Serbia if attacked, but then treaties in these days count for very little. They are kept so long as it suits the stronger party to keep them.

October 14 Thursday . . . A Zeppelin raid on London took place last evening. 8 people are reported killed and a number wounded. The Zep was over Cromer soon after seven in the evening. A notice issued later than the above says that 52 people were killed and 170 injured in this raid.

October 15 Friday Events are moving swiftly in the Balkans . . . It goes without doubt that we cannot let Serbia be crushed and the Allies one and all have decided to go to her relief. If this is to be done it must be at once and quickly. . .

THE DIARY OF JOHN COLEMAN BINDER

October 16 Saturday Very little news from Serbia to-day although many rumours are in circulation. . . .Our total losses in Gallipoli are officially stated at 96,000. A bad business this. The strategy was good and if it had been properly organised and carried out would I believe have been the end of the war, but it has been badly organised (from lack of co-operation) and I am afraid now cannot prove a success. I think the best plan would be to abandon it and transfer the whole of the forces to Serbia.

October 17 Sunday A new recruiting campaign is to be opened to-morrow with the object of securing 30,000 recruits per week. It is under the direction of Lord Derby, who will have the help of the Labour Party and all political organisations in the country. There will be placed at their disposal the names of all men of military age, as revealed by the National Register, and each of these will be visited and asked to enlist. It may be successful but I am rather doubtful. It will be tried for six weeks and if it does not succeed I am of the opinion that some kind of Compulsory Service will be adopted. This I think is the most serious question we have to face, and if Conscription is adopted it will do more to disorganise the whole nation more than anything else. It must enormously reduce our trade and consequently weaken our financial position. I think it is a choice between the two evils of Conscription and trade destruction.

A new field of activity has been opened for the navy in the Baltic. We know that our submarines have been there for some time and have practically cleared all German ships off that sea. One submarine going to the Baltic through the Sound on Friday was attacked by three German Destroyers. She turned on them and at once torpedoed one and sank her with all her crew. The others made off.

[The British Navy seems to have been very successful in capturing or destroying German submarines].

The price of cattle and sheep has fallen considerably the last month but pork is very dear and is now making 11/- per stone (14 lbs) in local markets.

Wheat continues to advance and is now worth 50/- again. This is chiefly due to a lack of shipping to bring the Canadian Crop over. Barley is very dear and has made up to 54/- and 55/- per quarter.

1915 October 18 Monday The chief item of news to-day is that the French have joined the Serbians and are now attacking Bulgaria. Serbia is hard pressed from the North.

October 19 Tuesday . . . Very heavy casualty lists are coming out each day just now. To-day's contains 3,016 names. Of course a great proportion of them are wounded only, but some of the wounds are horrible.

Percy North an Oundle boy whom I mentioned as missing after the last great battle has now written home to say that he is wounded and a prisoner at Munster in Germany.

Our prisoners especially English, (there are 25, 000 there to-day) receive very harsh treatment in Germany. Great quantities of food and clothing are sent out to them by their friends and also from public subscriptions here. Bread which is very much asked for by the prisoners is not very satisfactory when it reaches them if sent from England as it is nearly 10 days before it reaches them. For the payment of 1/- per week the British Legation at Berne, Switzerland undertakes to supply each man with sufficient bread sent from Switzerland.

October 20 Wednesday French wounded have reached Salonica from the interior so that is evident the Allies are now engaged in the Balkans fighting. No mention is made of any English at present but we know they are there also.

General Hamilton in command at the Dardanelles is ordered home to-day, indeed it is said that he has already landed in England. I think things are going not at all well there. There is much misgiving about this Dardanelles business.

What is regarded as the last effort in voluntary recruiting is announced to-day. If this fails I see nothing for it but compulsory service in some form or other. The scheme is as follows:

Every man of military age i.e. between 18 and 40 will be waited on and urged to enlist. If he does so he will be at once attested and enrolled and will be practically a soldier although he may not be required to join the colours at once but may have to await orders. These men as enlisted will be divided into 46 classes. The first 23 classes will consist of unmarried men and the other 23 of married men. The classes in each section will be called upon to serve in such order as may be deemed best, and each man will be given 14 days notice.

The scheme as to canvassing will be worked by Recruiting Committees -- the political agent of all parties and they will have at their disposal the forms of the National Registration. These relating to men of military age were in the first instance coloured pink but they are now blue. This work will all have to be carried out before the 30th of November. Personally I am doubtful as to its success but I sincerely hope it may do so. Conscription in this country will raise enormous difficulties.

October 21 Thursday A very strict censorship is exercised over news coming from Greece and Serbia and scarcely any reliable news is to hand. A rumour to-night says that England has offered Cyprus to Greece if she will fight on our side.

I hear that although no big naval action has occurred since last January constant minor actions with submarines are occurring. An Oundle man writes home that lately they have had to put into port 4 times for repairs.

October 22 Friday A big effort known as 'Our Flag Day' was made throughout the Empire yesterday on behalf of the Red Cross for our own Soldiers and Sailors. It is expected that a very large sum of money will have been raised. Apart from this effort 1 ¾ Millions has already been subscribed.

The whole world to-day is aghast at the judicial murder by the Germans of Miss Cavell an Englishwoman living in Belgium. She was arrested on August 5 and after having undergone a kind of trial at the hands of the German soldiers was condemned to death on October 11. In spite of all efforts made by the American and Spanish Ambassadors she was brought to execution at 2 am on the morning of October 12. It is said she collapsed on seeing the firing party and that a German officer shot her with his revolver as she lay on the ground.

The charge against her was that she harboured wounded English and French soldiers. This she quite admitted but at the same time she had been equally kind to wounded Germans and had helped them in many ways.

This brutal act has only added to the intense hatred of the Germans which has taken hold of all classes in this country and it will do them a great deal of harm in all neutral countries too.

1915 October 23 Saturday The news from Serbia to-day is grave and ominous. The Serbians are retreating slowly in the North and contesting every foot of the ground but the Bulgarians are thrusting at the lines of communication with Salonica. It remains to be seen what effect this will have. Greece still sits on [the] fence. She is said to require that the Allies should land 300,000 men at Salonica before she feels safe to declare herself on our side.

The Allied Fleet yesterday bombarded the Bulgarian sea ports in the Aegean Sea.

. . [.The Germans attacked Rheims but suffered heavy losses because they advanced in close formation].

THE DIARY OF JOHN COLEMAN BINDER

October 24 Sunday A dull Autumn day. No further news from Serbia to-day.

This recruiting scheme which I mentioned last Wednesday is now being thoroughly worked and is being brought home to everybody in this country. I think that now people realize what we are up against and in what critical and ominous times we are living. More and more each day is being brought home to them the seriousness of the situation (especially in the increased cost of living) and taking the situation as a whole I am glad to say they are meeting that situation bravely.

Men and women with whom you come in contact are anxious but there is no 'whining', and least of all is there any talk of giving way. It is recognised on all sides that there can be no compromise in this affair, and if we are to go under (which with God's help we shall not) we will go under fighting to the last. I am glad to say that it is freely acknowledged we have at last turned the corner with regard to munitions. Reports as to the battle of Hulloch say that the supply was ample and that when the battle died down the artillery had plenty left. This is satisfactory. Our supply will still increase as the new schemes of manufacture have not yet reached their maximum output. Japan is sending large quantities to Russia via the Siberian Railway, and the result is apparent in the way in which Russia is holding her own and in her power to advance again.

Wheat is again dearer on the week and Barley also. The latter has reached 50/- per qr. for grinding purposes and we paid 48/- for some (20 qrs) to Mr John Platt of this town this week.

All the railways in the country are still closely watched. This is mostly done by special constables. There are still plenty of people here who would only be too glad to help the enemy if they could. Another spy was shot this week and yesterday two men were charged with signalling to the Zeppelins on the night they came to London. These men wee handed over to the military authorities and will be court-martialled.

October 25 Monday

[*British submarines have sunk 10 German ships in the Baltic carrying ore from Sweden to Krupps*].

1915 October 26 Tuesday The Serbian news to-day is again bad. The Germans are slowly driving them back and the Bulgarians are pressing them on their flank. The situation is one of extreme danger and this was candidly acknowledged by our Government in the House of Lords to-night. . . .there are only about 13,000 British Troops at Salonica, what force the French have is not disclosed but it does not seem to be very great. I am afraid the Serbians will be crushed.

October 27 Wednesday The statement in the House last night has made a profound impression on this country and a good deal of criticism is directed at the Government, but the situation is a most difficult one and has without doubt been brought about by years of German intrigue in the Balkans.

Recruiting is going on very rapidly again especially in Northampton and other centres. Men in the shoe factories were not allowed to enlist last winter as they were all needed for army boots making but it seems as if they had turned the corner in equipment and men are now being released except those working particular machinery.

A British transport was torpedoed in the Aegean sea yesterday. All were saved except about 90.

Another spy was shot in the Tower to-day.

Admiral Sir Percy Scott who is in charge of the defence of London against air raids announces to-day that more and better guns are being mounted. It is also said that men who are accustomed to firing at air craft are being brought back from France where they have had much experience in this kind of warfare.

October 28 Thursday It is Red Cross Flag Day here to-day and a miserable wet day, but I believe it is quite a success. I hear that the amount realized by the sale of these little flags is over £30.

The Germans and Bulgarians have joined hands. It is true it is only a small junction but it must pave the way to larger movements and open a way through to Turkey . . . .

It was announced to-day that our own total losses are 497,000. Of this number over 100,000 are actually dead.

DAY BY DAY THROUGH THE GREAT WAR

October 29 Friday   The King is across in France. He has been there nearly a week reviewing troops and taking a look into all that concerns the Army. . . .

Friday Night   A telegram from France to-day says that the King was thrown from his horse yesterday at a review and badly bruised. The cheering of the soldiers caused the horse to rear and she rolled over. It is said that no bones are broken but the King was badly bruised.

A Memorial Service was held to-day at St Paul's in memory of Miss Cavell and was attended by the Premier and other Ministers and thousands of people. This murder has caused a most profound impression throughout the whole world and has given a great impetus to recruiting in this country.

October 30 Saturday   Vague rumours are current to-day that Roumania has been won over by the Allies as the result of certain large concessions which have been presented to her and that she will range herself on this side.

There has been a wave of depression over the country since this Balkan business has come up, but I think it has now steadied itself and the cooler heads are beginning to see events again in their true perspective. . . .It is not the end of the war for Germany . . .she has detached a big army from her other fronts and the result is the renewed offensive of the Russians, French and Italians . . . and the tightening of the grip of the British Navy . . . certainly the dominating fact in this war. These grim grey ironclads hid in the mists of the North Sea are slowly but surely strangling Germany and it is evident that the internal condition of her people is becoming much worse. The principal things she seems to lack apparently are wool, cotton, some kinds of metals, petrol and rubber and last but not least meat and fats of all descriptions. Meat is forbidden to be served in their restaurants four days in each week. Butter is 2/6 per pound . . and lard, which in England is still at 6d is 1/6 to 1/9. No wonder the people are said to dread the coming winter. All woollen goods are being taken for the Army in Russia and no private person is allowed to purchase them. . . .

1915 October 31 Sunday   The recruiting scheme under the control of Lord Derby is proving a great success. Many thousands of men have joined during this week and letters are being sent to every man between the ages of 19 and 41 asking him to enlist. If this is not successful he will be canvassed and urged personally to do so. These men will be divided into 46 classes, 23 married and 23 unmarried, and these classes will be called up from time to time as required, the unmarried going first (if they have not already joined, which they may do at once if they like). No man at work on Munitions will be allowed to enlist and a Committee consisting of about 5 persons will be appointed by each Town, Urban District or Rural District to consider the claims of men who are indispensable to their employers. A fortnight's notice will be given to each man before he is called upon to join the Colours.

These are the main features of the scheme, and upon the results of it will depend as to whether there will be some kind of Compulsion or not. It will be carried through before the end of November.

I think the objections to Compulsion are very weighty. The chief is the question of Finance. England to-day is financing not only herself but also France, Russia and also Italy. It is obvious if you requisition every man between 19 and 41 the whole trade of the country must suffer most severely and without trade there can be no means of keeping things going. Many trades are very much upset as it is and it is very difficult to obtain some kinds of goods. This is chiefly caused by the shortage of labour.

Another reason is that a great number of people are dead against compulsion and will resist it at any cost. This will cause a breach in our ranks which so far have shown an unbroken front to Germany. It is urged that almost every man in France is serving. This is possibly true and is just the reason that she cannot finance herself and we by our industries are compelled to do it for her.

General Joffre the Commander-in-Chief has been in London for 2 days and returned to the front this afternoon.

November 1 Monday . . .This is the usual day for all Town Council Elections but Parliament has decreed that no elections are to be held this year.   All vacancies are to be filled up by co-option.

November 2 Tuesday   News comes to-day that the Germans have captured the chief Serbian Arsenal, also that the French and Bulgarians have joined in conflict, but the battle which commenced on Sunday is still going on.

To-day the Prime Minister is to make a general statement as to the War. This is being looked forward to with much expectation as it is supposed he will disclose much that has hitherto been obscure, also that he will announce the formation of an 'inner Cabinet' which will have the supreme direction of the war so far as we are concerned.

The King returned from France last night. He is much shaken and bruised, but the accident is said not to be at all serious.

November 3 Wednesday Notice has been given to the Special Constables here that they will be required to guard the Railway Bridges in this district. This has been done by Special Constables in other parts of the Country for some time.

The Prime Minister's statement last night has on the whole satisfied public opinion although he did not meet all criticism that had been levelled against the Government. I think their chief faults are in the Balkans and the Dardanelles, but one can scarcely judge of this latter as it is impossible to reveal all the circumstances under which it was undertaken. At any rate, it is generally acknowledged to be a failure and I do not think it will be seriously undertaken again at present. It had certain advantages in that it drew off the attack from Egypt and also relieved the pressure on the Russians in the Caucasus but on the whole it is [a] disastrous and bloody business.

He also said that under the new recruiting scheme (which is going well) men will be called up according to age, the younger going first, and that if this scheme did not succeed compulsion would be used.

1915 November 4 Thursday The Serbians are fighting hard and dealing some heavy blows against the enemy. To-day British Cavalry are reported in action against the Bulgarians. Who these cavalry are is not disclosed but I imagine they are some of the Yeomanry who have been sent from Gallipoli. They were sent in the first instance to Egypt. After the danger was over there they went on to the Dardanelles leaving their horses behind and now I expect they are again mounted. . . .This whole Balkan business is quite bewildering and it is extremely difficult to sift false news from true. A telegram late this afternoon says that the Greek Ministry is again out of office. One can never tell what may happen in the quarter from day to day.

November 5 Friday The rumour of last night is quite confirmed this morning. The Greek Ministry wished to demobilise the Army. This was rejected by the Chamber so consequently the Ministry resigned. M Venzelis again dominates the situation. It would be folly to assume that this means Greece coming in on our side at once, but at the same time it may lead up to events which will compel her to do so.

The General Election was due to be held in January when the life of this Parliament expires but the Government announce to-day that no election will take place until the war is over. This is quite right as it is unthinkable that we should have all the turmoil and excitement of an election during this terrible war.

Later A rumour late to-night says that Lord Kitchener has resigned.

November 6 Saturday London appears yesterday to have been a city of sensations and to have had a bad attack of 'nerves' arising out of the report that Lord Kitchener had resigned. Certain rumours were abroad early in the morning and in the afternoon the Globe newspaper definitively announced that he had resigned. About an hour later an official denial was issued, and it was also stated that he had gone on a special and important mission and that the Premier would take charge of the War Office during his absence. So the incident closed, but to-day the authorities have raided the Globe Office and suspended it. This is done under the 'Defence of the Realm Act'. It would be quite as well if the Government would take similar steps against other notorious papers (such as the 'Daily Mail') who are always seeking to dishearten the nation, spreading these kinds of rumours. The Premier in his speech last Tuesday called them 'Professional Whimperers' and this they are. Speculation is rife as to where Lord Kitchener has gone. The prevailing idea is that he has gone to the Balkans. I think if this is so the mission is diplomatic as well as military. The fighting there is still fierce and continuous and the Serbians are giving way slowly. To-day we are informed that there are 40,000 of our (English) troops there and that they have been in action. They form the right wing of the French Army. . . . Along our own front things are fairly quiet but, as the men who come home tell us, there is always quite enough going on to keep them alive.

November 7 Sunday There has again been much 'Peace Talk' by Germany principally through the American Press, but her ideas (if they are authentic) are so preposterous that no responsible person in this county mentions them except in derision. For instance she suggests that we should give up our East African Possessions in exchange for her evacuating Belgium. That we should pay an indemnity of 1500 millions, and other similar nonsense. Also that Russia should give up Poland and that France should acquiesce in her retaining Alsace and Lorraine etc. etc. Of course it is all 'bluff' and 'bluster' and as such is estimated at its true worth in this country. There are   I think reasonable grounds for thinking that Germany is feeling the pinch although it is most difficult to get really reliable information as to what is taking place there. They claim they are self-supporting and can carry on the war for years. Possibly they may be self-sustaining in normal times, but she cannot take ten millions of men away from her industries (especially agriculture) and add them to the consumers instead of producers and continue in the same position. The end is inevitable whether it comes sooner or later.

We in England are very quiet but there is no slacking in our determination to see this thing through. Looking back over the last 16 months I am bound to think this great war was inevitable, although I did not think it would come in my time. Events have disclosed such ideas existing in Germany that a collision between their ideas and the ideas by which this country is ruled was inevitable. . . . Their sole idea as far as I can judge may be summed up in the words 'Might is Right', ours 'Right is Might' and these two were bound to fight.

It is a fixed idea here that until there is a change in Germany that there can be no living in this country, and no safety here. We feel we are fighting for our own preservation and we would rather go under fighting than we would be governed by German ideas or think that future generations in this our country should be either.

Many efforts are now organised for our soldiers and sailors. Things are much better organised than they were last winter and all voluntary effort is now directed by Government into the right channels. Of course the system is not perfect, but it is a great improvement on last year. In every town and village work is being done for the 'Red Cross' by the making of bandages, garments and other requisites. At Oundle the front room at the Victoria Hall is open all day on Wednesdays for the Ladies to go and work, and it is hoped to do much good by this.

Efforts (voluntary) are also being made to supply our prisoners in Germany with warm clothing and arrangements have been made at Northampton to send out a good and sufficient supply to all prisoners from the Northamptonshire regiments.

November 8 Monday . . .Lord Kitchener has gone to the Balkans. This is official. What he has gone for is not publicly known but great developments are expected in that quarter.

I think Kitchener has now got affairs into shape at the War Office and Lord Derby having taken over the recruiting business, he feels that he can be spared to do what is more important work in the Balkans. The storm centre to-day is certainly in that quarter.

The King is much better and no further bulletins will be issued.

November 9 Tuesday The Germans are slowly capturing the through line to Constantinople - only 30 miles of it remain in Serbian hands.

Major Riddell (whom I mentioned some months since) has again been to the Rectory for a week end on leave from the front. He says that the Germans are now using very bad ammunition. Many of their shells fail to explode and nearly all prisoners who have been taken lately are men of over 50 or quite boys. This shows the drain on German resources. Twenty Bulgarian prisoners were brought to England yesterday. This shows that we have been fighting there.

THE DIARY OF JOHN COLEMAN BINDER

Another German Cruiser (300,000 tons) was sunk in the Baltic yesterday by our submarines. Theses submarines have done remarkable work in the Baltic and the Germans are getting alarmed. They have prevented communication with the German armies in North Russia by sea and have also done much injury to their mercantile marine.

German submarines have succeeded in reaching the Mediterranean and have sunk several ships there. Yesterday they sunk an Italian liner.

1915 November 10 Wednesday   Weather conditions are now very bad along the fighting lines in Flanders. Men writing and coming home report they are smothered in mud. I do not think that much can be done there this winter. It will be a repetition of last winter but I hope the suffering and discomfort of the men will not be so great as things are better organised.

November 11 Thursday The sinking of the Italian steamer is about on a level with the Lusitania. She had a lot of women and children on board, about 300, also 25 Americans. . .I suppose America will still sit still with folded arms and make 'vigorous ' protests. This seems to be about all she is capable of. As for taking 'action' that is quite another matter.

One of our transports on its way to Salonika with the Lincolnshire Yeomanry was shelled by a German submarine in the Mediterranean last Saturday. 27 men were killed . . Amongst the killed is Lord Kesteven and several other men from the Stamford district. I saw to-day Mr C. Springthorpe, a miller of Luffenham, who tells me that he heard this morning that his son was amongst the killed.

Another huge Vote of Credit in the Commons last night £ 400,000,000, which will carry us on to the middle of February. The 'City' people are beginning to get very anxious about our huge liabilities.

Rumour says that we are going to withdraw from the Dardanelles.

November 12 Friday . . . Yesterday the first meeting here for the canvassing of men to enlist was held at the Victoria Hall, and arrangements were made to come on Lord Derby's scheme.

November 13 Saturday   Mr Churchill's resignation from the Cabinet is announced this morning. He is a man of much energy and power. Since the Coalition Cabinet was formed he has held no really responsible post and now that a small War Council (of 5 members) has been formed and in which he was not included he feels that his time is being wasted. He proposes to join his old regiment the 10th Hussars in France.

[Fighting continues in the Balkans]. The position of Greece is still most obscure and indeed over the whole of the Balkan business a veil of mystery seems to rest. Probably the whole truth will not be known for many years if it ever is.

Sunday November 14 A beautiful winter's day after a sharp frost. We have had a great downpour of rain this week in the Midlands and South and snow In the North, so we may fairly say Winter has commenced

The troops in this country are in much better circumstances than they were last winter. Huts have been built by the thousand. These have been made very comfortable and are well warmed and dry.

An announcement of very great importance concerning recruiting has been made by the Government this week. Under Lord Derby's scheme all men married and unmarried between the ages of 19 and 40 are being asked to join the army, but the Government now give notice that no married man who enlists will be called up for service until every unmarried man has been called up, and that if these unmarried do not enlist before November 30 conscription will be put in force against them.

Local tribunals (generally of 5 members) are now being appointed in each district rural and urban by the Rural and Urban Councils, and in boroughs by the Town Councils, for the purpose of hearing appeals as to enlistment. For instance a man may enlist but his employer may say that he cannot possibly do without him. His employers will then appeal to this Court which will determine if this is so or not. They may either say he is not necessary or that he is. In the latter case they may release him altogether or place him in a group which will only be called up much later. The supply of unmarried men will at any rate be exhausted before the married men are called up, and the same tests will be applied to them.

DAY BY DAY THROUGH THE GREAT WAR

Wheat continues to rise in price and is now worth about 55/- to 56/- per qr on rail. This is a rise of quite 12/- to 13/- since September. This has been brought about chiefly by one cause and that is the lack of ships to bring wheat and other corn to this country. It is an acknowledged fact there was never more wheat in the world than there is to-day. The seas are practically free from the enemy and yet we do not get the grain. The cause of this is easy to see. Our own Government have taken about one third of our ships for their own use. All German ships have been driven from the seas and are rusting in port, and a large part of our ships are plying between neutral countries without coming to these shores at all.

This is to be altered. In future, that is so long as this war shall last, all our ships are forbidden to ply between neutral ports exclusively and they will [be] compelled to bring cargoes to this country at least one way. This it is hoped will cause freights to decline and so lower grain prices here.

1915 November 15 Monday Grave reports are to hand this morning concerning the position of Greece. It is possible the Allies and the Serbians may have to retire on to Greek territory and Germany is trying to induce Greece to attempt to disarm them if they do so. Lord Kitchener is said to be in Athens and Greece is reminded by England and France that there is still the English Fleet to be reckoned with and that the Greek coast is quite open to bombardment.

November 16 Tuesday Mr Churchill's speech on his resignation is the chief topic to-day. I have read it very carefully and on the whole it is a brilliant Parliament speech but one to which there must be an answer at several points if other ministers could reply. He explains and reveals several matters about which little information had been given to us. Such as the Antwerp business which he says was not really his scheme, but Lord Kitchener's, although he went to Antwerp and ordered a naval brigade to be sent across. This was a distinct error on his part as this brigade had not been recruited more than six weeks and it was obvious they were quite unfitted to take the field.

His explanations as to the Dardanelles (for which expedition he has been much blamed) are conspicuous for one thing and that is the lack of agreement or working powers between the Admiralty and the War Office and it appears to the ordinary observer that that was the chief cause of the failure. These operations seem quite in abeyance just now, and we hear very little about them.

November 7 Wednesday I think the times grow more serious. The situation in Greece is most perplexing. The Serbians are being driven back and must eventually come on to Greek territory together with the English and French troops who are with them. It is much feared that the Greeks may stab us in the back and the Allies are putting pressure on the Greek King and his cabinet to come to some understanding. A big fleet is assembled at Salonica and it is quite prepared to act if necessary. The King is certainly acting against the feeling of the majority of the Greek nation and in defiance of the fact that M Venzelis has declared against his policy.

Last night Mr Asquith, Mr Balfour, Sir E Grey, Mr Lloyd George together with their military and naval advisers crossed over to Paris to confer with the French Government. This is practically a new War Council, and it is hoped and expected that Russia and Italy may also be able to come to these conferences. I think this fact alone shows how serious the situation is.

Lord Fisher made a reply in the House of Lords to Mr Churchill's speech on Monday. It is between these two men that great difference of opinion has arisen. Lord Fisher is to the Navy what Kitchener is to the Army and the present efficiency of the Fleet is due in a very great way to him. He is a sailor. His speech did not contain 100 words and I think will appeal much more to the country than the 4 columns of newspaper speech of Mr Churchill's. He just said he had been 61 years in the service of his country and was content to leave his record at that. He also strongly deprecated public discussion at the present time.

A Red Cross ship crossing yesterday from Calais to Dover with 385 wounded struck a mine or was torpedoed. Three hundred were saved by vessels which raced to her help on receiving the wireless message she sent out but 85 poor fellows were drownded. This is German 'Kultur' attacking helpless wounded men.

1915 November 18 Thursday To-day is 'Flag day' for the Russian Red Cross and the Russian Flag is being sold throughout the country. Over 2 millions have been prepared. It is a clear fine day and I think the ladies who are selling them are doing very well.

A rumour says that the German Fleet has been seen moving out of the Baltic. I hope they are coming out to fight. This I believe is the sincere wish of every British sailor.

November 19 Friday Events are extremely quiet all along our lines in France just now. This is partly accounted for by weather conditions which are very bad. A week's rain has turned the trenches into ponds and men writing and coming home say the trenches are quite two feet deep in water. Men who come home on furlough are plastered up with mud. They usually come straight away from the trenches and are given about four days.

END OF VOLUME FOUR

THE DIARY OF JOHN COLEMAN BINDER

Volume Five
20 November 1915 to 22 March 1916

1915 November 20 Saturday This commences another volume of this diary. I wonder how many more books it will fill. I am quite aware that these rough notes are fragmentary and disjointed, but still they may be of interest to some one in after years. Of this one thing who ever reads them may be quite assured and that is they were written down each day or at the most two days so that they contain such impressions as are now being made.

Of course these notes are very imperfect. The war is so huge and the interests involved so tremendous that we can only concentrate our ideas on principal events as they occur and it is rather difficult to take a long and true estimate of the war as a whole.

Glancing over the situation to-day there are some things which encourage us and other which dishearten us. The military situation is far from what could have [been] hoped or desired, but if this is so with us it is equally or more so with Germany.

Lord Haldane (than whom no living Englishman knows more of Germany) said the other day the Germans had quite expected to finish this war in three months and by that time to have imposed their will and rule on Europe. Looking back I think there are two chief events which frustrated their intentions. The first was the resistance of Belgium which allowed time for mobilisation and the other the intervention of this country. To us living to-day it appears that the turning point was the Battle of the Marne. Germany suffered there a fierce and decided check, and although rushing from East to West and North to South has never been able to regain a decided advantage. I should like to know if later years will confirm this opinion.

She may be gaining victories but I firmly believe she is losing the war. I am afraid so many of my fellow countrymen are apt to take such a short sighted view of this conflict and cannot truly estimate the world wide interests that are involved.

Lord Kitchener is at the Dardanelles. It is disclosed that General Monro who succeeded Sir Ian Hamilton in command there has recommended that our forces should be withdrawn. The Cabinet were not satisfied with this and asked Lord Kitchener to go out and make a further report. This is causing some discontent in Australia as the Australians have borne the brunt of the fighting there.

November 21 Sunday A regular November day, grey with a bleak East wind. Events are moving in the Balkans and it is on Serbia that all eyes are fixed. She is being slowly overwhelmed and the Allies have not sufficient force there to shield her. Many troops are being sent out from England and also from France and it is hoped and expected that Italy will soon be in a position to send effective help.

The recruiting campaign goes on and the time for closing it has been extended to December 11. It has suffered a back check this week owing to a misunderstanding or vacillation on the part of the Cabinet. They have now pulled themselves together and things seem more hopeful. I myself had hoped to do some canvassing, but felt compelled to withdraw as I could not conscientiously carry out the scheme as it then was and thousands of other canvassers thought the same. However the scheme is now fairly settled and will be given a fair field. It is obvious this is the last <u>voluntary</u> effort and if this fails there will be no alternative but compulsion. Although the Parliament would have to sanction that course, but I do not think there would be much difficulty about it, as I believe it would now be approved of by the vast majority of the people.

November 22 Monday The situation in Greece has now reached the breaking point. The Allies have practically given her 24 hours to say what she intends to do. Both Lord Kitchener and M. Cockin the French Ambassador have interviewed the King and have been unable to get any real answer from him. I believe the Greeks as a nation are decidedly in our favour, but the King and his party are largely under German influence and no doubt have received a good deal of money from them. As a precautionary

111

measure the Allies have boycotted or annexed all Greek ships in their ports for the time being.

1915 Tuesday November 23 Very little news from Greece to-day. This afternoon it [was] rumoured that the blockade has either been withdrawn or does not exist. The censorship of messages is very strict and it is difficult to get reliable news.

To-day the Government announce they intend to issue £1 Bonds bearing 5 per cent interest. This is to induce if possible the working classes to lend their money to the State. The amount invested by small [investors] in the War Loan is only 5 Millions and it is thought the reason is that it is a fluctuating Stock. I hardly think this is the true reason. The working classes as a whole do not realize they are living in a fool's paradise. Now everything is booming on account of the huge sums that are being spent (and often wasted), but it is certain that eventually after the war bad times will come as taxation will be enormous and I think it will be difficult to re-instate all the men that will be discharged from the Army.

I had a very interesting letter from one of my nephews who is on the French Front yesterday. He has just learned the art of Bomb Throwing and had been in the trenches for a good spell. He was delighted to get out as he was covered with Lice, but having had a good bath and clean up he felt much better. A company of Players had also given an entertainment about 20 miles behind the lines. His regiment (the Oxfordshire & Bucks Infantry) drew lots as to who should go, and he was one of the successful ones. They were taken in Motor Buses and had a real good time. Quite a change for them.

November 24 Wednesday There have been persistent rumours the last few days that the enemy are again massing large bodies of troops on the Western front and that they were about to make another attempt to break the Allies' line. I do not think this is likely. I think it is more probable they were thoroughly alarmed by the last battles in September and October and are afraid we should smash their line. It is now generally known that we came within an ace of doing so and it was only the failure to bring up supports that prevented [us] from quite breaking through. The reports from our people both men and officers there are very sanguine, and they feel quite confident when the time comes they will be able to give a good account of themselves. It is quite certain that we are now superior to the enemy in munitions and are able to send two or three shells to their one. The revolution in the manufacture of munitions during the last 4 months has been almost incredible, and even now we have not reached our full output. Not only has the number of factories been much increased but the output has been speeded up in all directions. Thousands and tens of thousands of women and girls have been engaged and are doing as well as the men. Russia is getting huge supplies from Japan.

Thursday November 25 The Greek difficulty seems to have been allayed as the embargo on Greek Shipping has been withdrawn. The German Austrian Army has over run nearly the whole of Serbia . . .This Balkan business is an awful tangle and may take some time to straighten out. Russia is reported to have concentrated an army of 400,000 men on the Danube and is only waiting to come to an agreement with Roumania before going to the help of Serbia.

November 26 Friday Very little news to-day. Events, except artillery duels, continue very quiet in France. The men are now coming home on 3 or 4 days furlough in batches of 50 at a time.

I saw letters to-day from one of [my] nephews who is at the Dardanelles with the Bucks Yeomanry. They are having a very rough time, not so much from the enemy as from the climate and from dysentery. He says that of the men who originally went out with the regiment only 25 per cent are now available. The men out there do not get the same comforts as those in France. When out of the trenches they have to live in dug outs and these are not at all conducive to health, and from what I can gather the food is not nearly as good as the men get in France.

1915 November 27 Saturday Last night and to-day news has been published of some very stiff fighting in the Persian Gulf campaign. The English Force which has been engaged there against the Turks since last year has had some heavy work and has done very well and is now within about 10 miles of Bagdad. . . .Our losses are given at 2500 wounded. The killed are not yet known. Our men took 1500 Turkish prisoners and made good progress towards Bagdad.

THE DIARY OF JOHN COLEMAN BINDER

This campaign is a very sore point with the Germans as Bagdad has for the last 20 or 30 years been the 'Ultima Thule' of their ambitions and has figured largely in all their dreams of an Eastern Empire. They secured some years since a concession from the Turks to enable them to build a railway to the place. This England withstood for a long time and it was only just before the war that an agreement had been arrived at concerning it. This is now all done with and Germany sees one more of her most cherished ambitions falling to pieces.

Sunday November 28 A very cold winter's day. Snow has fallen heavily in the North and during the last 48 hours we in the South have had sharp frosts 16 degrees [Fahrenheit] yesterday and 15 this morning. Winter has come early this year and we have already had more frost than we did during the whole of last winter.

Men home from the front say it is bitterly cold out there and there have been heavy snowfalls in North France.

I note some curious changes caused by this war, one or two of which I will mention. One is the habit of going to bed earlier. This is caused by the darkening of the lights in the streets which causes many people to remain in their own homes. Many theatres are making the Matinee commencing at 2.30 the chief performance of the day and in some theatres no evening play is held.

Another is the partial breaking down of class distinctions. Both rich and poor, young and old, have a common cause to work for, and this has caused party bonds to give way and all parties from ultra Tories to Socialists are frequently joined together in these efforts. Another effect is the slump in the Publicans' business in these smaller towns. This was bad enough before the war but it is much worse. Most of the young men are away and those that are left have, owing to [the] high price of all commodities, little money to spare in drink. This does not apply to areas in which munitions are being made as there there is any amount of money to be fooled away, and the Board of Control (established under the Defence of the Realm Act) has had to rigorously curtail the hours of opening. In London this week they have announced that all licensed houses will only be allowed to open from 5 am to 7, from --- --- and from 6.30 to 9.30 and that no woman must be served with drink before noon. In a good many instances the separation allowance to a soldier's wife has been a veritable curse to her, and she has now more money than ever she had. Consequently she spends a good deal in liquor.

The congestion of traffic on the Railways is still very bad and I am afraid I cannot see any hope of improvement. A great many of the best of the men have enlisted and it is only with great difficulty that anything like a service can be carried out.

November 29 Monday No important news to-day from any seat of war.

Roumania is said to be preparing to intervene on the side of the Allies. Time will prove.

November 30 Tuesday The drastic order for closing public houses in London came into force yesterday and according to all accounts worked very well. Intoxicants can only be sold from 12.30 to 2.30 and from 6.30 to 9. Non-intoxicants and food can be sold during the usual hours.

Serbia is now almost entirely in the hands of the enemy, but winter has put a stop to the campaign. Great numbers of our troops are being sent from France to Salonica. This is not generally known, but is surmised from the fact that many people have not heard from their sons etc. who are supposed to be in France for some two or three weeks.

A report is current to-day that the old Austrian Emperor is anxious to conclude a separate peace and that the Kaiser is at Vienna endeavouring to dissuade him. The Pope is said to have induced the King of Spain to try to bring this about.

1915 December 1 Wednesday Lord Kitchener arrived back in London yesterday and will be able to place some definite propositions as to the Easter campaign before the Cabinet. Very little is being done in the Dardanelles. I believe we are simply marking time there.

The French government is raising a new loan. About 50 millions are offered in this country. It is offered at 88 per cent and at present will pay 5-12-8 per cent but if the exchange regains its normal position it will pay 6 ¼ per cent. This is a big return.

December 2 Thursday A report is current to-day that a Russian Army has crossed the Danube and is moving through Roumania to attack Bulgaria.

Events in Greece remain very obscure and even now it seems uncertain as to what part she will play in this affair.

A bold stroke by an English Airman yesterday. He dropped a bomb on a German submarine off the Belgian coast and split her in two. She sank at once.

December 3 Friday . . . Germany has now over run practically the whole of Serbia and apparently is about to make a move in another direction either to cope with the Russian Army or to turn on the French and ourselves. I can only hope that we shall have sufficient men out there to cope with the situation. Italy has declared that she intends to lend a hand, and now that Russia is moving we may hope that matters may improve there. At any rate we are certainly better prepared for a winter campaign than Germany is. It is generally understood that the equipment of our men is excellent and that there is no lack of warm clothing, boots etc. Some of the men who have been home lately have come in their sheep skin coats which appear to be very warm and comfortable.

December 4 Saturday The appearance of the Russian Army in Bulgaria is announced with assurance this morning.

Lord Kitchener has resumed control at the War Office. Late to-night a telegram is posted announcing a bad set-back to our forces close to Bagdad. No details are given but the casualties are very heavy, 4500 killed and wounded. A German message says it was owing to the treachery of the Arabs, but we can only wait and see. This is very unfortunate as great hopes had been aroused that Bagdad would soon be in our hands.

December 5 Sunday There is no news from the Persian Gulf this morning.

Looking back over the past week I cannot but think there have been decided movements towards peace by Germany . . . .It is known that she has offered to make a separate peace with Serbia. This has been promptly declined. She has tried this plan with all the Allies except England and in each case has met with a prompt and decided refusal. England France Russia Italy Serbia Japan and Montenegro are now united in a treaty not to treat for peace without the full consent of each and all of them. This has greatly disheartened Germany who thought to divide them up. . . .I can only say that firmly definitely and without fear of contradiction that they will meet with no response . . until the conditions laid down by our Premier at the beginning of the war are fulfilled and that is that Germany shall not have one inch of territory belonging to other nations which she now occupies, and that compensation has been accorded to Belgium and other countries for the injuries which they have suffered.

. . . Some people who are informed think [the breaking point] must come next spring. Myself I cannot think this. I am afraid that next spring and summer will see some great fighting, and that at any rate we shall see no serious peace negotiations until next autumn at the earliest. I hope I may be mistaken but this is my own conclusion . . .

1915 December 6 Monday The reverse at Bagdad is quite confirmed this morning. The Turks had been much re-inforced and consequently got the upper hand. Our troops had to fight a severe rear guard action but according to advices to-night are back at their fortified camp some 80 or 100 miles from Bagdad.

Economy is quite the order of the day, and is being preached on all sides. I am afraid there is much more preaching than practising. It suggested to-day that the Cabinet Ministers may relinquish 1/3rd of their salaries to set an example to the Nation. I think this would be a wise thing to do. Reports received from all centres where trade is good confirm the belief that money is being spent in a most reckless way by the wage earners, especially in furniture, plants/ pianos? cheap jewellery and expensive food. A great effort is to be made to try to get them to save and various schemes have been suggested. The most promising one

THE DIARY OF JOHN COLEMAN BINDER

according to my idea is that house-to-house visitations should be made early in each week to collect the savings. I believe this would be the best way. Ninety per cent of the wage earners do not know the way to save, and unless they place their ready cash where they cannot get it at a moments notice they squander it.

A plan like this is being adopted in Birmingham where almost incredible sums are being paid in wages.

December 7 Tuesday Great efforts are being made to ensure the success of Lord Derby's enrolment scheme. It closes definitely on Saturday. Personally I am not very sanguine as to the result. I believe it has gone well in some places but not in others. No indications as to the result have been allowed to be published, so at present it is all guess work. If it should not succeed I do not see any alternative but some system of modified compulsion.

Very little war news to-day except the daring exploits of a submarine in the Sea of Marmora. This vessel managed to slip in there and during two days caused havoc amongst the Turkish shipping.

Reports from both Russia and France are very meagre. In both countries it seems almost as if winter had put a stop to the warfare. In Belgium all along the Yser the floods are very bad and the Germans have been obliged to abandon some of their trenches.

American Congress meets to-day. The President's speech is eagerly awaited in almost every country. He is expected to take a strong line, especially towards the plotting and threats of German agents in the States. These men have done all they could to stir up strife, and almost carried on war against the State. There have been continual explosions in works where munitions are being made for the Allies, and other acts of a like description. Some of the culprits have been caught and tried and sentenced to imprisonment. It was proved without doubt these plots were being engineered by persons connected with the German Embassy and on Monday last the German Government was requested to recall them. Yesterday an explanation of this procedure was asked for by the Germans and to-day the Americans reply by <u>ordering</u> the men to clear out. Temper is rising on both sides and a quarrel may yet come in spite of all President Wilson's efforts to prevent it. I think he has gone as far as any man who has any backbone can go.

December 8 Wednesday The American President spoke very strongly yesterday and urged Congress to take steps to put a stop to all this plotting and doings in the States. I think America has her hands full just now as well as we have.

December 9 Thursday [Set backs and very cold weather in Serbia].

The result of the collection for the Red Cross on "Our Day" which I mentioned as being held in October throughout the Empire is published to-day. It amounted to £800,000 on that day alone. It is indeed marvellous where all the money comes from.

1915 December 10 Friday The debate in the German Parliament on Peace last night did not disclose anything new and as far as I can see will lead to nothing. Indeed I think it is all a 'put up' affair. The principal thing in it was that as usual 'England is the sole enemy. She alone is the cause of the war, and she alone wants it to continue' and all this kind of nonsense.

The position of the Allies in Serbia to-day looks very threatening. The Bulgar German troops have been trying to envelop them but did not succeed. They withdrew to other positions after a good deal of fighting and are now close on Greek territory. I think these Greeks will only be deterred from attacking them by an overwhelming display of force both on sea and land. Troops are being sent there in large numbers but very little is said in the daily papers about it.

December 11 Saturday A good deal of anxiety is felt about the position of our men in Serbia or Greece. Probably they will be able to retire to a safe position as there is now [no] object in remaining in Serbia. Of the Serbian Army about 250,000 are still in fighting form, and it is proposed to give these time to recuperate and re-arm before much else is done. A situation of great danger would arise if the Bulgars should follow the Allies on to Greek territory as the Greeks and Bulgars are sworn enemies. Any moment may bring dramatic moves in this Balkan business. To a looker on it looks like a vast seething pot.

To-day is the last day under the Derby enrolment. Extraordinary scenes have been witnessed all over the country this week as hundreds of thousands of men have flocked to be enrolled. In many cases they have not been able to be medically examined but have simply been enrolled and the examination will be taken later. The principal time is in the evening and in many places the offices have been kept open all night to deal with the rush. The place of enrolment here is the Victoria Hall and each night this week scores of men have come forward. An order issued this afternoon from London announces that men will be able to enrol up to 12 o'clock tomorrow (Sunday) night.

Whether this scheme will meet the requirements of the Government cannot be known for a few days until all the returns have been completed. Up to the present I do not suppose there are half a dozen men in the country who have any real knowledge of the facts.

Lord Derby hopes to place the full figures before the Cabinet by Wednesday and there is to be a debate on Recruiting in the House during next week when it [is] said that some declaration will be made on the subject.

I think the great majority who have now enlisted have done so with the genuine desire to save the nation from conscription and because they realize that by no other means than this could it be done. Much as this war is hated and deplored it is clearly seen by the bulk of the nation that [it] is no time for peace at present. The strain is great and is increasing day by day, and I firmly believe that as regards the inconvenience and dislocation of civil life it will be much worse. Trade is hampered and restricted on all sides. The railways are congested and civilian goods traffic is very much in arrears. A firm of Millers at Hull (Ranks) told me this week that they were quite unable to get railway wagons without great difficulty. They had been very short of them for some time, but one day last week they had 300 sent them. All of these (each holding from 6 to 10 tons) were loaded and dispatched within 24 hours.

In many other industries similar conditions prevail and when these new men are called up I think matters will become worse.

It is generally thought that the first groups i.e. young unmarried men of 19 to 22 or 23 will be called to the colours directly after Christmas.

December 12 Sunday   A typical December day. Sharp frost and snow this morning.

Two Oundle men have been killed this week, one named Fox and the other Leveret.

Last week I enrolled as a member of the Special Constables. They have been asked to guard the three Railway Bridges here (Fotheringhay, Black Bridge and Cherrymill) during two nights each week. One cannot see the necessity of this at all as conditions are quite normal, but it is possible the Army people have some information which they cannot disclose. I should have [thought] it would have been quite sufficient if they had been guarded at the time munition or troop trains were on the move. However it is little we civilians of 50 or so can do and one does not like to back out at the first time he is asked to do anything.

Christmas is approaching, but one hears very little about it except so far as it concerns the men at the front. It will be a sad and sorrowful Christmas to thousands in this country and indeed every war country. The Germans Censors took elaborate precautions not to allow details of their Peace Debate except such as they wished to be sent over here, but in spite of this it has come out through Amsterdam and Copenhagen there were riots and other disorder after it.

Food prices in some directions continue to rise, but the Meat trade is not so dear, although there has been no general reduction in the retail prices.

It is a curious fact that in spite of all difficulties sugar is cheaper to-day in England than anywhere else in the world.

A contested election, almost the first since the war commenced has taken place this week in the Cleveland division of Yorks. The Election which was fought on the restrictions imposed by the Government on the liquor traffic resulted in favour of the man who supported these restrictions by a majority of 6000. Clear evidence this of what the country thinks about them.

THE DIARY OF JOHN COLEMAN BINDER

December 13 Monday   The news from Serbia this morning is bad. The Allies have had to retreat being outnumbered by 10 to 1 and owing to bad roads had to abandon 8 guns. There was no rout or anything of that kind. The battle was furious but the retirement was quite orderly and was covered by 3 Irish regiments who suffered very severely. They were the Munster and Dublin Fusiliers and Connaught Rangers.

The recruiting campaign finished last night and it now remains to be seen what success has been gained and what proportion of unmarried men have enlisted. It has been fairly well organised and Lord Derby is to [be] congratulated on the great energy and tact he has shown, but some bad mistakes which might have been avoided. I understand that 90 per cent of the unmarried men here who were eligible have joined.

December 14 Tuesday   The Allies after due consideration decided to hold Salonika at all costs. It is said the Austro- Germans will advance against them but the Bulgarians will not cross the frontier.

The persistent reports as to the concentration of the Germans in France still continue, and it looks as if they intended to make a big fight.

December 15   Rumour says the Recruiting Scheme has been a success. The Labour Party say they are quite satisfied with the result, although no announcement can be made after a few days.

Attention is being turned once again to Egypt. The Turks assisted by the Germans are making preparations to attack the Suez Canal. Travellers coming that way say that thousands of men English and Egyptians are throwing up earthworks to protect it.

December 16 Thursday   To-day is Serbian Flag Day here and the Serbian Flag is being worn by almost every person. A Whist Drive in aid of the funds was held last night in the Victoria Hall. The amount realized yesterday and to-day is £87.

The Red Cross work room at the Victoria Hall is open every Wednesday from 10 am to 7 pm. A good deal of work has been done for the wounded soldiers. This will [be] sent to the County depot at Northampton and is being used at the different hospitals in the County.

All the patients have been removed from Berry Wood Asylum to other Asylums and it will be used as a Hospital for the wounded. It is hoped to get it ready early in the new year and a thousand or 1100 can be nursed there.

Sir John French has relinquished the command of the Army in France and will be in command of the Forces in England. He is getting on towards 70 and the strain on him during the last 18 months must have been very great. He has done well in France.

Sir Douglas Haig, a man who has made a name for himself during this war will succeed to the command. He is 54.

Events are very quiet all along the lines in France just now. They cannot very well be otherwise. The mud is frightful. My nephew writing home the other [day] said the men had to <u>pull</u> each other out of the trenches as they are quite knee deep in mud.

1915 December 17 Friday   Quite a new departure in finance is announced to-day. Five year Exchequer Bonds bearing interest at 5 % are to be issued. They will be in 100£ and multiples of the same. They are issued at par and this should be an attractive investment.

December 18 Saturday   A Proclamation is posted to-day calling up for service Group 2 to 5 under the new scheme. Individual notices will be sent to each man as to when and where he will have to report himself and all under these groups will be embodied by Jan 20 1916. Group 1 is men between 18 and 19 who have been enrolled but are not liable to active service until they reach the age of 19.

Curiosity is much excited as to the actual numbers which have enrolled under the Derby or Group scheme and the Prime Minister is expected to disclose this in the House on Tuesday. Recruiting has been resumed under ordinary conditions and some thousands have joined this week.

. . . Immense quantities of all army supplies are being made in this county for the Allies. Northampton and district are now very busy on an order for a million pairs of boots for the Italians and as soon as this is completed there are other orders awaiting them.

December 19 Sunday Very little news again to-day from any war area.

Every body who has friends at the front has been busy during the past week sending out Christmas Parcels. The last day for doing this was Thursday. At first 11lbs in weight could be sent, but since Nov 1 no parcel must weigh more than 7lb and the postage is 1/- to France and about 2/2 to the Dardanelles and Greece. Usually a train load of these parcels are sent to the Army each evening but it will take many trains to carry all the Christmas Gifts.

The Postal Authorities will be much handicapped this year, owing to the number of men who have enlisted. Women are being employed in large numbers (in Northampton there are now 10 women delivering letters) and the number of deliveries is being reduced.

This labour business is causing much inconvenience and delay in all trades and it is difficult to get many articles especially those in which much labour is required to make them. Such articles as string, coiou [coir] mats and matting, sacks etc are difficult to get. Glass bottles (great quantities came from Belgium) are also very scarce.

Mechanical toys which were imported from Germany are at a great premium. The dolls are perhaps a little better than the crude affairs of last Christmas, but even now we cannot produce the porcelain faces for these in England. Germany seems to have had a monopoly of them.

Labour is also scarce amongst farmers but the War Office have made it possible for men to be allowed to come home from some of the depots to help in threshing work. There are about 30 available for this at Northampton now.

12,000 men of the Middlesex regiment are coming to Northampton for training.

1915 December 20 Monday There seems to be a vague idea that the end of the war is not very distant although I cannot myself share this view. Sir John French in bidding 'Goodbye' to his Army in France refers to-day to the 'glorious end to heroic efforts not far distant' and Lord Derby yesterday made a remark to the same effect.

The Expedition to Gallipoli or the Dardanelles has been abandoned and the men have been transferred to Egypt and Salonica. This is announced this afternoon. This affair has been the costly and bloody mistake of the war on our side and there is a good deal of blame attaching to somebody, but at present the general public does not know who it is. Mr Churchill said   (and he should know) that it was a risk and a gamble. So it was and a most disastrous one too. The strategy was right but the tactics were bad.

We shall have much jubilation in Germany over this affair.

I heard to-day from one of my nephews who has been in this expedition (he is in the Bucks Yeomanry). He says the sufferings of the men have been terrible. He himself has been very ill (has not been wounded) and has lost his finger nails. They are thankful to be back in Egypt.

Of his regiment there are only 20 per cent of the original members now left.

I have to-night been appointed a member of the Local Tribunal for hearing appeals for exemption from Army Service. These appeals can be made by men who are considered by employers to be indispensable to them. There are also various other reasons for which they may appeal.

December 21 Tuesday The Germans launched a gas attack against our lines at Ypres yesterday, but our artillery dropped 40,000 shells on to them in 30 minutes and this in some measure drove the gas back on to the enemy.

A further announcement late last night modifies somewhat the affair in the Dardanelles. We have abandoned Suvla Bay and the Anzac region, but intend to hold fast on to the Kuthia lines. From this it is clear that no further attempt will be made to capture Constantinople but we shall prevent Turkey receiving any supplies by sea.

THE DIARY OF JOHN COLEMAN BINDER

The withdrawal was most skilfully managed. The enemy were quite unaware of what was being done, and no action had to be fought to cover the embarkation. It was most cleverly done by the Navy and much credit is due to them; only about 20 lives were lost.

A fight is reported between the Bulgars and the Greeks.

December 22 Wednesday   A keen debate last night on the Army in the House. Reading between the lines of the Prime Minister's speech one can see that the response of the unmarried men to the recruiting appeal has not [been] altogether satisfactory, and the pledge was renewed that these should be called up first and compulsion in some way was foreshadowed.

The 8th Northants Regiment are under orders for Serbia. The officers and men have been for 24 hours to say 'Goodbye'. The regiment was raised 12 months since and has been quartered in Cornwall and lately at Colchester. Amongst its officers is M. Watson son of Mr Watson Cashier at Barclays Bank. He is an old Oundle School Boy.

December 23 Thursday   There has been strong action by the French along their lines in Alsace the last two days. They have attacked the German trenches and have captured 1200 prisoners and 21 officers.

Last night 80 men who had been interned in Germany since the war commenced arrived back in England. They were principally men who were sailors and also men who were residents in Germany. Their treatment has been very harsh and they declare that they were only kept alive by the food which had been sent to them from their friends here. They brought some of their prison food back with them and it is said to be abominable. The bread is principally potatoes. They say that great depression exists in Germany and that peace is much desired amongst the people, but I doubt if the leaders want it.

1915 December 24 Friday   The Kaiser is reported to-day to be unwell and that ear specialists have been summoned to Berlin. Rumours crop up from time to time that he suffers from a malignant growth in the ear which so affects him that he has to be placed under restraint. This may only be a canard but at the same time it may explain some of his mad actions.

To-day the Germans announce that they intend to be in Salonica by January 15th ! !

December 25 Saturday   To-day Christmas Day and what a satire on Christianity. The whole continent of Europe (with few exceptions) a good part of Asia and Africa plunged in this frightful war.

The day for England is a very gloomy one from the point of weather conditions. It has rained nearly all day and has been very dark. Almost everybody has been indoors. Christmas this year has been shorn of much of its usual rejoicing. It is generally recognised that it is not a fit or suitable time for merry making situated as we are in such a terrible crisis.

Trade is fairly good and where munition work is being carried on there is a great quantity of money to be spent but there is no real heart in it at all. So many homes are desolate and if they have not lost anyone in 99 cases out of 100 they have relatives who are in the fighting line.

Amusements are very much curtailed and where they are held it is chiefly in aid of War funds. Hunting is almost in abeyance and is followed by very few. What is done is chiefly for keeping down the foxes but this is not done very thoroughly and there are long and deep complaints from the farmers as to the damage they cause.

Enormous quantities of food and other things have been sent to the men at the front this week by their friends at home, and also from other organisations. One paper (the Daily News) collected £24,000 to supply them with Plum Puddings. This helped but was not sufficient. We have now 1,250,000 men in the fighting lines.

The men in France are sending home many souvenirs made in France. They are dainty and exquisite work and are done in silk. They usually cost 6d or 10d.

December 26 Sunday   We are quite cut off from the outside world yesterday and to-day. No newspapers have been published and only a few of them will be published tomorrow.

119

DAY BY DAY THROUGH THE GREAT WAR

It is a much brighter and better day to-day and people seem more cheerful.

December 27 Monday There has been no informal Christmas truce along the lines this year, but fighting has been continuous although not very violent except in the French section in Alsace.

The King sent a cheery message to the soldiers in which he spoke of "The Goal drawing nearer into sight". We all hope that it may be so but I am doubtful.

Great efforts are being made to find labour for the new munitions factories which have been erected by the Government. Eighty thousand skilled workmen are required to man them and the Minister of Munitions Mr Lloyd George has been addressing meetings during the last few days, urging the Trades Unionists to relax their rules so that women may be able to do some of the less skilled work.

There is a minority of Trades Unionists who I am afraid are so blind and stupid that they continue to place these Trades Unions before the needs of their country and are saying that these Unions shall be first and everything else second. They are chiefly Socialists of the extreme type but nevertheless have a good deal of influence amongst a certain class. A violent gale to-day. Much damage done.

December 28 Tuesday A smart skirmish took place on Christmas Day close to Bagdad at Kut-el-Amara. The Turks lost about 900. Our casualties were about 190.

The Indian Troops are being removed from France. Their destination is not stated but most likely it is Egypt where preparations are being made to repel the invasion which the Germans say they intend to make.

1915 December 29 Wednesday A step of great and grave importance is announced to-day. The Cabinet have by a majority of votes decided to ask Parliament to make military service compulsory. This step has been caused by the number of young unmarried men who have refused to enrol. What the number is is not at present declared, and what form conscription will take is still not decided.

December 30 Thursday The Conscription business is almost the sole topic of conversation amongst all classes. Christmas has speedily been forgotten and all thoughts are now turned again to the war. On the whole there is not much outcry against conscription at present, but I imagine if force is actually used to compel some of these men to serve there will be a good deal of disturbance and besides this these who will be forced to go will be of very little use as fighters.

The Austro-German Bulgaria Army has not moved against Salonica at present. The lines around it which extend roughly about 70 miles are being strengthened every day and it seems probable that great events may take place there. At any rate it will be a great menace to any German Army which may try to invade Egypt.

December 31 Friday The last day of the old Year. A year in which we have faced many trials and many difficulties and a year which has brought many disappointments and much sorrow and suffering, but also much that we have to be thankful for. Through God's mercy our enemies have never been able to set foot on our shores, and even if they have come over with their airships it has only been by stealth and under cover of the night. In looking round to-day and comparing our position with that at the beginning of the year I see some decided and great changes. I think I see a more united and self-reliant nation, a nation less given to brag and show, but a nation and an empire that has made up its mind to endure to the end and through God's mercy to conquer.

I think I see in every class a desire to sacrifice themselves and to do what is possible to, carry this thing through. I am now writing of the vast majority of this nation, of course there are some who are content to do nothing and to hinder other people, but happily there are not many of them.

In all classes I see a decided longing for Peace, but even the least well read can see that at present a lasting Peace cannot be made and they are willing with others to carry this burden. Looking round all over the vast theatres of war and considering it in all its varied aspects I am afraid that the end will not be next year. This is my opinion. I may be wrong. I hope I am. That Germany desires peace and that she would like it on her terms is patent to all of us. I admit that she has some reason for her optimism. Her armies stand victorious in many countries and she is now at the high water mark of her ambition, and she

THE DIARY OF JOHN COLEMAN BINDER

is puzzled to know why <u>we</u> do not ask for peace. This is a superficial view. Her victories are patent to us all but her defeats which are none the less real are not so apparent. First is her defeat by our Fleet. That is the outstanding feature of this war. . . .The second great factor is Germany's decline in food and manufactures and her rotten system of finance. Each of these is playing a great part in this struggle.

We have made mistakes and huge mistakes and if we have the sense to learn by them we shall do better in the future.

The bloody Dardanelles business has been an awful fiasco and has only [been] redeemed to some extent by the successful withdrawal from Suvla Bay and Anzac.

The battles of Neuve Chapelle and Loos were victories in one sense and defeats in another.

Rumour says that Sir John French was largely responsible in both these actions for their failure. It is said that he would not allow the divisional Commands to control the Reserves and in consequence of this they were not at hand when required and hence his retirement from the Command.

The year ends to-day almost as it began with a naval disaster. HMS Natal has been sunk in harbour by an internal explosion. Three hundred are missing. Without doubt it is the work of the enemies' spies.

1916 Saturday January 1   A day of Storm. One of the worst gales of recent years has been sweeping over the land to-day accompanied by terrific squalls of rain. Letters received from France say the trenches are awful. They have had much rain there.

. . . . News is posted this afternoon that a P&O Liner has been sunk in the Mediterranean (probably by an enemy submarine or a mine). I should think they will now send them round by the Cape, as most other countries are now doing. Two Japanese liners have recently been sunk in the same sea.

January 2 Sunday   A day of Intercession and Prayer throughout the whole Empire. Every Creed and Denomination is uniting in this act. No news is posted to-day.

The Conscription business is likely to become very acute this week when Parliament meets again on Tuesday. I see signs of a gathering storm especially in Labour quarters and unless   this question is very carefully handled it will split the country into two warring camps.

The chief objection raised by the Labour people (and I am inclined to think it is true) is that Conscription will be used by the governing classes as a weapon to crush them. It is almost certain that Compulsion once placed on the Statute Book will not be removed in this generation.

Affairs locally go on much as usual. The School workshops are still working hard at munitions and considerable additions are being made to their machinery during these holidays to enable them to turn out better and more efficient work.

The Local Tribunal (in the Rural district) meets this week to hear appeals. I believe they have about 40.

Severe restrictions with regard to Lighting come into force with the New Year especially as to vehicles. Every vehicle (including perambulators) must carry two lights. No motor may have more than two and these only of a subdued kind.

January 3 Monday   Four hundred lives were lost by the sinking of the P&O Liner Persia. She was torpedoed without a moments warning and is reported to have sunk in about 10 minutes. Americans were on board and it is reported officially that one of them who is American Consul at Aden was drownded. As usual America protests!! And the President is said to be considering the matter!!! and refuses to say anything. Whenever will the United States have the courage to act and not to talk. She is losing the respect of the whole world by her cowardly ways. I believe much of it lies with the President, if they had had a stronger man he would have struck before this and talked less.

January 4 Tuesday Some very severe fighting is taking place along the South Russian lines. . . .Another German Colony (the Cameroons) has been about demolished and the capture of its capital (Yaunde) is announced to-day.

DAY BY DAY THROUGH THE GREAT WAR

January 5 Wednesday To-night the Conscription Bill is to be introduced into the Commons and we shall then know what the Government propose to do.

A proclamation is posted to-day calling up Groups 6, 7, 8 and 9. They will have to join the colours early in February.

1916 January 6 Thursday The Conscription Bill was brought in last night and met with a mixed reception. All unmarried men between 19 and 40 who have not attested will be compelled to do so. According to the report presented by Lord Derby there are 650,000 but this is a fictitious figure as from it would have to be deducted men who are starred, the indispensable, and the unfit (i.e. physically) This would certainly reduce the numbers to about 250,000. Is it worth upsetting the voluntary principle for this number [?] I don't think it is. There are also exemptions allowed viz Ministers of all Denominations. (I cannot see why they are exempt) and Quakers, although these will be called to the colours and assigned other work. I am afraid that it looks very much as if we should have a General Election over this business before it is carried. This would [be] the worst that could happen to plunge the whole country into the turmoil of an election during the war. Besides it is manifestly unfair as the Register is already two years old and an enormous number of men are away on Army Service.

The Labour Party met this afternoon in London and decided by about 2 to 1 to oppose the Bill.

The Russians report to-day a small advance, but I do not think we can look for anything very decisive there at present.

January 7 Friday To-day we have published the full dispatches relating to the Dardanelles, giving an account of the operations from June to October. They are all from Sir Ian Hamilton, the General in command and give a very clear and explicit account of the operations and show where the cause of the failure lies. We came almost within a measurable distance of success and the blame for want of it must be laid partly on Hamilton himself but chiefly on General Stopford and his two Brigadiers.

The bravery of the troops both Australian and English is simply marvellous, and I think if any thing deserves especial notice it is the charge of the English Yeomanry at Suvla Bay.

I cannot think that Sir Ian Hamilton is without blame. When he arrived at Suvla Bay from his headquarters on Aug. 8 he should have taken supreme command.

The Conscription Bill was carried in the House last night by a majority of 298. It is quite possible that some compromise may be arranged before it is brought into operation. Already Lord Derby's scheme has been re-opened and men can now enlist again under the Group system.

January 8 Saturday Strong and persistent rumours have been in circulation this week concerning the Kaiser's health. It is officially given out from Berlin that he is suffering only from cold, but rumours say that it is cancer in the throat and that already an operation or operations have been performed. If this is the case the end is inevitable sooner or later, for to-day there is no permanent cure for this dread disease. I imagine that whether he lives or dies it will make but very little difference to this war. His heir the Crown Prince is a most detestable man, and a greater fire-eater than his father, and besides this the German people are in the grip of a military caste and there can be no permanent peace until this caste has been shattered.

The Russians are making great efforts to capture Czernowitz, a city in the Bukhovina close on the Roumanian border . . . .

There is some talk to-day of a Referendum on the Conscription Bill but I do not think it will come to anything.

General Stopford has asked for an inquiry into the whole question of the Suvla Bay Landing.

January 9 Sunday Reports late last night say that fierce fighting has broken out in some American cities between Austrians and that serious loss of life has taken place.

The second groups of Conscripts will have to join the colours on Feb 20. They are men from 23 to 26. The first groups received their official papers to-day.

THE DIARY OF JOHN COLEMAN BINDER

I am quite sure the labour problem will become very acute. It is impossible to secure a man in any trade or business and as these new groups are called the difficulty will be much increased.

Crime is almost non-existent in the county to-day. At the quarter sessions this week at Leicester, Peterborough and Northampton there was not a single person for trial.

Wheat continues to rise in price and 60/- has been paid for it at Peterboro yesterday. Bread is raised to 8d per 4lb loaf tomorrow here. The London price is 9d.

Public work is very slow now as all Public Bodies are only marking time. The Government has forbidden the issue of all new Loans consequently work has ceased.

The Oundle Board of Guardians in common with many other Boards decided on Wednesday last to hold monthly instead of fortnightly meetings.

Germany has during this week been trying to get Russia and Japan to treat for Peace, but each of them has declined and say that they intend to fight it out to the end.

January 10 Monday At 9.40 last night the Press Bureau officially announced that the whole of the Dardanelles Peninsula had been evacuated. It was well and cleverly done without the loss of a single life and all stores were also brought off. So ends this ill-fated ill-starred adventure. From its very inception I was always most doubtful as to its success as will be seen if this diary is referred to. It has been marked by the splendid heroism of the men and by the incapacity of some of the leading officers. The name of Australia and New Zealand will be associated with it for all time, for upon them has fallen chiefly the brunt of this affair. There is one redeeming feature in this expedition and that is the way in which the evacuation has been managed. Not a man has been lost, no battle has had to be fought and only a few worn out guns were abandoned (One ship was sunk probably to which I will refer later). The Turks were bluffed once, and again allowed themselves to be bluffed. The Government I think are to be commended that having made up their minds (they were a long time doing so) to withdraw they did it promptly and everyone seems thankful that we have got away from this horrible place. It is generally assumed the bulk of the men have been sent to Salonica and Egypt.

The loss is announced this morning of the battleship King Edward VII. Where she sunk is not told but most likely it was during the withdrawal from the Dardanelles. She struck a mine and had to be abandoned. Every man was brought off which is much to be thankful for. Of course the loss of the ship is great but we shall be able to replace that.

The furious battles along the south Russian lines still continue. . . .The Russians appear to be well equipped especially with artillery. A lot of guns have been sent to them from this country. They were bought in America. Some men who come from close here have gone with them.

January 11 Tuesday There has been a sharp battle in the Bagdad campaign and the Turks have received a set-back.

Very little news is now coming through from our own lines in France but all letters and also the men home on furlough say that at present it is impossible to do anything as the weather conditions are so bad and the mud is awful.

In Alsace the last few days the French have been attacked by the enemy and some sharp fighting has taken place. . . .

It seems as if the Country had made up its mind to accept Conscription and I think the Bill will go through without much opposition. Judging from the comments in the German Press this has caused them much annoyance. This decision is I think good in one way as it is an evidence both to our allies and to our enemies that we are determined to fight this was out to the end and are prepared to make great sacrifices to do so.

1916 January 12 Wednesday Some anxiety is felt for the troops against Bagdad. The relieving force has not reached them, and the Turks are pressing them hard.

DAY BY DAY THROUGH THE GREAT WAR

There is no cessation in the Russian offensive in the Batshina. These battles have at present prevented the Austro- Germans from advancing to Salonica. They are constantly sending out statements that they intend to do so. I think these Balkan people are all rather alarmed (i.e. the Turks and Bulgarians) at the proceedings of the Germans. They seem as if they had determined to stay in the Balkans and the Turks are afraid lest they should seize Constantinople. Once they assumed control there the Turks are aware they could not be got rid of without much trouble.

January 13 Thursday The Conscription Bill was passed in the House last night by 439 to 29 so there is no doubt that it will now become law. There are not many here whom it will affect and these will have the chance to join voluntarily before the act comes into operation. They will also have the right to appeal. It is probable that about 5000 men will shortly be billeted at Wellingborough. Northampton has now about 12,000. There are very few at Peterborough but a large number at Bedford.

Berrywood Asylum is nearly ready to receive the wounded. It will provide accommodation for about 1100 patients and the people in the County i.e. ladies are working to equip it with the necessary articles such as sheets, bed jackets etc.

The patients (i.e. lunatics) have been sent to other Asylums in Derbyshire, Lincolnshire etc.

January 14 Friday One of the tragedies of the war has been taking place this week and that is the over-running of the small state of Montenegro by the Austrians who to-day have occupied its capital. It is easy to cast blame, and one does not know what is behind the scenes but it does really seem that the Allies have been very much to blame in allowing this to take place, besides it is a great blow at the naval position of Italy in the Adriatic, especially as the enemy will now have the use of the harbour of Cetinje.

January 15 Saturday The meetings of Local Tribunals to deal with claims for exemption from Army Service are now being held in all parts of the country. There is such a long list of men who are 'starred' as being indispensable and can claim to be put back for the present that I am afraid that the numbers will fall short of what is expected. I think these lists will have to be revised and the net will have to be drawn closer or many men will slip through. We hold our first meeting of the Oundle Urban Tribunal on Tuesday next at the Council Offices St.Osyth's Lane, but there are only two disputed cases under the first four groups.

The Rural Local Tribunal meet on Monday at the Board Room at the Workhouse. Their area being much larger they have more cases to deal with. I believe there are about 20 cases down for hearing.

Most contradictory reports are in circulation as to the Kaiser's illness. From Berlin the German Government have issued a statement in which they say (as they naturally would) that he is only suffering from a 'harmless boil', but unofficial reports coming from neutral countries such as Denmark, Holland and Spain (which country is in close touch with Germany) declare without doubt that it is cancer in the throat and that the larynx will have to be removed. This may prolong life, but if it is cancer the end is as certain as tomorrow's sunrise, for science has at present discovered no remedy for this dread disease, although hundreds of thousands of pounds has been spent on research.

January 16 Sunday. Some of the Yeomanry are at home again to-day for the week-end. They look very worn and war -strained, but on the whole look very fit. They are doing trench work but still have their horses with them, which of course are some miles behind the lines.

The second regiment of Northants Yeomanry which was raised at Towcester and has been quartered at Luton for some months is now under orders and will sail for Egypt on Wednesday. A third regiment is being formed and the Depot is at Towcester.

English wheat has remained at about 60/- during this week, but foreign is dearer and maize has risen to almost a prohibitive price. It is now quoted at 51 /- to 52/- in Lynn, which means 54/- at this station. All feeding stuffs are extremely dear. The millers quote sharps @ £11 per ton. The pre-war price was about £6. There is not much change in Meat. Beef is a little dearer again just now. Pork is about 10/- to 10/6 per 14lb.

Farm labour is becoming scarce and yesterday the War Committee (a body created by the Board of Agriculture) meeting at Northampton, acting on the advice of the Board, decided to make a thorough canvass to see what labour is required and also to ascertain what female labour could be acquired.

1916 January 17 Monday Hot fighting continues along the Russian lines, but St Petrograd says "There is nothing fresh to report". This is the usual Russian way to conceal their movements.

A curious and comic incident occurred at the end of last week. Von Papen a German attaché who had been bundled home from America on account of his plotting and stirring up of sedition and whose safe passage had been guaranteed by the English Government came into Falmouth on a neutral vessel and was fool enough to bring with him most incriminatory letters and documents. They were of course seized by the detectives and some of them are published to-day. They throw a very clear light on the way in which money has been used by the German Embassy in the States to pay people to blow up the Munition Works and ships and do all the damage they could to injure us by destroying goods intended for the Allies. America is furious. He must have been a simple fool to carry such documents with him knowing that he would have to put in to an English Port, but I expect he did not expect to have his baggage searched. How galling it must be to the Germans to know that not one of their people can cross the seas without our permission and this in spite of all their vaunted power on the sea.

January 18 Tuesday Not much war news to-day from the front except that the Italians and Austrians have been knocking each other about.

The Conscription Bill got into Committee last night in the House, and there was some keen debating although the Government majorities were overwhelming. The Conscriptionists have carried their point of enrolling men at 18 years old now want them to be called up at once. A very hot debate ensued on this.

January 19 Wednesday There are startling rumours current to-day to the effect that the Montenegro business is all a 'put up' job, and that the King had made a secret Treaty with Austria some two months since. That the Allies were aware of this and of course made no effort to save the State. This may or may not be true.

What was left of the Serbian Army has been transported to the island of Corfu by the Allies to give it rest and to recuperate. It will probably be brought into action again later in the Spring. No attack has at present been made on Salonica by the enemy. General Sarrail, a Frenchman, is in supreme command and it is confidently said that adequate precautions have been made to defend the place. It is certain that the Russian onslaught has taken off the pressure in this quarter. The Russians also are shaking up the Turks in Asia Minor again.

There are rumours that the Germans are preparing to come over with a fleet of Zeppelins as soon as the weather permits.

January 20 Thursday The price of all kinds of food stuffs continues to rise. The principal cause of this is the cost of transport and freights from all parts of the world to this country are enormous, in some instances seven or nine times as much as they were in the pre-war times. For instance, freights for grain from South America have risen to 140 shillings per ton and are still rising. I think some means will have to [be] devised by the Government to deal with this question or goods will rise to famine prices. It is said that not more than 50 per cent of the world's mercantile shipping is available for ordinary transport. The remainder has either been driven off the seas as in the case of Germany and Austria or has been commandeered by the Admiralty for transport purposes.

1916 January 21 Friday The Montenegro affair remains very obscure and it is impossible to form a definite opinion as to what is or has taken place. It is now said that they will still fight the Austrians.

The fighting in Bukhovina between the Russians and the enemy continues with the greatest fury. The Germans have lost very heavily, but according to Petrograd to-day the Russians are quite satisfied with what they have accomplished.

The relief forces going to the aid of our army near to Baghdad have [almost] reached them after a series of engagements. They are now only seven miles away but a considerable force of Turks is opposing them still.

The 1st South African Brigade has arrived in Egypt. They have quite cleared up all their fighting in S. Africa and now going to help us in E. Africa and Egypt.

January 22 Saturday Very little news to-day, that is real war news, except that we have about finished the capture of the Cameroons in West Africa.

The men in the first groups have joined the colours the last few days. There has been no confusion. Each man received a paper telling him where he was to join also the date and hour, and a free railway pass. The men from this County joined at Northampton. They were at once equipped and clothed and received their day's pay. They were not allowed out of barracks that [night] and the next morning were sent to the various depots of the regiments they had chosen to join. As far as possible this privilege was allowed them.

January 23 Sunday A very drastic measure has passed through Parliament this week giving the Board of Trade power to close down any business run by enemy subjects in this country. If this is properly used it will put an end to a good deal of money that has been going to Germany in this way.

We seem just now to be passing through one of those periods of depression which have recurred from time to time during this war. One cannot say what is the cause of it, but on the other hand there is nothing very much to encourage us. I suppose the period of suspense is always more trying than the time of action, and most people are now looking forward to a time of great movements during the coming spring and summer. If these take place it is clear that the losses on both sides will [be] terrible, and it is difficult to see how victory can be gained without these battles. We hear from time to time of the bad economic position of the enemy. Possibly it is true, and we also see that neutral countries are beginning to lose faith in the ultimate victory of the Germans. This is clearly proved by the gradual but persistent and steady fall of the exchange. Most financial experts both in this country and also in neutral countries declare that even if Germany were to prove victorious she is ruined financially. She had built such hopes on a huge war indemnity to be wrested from the Allies that when events began to go against her it upset all her calculations. One cannot say with certainty what is in the future but it seems almost certain that she will never receive a single shilling in hard cash from any one of them.

The new taxes in this country are now being collected and they are enormous. Roughly speaking they are two and a half times as much as they were before the war, and are hitting many people very badly especially those whose income is declared as 'unearned'. It is now beginning to dawn on the general public that we shall have to live a very different life in this country from that to which we have been accustomed and that neither this nor many succeeding generations will be able to afford the luxuries they have been used to during the last 30 or 40 years.

January 24 Monday The first air raid this year took place during Saturday night on the Kentish Coast. An aeroplane came over and dropped some bombs. One man was killed

and 6 women and children injured. This was followed at mid-day yesterday by another raid by a sea plane, which was quickly driven off by our air men. No damage was done. There is a growing demand by the public that if these air raids take place on unfortified places, we should retaliate. Sentiment has been against but I am afraid we shall have to do it. The Germans will [not?] listen to argument. All they fear is force. When the French retaliated last year by raiding Karlsruhe they were furious, but it stopped the raids. They talk about their empire of Blood and Iron. What they want is their iron and other people's blood.

There are rumours that the Government will shortly prohibit the import of all kinds of luxuries. There are two reasons for this. One is to make the nation economise and the other to release more ships for the carrying of necessaries such as grain, sugar etc.

1916 January 25 Tuesday The Germans made a heavy move against the French on the Yser yesterday. 20,000 shells were thrown, the French line was pierced but the enemy was quickly driven out and the losses on both sides were very heavy.

January 26 Wednesday Considerable anxiety is felt for the Forces near to Baghdad. The relief column has not yet reached them. The weather conditions are bad and the Turks are in strong force. Last Sunday a battle took place between the Relief Force and the Turks and our losses are said to be heavy.

THE DIARY OF JOHN COLEMAN BINDER

Yesterday the Germans again tried to pierce the French lines farther south in Artois at Neuville St Warl. Fierce fighting ensued but they were repulsed. It looks as if they intend to make a big fight on the Western front as the weather improves.

No attempt has been made to attack Salonica, but on Monday the allied airmen attacked the enemy's position at Monastir with nearly 50 aeroplanes and did very great damage.

January 27 Thursday The German attacks in France seem to have ceased for the present.

Last night was a great night in the House. Sir Edward Grey defined clearly our position with regard to the blockade of Germany. Much annoyance has been caused to neutrals by the way in which we have held up and seized contraband going to Germany. A good deal has found its way through neutral countries such as Sweden, Holland etc. but still not so much as one would expect, the Navy keeps too sharp a watch, but it is amazing the things that the Germans attempt to smuggle in through the mails. Goods of all descriptions. Only last week 8,000lbs of rubber (of which the Germans are desperately in need) was found in mail bags consigned to one man in Sweden and he would have forwarded it to Germany. Of course it was seized and condemned as a prize. This is only one example, scores of others might be quoted.

Sir Edward Grey re-stated our position in most clear and emphatic terms, and declared that the Allies would never lay down their arms until German Militarism was destroyed.

January 28 Friday An announcement of the greatest importance was made late last night in the House. The Government said that very shortly they intend to prohibit the import of paper making materials (which are very bulky) unmanufactured tobacco, building materials, furniture, wood and some kinds of fruits. This is on account of the shortage of ships and the absolute necessity of increasing the import of grain and other foodstuffs. It is a very drastic step, and I am not quite certain that the remedy will not be worse than the disease. Trade relations are so mixed and delicate that the less Governments interfere with them the better. Already there is an outcry from the tobacco manufacturers in this country who point out that we derive 24,000,000 in taxation from this article.

January 29 Saturday President Wilson of the United States has startled the world to-day. He has declared last night that America was ready to fight and that he did not know what the conditions would be during the coming days. This is taken to be a warning to Germany that the patience of America over the Lusitania and the other like affairs (which are still unsettled) is almost exhausted. Judging as an outsider, I do not see things in this light. I am inclined to see in this latest speech an electioneering move. I think Wilson is becoming aware that on the whole American opinion is decidedly against his pacific policy and as the Presidential Election takes place in November and he will probably be a candidate again, he has taken this step to conciliate public opinion. As I have often said in this diary I do not believe the intervention of America would benefit us very much. She has no army of any account and her fleet is extremely limited for a country of her size. Besides I think the German - American in her own cities is a danger which cannot be lightly disregarded.

The Germans made a big attack on sections of the lines in France and Belgium yesterday, but they gained no advantage, and were driven back into their own lines. One never knows what regiments or divisions take part in their encounters until weeks afterwards and then only from private letters. We have only learned this week that the 6th Northants had a very heavy time of it on Dec 29. They lost 20 men out of their 'A' company by being gassed and taken prisoners and about 40 killed and wounded. This world war is far reaching and I am glad to think that Oundle men are taking their share in every place and climate. To-day I learn that one of them named Streather is out with his regiment on the far distant frontiers of Western Egypt where a force is holding up the hostile Arabs from joining hands with the Turks. There was a severe engagement out there on Christmas Day and another one this week. I believe it is seriously thought that the Turks backed by Germans intend to make an attack on Egypt and a large army is being concentrated there to oppose them. If they do try this it will be a most hazardous affair, as they are bound to cross the Desert to get there.

1916 January 30 Sunday The announcement that the import of certain articles would [be] prohibited was the chief topic of conversation yesterday. Paper is the one that appealed most to the general public as this is an article of such general use, and I think has been very much wasted of late years owing to its cheapness. It will affect all classes. The newspapers to-day hint that their size may be reduced and that possibly the price may be increased from ½d to the old price of 1d. Of course some papers have never gone lower than a penny and have an enormous circulation many of them selling nearly a million a day.

I quite expect that means will be adopted to collect old paper so that it may be re-pulped and used again. The great difficulty will be the transport of it as it is quite certain the railways will be unable to carry it as they are more than congested now.

This week most of the great Banks have been holding their annual meetings, and the speeches of the various Chairmen make most interesting reading. They one and all declare that the enemy is ruined financially and that if the war is prolonged the crash when it does come will be terrific. These men should know what they are talking about and I think we may safely conclude that they are correct in what they say.

The local Tribunals are now dealing with claims for exemption from Army service. There were only two disputed ones in this town in the first four groups. A second meeting is to be held to-morrow night to deal with the next 4 groups. I believe there are 5 cases for hearing. This tribunal cannot exempt a man altogether, it can only give him a release for 10 groups, which means that he will have a respite for about 2 months. He will then be called up again and will have the chance of appealing again.

These men are being quietly called up without any fuss or excitement and are joining the colours so many each day, and are then drafted to various regiments.

The long drawn out Session of Parliament came to a close on Thursday. It has lasted with short intervals from Nov 1914 and I think has been solely occupied with War affairs. A new Session will commence on Tuesday fortnight. I wonder if we shall have an Election in the Autumn.

The reports as to the Kaiser's illness have subsided. It is most difficult to learn the truth about it. A correspondent writing in the Times who saw him lately at Nirk [?] declares that he is an old and broken man.

1916 January 31 Monday Notices are issued to-day calling up attested single men from 27 to 30. They will have to report themselves on Feb 20.

The French report that fierce fighting has been proceeding on their lines for the last 72 hours. The Germans also say the same. They made ten separate attacks on the Allies lines last week, but have made very little gain. The French say that they (the Germans) have lost a whole Division. The dead have been left unburied and the wounded have been left to die. The fiercest fighting has been near to Neuville St. Warl, which has been practically wiped out. It looks as if the enemy mean to force the pace. My own impression is that they are getting desperate, as they can see that time is on our side. Reports from Berlin say that they cannot understand why we have made no response to their "Peace Kites". This is not true. We have answered them but in our own way, by adopting Compulsory Military Service, thus showing them that we intend to fight this out to the last man. Zeppelins were raiding Paris on Saturday night and again yesterday

Since writing the above we have had Zeppelins much nearer home. About 7.30 the police received warning that they had been sighted off the coast at 5 o'clock and were then coming in. The police did not create a panic and as a matter of fact very few people knew that there was any danger but about 9 they received further messages saying that they were coming inland. The few street lamps that were alight were turned out and this led people to think there was something wrong but nothing was seen of them and the night settled down as usual.

February 1 Tuesday The Zeppelins came during the night about 2 o'clock this morning. So war has been very close to us to-day. I myself did not hear it or them, but many people did. They could not be seen as it was very foggy but the noise was very much like a railway train. No bombs were dropped here as at that time there would not be a light to be seen. The Police who were about tell me that it was very low down and quite over the town. Some excitement was caused this morning by these facts but no dismay. Two bombs were dropped near to Islip Furnaces. They were not incendiary bombs. There are no reports in the London morning papers, but reports are coming to hand by word of mouth from various places, and a considerable loss of life was caused. Peterboro, Northampton, Kettering, Wellingboro were all in total darkness, and main lines were stopped running. They appear to have been at Derby, Nottingham, Loughborough, Burton -on-Trent etc. No details of these reports are now allowed to be published. Why this is so nobody appears to know. All the details of the Paris raid are published in the London morning papers. An official announcement is issued to-night giving an account. It is said this has been by far the largest raid yet attempted. Six Zeppelins came over and bombs were dropped in six counties. 59 people were killed and 101 injured. This is not quite accurate as no mention of bombs being dropped in this County as they certainly were at Islip. London does not appear to have been touched.

February 2 Wednesday We have to-day Berlin's account of the raid. To show how difficult it is for these Zeppelins to locate where they are or have been I may mention that they claim to have been to Liverpool and Manchester when as a matter of fact they were nowhere near these places. The 'Black Country' suffered severely. Birmingham was their object (or one of their objects) but it was almost in total darkness and no doubt they mistook the glare of the blast furnaces in Staffordshire for that place.

One of the most curious and dramatic incidents in the war comes to hand this morning. For the last week great anxiety has been felt for the safety of the Elder Dempster liner "Appam" homeward bound from West Africa carrying about 300 people (including crew). She had almost been posted as missing, as nothing had been heard of her since Jan 18th except that one of her boats had been picked up. About midday yesterday she put into New York flying the German ensign! ! and in charge of a German prize crew of eleven men. She had been captured by a German Raider off the coast of Madeira and as it was absolutely impossible to take her to a German Port they had run across to America. Where this raider came from is at present a mystery. She appears to have fought several actions and sunk some merchantmen, but I guess now that she is once discovered her career will not last very long. What will become of the "Appam" remains to be seen, as it raises very nice points of international law. The Passengers will soon come home.

People coming in to-day report that they heard the Zeppelins in all directions chiefly between 7 and 9 in this district and in a few cases they were seen, so it was evident they missed us when coming in and passed over here on their way as they came from the North West and were going East. The Pheasants were much upset by the noises and were 'clucking' all night. They seem to possess a very acute sense of hearing.

Many of the blast furnaces received warning early in the evening and were damped down. This can be done in about 5 minutes in those recently built but in the older ones it takes much longer.

1916 February 3 Thursday The mystery of the raider is not yet disclosed. It is suggested she has fitted out in some neutral port. If this is so it will lead to further complications. It is estimated that she has already sunk ships and their cargoes to the value of 1 ¼ millions. In one case the merchantman attacked (the Clan McTavish) put up a real good fight and only surrendered after having 15 men killed.

February 4 Friday Good news this morning. One of the Zeppelins has been destroyed and all the crew drownded in the North Sea. At present it is not very clear where she came from. Whether it was one returning from the raid or another one coming is not stated. We know that they were pretty well peppered by our people on their way home, and they claim to have put one of our batteries out of action. Possibly it was winged by one of these guns. As they were flying back they crossed Holland and this being neutral territory the Dutchmen gave them a warm reception, so that she might have been injured there. It does not matter much where, the principal thing is she was sunk. She was seen floating on the water by a fishing smack and the crew which numbered about 20 begged to be taken off, but as the crew of the smack numbered only 4 men they were wise enough not to take about 20 Germans on board, consequently they were left to their fate.

February 5 Saturday The death roll of the raid has now been raised to 67 as the result of further deaths owing to injuries. Some of the details which one hears from friends are perfectly ghastly. In several instances people were absolutely blown to atoms.

DAY BY DAY THROUGH THE GREAT WAR

The stubborn war on the lines in France still goes on with unabated violence. According to such reports as we get the Artillery contests have of late been very severe. Possibly this is the prelude to further offensive. We have made no big move now since the battle of Loos, and indeed it has been quite impossible to do so owing to weather conditions.

At Salonica events remain fairly quiet with the exception of air- raids, and the same may be said of Egypt. Our force near to Baghdad is still beleaguered as owing to very bad weather no further attempt could be made to relieve them, but fairly good news has been received from them and less anxiety is felt for them.

The Russians have lately shaken up the Turks severely in Asia Minor and have done some remarkable work in spite of the awful wintry weather. Numbers of the Turks have perished by frost but the Russians are much more inured to it. There is a report to-day that the Turks have abandoned Erzerum their chief fortress in Asia Minor.

No further news has been heard of the German Raider, but I quite expect she will turn up again before long, and it is possible and it is possible she may do much damage before she is captured.

February 6 Sunday Quite a new departure is taking place here to-day. As a result of a <u>request</u> from the authorities i.e. the police no evening services will be held in the various places of worship. The service will be held in the afternoon at 3 or 3.15 instead so that it may conclude before dusk so that there may be no lighting. I think this is a most sensible precaution, as it is an undoubted fact that the Zeppelins are attracted by light, and they seem to have dropped their bombs on the places that were brilliantly light. The Military Authorities have control of the lighting over the whole country and they have proclaimed certain districts as being especially liable to danger. In these districts most drastic orders are in force, and the police see to the inforcement of them. I think it would [be] quite wise if the whole of the country were put under these restrictions. At present Northampton and Peterborough are the only places so proclaimed in this County.

We quite expect these raiders will come again, and that damage and loss of life will occur, but this we expect and it does not dismay or frighten us, at the same time I think the War Office might take more efficient measures for fighting them than they did. These raiders were off the Coast for at least two hours in daylight and surely something could have been done to meet them.

These services will be held in the afternoon until further notice. It is probable as the days get longer the evening services will be resumed.

As the days go on, we are all looking forward to the future. I am convinced that we shall have a period of great strain and stress during the coming 12 months, and we must brave ourselves up to meet it. Germany is going to put forth all the force she can command during this summer and it is against England that she is chiefly going to use it. She knows that we are the cornerstone of the Allies and if she could only knock us out the rest would fall to pieces. It does not benefit her much if she defeats France or Italy or Serbia or Russia for she knows that as long as we are holding out the war will go on, and the longer it goes on the more certain her defeat will become. Men are very grave and serious in these days, and I think there are few who do not realize our peril. They realize it but I can confidently say they are not dismayed or downhearted. They are quite aware that we are fighting for our lives, and when a man is doing that there is nothing more to be said.

1916 February 7 Monday No fighting news of importance to-day, only a crop of rumours which we now estimate at their value. These include a threat of the Germans to surprise us with a new torpedo, to attack on a big scale in the West, and to attack Salonica.

A big explosion caused by melinite has taken place at the great Austrian Arsenal at Skoda where some of the biggest guns and mortars used during the war have been made. The Germans used guns made at this place when they battled their way through Belgium in August and September 1914. Two hundred men were killed by this explosion and much of their plant destroyed.

I attended a meeting of the Military Tribunal to-night. Five appeals were before us. Three of the appellants were placed back 10 groups and two were disallowed. These two can appeal to the Central Tribunal if they like. The hearing will be held in London.

I have to-day insured all my property against damage done by aircraft. This includes property of all kinds: Houses, Stock in Trade, Furniture and live stock. It is insured through the usual Insurance Offices who act as agents for the Government and the amount insured is the same as that for fire. The premium varies from 2/- per cent (for private dwelling houses and their contents) to 7/6 per cent for the most hazardous classes such as Railway waggons and timber stored in the open. Small amounts up to £100 can be insured through any Post Office.

Tuesday February 8 A renewal of the Russian fighting in the south close to Roumania is announced this morning. Not only artillery but bayonet work.

The Government to-day issue a notice saying that owing to lack of ships less sugar will be imported, and asking people to use less, also less of jam, marmalade, biscuits etc. In spite of the doubling of the price since war began there has actually been an increase in the consumption. I am afraid this request will be of very little use.

1916 February 9 The Lighting which applies to danger zones has been very much extended to-day and we are now coming under it. The proclamation has not been received here at present but it will come very shortly. There has been a growing demand by the public for this since the raid of Jan 31, even now it is not applied to the whole country as it should be, but only to specified areas.

Under the provisions of this order all lights must be obscured at 1 hour after sunset. No ray of light must shine from any house or building direct into the street, all rooms which use lights at night must have their windows darkened by dark curtains or blinds and the same applies to all skylights. Motors of all descriptions can only carry one obscured light in the front and one red in the rear. These are the principal provisions and the enforcement of this order lies in the hands of the Police who have full power to act and summon offenders. The penalties can be inflicted up to £100. To-day at Northampton (where these orders have been in force about a month) a tradesman was fined £20, which he richly deserved.

I have to-day lodged all my deeds and papers at Barclays Bank and the Northants Union Bank as I do not think the ordinary fire-proof safe is enough protection against bombs.

Another Zeppelin scare to-night. About 7.15 pm the police received warning that they were off Scarborough at 6.30. It is fairly light to-night, the moon being in the second quarter. All lights i.e. lamps (street) were at once put out, also in many private houses and even where they were not put out the windows are shaded by dark curtains. I have just been for a walk round the town and but very very little light is visible.

10 pm   The police have received no further warning so probably they have gone to the North.

February 11 Friday Nothing was heard of the Germans during the night and to-day people are saying that it was a hoax. I can confidently say that it was not. I am told by the police they received their warning from Peterboro' and that it had come through from the Military Authorities on the N.E. Coast. Possibly the Zeps turned back or were driven off.

Germany to-day threatens to sink all merchantmen at sight as lately some of these vessels have put up most determined fights against submarines. We shall meet this new menace by heavier arming of our merchantmen.

The Russians have won a notable victory and are again across the Dneister.

February 12 Saturday Almost a complete dearth of real war news. With the exception of the usual trench warfare, things are very quiet. It seems almost like the quietness before the storm bursts. Whether it is time alone will prove.

The children of the schools in Baden were give[n] two days holiday to celebrate the glorious victory of the Zeppelin raid on Jan 31. A victory which only resulted in the murder of non-combatants and did not entail the death of one soldier nor the destruction of any military stores or munition works. So much for

DAY BY DAY THROUGH THE GREAT WAR

German victories. We are learning to estimate these claims at their true value.

February 13 Sunday   I think the chief interest during the last week has centred on all sides in the Air raid business and this chiefly because it has brought home to many people especially those living in the Midlands that we are at war, and at war with a most unscrupulous and deadly enemy. Whilst one cannot but sincerely deplore the deaths that have resulted from these raids, one cannot conceal that it has shaken people out of their lethargy, and has brought war home to them.

   Of course precautions will be taken as far as possible to minimise the effects of these raids and also to combat them, but at the same time I can truly say there is nothing in the nature of   a panic. Some resentment is felt that we are not in a better position to fight these Zeppelins, but I am confident that means will be taken to meet this deficiency. Twelve months ago the Germans boasted they would drive our commerce off the seas and starve us out by the aid of their submarines. To-day they acknowledge that this threat has not and cannot be carried out as we have been quite able to check-mate them by the means which have been adopted, and I have no fear [but] that we shall do the same as regards Zeppelins.

   Measures are being concerted by all Local Authorities as regards warnings, extinguishing of lights etc. etc. In many places the electric light is switched off at the power station on the first warning, and the same thing applies also to gas. I have friends living in Norwich, which owing to its situation is probably the most dangerous place in England, but which , owing to the excellence with which the lighting and other restrictions are enforced, has never been attacked, although other towns and places in Norfolk have been bombed. In Norwich a match even is not allowed to be struck in the streets and the least ray of light from any shop or dwelling house speedily results in a visit from the Police. I think it would be an excellent thing if these means were adopted with the same thoroughness throughout the whole country.

   Prices of grain remain about the same. Wheat keeps at about 58/- to 59/-. Some two months since the Authorities sent a letter to all Millers asking them what quantity of wheat they could store, and on the strength of the replies received they (the Government) have bought largely. This is now beginning to arrive here and will be stored as reserves. The Miller storing this wheat will have the option of buying at the day's price when the Government decide to sell, meantime the Miller will be paid a small sum per week per quarter for storing it.

   Almost every other article I could mention is gradually getting dearer. Manufactured goods especially so.

   Livestock of all kinds maintains its high prices. Pigs a short time since were a little cheaper, owing to the fact that, offals being so dear, everybody was wishing to sell, but now they have reverted to their former price and indeed in some cases above it. In Wellingborough this week they are quoted at 17/- per score. Mutton is about 11 ½ d to 1/- per lb Beef 9 1/2d These are wholesale prices.

1916 February 14 Monday Much regret was caused this morning at the sudden death of Mr J.H. Smith of Cobthorne, which took place about 1 o'clock this morning. Mr Smith had taken the leading place in the public life of the town. He had also done much work for recruiting during this war. His only son an officer in the Manchesters was killed at La Cateau on the retreat from Mons. He will be buried at Stoke on Wednesday.

   Very little war news to-day, although there seems to be a gradual waking up all along the various fronts. The cruiser Arethusa has been sunk in the North Sea to-day. She struck a mine. Ten men were lost, the remainder were saved.

February 15 Tuesday   The Russians are shaking up the Turks in Asia Minor and to-day comes the news that they have captured one of the forts at Erzerum. Should they capture this place it will be a notable success.

Parliament meets again to-day and will [be] almost entirely devoted to war finance. I think I can see a growing demand for protective duties especially after the war, and I believe these will be levied against Germany very heavily.

February 16 Wednesday   News of heavy fighting in France is published to-day, and I am afraid it has gone against us in some measure. Sir Douglas Haig reports that close to Ypres the enemy have occupied 600 yards of our trenches, but have not pierced the line. He does not say anything about casualties but they must be heavy.

Grave warnings were spoken by the Prime Minister last night as to our finances. He foreshadowed further taxation. Lord Kitchener speaking in the Lords was quietly confident. He said very little as he generally does, but what he did say was to the point.

To-night a small committee of the Urban Council (including myself) met the Superintendent of Police to arrange as to the public lighting. Further reductions in the number of street lamps will take place, and in those that remain the glass will be painted 2/3rds of the way down the sides and on the top, ordinary burners will also be substituted for incandescent ones. There will only be about a dozen lamps in the whole parish. These can be quickly put out and in about ten minutes after the police have received warning the place will be absolutely dark.

Mr Smith was buried to-day at Stoke after a service in the Parish Church here. There was a large attendance of the Urban Council, Guardians, Special Constables and the general public. It has been a most stormy day. Early yesterday morning we had a sudden fall of snow about 4 or 5 inches but fortunately it turned to rain last night so that the snow had gone. The wind was so high to-day as we were going to Stoke that one of the windows of the carriages was blown in.

1916 February 17 Thursday News reached London last night that the Russians had captured Erzerum after 5 days hard fighting. This is the best news we have had for some time and I think must have an important bearing on events in Asia Minor.

February 18 Friday An appeal is issued to-day by the Government to owners of Motor Cars who are simply using them for pleasure to discontinue their use and hinting strongly that unless they do that they will be compelled to do so. This is quite right. Some millions must be wasted every year in this way and considering the present financial strain it is only right that this form of pleasure should be put down.

February 19 Saturday The work of the military Tribunals under the Derby Group is now in full swing and I think on the whole is proceeding satisfactorily although there are complaints there are too many exemptions.

Appeals under the Conscription Act will be heard very shortly and there is some idea that <u>young married</u> men who have attested may be called to the colours before long. Great care and discretion will have to be exercised in these matters or the business of the nation will become completely disorganised. It was stated in Parliament this week that men who had enlisted from some of the docks and wharfs have had to be brought back again as the congestion in these places is so great. I myself have had some goods lying in a ship in the Thames since Dec 1, and which did not get unloaded until Jan 24th. The same thing occurs in many other ways. Much as we want men it is clearly impossible that all should be called if the business of the country is to be carried on.

I attended a meeting of Special Constables at the Police Station to-night to make arrangements for the carrying out of the new lighting regulations. Four special Constables will be on patrol each night from seven to ten, and the whole of them (about 40) will be summoned to duty in case of an air raid. It has been decided that no warnings of these raids shall be given in the district by 'Hooters', Whistles or Church Bells as it is considered that [it] is not wise to cause unnecessary alarm. Constables will be [on] duty to do what they can in the way of advising people etc. They will also have power to hold up Motor Cars which may be travelling through the town.

February 20 Sunday   No special news to-day. The tremendous blow struck by the Russians at the Turks which resulted in the capture of Erzerum continues to re-echo throughout the world. The fighting was terrific and was carried out under terrible weather conditions, 50 degrees of frost being registered. The final assault lasted without ceasing for 24 hours and then the Turks were completely overwhelmed. They were not all captured [but] fled, and tried to rally 10 miles from the city but the Russians were close upon them, and before they could re-form had again beaten them. Full details have not reached us yet but the spoils are said to be enormous. It is much too soon the estimate the consequences of this victory, but that these will be very great cannot be doubted. Already they are coming to light. The King of Bulgaria was in Vienna. He has immediately rushed back to Sofia, as the Turkish troops may now be much weakened in the Balkans, and it is quite possible that we may see most dramatic events there. The Allies are constantly being re-inforced at Salonica and may some day strike very hard. The remnant of the Serbian Army is in the island of Corfu. (There are 100,000 still remaining) and will be quite ready for service again by the end of this month. I may mention that this county of Northamptonshire has every reason to be very proud of the part they played in that great retreat of the Serbs. They (the Serbs) were shod in boots made in this County and it is reported that the men were willing to abandon everything rather than their boots, and that the boots were all that could be desired.

Roumania is also making every preparation so that it looks as if the Balkans would once more become the centre of attraction.

To-day I received a letter from one of my nephews who with the Bucks Yeomanry had been through the Gallipoli business. They are now on the Western borders of Egypt keeping quiet the Senussi Arabs who the Turks (with German assistance) have been stirring up to attack us in Egypt.

A woman spy was tried by Court Martial this week and condemned to be shot, but this was commuted to penal servitude for life. She had only been here six days and during that time her every movement had been noted and all her letters opened.

1916 February 21 Monday A Proclamation is posted up to-day calling up the youngest class of the "Derby Group" i.e. young men who had reached the age of - - on the 14th August 1915. These had not been called up before but the exemptions from the other classes have been so great that it will be necessary to call up almost every man. It is rumoured that the first groups of <u>married</u> [men] will be called up early next month.

The Russians are keeping the Turks on the run in Armenia. After the capture of Erzerum they made a sweep forward of another 150 miles and have captured other important strategic positions. Germany is growing very restive about this and their newspapers (entirely controlled by their Government) are severely blaming the Turks. It is quite obvious these successes must have far reaching consequences.

February 22 Tuesday Yesterday 24 of our aeroplanes raided the German lines of communication in France and did much damage to them. The airmen all got back safely.

Another huge vote of credit in the House to-day bringing up the war expenditure to over two thousand millions. It is as the Prime Minister said: no mind can adequately grasp these stupendous figures.

February 23 Wednesday A furious battle is raging in Artois not far from Verdun. The Germans claim considerable success and these claims are to some extent acknowledged by the French although they have been bought at a terrible cost. It looks almost as if the Germans intend to make an attempt to capture Verdun, the great French fortress, but they are making an offensive all the way along the lines. The weather conditions are very bad and snow is continually falling. We here in England are now having the worst weather we have had this winter. A regular blizzard to-day.

Yesterday the French brought down a Zeppelin. About 8 pm it was sighted sailing over their lines without any lights. Chase was at once given by motors armed with aircraft guns and the second shot fired by one of these pierced it setting it on fire. It at once collapsed and came to earth burning like a huge torch. There were 30 men on board and when they reached the ground every one was a charred corpse, without a rag of clothing.

February 24 Thursday The great battle near to Verdun which began on Monday still continues. The German Crown Prince is in command of the Germans who (we are told) have gained only slight successes. Only general news of these battles is published. It is some weeks before we get any details of them.

February 25 Friday Still the great battle is continued. The losses are reported to be appalling. Verdun seems to be the objective of the Germans. I think they are trying to make a set off to counteract the effect of the fall of Erzerum.

THE DIARY OF JOHN COLEMAN BINDER

1916 February 26 Saturday   There was a slight lull in the great Verdun battle on Thursday but yesterday the fighting was again renewed with all its former vigour. This great conflict which commenced early last Monday has now lasted four days and is engaging the attention of the whole world. Both the Kaiser and that wretched son of his the Crown Prince are there and it seems as if the Germans had decided to forestall the offensive which <u>must</u> come during the early summer. The French say that they are confident of being able to retain their positions but nevertheless one must view this battle with some anxiety as it is certainly the greatest conflict we have had since the great battle at Ypres some twelve months since, and is certainly fraught with great issues. Rumours of the coming conflict reached London early last Monday morning and it is quite evident that the French were quite aware of what was coming. Rumour says that one of the chief reasons for this new offensive is that Germany is about to issue a new War Loan and it is very necessary that she should secure a victory to ensure the success of it.

To-day the Germans claim they have taken 10,000 prisoners since Monday and have advanced about 3 or 3 ½ miles on their right. From French reports we learn the Germans utterly reckless of human life are fighting in their usual close formation and have had whole regiments swept away by the deadly fire of the French 75's. That it is a most bloody and costly affair even we at this distance can see.

The French Official report issued in Paris this afternoon says that the battle has continued all night and is still going on.

Comparative quiet reigns all along the remainder both of our front and the French.

The Russians report to-night another well-earned victory in Mesopotamia.

February 27   No reliable news is to hand to-day of the great battle. We eagerly await to-morrow morning's papers. These newspapers are beginning to reduce their size as owing to the restricted import of paper they will only get ⅔rds of their normal supply.

We are now beginning to feel the pinch of war in many ways and I think we have much the hardest time coming. Supplies of many articles are dwindling and it is certain they will continue to do so. We shall [have] to put up with the loss of many things which we have regarded in past years as necessities.

Sugar especially is getting very short and it is only by the utmost prudence that grocers are able to supply the normal requirements of the public. The Government of course control all this business and for the last 14 days they have absolutely refused to sell any. On Thursday two of the largest dealers in sugar in the City of London had not a single bag to sell and I believe this was the case with all the other wholesale houses. I quite expect the Government are trying to reduce stocks in the hands of the retailers and then clap on a very much heavier duty in the next budget which by the way is due at the end of March.

We have had some very bad weather this week. A regular blizzard on two days and the snow is very deep in some places but I am glad to say to-day it is thawing but is very cold.

February 28 Monday   The terrible battle around Verdun still continues and has been fought with unabated vigour through the week end. The French we fear have not done as well as we could have wished, but they are fighting every inch of the ground, and express themselves quite confidently as to being able to prevent the capture of Verdun. The Germans have lost terribly, much more heavily than the French, and seem utterly reckless of human life. They boast they are prepared to lose 200,000 men in this attack. The belief is gaining ground that this is the beginning of their big offensive, and I think there is some truth in it. They can see it is Now or Never, and are making desperate efforts to deal a big blow. They have reached their utmost strength and will never be able to replace the men they are now losing. On the other hand, the Allies can still put huge reserves of men into the field. The Germans knowing this will I believe make desperate efforts and I quite think we are on the eve of great events. It is quite possible if they won this battle that they may think it an opportune time to bring out their fleet and I am certain that they will send the Zeppelins across again. We can see all this and must make up our minds to fight it out with all the power and strength we can raise.

Amsterdam advices say that the German dead and wounded are so great that all their hospitals are full and that the wounded are lying in the streets.

DAY BY DAY THROUGH THE GREAT WAR

Yesterday the "Maloga" the largest ship in the P & O service outward bound to Bombay struck a mine two miles off Dover and sank in half an hour. In spite of all the help rendered to her 47 lives were lost and another vessel (a collier) which went to help her was also mined.

To-night's telegrams from Paris say the battle still continues but that the position is practically unchanged. War reports are issued in Paris each day at 3 pm and again at midnight.

1916 February 29 Tuesday Some details of the immense battle are beginning to come through and they are almost incredible. The valour displayed by both sides beats all description, but I think it will be admitted that the Frenchmen carry off the palm. One of the old dismantled forts "Dounament" to the north of Verdun seems to be the chief point of attack. Three times the French lost and won it back again and it is now in German hands but the French have now completely surrounded it and have shut up in it a German Brigade. It is reported that the Germans have hurled 800,000 men along this line of battle which extends 25 miles.

Competent critics believe this battle is only the preliminary to a much vaster move. Indeed the Germans yesterday made another attack farther along the line in Champagne. The French fighting is splendid and although anxious they are quite confident of their ability to hold their own.

March 1 Wednesday There is a lull in the Verdun battle yesterday although the further east there was some fighting. It is too early to say that the German attack has faded but it looks very much as if it had. The German regiment which captured the old fort of Donaument is still shut up in it and is surrounded by the French. To-nights reports say that the Germans have had 30,000 actually killed and it is rumoured they are carting them away to some blast furnaces to burn them, which perhaps after all is the best thing to do. The French do not at present give any account of their losses. Without question this is the greatest battle we have had on the Western front during this war.

A meeting of the Military Tribunal for Oundle was held here to-night at 8 pm. There are seven members, six of whom were present. The Public and Press were admitted. We had eight appeals before us which were dealt with in 2 hours. Only one exemption was given. A son of a widowed mother, whose business was entirely dependent on him. The proprietor of a Kinema who had been put back for 2 months now appealed for further extension. This was refused and he will have to go. In one or two other cases young unmarried men who are in business for themselves were put back two months to allow them to make arrangements.

March 2 Thursday Fighting to the east of Verdun has been resumed, but on the north where the real battle lies it has been quiet. The Germans are digging themselves in, and are said to be moving their heavy artillery up to recommence the attack. Even they admit that the bravery of the French is magnificent.

March 3 Friday Yesterday our own men made a move on the Yser and won back the trench which the Germans captured a few weeks since taking 180 prisoners and 4 officers.

To-nights telegrams from Paris say that the great battle for Verdun has been resumed with increased ferocity if that is possible. The Germans have again attacked the village of Dounamont and have gained a footing in one end. The village consists of one narrow street and hand to hand fighting is going on across this narrow place.

March 4 Saturday To-days news is a repetition of yesterdays. The fierce battle for Verdun is still going on and is being watched with intense interest throughout the whole world. Besides this battle all other contests on this Western front are small. It is impossible to give any reliable estimate of the losses, but the latest figures say that up to Wednesday last the enemy had lost 45,000 in killed alone and all reports agree that the slopes where they attacked are literally covered with dead men. Opinions are divided as to what caused the Germans to make this great blow just at this moment. In some quarters it is urged that as they are about to issue a new war loan, and it is imperative that [they] should be able to parade a victory to insure the success of it. Others urge that of course they are quite aware the Allies would move as soon as possible and they decided to get the first blow in if possible. It is quite certain they have been preparing for this for some months, in fact it is said the whole business had been rehearsed twice and then came

THE DIARY OF JOHN COLEMAN BINDER

the Kaiser to Mezieres to give the word to launch the attack. We do not know who is in command of the French but to-day it is disclosed from Paris that he is quite an unknown General. Whoever he is he has done splendidly.

1916 March 5 Sunday Last nights late news still continues the tale of this battle. Paris says that the battle is unabated. Another week of tense expectancy. We do hope and pray that the Germans may fail in this attack as it may have a tremendous influence on the future course of the war. Some of their military writers are now beginning to cry out at the huge slaughter and ask if it cannot be stopped. Much as we deplore it, it cannot be stopped until Germany acknowledges herself beaten. Of this all the Allies are determined. Other nations in Europe - to wit Roumania, Greece and even Bulgaria and Turkey are watching this fearful battle, and it is quite possible that if success inclines to our side, they may be induced to join us, and this would mean a much earlier end to the war.

In civil life here events go on much as they have done except that the one sole topic of conversation is the war, and this is being increased as these recruits are being called up, and the Tribunals are giving their decisions. Two more sittings are to be held here this week on Tuesday and Friday.

Some comment has been caused by the number of postponements and exemptions that have been granted generally, especially in the case of farmers, and it is probable that all these cases will be sifted through again. It is a most difficult and thankless business. It is quite impossible to reconcile the demands of the Army and also to satisfy all civil requirements. There must be compromise and the only way to do it is to balance the individual cases as equally as possible. I am certain we shall see much hardship suffering and inconvenience during the remainder of this war.

Lighting regulations are now strictly enforced (with the aid of Special Constables). After dark the streets are quite dark and the vehicular traffic almost ceases. All shops now close at 7pm and after that time very few people are about.

We have the whole business well in hand now if a Zeppelin raid does take place. Special Constables, Fire Brigade and Ambulance all know their appointed places. I think there will be many raids during the coming summer.

March 6 Monday A strange co-incidence occurred last night, after writing up this diary for yesterday. I had gone to bed and was fast asleep but was roused by the police at 11.15 and was informed that as a Special Constable I was to go on duty at once, as Zeppelins were in the neighbourhood. I was told to call about eight other Constables and then report to the Police Station. I did so, and was then ordered to see that <u>every</u> light in the town was out. Whilst carrying out these duties I heard a Zeppelin but it was some miles away. Another Constable heard bombs, but these I did not hear. This was all that was heard of them here. After waiting until 3 am this morning we were dismissed.

We understand they were at Hull, Grimsby, Grantham etc but at present we have received no confirmation of this. All orders are now given from London with regard to these raids. If they appear off the coast information is at once sent to headquarters in London and from that time they are kept under close observation, and every movement is reported, and warnings are sent from London to all parts as to where they are. It was only after receiving orders from London that we were dismissed this morning.

Cheering news comes from Paris this morning. The Germans have been fought to a

stand still, and although the situation is still critical the French say they are quite confident now. Hard fighting is still going on especially at Donaument which is the real storm centre.

The Russians continue to make fine progress in Asia Minor and have dealt the Turks several heavy blows lately.

1916 Tuesday March 7 Thirteen people were killed and 33 injured in yesterday mornings raid. Three Zeppelins are said to have been here and they sailed over the counties bordering the East Coast from Yorkshire to Kent. They do not appear to have [reached] any further inland than Wansford about ten miles from here and that was when I heard them. Great damage was done at Hull where they dropped an aerial

137

torpedo wrecking a terrace of houses. The Railway Station also suffered very much.

We are quite expecting they will come frequently as soon as the weather permits but at the same time there is a good deal of criticism of the Government that some means cannot be devised to check them. They were caught in a snow storm but as far as we can learn appear to have reached home in safety.

The weather for the last three weeks has been very very bad. Great falls of snow, which have thawed very quickly making big floods. The wind also has been extremely searching. Similar conditions are said to prevail in France.

Another Military Tribunal meeting was held to-night. Eight appeals were heard. Four were refused. Two adjourned and two granted 3 months relief.

March 8 Wednesday The Germans having failed in the centre of their attack on Verdun are now battling hard on the wings and have made some little advance but they admit their losses are very great.

It is evident the Zeppelins which came over on Sunday were surprised to find such cold snowy weather, and as they cannot do much in snow they unloaded their bombs indiscriminately and went off home. Bright fine sunshine has prevailed over the northern part of Europe but here and in France winter has got a firm grip. Before the war, weather forecasts were published every day in the newspapers but now they are quite done away with as they might be of much use to the enemy.

March 9 Thursday There was a lull again yesterday in the Verdun fighting. This great [battle] dominates every other event at the present time. I think that if this business fails it may possibly mean the beginning of the end. Even if the Germans take Verdun, it will be a show victory only as this war has quite proved that fortresses are of little or no use against modern artillery. As a matter of fact all the fighting now is not at Verdun, but at from 4 to 8 miles away from it.

Friday March 10 It is quite confirmed by Dutch and other neutral vessels coming in from the North Sea that the German Fleet of about 50 ships was outside the harbours on Monday and Tuesday. It was accompanied by one or two Zeppelins. I wonder if they will ever risk a real naval battle. Since they came across 12 months last January and were quickly sent back we have heard little or nothing of them, but we cannot reasonably suppose they have been doing nothing all the time. I expect [they] have been preparing some stroke which they hope to bring off.

March 11 Saturday To-day is the 20th day of the great Verdun Battle, and it still goes on. Violent fighting is taking place especially on the west banks of the Meuse. The issue is not yet decided, but every day the Germans are held up is a day of victory for us.

To-day Portugal enters into the war, on our side. Certainly she cannot be of much use to us in Europe but in Africa her help will be most valuable. The South African Boer General Smuts drove the Germans hard in his East African campaign and before long there will not be a foot of German Colonial Empire. This is a terrible blow to them as they had expended enormous sums of money on these affairs and now they have all been captured.

1916 Sunday March 12 Cheering news comes from France this morning - the Germans are still held up. We offered to send them men but they say they are able to hold their own.

Yesterday 31 Aeroplanes from our lines did much damage in the interior of Germany.

The bad weather still continues and we have now had a month of snow and rain. To-day it is a little better as all the snow has gone.

Men are now joining the army under compulsion in large numbers. The first lot of married men are due about April 7 and I am afraid is going to cause much distress and the breaking up of many homes. The curse of this dreadful war is now being brought close home to us, and we are feeling its effects in all directions. I think the next six or eight months will be the crucial time. We are certainly expecting that the Zeppelins will raid us in increasing numbers as soon as the weather improves. Much as they may do this they will not cause us to flinch from seeing this war through to the end.

THE DIARY OF JOHN COLEMAN BINDER

Many articles are getting very dear. Sugar is getting very limited and at the present moment it is not possible to buy any sugar from the wholesale people in London. It is rumoured it will be raised to 6d per lb by the next Budget in April.

Pigs are making record prices and are quoted at 12/- to 12/6 per stone in local markets. In many places they are making up to 14/- Mutton is quite 1/1d to 1/2d per lb wholesale.

March 13 Monday There has been no infantry actions at the great battle at Verdun since Friday when the Germans attempted to capture the village of Vaux and suffered ghastly losses. Attacking in their usual close formation they were simply mown down. According to reliable accounts the dead and the living simply rolled down the slopes together. What a frightful business.

Affairs are going from bad to worse in Turkey. There is chaos everywhere, and I quite think it possible that a revolution may occur there and Turkey ask for a separate peace.

Russia advances steadily in Mesopotamia and is now only 130 [miles] from Baghdad.

March 14 Tuesday There is much unrest and dissatisfaction amongst married men who enrolled under the Derby scheme. They contend that so many unmarried men have been postponed and exempted that they (the married) are being called up much earlier than they anticipated. I think many of these men enrolled under the idea that they would not be called up at all and now that the call has come they are not very willing to go. It is quite certain that there will be very many hard cases when these men do come up and that the work of the Tribunals will be very difficult. It is quite true that many more unmarried men will have to go and steps are being taken to sift them through again.

March 15 Wednesday The artillery action continues very violent along the Verdun sector, but there is a long pause in other operations. It is generally thought the Germans have not abandoned this battle but are only waiting to get up more men. It is not easy to ascertain what their losses along there have been during the last three weeks. Some authorities place them as high as 250,000 men. At any rate it has greatly shaken them and also caused great depression in Germany and has much encouraged the Allies. The fighting of the French has been magnificent. I hope ours will be as good when our turn comes.

March 16 Thursday The Germans are again attacking Verdun from the West of the Meuse but make no appreciable gains.

March 17 Friday Yesterday the Germans repeated their great assault on the west of the Meuse to capture a ridge called Mort Homme and received a terrible set back from the French. The attack was a complete failure and their losses are terrible.

1916 March 18 Saturday Again the Germans are launching fresh attacks at Verdun. Yesterday afternoon and evening they were attacking Vaux west of the Meuse and again it is the same tale - they were quite without success. These or this battle, for it is really one long battle engages the attention of the whole world, as it seems to us all that it is the climax that is being reached. The carnage is frightful, even the Germans admit this. Good authorities say that they have lost 300,000 men in the last four weeks.

Sunday March 19 The last telegrams last night confirm the repulse of the Germans before Vaux. How these Frenchmen do fight. Looking back over this week I think I can see a distinctly more hopeful feeling amongst all classes. This 4 weeks battle at Verdun has gone badly for the Germans and we are beginning to see more hopeful times ahead. We recognize that Germany is not yet beaten, but we quite believe that a good beginning has been made. Reliable reports coming from Germany, especially from the Portuguese Ambassador who has been recalled this week go to prove that the truth is beginning to dawn even on the obtuse German people that they are being beaten and that it was necessary to fight this great battle at Verdun to encourage them. Now they are being beaten there, and this will create further discontent. What neutral countries think of this battle is shown by steady decline of the value of the German exchange which [is] now at a discount of nearly 35 per cent in nearly all countries. In addition to this we know that the internal condition of Germany is far from good. The steady relentless pressure of our own fleet is the solid bed rock on which we build, although many people do not seem to realize it. 400 ships up there on the north coast of Scotland are slowly but surely starving Germany and with God's help will bring her to her senses.

Of course we do not think that the war is won and over. I still think that there will be some terrible battles this spring and summer but I am distinctly hopeful that the war may end before another winter, but we can only hope this. It would be the utmost folly to conclude a premature peace. There is not the least doubt we could have peace to-day on Germany's terms. (She has been putting out peace terms again this week, but they are certainly such as we could not dream of accepting). Peace when it comes will have to be on the Allies' terms not on Germany's. Unless she is crippled she will go through all this business again in a few years hence.

March 20 Monday An aeroplane raid took place yesterday afternoon over Deal and Dover. Thirteen people (mostly children) were killed and a number [of] English airmen quickly rose in pursuit and after a smart battle over the sea one of the enemy aeroplanes was forced down and the aviator shot. The other two got away.

The attacks at Verdun grow much feebler. It is too early to say they have failed altogether but it is certain they have had a very bad set back. It may be they are only taking breath.

Late to-night we learn that our airmen, English French and Belgian, smartly retaliated for the Dover raid. 68 aircraft starting about 1 a.m. from our lines in Belgium went to Zeebrugge a small port now held by the Germans on the Belgian coast and dropped 5 tons of bombs on it. This will keep the Germans quiet a few days. This Zeebrugge is a regular nest of submarines and aeroplanes. All our men returned safely.

Tuesday March 21 A running naval fight took place off the Belgian coast yesterday morning. Two German [?Destroyers] on outpost duty were sighted and after a few shots they ran and made for Zeebrugge. Dutch telegrams say that some wounded sailors were seen so that evidently our men found their mark. Our casualties were 4 wounded.

Late to-night most hopeful news comes from Russia. She has made a strong attack both on the extreme north and south and in both cases has been successful. Both Berlin and Vienna admit this.

Wednesday March 22 A big attack on Verdun was made last night much further west and the enemy gained some ground but at a fearful cost.

Fresh regulations are announced to-day with regard to conscription. All the unmarried men will be called through again, the number of reserved occupations much reduced and even in these only men of certain ages will be allowed to appeal for exemption.

Now that conscription is being enforced the people of this country are beginning to realize what conscription means. It will cause much distress and ruin, especially amongst men who are earning from £200 a year and upwards. At present these men are only to receive 12/6 a week for wives and 1/6 per head for children. Of course this means the entire breaking up of the home and consequent ruin. I look with much apprehension on the course of affairs in this country unless some relief is given in this conscription business.

End of Volume Five

THE DIARY OF JOHN COLEMAN BINDER

Postcard sent to Percy Knight (stepson of J.C. Binder's sister Annie).

THE DIARY OF JOHN COLEMAN BINDER

Volume Six

23 March 1916 to 13 December 1916

1916 Thursday March 23   I am writing this day's diary on Sunday March 26 as I have been quite unable to get a book like the previous ones and am unable to do so now. These books are made in Scotland and the bookseller assures me that he has had some on the way for weeks. This is a single instance of the congestion of traffic. I myself have had goods on the way from Hull for quite three weeks and can get no tidings of them. The labour difficulty is growing very acute and must of necessity do so as more and more men are called to the colours.

I am much concerned that the breaking point will be reached if no check is put on this continued draft of men. Out of about 14 million workers in this country it is confidently asserted that 6 millions are entirely engaged in this war.

The attacks at Verdun continue, but they are child's play compared with those of a week or two since. It is generally conceded that the Germans have had a bad set back there. Possibly that wretched Crown Prince and his equally wretched father may send another quarter of a million men to be slaughtered but there is very little chance of victory for them.

To-night 30 of the National Reserve arrived here for the purpose of guarding the railway bridges in the vicinity. These are all old soldiers of about 50 to 60 who have re-enlisted for service during the war.

March 24 Friday The Russians are doing exceedingly well both in Asia and in Europe. It looks very much as if we shall soon see this trench warfare come to an end on the Russian front and it looks very much as if we are on the eve of great events.

I attended a meeting of the Local Tribunal to-night. We had many difficult cases (14) before us and sat from 7 until 11. We did what we considered best, but it is a very unpleasant business and one which I do not like at all, but shall not shirk it.

March 25 Saturday Very little news to-day except that a cross channel steamer has been sunk but all aboard were saved. To-night the first man in this neighbourhood to be arrested as a deserter under the Conscription Act was brought into the prison here. He came from Laxton and had failed to take any notice of his call or summons.

March 26 Sunday A bright day with sunshine, but bitterly cold. It is drying well and that is what is now required. All agricultural work is terribly backward as we have had real winter the last 7 weeks and nothing whatever has been done on the land. It has been the worst March in my recollection. I am afraid that much seeding will go undone this year as the land is so wet and also on account of the shortage of labour.

Persistent reports are again going about of the activity of the German Fleet. I often wonder if they will ever risk an action. Preparations have been made all down the east coast for a raid and all arrangements are now well in hand should this fleet succeed in getting through. Civilians would be moved inland and all arrangements have been made as to the routes by which they would travel, and also as [to] their food and lodging. We Special Constables have been quietly warned as to this. Personally I do not much fear invasion. It is not impossible but I do not think it is probable. The time has gone by for it. Germany has more than she can do to maintain her armies on both fronts without trying to send another army here.

I have no doubt Zeppelins will come and come in increasing numbers, but although these do much harm and cause loss of life they do not at all influence the course of the war.

1916 March 27 Things are getting very lively in the North Sea. Last night the Admiralty reported that on Saturday a squadron of our seaplanes escorted by warships raided the Zeppelin base behind the Island of Sylt. They came into contact with German patrol ships, two of which they sunk. One of our torpedo destroyers collided with another ship and foundered, the crew was saved. The Zeppelin sheds were much injured. Unconfirmed reports say that another naval action was fought yesterday. I do not think there is much doubt but that many German submarines are out, also the sea is strewn with mines. The Dutch Admiralty say to-day they will convoy their own ships across once a day, and that the convoy will be preceded by a mine sweeper. It is quite evident that events are now going to move. Germany is getting desperate.

1916 March 28 Tuesday A terrible day to-day. The worst snow storm and blizzard we have had for 40 years. Snow began to fall last night about 8 and did not cease until 5.30 to-day. From 2pm to 5 to-day it blew a regular hurricane. An immense amount of damage has been done. Trees uprooted, telegraph posts and wires are down in all directions. Altogether the worst snow storm which I recollect since Good Friday 1876.

Our men made a step forward yesterday and captured 600 yards of German trenches at St Eloi. The enemy still continues to hammer at Verdun but quite without effect.

March 29 Wednesday Since last Friday there has been quite an outbreak in the submarine warfare and several big vessels have been sunk without the least warning. On one of them, a cross channel steamer the 'Sussex', which was torpedoed last Friday, were several Americans. This has again aroused America, but I am very doubtful if she will really do anything.

Reports coming in from all the surrounding districts describe the disastrous effects of the hurricane yesterday. In many places the roads are impassable and the villages quite isolated. In one place on the Great North Road near to Waternewton there are 30 telegraph poles down altogether. The drifts between Benefield and Brigstock are between 8 and 10 feet deep.   I sincerely hope the Germans will not be tempted to make a raid just now, as it is quite impossible to telephone or telegraph.

I think this storm will be known as "The Great Storm of the Great War".

March 30 Thursday We still hold our gains at St Eloi and yesterday the French made a determined assault on the enemy 10 miles N.W. of Verdun and drove him back some 300 yards.

The thaw which has set in in Russia is hindering the fighting and it is probable that both sides will have [to] remain quiet until the ground dries although the Germans are said to be about to make a raid on Riga by sea.

Labour troubles are again in evidence on the Clyde. The extreme section of Socialists (which are quite repudiated by the Trades Unions) are trying to delay work on heavy guns and so compel the Government to repeal the Conscription Act. They have been doing this for some time. At last the Government has moved quickly and has deported some of the leaders. They were arrested by soldiers and carried off to some unknown place. I expect there will be much trouble there with these men.

March 31 Friday As reports come to hand the enormous damage caused by the storm is being realized. I am sure that no one living can remember such widespread loss that has taken place. To give only one instance, on the Great North Road between Norman Cross and Wansford there is scarcely a telegraph pole standing. On the Midland Railway they are down for miles and to-day the trains are only crawling from one signal box to another. We are now having perfect summer weather but there is a[n] immense amount of snow to thaw. At Northampton on Wednesday there was no market, an event without precedent. What stock was at Thrapston on Tuesday could not be got away and was only removed yesterday afternoon. They were fed in the Cattle Market.

April 1 Saturday Yesterday the Germans hurled furious attacks on the French position N.W. of Verdun and succeeded in gaining the village of Malancourt, but suffered fearful losses in doing so.

The Zeppelins again came over last night but did not reach this pat of the country. The police here did not receive any warning as we are almost isolated as regards telephone and telegraph. All trains were stopped in the London district and the railways were much disorganised. There is a very short announcement in the Times issued this morning by the War Office at 1.25 a.m. which says they visited the Eastern Counties and the North East Coast and that so far 90 bombs were reported to have been dropped. 5 Zeps are said to have come .

THE DIARY OF JOHN COLEMAN BINDER

Saturday Evening   An excellent piece of news is published this afternoon. One of the Zeppelins came down in the Thames Estuary this morning about 9 o'clock. It is not said whether she was shot or how she came down, but she was at once surrounded by Patrol Boats and the crew surrendered. The Boats attempted to tow her ashore but the beastly thing sunk, much to the grief of the boatmen. This is really a good augury for the coming Zeppelin season.

To-night the Police here have issued a special warning enjoining people to be especially careful as to their lights as, owing to being so cut off, no warning can be given when a raid is likely to occur.

The War Office to-day forbids the ringing of all bells and clocks between sunset and sunrise as these sounds enable the Zeppelins to locate towns and villages.

1916 April 2 Sunday A glorious April day, warm and bright, without a cloud to be seen. Snow is still to be seen in drifts under the hedges, and the floods are rising very rapidly. There are immense quantities of water coming down the valley. All field work is very backward, but the land is rapidly drying, and I should think if it continues to do so seeding will be possible on the light lands in a few days.

Yesterday the Army Authorities issued a notice commandeering all hay, straw and clover forage. A farmer may use what he requires for his own stock, but he will not be allowed to sell to any other farmer or dealer without the consent of the Army people. Great quantities of forage have been bought in this district ever since the war began, and every day one can see it being loaded up at the Railway Station.

All seed corn is very dear. Seed Barley is fetching 60 to 65 /- per quarter. Sheep are fetching record prices. Some tegs at Thrapston made 104 /- last Tuesday week.

April 3 Monday For 3 nights in succession the Zeppelins have raided this country. Sixty -six people have been killed and 166 wounded. As I predicted last Wednesday the enemy is well aware of the breakdown in the telephone service and has taken advantage of it. They have not come into this district and no alarm has been given. From what one can gather it is principally the eastern counties that have suffered. I should not be at all surprised if they come again to-night, it is quite calm and fine.

The intense fighting around Verdun continues. <u>That</u> is the storm centre. These Zeppelin raids are very bad but they will have no real influence on the war. Verdun can and will have but I think the general public do not realize this. They are far more concerned about raids than about the real great battle that is in progress.

Russia last week ordered 3 Million pairs of Army boots in this country. Most of them will be made in this county and it is said each pair will require 9 square feet of leather.

Another air raid to-night.

April 4 Tuesday   Great numbers of troops are being moved down into the Eastern counties . Rumour again says the authorities again think it possible that the Germans may make a raid on the coast with their fleet.

The air raids continue. The Zeppelins are again off the coast to-night. The police have received warning but so far they have not come into this district.

Very little information is given as to the means taken to fight them, but I think we may assume that some of the measures taken have proved a success. They have not touched London lately although it is well known they have tried to do so.

1916 April 5 Wednesday Budget Day to-day. The figures are real staggering. 500 Millions to be raised by taxation during the next 12 months. It <u>must</u> mean that everyone will be very poor. Income Tax up to 5/- in the £. The price of Matches doubled. A tax on entertainments (a very good thing) The Cinemas are frequented by hundreds of thousands of people every night and can quite afford to pay a tax. Big Motor Cars for pleasure a[re] very heavily hit. A 60 HP will have to pay a tax of 126£ per year. This will mean that many of them will be laid up. Of course many other goods will raise in price, for instance soap, hardware, cutlery have all risen very much in price as the import of them is stopped. The import has been stopped rather than put a duty on them. The constant sinking both of our own and also neutral ships is limiting the ships available, and all ships coming from America are compelled to bring a certain amount of wheat.

April 6 Thursday The Budget is accepted without much grumbling as people know that it is inevitable and appear willing to shoulder the burden. I am sure it will have a big effect in Germany as it will show them that we are determined to see this war through to a successful end cost what it may. It will be very interesting to read what they will have to say about it. They themselves are financing this war by constant borrowing and have made but very little provision for even paying interest on their loans, let alone repaying them. In fact they have only raised about 20 millions a year by new taxation whereas we have raised --- millions.

The chief fighting interest this morning is again shifted to the Baghdad force, which has now been besieged at Kut for 120 days. To-day it is reported that the relief force has advanced some distance and has captured important Turkish positions.

April 7 Friday The air raiders attacked the North east coast again last night. They killed one little child ! ! They did not remain long as the place they attacked was provided with air craft guns and they were soon driven off.

Again yesterday morning the Kut relief force made a good advance, capturing Turkish positions by a great bayonet charge. This brings them appreciably nearer to Kut.

Much fighting has been going on in our positions in France the last two days especially round St Eloi which was captured by us from the enemy about 3 weeks since and which he is now endeavouring to take again. After a comparatively quiet time the wounded are now arriving here in much larger numbers.

Saturday April 8 The first married men who attested last November are joining the colours to-day. They are men up to 27 years old. There are a number of them from this district and they have to go to Kettering. More are going on Monday and each day next week. There is a party in the Country chiefly represented by the "Times" which would stick at nothing to make conscripts of <u>all</u> men married or unmarried up to at least 45. This crew is the curse of the country just now and has more to sow discord than any other section of the people. As they were told by a Conservative member in the House on Thursday (Mr Duke) they 'want a cabal every afternoon and a Crisis every other day' All they care about is winning a victory for Conscription , Protection and against Home Rule and very little about the defeat of the Germans.

The Germans have re-captured (from the Canadians) part of our gains at St Eloi and last night fighting was going on strongly.

April 9 Sunday Yesterday some forage which was being offered for sale at Northampton was seized by the Army Authorities under the regulation which I mentioned last week.

The Great Battle at Verdun still continues. There is no question that this is the greatest battle in this or any other war. It is now known that for 6 months the Germans have been preparing for it. It is being closely watched in this and also in all Neutral Countries. Up to the present it is decidedly a defeat for the enemy, as he has not gained any great advantage and has suffered enormous losses. At the same time he is compelled to fight on, as he well knows that to give up would be an acknowledgement of defeat, and would be regarded as such amongst all neutrals.

The new taxes are accepted with good grace, but some of them are not workable in their present form, especially the Matches Tax. The duty is 4d on every hundred matches but as the number varies so much in different boxes and different makes it is most confusing. In fact it has brought the wholesale match trade to a deadlock. Evidently the Treasury did not consult any one who had a knowledge of the business and so have very much confused the affair. The protest is not so much against a tax on matches but against the way in which it is proposed to levy it.

The Snow of the Great Storm has not all gone yet, in fact it is quite deep in some of the cuttings, and is still lying about under the hedges.

THE DIARY OF JOHN COLEMAN BINDER

A number of people were fined at the Police Court this week for failing to obscure their lights. This is quite the usual thing at Courts now. At Wellingboro on Friday 60 were summoned. The penalties usually vary 7/6 to £3, but a fine of anything up to £100 may be imposed. As a rule the Order is well obeyed, and [it] is chiefly through carelessness that the offence is committed.

Perhaps it might interest some-one in later years if I gave some of the prices of articles of food which are now current. Taken altogether I think they may [be] regarded as very moderate when all the circumstances are considered, although people grumble and say how dear e is. It is quite true they are dearer than we have been used to.

Bread	8d per 4lb loaf
Potatoes	10d per 14lb
Flour	2s 10d per 14lb
Salt (wholesale) (a rise of 50%)	50s per ton
Cheese (Canadian)	1s per lb
" (English)	1s 2d to 1s 3d
Butter "	1s 6d
Sugar (granulated)	5 ¼ d per lb
" (loaf)	6d very scarce
" (Demerara)	5 ¼ d
Rice	2 ½ d to 4d
Soap	4d to 5d
Bacon (American)	11d to 1s
Bacon (English)	1s 2d to 1s 4d
" (Danish)	1s 5d to 1s 6d
Milk	5d per quart (London 6d)
Tea	2s 2d and upwards (duty 1s per pkt)
Coffee	1s 6d (since added duty of 4d)
Cocoa	1s to 3s
Lard	10d (a big rise in this since 1915)
Beef	1s to 1s 3d (dearer in large towns)
Mutton	1s 1d to 1s 2d " "
Pork	1s to 1s 2d " "
Candles	6d per lb (used to be 3 ½ d)
Paraffin	11d per gallon (" " 8d)

Roughly all clothing woollens etc. have advanced 25 per cent, as also have all cotton goods. Paper is also very dear and in some cases has advanced 150 per cent. All newspapers are smaller, the quality of the paper is also very poor, consequently the printing is bad.

Boots are much dearer. It is rather difficult to get any quantity of civilian boots - the manufacturers are overwhelmed with Army work both for our own Army and also for the Allies.

1916 April 10 Monday The intense fighting was again going on at Verdun yesterday. The attack was on a front extending 12 miles. A small advance was made at a terrible cost by the Germans in one place and they were compelled to retreat at another. Yesterday was the 50th day of this fighting round Verdun. All the points of the attack and the names of the places are quite household words in this country.

April 11 Tuesday Details of Sundays battle at Verdun came from Paris last night. A most ghastly affair. The Germans launched 3 attacks after a bombardment which had lasted from midday on Saturday. Each of these attacks was repulsed with awful slaughter, and in no case did the Germans get within 100 yards of the French. They were simply mown down. Thousands of dead and dying were left on the ground and the others fled. What a hellish thing that one man should have the power to send men to death in this senseless way. The real facts of these or this battle of Verdun have been carefully concealed from the people of Germany. They only see the official reports issued from Berlin and we and all other countries know that in most instances these are carefully 'cooked' so that they shall not reveal the real state of affairs. I cannot help thinking if only the German people knew the real state of affairs they would demand that useless slaughter of this kind should cease.

Much uneasiness is felt for our troops which are beleaguered at Kut on the Tigris. It was hoped on Saturday that the final effort which was to [be] made on Sunday to relieve them would be a success but this morning news is published that it failed. These people have now been besieged 120 days and it is feared they are getting very short of food.

April 12 Wednesday The Germans have been using liquid fire against the French at Verdun but in spite of this they do not make any progress. It is said on good authority they have lost 30,000 men since Sunday.

April 13 Thursday There is no news again to-day from Kut. It is believed that bad weather and the floods of the Tigris have much impeded operations there.

The attacks at Verdun have ceased since the last big ones on Sunday and Monday. The French do not publish their losses but it is generally thought they have lost about 40 thousand men since February there.

There has been a renewal of the fighting on our own lines the last two days more especially at St Eloi

April 14 Friday Once again America has come into the situation over the torpedoing of neutral vessels. The Germans have sunk dozens of these without the least warning, and America now says that her patience is exhausted and that she will stop this kind of thing. She has said this so many times that she is only laughed at by the whole world. Perhaps she may be forced to take action <u>some</u> day.

April 15 Saturday The relief force has advanced a little way to Kut, about 3 miles, but the situation there is very critical, and I am almost afraid that the beleaguered men will be forced to surrender.

The fighting at Verdun has died down very much compared with what it was last Sunday Monday and Tuesday, but it is thought that the Germans will attack again, as to give up would be an acknowledgement that they have been defeated.

I do hope that the Allies will not be tempted to take a premature offensive. There are a number of people here who are clamouring for this. I think it far better tactics to let the Huns dash themselves against our defences and so destroy themselves. The time <u>will</u> come when it will be quite advisable to attack, but I do not think it has come at present.

1916 April 16 Sunday Little or no news to-day. The weather continues cold with biting winds. The snow from the Great Storm has disappeared down here in the valley but there are still considerable drifts on the uplands.

THE DIARY OF JOHN COLEMAN BINDER

Recruiting is still a burning question in this country. A cry for compelling all married men up to 41 years of age to enlist has been raised but I do not think it will succeed. Of the married men who attested last November only those from 19 to 27 have at present been called to the colours.

I think it more likely that the following scheme will be adopted. All men on reaching the age of 18 will become soldiers and will be at once enrolled, but will not be sent abroad until they are 19. Under the Conscription Act now in force only men who had reached the age of 18 on the 15th of August last are compelled to join. There are a considerable number who have attained that age since then. It is estimated there are 360,000 and I think it is most probable these men will be compelled to join.

The Prime Minister is to make a complete statement on Tuesday.

We have had no Zeppelin raids since Wednesday week for one thing the moon has been very bright and these raiders do not like moonlight. They are seen so very easily.

From information which reaches me from various sources I am quite sure that the Authorities still think that the enemy may make a dash to land troops in this country. Lord French is in supreme command of all the arrangements here and from what we know is quite satisfied that he will be able to cope with any landing. Large bodies of troops are being massed all down the East Coast. This is being done very quietly and it is only from word of mouth or letters that one can gather what is being done. For instance some of my friends write me from Norwich and say there are 50,000 men quartered there. These are principally Scotch regiments and I hear of many like incidents.

April 17 Monday The enemy continue to sink merchantmen of all nations without any warning. I view this continual sinking of ships with much uneasiness as tonnage is already scarce and freights are continually rising especially on neutral vessels. Yesterday 167 shillings per ton was paid for freight of grain from the Argentine to the French ports. This will give some idea as to [the] great increase there has been (in normal times about 40/- to 45/-). I think we may soon see some relief from this situation as America seems at last to have made up her mind to stop it and to-day has sent what is practically an ultimatum to Germany although no time limit has been fixed and she is preparing to enforce her demands by getting [ready] for war. I do not think it will come to that.

April [18] Tuesday The Russian Campaign in Asia Minor is going well and the Russians are now only 12 miles from Trebizond, the Turkish Black Sea Port. Affairs in Turkey go from bad to worse. Germany keeps a small army there of about 50,000 men and these assisted by the German officials in all the chief places in Government terrorize the whole country. Turkey is absolutely rotten and I quite believe will be wiped out as a European Power before the end of this war.

April [19] Wednesday The welcome news that the Russians have captured Trebizond is announced this morning. This is indeed good news and is a fine augury for what the Russians may do when they are able to move in other directions. I only wish the news to-day at home was as good, but it is not so. It is bad, decidedly bad. As I have foreseen from the very beginning a crisis has come over this Conscription business and it is quite possible that it may wreck this Coalition Ministry. Perhaps it is not quite accurate that the Conscription business is the real reason, but it is being used by the extreme section of the Tory Party headed by the "Times" as a means for getting rid of Mr Asquith. This faction is demanding that <u>every</u> man between 19 and 41 shall be compelled to join the Army. I am firmly of opinion that if this is done, it will bring the commercial business to a standstill. Money is the real backbone of this war. This country by its trading is making money and so helping to finance all our Allies. We have already lent them 800 Millions. Much as we admire the splendid bravery of the French it is quite certain that they, having called up every available man, would soon be compelled to give in unless they were backed by our money, and if we cease to trade we shall soon cease to fight. I hope some compromise may be arrived at but to-day things look very very awkward.

1916 Thursday April 20 At a late hour to-night it is announced that a compromise in the recruiting business has been arrived at and that the details will be told to a secret session of both Houses on Tuesday next.

149

DAY BY DAY THROUGH THE GREAT WAR

Friday April 21 To-day is Good Friday, but there is an entire absence of any holiday making.

It really seems as if events had now reached a crisis between America and Germany. America has sent a Note to Germany demanding that these submarine attacks upon neutrals shall cease at once and threatening that if they do not she will immediately break off relations with her. Various precautions are being taken in America for dealing with the large numbers of Germans and some Germans who are resident there.

April 22 Saturday It is said 'Everything comes to him who waits' and to-day we have a real confirmation of this. As I recorded in this journal during the Autumn of 1914 there were persistent reports that a large force of Russians were passing through England on their way to France. This was really a 'canard' but it was most widely believed in this country. However to-day it *is* true. We are told officially that a force of Russians has landed at Marseilles [and] are now going to join the French (probably at Verdun). We are not told how many there are, but I imagine there is not a great lot, and I think it has been done more to show the unity of the Allies than for any other purpose. Speculation is rife to-day as to how they reached France and it is generally thought that they embarked at Archangel, were taken well out into the Atlantic and then made for the Mediterranean, so missing our submarine infested waters.

There has been much trench war along our own front the last few days. It is said the Germans are about to attack us as they have done at Verdun.

April 23 Sunday Easter Sunday - What a grim satire on this Easter Day. Anywhere from 20 to 30 million men flying at each others throats and all the rest of the world only waiting for the opportunity of joining in the fray.

We have settled down to this war as a normal state of affairs although each day brings it home more closely to us in the dislocation of the ordinary times of peace. The price of articles is steadily rising. Some of this caused by artificial means such as taxation and the rest from natural causes such as lack of freight and congestion of the railways. Small quantities of goods are a very long time in coming through, some as much as a month in coming from Hull. There is also much stealing on the Railways. This is said to be due to the class of men that are now being employed.

Meat continues to rise in price and the best mutton is making about ¼ to 1/6 wholesale. Pork is also very dear. I have this week sold 21 Hogs which I quite think will cost the buyer 1/- per lb when he gets them killed.

We have had a little better week as regards weather, although we had a very sharp frost this morning. The fruit trees promise well but I am afraid if they come to perfection the fruit will not be much wanted as it is very very difficult to get sugar, and it looks as if this difficulty would increase as the war proceeds. Six cargoes have been sunk within the last few weeks. I am quite sure this submarine business is a great and growing danger to us and unless we can counteract it may yet cause us much suffering and distress.

Zeppelin raids are quite 'off' just now. They have not been over here for more than a fortnight. I quite think the means which have been adopted to repel them have been effectual.

Thousands of the Royal Engineers belonging to the Army are being used to repair the telephones and telegraphs destroyed by the Great Storm.

1916 Monday April 24 The relieving force on its way [to] Kut is again held up. The Turks have great natural advantages on their side and are making the most of them. This beleaguered force at Kut is causing much misgiving.

The demand of America that this sinking of neutral vessels shall cease seems to have made some impression in Berlin but I am very doubtful as to whether they will cease to use these submarines.

Tuesday April 25 A day of sensations. Enough events have been crowded into to-day to have lasted us a 12 months in ordinary times. I will chronicle them in the order in which they were announced.

An attempt of the Germans to land arms in Ireland by means of a vessel disguised as a merchantman. On board this vessel was Sir Roger Casement, a renegade Irishman who has been in Germany since the war commenced and has been trying to induce captured Irish prisoners to enlist in German service. The vessel was sunk but fortunately Casement was saved and captured. Event No. 1.

Event No. 2. About 11 o'clock it was announced there had been a Zeppelin raid over the Eastern Counties last night. This we knew as warnings were received here, but we did not come within the danger zone.

Event No. 3. About 2 o'clock the Admiralty published the news of a naval skirmish off Lowestoft. A German battle cruiser squadron appeared off that place about 4-30 this morning and after a fight of about 20 minutes with the local naval forces returned to their base. This on the face of it appears to be most unsatisfactory, that a squadron of this size should be able to come so close in and not be intercepted. Apparently there were no naval casualties but we await further information. Four people were killed on shore.

Event No. 4. About 4 o'clock the Irish Chief Secretary announced in the House that rebellion had broken out in Ireland yesterday. Serious disturbances had occurred in Dublin and that some parts of the City were in the hands of the rebels. Troops were being hurried up from the Curragh Camp and it was known that 12 soldiers had been killed. Owing to the Great Storm telegraphic communication is very much broken with Ireland still and up to the present these appear to be all the details that have come through.

And to finish up with the Secret Session of the House to settle if possible this Conscription business. Surely a wonderful day and although numbers of people gather to read the telegrams and discuss the news there is not great excitement. We await eagerly tomorrow's papers. Very late to-night. Zeppelins are reported over Woolwich.

Sir Roger Casement has been brought to London.

April 26 Wednesday This battle squadron of German Ships bombarded Lowestoft for about 20 [minutes] but it is admitted that their gunnery was bad. They ought to have blown the place to atoms in that time. It is surmised they came [from] Borkum which is only about 7 hours steaming from Lowestoft. Of course it is impossible to have a fleet all the way down our coast but the disquieting feature of this raid is the fact that the enemy must have known the dispositions of our ships so as to be able to make a dash like this. Probably a good deal of their information is gathered by means of their Zeppelins which are of far greater value as Scouts than as engines of war.

More information comes through from Dublin to-night. The rebels are ringed in the middle of the City. Eleven have been killed, and about 10 or 12 soldiers. The rest of Ireland is quiet. The best feature of this business is that the National Volunteers which is really a Home Rule organisation turned out to support the soldiers.

Thursday April 27 Up to an early hour this morning the rebels had not surrendered in Dublin but their Headquarters had been knocked to pieces and the Military had occupied it. Martial law reigns in Dublin.

The Conscription business has been settled for the time being. All boys as they reach the age of 18 will have to join the Army, and if the recruits amongst the unattested married men do not reach 200,000 before the end of May, compulsory powers will be put in force to call up all men up to 41 years old.

Much damage was done at Lowestoft by the bombardment, about 200 houses injured.

1916 April 28 The whole recruiting business is again in a state of chaos. A bill to embody the provisions I mentioned last night was introduced into the Commons yesterday but was withdrawn in less than 2 hours. It met such a hostile reception on the ground that all time expired men would be retained in the Army until the war was over. These constant upheavals are having a most disastrous effect on the country, and discontent is being expressed very openly. A new bill will probably [be] introduced next week, but it is shaking the Coalition Government and quite possibly may mean its downfall.

There is no improvement in the Irish situation. All Ireland has been put under martial law, and Sir John Maxwell has been sent to take command. The rebels still hold some of the principal buildings in Dublin and fighting continues in the streets.

April 29 Saturday   Late to-night comes almost the worst news of all. Our army at Kut near to Baghdad has been starved out and has been compelled to surrender. No details are given so we shall have to wait for Monday's papers. We have been hoping that this might be averted and it is quite possible that it might have been had it been a normal season on the Tigris, but the elements were all in favour of the Turks and against us.

April 30 Sunday   What a week we have gone through. It is a mercy we cannot see what is coming as we should be frightened to death.

Since last Sunday - Irish Rebellion, a naval raid, a Cabinet Crisis, not yet over, and to finish up with, the surrender at Kut. I think this has been the most depressing week of the war and it is only by taking a long view and quietly thinking and counting up the essential and real factors that one is able to withstand all this strain and reverse.

The real and outstanding fact to the credit side of the Allies is the undoubted fact that the Germans have been beaten at Verdun. Fighting is still going on, but it is hopeless from the German side and it is quite certain they would be glad to withdraw but they cannot do so. They attacked the wolf and the wolf has got hold of them. A most conservative estimate places their losses at 300,000 men [and] the French loss at 100,000. What an awful struggle. It has now lasted 66 days, with very brief interval. It is true the armies do not retreat from the field as they did years ago, but nevertheless defeat is quite as decisive. Another cheering feature for us is the stand that America is making about submarines. Either Germany has got to drop this business in its present form or America will go to war with her. The issue is clear and specific now, but it still trembles in the balance. An answer is expected from Germany to-day. I am inclined to think some way will [be] found to compromise.

These are some of the redeeming features of this terrible time. I think almost every one is now realising that we are in a grim death struggle with a most deadly and unscrupulous foe. We do not despair and we are not shrinking from it but we recognize that it will require all our coolness courage and dogged tenacity to win through.

The Irish business is a bad one, and never ought to have been allowed to reach its present stage. Firm and decisive measures six months since when these extreme men began to organize with the help of German money would have saved much trouble to-day. One happy thing about this is that it is condemned alike by Home Ruler and Ulsterman and I hope may soon be put down, but today's advices do not hold out much hope at present. The chief rebel centre is certain public buildings in Dublin and I imagine the authorities do not wish these to be injured, otherwise they could soon rout the rebels out of them. We await tomorrow's papers with much anxiety.

Yesterday Mr McMichael of this town received word that his son Douglas McMichael had died from wounds received in action in France. He was a 2nd Lieutenant in the Bedfordshires. This regiment was in a very tight place last Wednesday week and suffered severely. He was then wounded and died the next day.

1916 Monday May 1   Better news from Ireland this morning. The rebellion [has] been broken after grim fighting in Dublin streets. The leader has been killed (so he will not cause more trouble) and others wounded. Immense damage has been caused by fire. These rebels resemble more the Communists of Paris in 1874 than true rebels. The Post Office has been burnt down and Sackville Street is in ruins, but there are so many incidents that I cannot write them down. I will keep to-days newspapers where they are fully described. This outbreak has not caused much alarm in England as it [is] generally looked upon as [a] crazy brained plot engineered chiefly by German fools who seemed to imagine that England would be diverted from her main purpose by these means.

The surrender at Kut has caused much regret but no great dismay [as it] had been generally anticipated. These brave men had made a most gallant stand, and it was famine alone which caused their surrender. Of course Germany is jubilant, but it is quite possible that the captors may yet be captured as the Russians are rapidly cutting off the Turkish army from its base, and our relief army is also advancing.

THE DIARY OF JOHN COLEMAN BINDER

To-day about 500 of the Irish rebels have been brought across to this country.

May 2 Tuesday Not much news this morning from the war areas. Of course the fighting goes on from day to day more or less violently, but our front was comparatively quiet yesterday.

Zeppelins are about again to-night.

May 3 Wednesday To-day the Government have taken the plunge and decided on conscription for every man between 18 and 41. I still think it is unnecessary. We have to-day over 5 millions under arms, and if many more men are withdrawn from industry it will [cause] financial collapse.

Three rebel leaders in Ireland have been court-martialled and shot to-day, and the Chief Secretary (Mr Birrel) has resigned. A man of good and great ability, but too lax and easy going to deal with these extreme men in Ireland. The trouble ought to have [been] nipped in the bud. This rebellion is most certainly a direct result of allowing the Ulstermen to arm nearly 3 years since when they did so to oppose Home Rule.

May 4 Thursday The raid on Tuesday night caused the death and injury of 36 people chiefly in Yorkshire and Durham. It is said that at least five air ships were about. One was winged by our guns and came to grief in Norway. It was so badly damaged that it could not be steered and finally smashed up. One less!

There is much resentment to-day amongst business men at this last conscription call. If it is pressed to its utmost it will certainly mean the closing down of many businesses. I think the Government has given way to newspaper clamour, which they ought to have withstood.

May 5 Friday A hot debate last night in the House on Conscription which was carried by a majority of 297. After carefully reading the debate I am quite of the opinion that the minority was quite justified in opposing the last call. They contend that we are coming perilously near to the breaking point in industry and finance.

Excellent news from the war areas to-night. One Zeppelin was destroyed and smashed up by our fleet off the coast of Germany and another in flying over the harbour at Salonika was also knocked to pieces by the Allies warships there. Not a bad bag this, three Zeps in two days.

May 6 Saturday Germany's reply to America about submarine warfare was delivered last night. I can only describe it as 'shuffling'. It tries to evade the issue and quibbles and procrastinates. It is said in America that it will not satisfy them at all. This remains to be proved. They are taking precautions to deal with the Germans in America should a rupture ensue.

Three more rebels were executed in Dublin this morning. These leaders deserve their fate and no sympathy whatever is felt for them. They have behaved most abominably. They have caused not only the death of brave soldiers but also of many innocent women and children, and so have richly deserved what they have now got.

1916 May 7 Sunday Further reflection does not lessen my aversion to this last move as to conscription. I feel quite sure that if pressed to its full power it may cause the loss of this war. So many men will be withdrawn from industry and commerce that it will mean a financial and economic breakdown. The idea of those who are pressing for it seems to be that we should make a great offensive on our Western front and 'smash' as they call it the Germans. This I regard as quite impossible. If the Germans after 6 months careful and elaborate preparations have failed (and they have failed) to break through at Verdun how can we hope to do so. Looking quietly and calmly at this great struggle it appears to me to be a struggle of endurance, not of smashing blows, and I firmly believe that the side that can hold out the longest will win. These were the views of the now Minister of Munitions (Mr L. George) when he was Chancellor 12 months ago and although he has now recanted them I think they are quite as sound to-day as they were then. I believe it is the food question, the paying of taxation and the equipment and financing of our Allies together with our supreme navy that are the cardinal and vital factors in this war. These are far more important than pressing every available man into the fighting line, irrespective of the fact as to whether they will make good fighting material or not. These are views I hold and hold strongly and, as a member of a Local Tribunal, I shall do my utmost to prevent <u>every</u> man being conscripted.

DAY BY DAY THROUGH THE GREAT WAR

To-day I had an interesting talk with one of the men home from the front in France. He is an Oundle man named Craythorne and is in the 6th Northants. He says they are just opposite the Bavarians whom he described as good fighters at a distance but when cornered always ready to throw up their hands and surrender. He says nothing delights them more than to kill the wounded. Stringent orders have been issued that none of these Huns are to be made prisoners.

May 8 Monday   Just as everybody had concluded that the battle at Verdun was ended it burst out again on Saturday with all its former violence. It is said that no such rain of shells has ever been seen as that launched by the Germans, but in spite of all this they only advanced a few yards.

The situation in Ireland has much improved but the rebellion is still flickering, not in any organised form but 'sniping' still continues in Dublin at night.

May 9 Tuesday   America has once more accepted the German apology. Germany has promised that in future she will not sink merchantmen or passenger ships without warning. This remains to be seen. America says if she does she will practically declare war. So far so good. If Germany keeps her word it will ease this country very much, as really I believe this continual sinking of food vessels is our greatest danger.

We are to have daylight saving. On Sunday week, May 21, the clock will be put forward one hour. It will seem queer to go to bed by daylight. This change has chiefly been brought about by large consumers of artificial light who can see it will save them much money. The general public does not at all desire it but will quietly acquiesce as they think it will help to save. I believe it will cause much confusion especially amongst the lower classes for the first few weeks.

May 10 Wednesday   Public opinion is beginning to deprecate any more executions in Ireland. Twelve leaders have now been court-martialled and shot and a great number sent to penal servitude.

1916 May 10 continued.   Peace rumours are rife in all directions again just now. I pay very little attention to them. There can be no hope of peace until Germany has cleared out or been driven out of the territories she has taken.

May 11 Thursday   I wonder how long this great battle at Verdun will last. The fighting is as violent there as ever it was. Almost incessantly the dreadful carnage is going on. On Monday Australian troops brought from Egypt landed at Marseilles and went up to the front to take over part of the French lines, exactly where is not told but probably not at Verdun.

May 12 Friday   Mr Asquith announced last night that he was going to Ireland. There is a growing feeling that enough of the rebels (16) have been shot and that it is time something else should be done. Soldiers are good servants but bad masters. The dangers of a military rule are shown by the fact that a man walking along Dublin streets was arrested, taken to Portobello Barracks and shot without any trial whatever. This has caused a great sensation.

May 13 Saturday   There has been a fierce attack on our lines yesterday by the Germans, they succeeded in capturing 500 yards of trenches which we partly regained.

There is much talk again about Germany being short of food. Possibly she is, but one is very sceptical after the fiasco of 12 months when they said they were nearly starved out. This was done with the intention of deceiving us, and probably the same thing is going on now. It is quite impossible to give any credit to the reports which come from Germany, either civil or military. Most of them are deliberate lies, published to mislead us. It is quite easy to [disseminate] these reports as the whole Press is under Government control.

May 14 Sunday   This week meetings have been held in different towns and villages throughout the Country to try to enlist women for farm work. Such a meeting was held here last Tuesday, but was not a great success. The pay offered is not bad 3d per hour, but there are very few women who have a liking for work of this description.

It is also intended to get young Danes to come over to do farm work. There will be an agreement with them for 12 months and they will have to [be] paid 18/- per week and lodging. Mr Nunnelly of Wellingboro has been across to Denmark with other farmers trying to start this.

These facts will show how very short we are getting of labour and this applies not only to farms but to every other occupation.

Much speculation is taking place as to whether Germany will keep her promise to America and discontinue submarine warfare as she has hitherto carried it on. It is clearly seen that Germany has received from America a decided blow. She wished to make conditions but America said 'No conditions. This is contrary to international law and must cease or we break with you'. Germany had to give way but it has been a bitter pill for her. It remains to be seen if she will keep her word. I am not very sanguine: If she does it will be an immense [gain] to us, as this sinking of merchant vessels has been the greatest weapon she can use against us.

Meat is touching record prices I paid 1/5 per lb for loin of mutton this week. This is prohibitive and in future we shall have to buy very little of it. Fat beasts have made up to £59 and £60 this week. Pork is practically a shilling a pound.

The trial of Sir R. Casement for Treason commences to-morrow in London.

May 15 Monday   Very little fighting news this morning.

Casement's trial for Treason commenced to-day. There was nothing very new in the evidence. It was shown that he had been attempting to form an Irish regiment amongst the Irish prisoners in Germany, but that he met with very little success. Only 52 out of 3000 having joined it. And as regards his mission to Ireland to raise insurrection it was a clumsy fool's business, and doomed to failure from the very beginning.

1916 May 16 Tuesday   Russia has made a sudden move in Mesopotamia and has advanced to about 100 miles from Baghdad. A small naval action off the Belgian coast. No English casualties.

May 17 Wednesday   There has been much fighting on the Italian frontier, and the Austrians claim they have had a big success, but we have not yet received the Italian version.

The latest groups of the Married men from 27 to 41 are now being called up. These are the men who attested last November. This is causing much distress and breaking up of homes. It is utterly absurd to call up many of these men as they are quite unfitted for soldiers. The Government seem determined to force every man fit or unfit into the Army. It is difficult to get any real information but I imagine from inquiries that I have made that there must be at the present time over 2 Millions of men under arms in this country alone.

May 18 Thursday   Some hard fighting has been going on along the British lines the last two days. We have captured 250 yards of trenches on the Vimy Ridge.

The National Register which was made last August is now being brought up to date. The work here is being done by the same people who had charge of it at that time.

May 19 Friday   It has become clear that the Italians have met with a severe repulse on their front, although the Austrians have had to pay very dearly for it.

The chief fighting still continues round Verdun where the Germans are continually bringing up fresh troops, and where they have not advanced a mile after nearly 90 days almost continuous fighting. It is without doubt the bloodiest and longest battle ever known, and there does not seem at present any prospect of it ceasing.

May 20 Saturday   In spite of all German precautions our submarines have again slipped through into the Baltic and to-day it is announced that two enemy vessels have been sunk.

There is a curious lull just now (except Verdun) and again the public is becoming impatient and is asking 'What are we doing'. For myself I do not look to see any bid movement this summer at all, and I think it is quite possible that the war will continue through next winter, and well into the year and even longer. Germany may be getting short of food, but at present as far as one can hear not a single person has died of hunger. I am far more inclined to think that the real first break up will come from the downfall of Turkey.

May 21 Sunday   We have to-day started what is known as 'Summer Time'. Before going to bed last night I put the clock on 1 hour. Of course it has not been at all noticeable to-day, but it is to-night when we require very little artificial light and are practically going to bed by daylight. I usually go to bed at ten o'clock but now it will be really nine and it is scarcely dark at that hour. Of course we get up an hour earlier in the morning. These arrangements will continue in force until September 30 when we shall put the clock back one hour and so revert to ordinary solar time. There is not much disposition to contest this change except amongst farmers. I think they will get over it by beginning work by the new time of 7 (which will be really 6) and so adhering to their present arrangements which are certainly far better suited to their needs than the new ones.

Zeppelin warfare has been very quiet lately and we have had no raids. Enemy sea planes were over Kent about 2 a.m. yesterday morning. Two people were killed and some little damage done.

May 22 Monday   According to reports this morning the fighting around Verdun on Saturday was simply awful. Thousands were killed and wounded. All the advantage the Germans gained was the capture of one part of a trench. The battle was resumed again yesterday in fact had last[ed] all through Saturday night.

The Russian Cavalry have joined hands with our forces which were sent up to relieve Kut (but which did not attain their object). This is a very smart and dramatic business but I do not think it is of any great value from a military stand point as the country through which they marched is said to be quite impracticable for either infantry or artillery, but it will certainly impress the Turks. The Turkish Empire is slowly but surely going from bad to worse. Its internal condition, reports of which we get through authentic American sources, is appalling, and it seems inevitable that it will drop to pieces.

1916 May 23 Tuesday   Hard fighting yesterday on our front and we have had a set back. The trenches which we gained on the Vimy Ridge last week from the Germans have been lost. This part of the line is [of] considerable importance and during the time the French faced the Germans here there were many fierce struggles for these trenches and they changed hands many times.

Some details of the details of the Verdun battle of the last few days is given from Paris to-day. The fighting seems gradually to have increased in violence from last Thursday up to 1 p.m. on Sunday. The slaughter must have been sickening. On the German side the Bavarians were chiefly engaged, and even Berlin acknowledges they lost three parts of their men. The net result is comparatively small. The French confidence is unabated. We cannot learn if either Australians or Russians are fighting on this section.

A very grave and serious warning was given by the Minister of Agriculture last night in the House, respecting our food supply. He said that we had reached the danger point and it was absolutely dangerous to withdraw more men from agriculture. This warning was really addressed to Local Tribunals, many of which seem obsessed by the idea that their sole function is to procure men for the Army and to ignore the production of food altogether. I am glad the Government has at last recognized this danger. To any one living in an agricultural district it has been patent for long enough. As I have said many times before in this Diary, I believe this food question is the greatest one we have to face, and if not very carefully handled may yet cause us to give way. One Member (Prothero) last night urged the Government to grapple with this question and to put the whole nation on limited rations.

May 24 Wednesday   Yesterday the French taking advantage of the German attacks further west suddenly attacked the enemy towards Douaument and captured the Fort which the Germans had held since February. This was a great victory but the fighting was terrible.

May 25 Thursday   The Germans appear to have been raised into absolute frenzy by the reverse which they sustained on Tuesday and yesterday launched almost incredible attacks on Douaument. Whole divisions were flung into the fight time after time. The carnage baffles all description. The ground is said to be absolutely covered with the dead. The defence of the French is magnificent. To-night's report says that the enemy succeeded in getting into what is called the Fort (but which really now [is]a series of trenches) but that the French hold all the approaches to it. It does not seem possible that fighting like this can continue long.

A Meeting of the Local Tribunal was held here to-night. There were 16 claims before us either for exemption or asking to be put back for a time. It took us about three hours to deal with this business. I am glad to say that the members of this Tribunal are getting a little more reasonable and are beginning to see that it is their duty to deal fairly between the Army and the People and not to force every man who comes before them into Army service. Another meeting is to be held to-morrow night.

May 26 Friday   The battle at Verdun still goes on. The French hold their ground and make the enemy pay an awful cost for every inch they give way.

Another meeting of the Local Tribunal was held to-night. 14 cases were gone through. Several tradesmen who appealed were given 'Conditional Exemption', that is were exempted on condition they continued in the business in which they are now engaged. Several masters asked to be allowed to retain their men as they were absolutely necessary to their business. In some cases this was allowed and in others from two to three months exemption was given. Although I am a member of this Tribunal it is most distasteful business to me. Some of the cases are most difficult and it is only the thought that we are in much danger and that [it] is necessary that every man should do his part (although it may be unpleasant) that makes me continue to do the work.

1916 May 27 Saturday   The intense fighting at Verdun has died down during yesterday although great artillery fire on both sides continues. I wonder what the Germans have lost there during the last month. Perhaps we may never know. I believe they dare not publish their actual losses. It is currently reported to-day that [they] have had to withdraw troops from opposite the British front to feed this furnace at Verdun. A dangerous game this.

May 28 Sunday   A beautiful May day. The Country is looking very beautiful and there is every prospect of an abundant hay and clover crop, if only labour can be got to gather it. Farmers are beginning to complain bitterly of the depletion of labour by the Army and meetings are being organized to protest against it. A large meeting was held at Peterborough this week. Women are being freely used in field labour. This is allright but they cannot do the work of men. I am quite certain that to withdraw more men from agriculture would be very dangerous.

'Summer Time' has worked very well since it was begun last Sunday. Every one appears to have got used to it, and it has been accepted with very little comment.

May 29 Monday   The French have again driven back the enemy at Verdun and recaptured some of the ground the[y] lost last Tuesday.

May 30 Tuesday   Things are going rather badly in Italy. Austria has made a strong thrust and has dealt Italy a bad blow. I think it will take her all her time to hold up against it.

Another new factor enters the war - yesterday the Bulgarian Army officered by Germans has invaded Greece. They claim this as compensation for the Allies holding Salonica. The Greek King is said to favour this invasion but the people are protesting against it. It is quite possible this King may get toppled off his throne before this war is over.

According to to-nights advices grim fighting is again renewed at Verdun. This makes 100 days this mighty battle has continued. It is safe to say that no such battle as this has ever been fought in the world's history.

May 31 Wednesday   Reports this morning say that the Germans having failed to break through at Verdun are now calling the Austrians to their help.

Much resentment is felt in this country against the American President for the attitude he has adopted the last few days. Speaking the day before yesterday he said "With the objects and aims of this war America had no concern." America will find to her cost if we are defeated that these things do concern her very much for she will be the next to be attacked by Germany, and we are fighting just as much for America as we are for ourselves.

June 1 Thursday Verdun is still the greatest centre of interest in these days and the attention of the whole world is fixed upon it. The battle is so great that really few details come through. Only the broad outline is published. It looks almost as if Germany had determined to win here or to confess defeat. It is certainly a mighty struggle between two peoples and I think involves far more than is apparent to us just now. It is generally thought that the French are receiving powerful help both from ourselves and the Russians.

We are gradually rounding up the Germans in East Africa and it will not be long before their last Colony is taken from them. This campaign is being admirably fought by General Smuts the Boer leader from S. Africa. He has also a considerable force of Englishmen under his command. The continual capture of these colonies must be very galling to Germany. She had spent such huge sums on them and was always bragging of what she was going to do with them.

June 2 Friday The fight at Verdun goes on with varying fortune. Give and take. Here a trench lost, there a trench won. I hear that at the back of the French lines, there are reserve forces of English and Russians.

Late to-night I hear of a naval action in the North Sea.

1916 June 3 Saturday We have a blow full in the face this morning. A great naval battle commencing on Wednesday afternoon lasting all night and part of Thursday has been fought off the coast of Jutland, and we to say the least of it have met with a great repulse. According to the statement published by the Admiralty at one o'clock this morning we have lost a total of 16 vessels including 3 Battle Cruisers. The Queen Mary, Invincible and --- and also destroyers. Very few details are allowed to be published at present but it is indeed a heavy blow, and one seems almost dazed by it. It is useless to try to form any judgement on it until we hear more information. As far as one can tell this morning the Germans appear to have lost about nine vessels. It is certainly the greatest naval battle since Trafalgar. Judging from what one can see we have lost about 5000 skilled seamen. The only thing one can do is to try to bear up bravely under this defeat. If I know anything about Englishmen it will only cause us to stick closer to this war and not to give way an inch. It is quite impossible to estimate what influence it may have, also to know what brought about this battle and the reason why we suffered so heavily, but I can only think our ships must have been drawn into the enemy's mine field.

No more news than the above has been published to-day. Rumour says the German loss is heavier than at first reported, also that our loss is reduced to 11 vessels. I am afraid we shall have to wait until Monday for more news.

June 4 Sunday No real news to-day only rumours.

June 5 Monday Much better news to-day. What appeared on the face of it to be a defeat of our fleet is quite the reverse and we can certainly claim the victory.

The impression of defeat arose from the bungling way in which the Admiralty issued their report late on Friday but now more authentic reports are issued it is quite clear the Germans have come off second best. It was a mighty battle and even to-day one cannot grasp it. At present it is not at all clear how it arose, but there is one very significant sentence in the German report which says " during the enterprise directed northward". This is generally taken to mean that the enemy had come out to raid our coasts and were caught. It is quite evident they were driven back although our losses in doing this were terrible. They were much superior to us at the outset, but our men and ships went for them and held them engaged but directly our heavy Dreadnoughts came up and made affairs equal the enemy bolted and ran pursued furiously by our ships. Our fleet swept the seas all day on Thursday but the enemy declined to come out again. They lost 17 ships and also great numbers of men. It has been a great battle but has not helped the Germans one ounce. The blockade is still as strict as ever and quite unbroken, and our Grand Fleet still sails the seas.

There is much grumbling to-day that the Admiralty allowed such a garbled [report] to be published on Friday and so cause such depression on Saturday and Sunday. They say to-day it was because Admiral Jellicoe had not returned to port.

THE DIARY OF JOHN COLEMAN BINDER

Much uneasiness was caused on Saturday by these reports as we have such unbounded faith in the Navy and know that it is our chief and strongest defence against this ruthless enemy, and it was felt that if we were to lose confidence in it we might as well throw up the sponge, but to-day confidence is quite restored and although we mourn the terrible loss of men we feel quite secure behind our line of defence.

This naval battle has drawn off attention the last two days from the great battles in France, both at Verdun where it is said the crisis is coming and also at Ypres on our own lines where another great battle has commenced. It looks as if the Germans had made up their minds to do something this summer. It is quite evident they are being pressed very much in their own country and do not want another winter of it. I think they will get another winter.

1916 June 6 Tuesday It is said that it is the unexpected that generally happens. This is certainly so to-day. Much consternation was caused this afternoon by a report issued by the Admiralty which stated that HMS Hampshire which was taking Lord Kitchener and his staff to Russia was either torpedoed or struck a mine off the Orkneys last night about 7-30 and that he and all on board have perished. It occurs to me that it was known to the enemy by means of spies that he intended to go to Russia and that it was determined to kill him if possible. We are still infested with these spies and the authorities are much to blame that they do not take stricter means against them. There is still one of these German fellows Van Rosa acting as a master in the School here and going about most unconcernedly. It is a crying shame. He ought to be under lock and key.

This death of Lord Kitchener is certainly a heavy blow to us, as he was probably the best organiser that we have, and we owe a great debt to him. He was a man of iron will and had gained his high position by sheer ability.

The Russians have made a quick move and heavy one the last two days. As is their wont they have been very quiet lately but to-day a curt telegram from Petrograd announces a great victory over the Austrians on the borders of Roumania. They captured 13,000 prisoners. The Austrians admit this. This will help to draw off the pressure of the Austrians upon the Italians where affairs have not been going at all well lately.

1916 June 7 Wednesday The whole Empire to-day is mourning the death of Lord Kitchener. On all exchanges and markets yesterday business was at once suspended as a mark of respect to him. He possessed to a most remarkable degree the confidence of the nation more especially of the middle and lower classes. The upper classes did not take to him so much as they found he was a man who could not be moved by their influence to favour their own class. He was a silent solitary figure, standing alone and having but few real friends, but we knew and trusted him and felt that he represented just that British courage and determination which is required to bring this terrible war to a successful issue. It is said that when war was declared he said it would last three years and I quite believe his foresight will prove to be right. I am thankful that his end did not come sooner as his great share of this conflict has to a large extent been done. The vast army which we now have in every land is his best monument and must ever remain associated with his name. Indeed when war commenced and new levies were being raised they were always spoken of as 'Kitchener's Armies'.

The Russians announce to-day they have increased their capture of prisoners to 40,000 and 134 guns. This victory is already causing Berlin and Vienna much concern as they see in it the first signs of the coming storm. 900 officers were taken prisoner.

June 9 Friday The fort at Vaux about 7 miles from Verdun which the Germans said they had taken last March has been levelled to the ground and the Germans are now occupying the site.

The war seems to increase daily in volume, and this and every other county is filled with its noise and clamour.

June 10 Saturday Events are moving fast on the Russian front, and it is now certain that they have delivered a real smashing blow at the Austrians. They have broken down the Austrian trenches (really scientific affairs) for 100 miles and are closely following the retreating enemy. Up to to-night they announce they have captured 66,000 prisoners since last Sunday, including many Germans. This shows that other troops have been rushed up to help them.

DAY BY DAY THROUGH THE GREAT WAR

We know to-day that [there] are 12 survivors of the ill fated 'Hampshire'. They came ashore on a raft and report that Lord Kitchener was lost through the swamping of a boat in the heavy sea.

The Government have commandeered all the wool in the Country. Merchants have had [to] make a return of all the stocks they hold. The local sales of this year's clip was about to be held. In fact it had been pitched at Kettering yesterday when an officer from the War Office stopped the sale and ordered that all the farmers should take it back home, saying that the Government would purchase it. I am told they are likely to pay about 42/- per tod for it. This is a little under last year's price. I quite think if it were sold on the open market it would make 56/-.

1916 Sunday June 11 Whit Sunday, but no holidays this year, or very little. All munitions works are going without ceasing as the demand is still great and urgent. Only one days holiday in the shoe making places for here the huge Russian orders are being got through and the work is ceaseless. Manufacturers even now are behindhand as labour is scarce. Every man is engaged on army work and civilian boots are not easy to get.

Surely the last ten days have been more crowded with events than almost any other period of the war. They succeed each other like scenes on a cinematograph. Before one can fully grasp one another has succeeded. The huge battles at Verdun, on our front at Ypres and Hooge, on the Italian front, now the tremendous blow on the Russian and the fierce naval battle of Jutland or Horne Reef as it is sometimes called. All these events make it difficult to keep a true and calm survey of this tremendous struggle.

One thing I can affirm without fear of contradiction and that is as time passes it is quite certain that ours was the victory in the North Sea. It is now clearly seen that in spite of our losses the Germans did not succeed in their main object whatever it was, either the raising of blockade, the getting of fast cruisers into the Atlantic or the raiding of our coasts. They were driven back without ceremony to the shelter of their mine fields and ports and have sustained such damage that it is doubtful if they will ever come out to risk another battle, we all hope they will. Our ships are all ready again. Within four hours of Jellicoe's return to port he had coaled and was again ready to fight. The blockade is tighter than ever and not a single shot was fired on our coasts, and yet the German Emperor is screaming about victory ! ! We have learned to estimate all these German claims at their true value and we simply tell them they are liars.

The last few days a feeling has got abroad that we are nearing the close of the war. People are saying that it will not go through another winter, and that Germany is trying hard to force a decision. Personally I do not share these views (I wish I could) but at present I can see no end in sight. Germany may be getting into a bad state, but she is not beaten, and certainly is not ready to accept our terms of peace.

June 12 Whit Monday . A cold wet stormy day.

Remarkable news comes from the Russians this morning. They are still continuing their hammer blows on the Austrians and on Saturday captured 35,000 more prisoners and an enormous amount of booty. They seem to have got the Austrians fairly on the run and we hear of cavalry charges, capture of batteries etc quite in the old style of warfare, instead of this everlasting trench business.

What effect these victories will have on the political situation cannot be seen at present, but it is quite certain they will have a decided bearing on the military aspect of affairs, and must upset the enemies' plan of campaign for this summer. Already the situation in Italy has been eased very much.

June 13 Tuesday The Austrians aided by the Germans have at last pulled themselves together and are making a bit of a stand in several places, but in others are still in headlong flight.

This last strike of the Russians has been managed exceedingly well. It is probable the Austrians had no idea they were about to strike. In fact some of the Austrian generals narrowly escaped capture last week as the Russian cavalry was close upon their heels. The Russians are now much better armed with artillery than they were last year (it has come from us and also from Japan) and are making good use of it.

June 14 Wednesday The great fighting still continues at Verdun and has extended also to Ypres where our own army is heavily engaged. Last week terrific fighting took place on the section held by the Canadians. Their losses were very heavy and they had to retire from some of their trenches, but to-night comes the news that they have recaptured all of them.

THE DIARY OF JOHN COLEMAN BINDER

I think the food question must be causing the enemy much anxiety. Writing home to his people a man named Butt who has been a prisoner in Germany since Sept 1914 says their rations are very very small, and asks that the parcels of food may still be sent to him. He says that the women beg the English food from the prisoners to give to their children.

It is no exaggeration to say that thousands of pounds worth of food is sent every week to our prisoners in Germany, and men who have been exchanged say that the prisoners are chiefly kept alive by this food. The next two months in Germany must be a very critical time as regards food.

1916 June 15 Thursday The total of prisoners captured by the Russians up to yesterday is 140,000. A part of the Austrian Army is in a very tight place and may yet have to surrender.

June 16 Friday Yesterday afternoon after a few days of comparative quiet the great battle at Verdun was renewed in all its former intensity. Some people appear to see this as the last real attack. I am doubtful. Germany is fighting there to gain time and to try to break the French before Russia could resume the offensive, but she has been deceived and Russia is now moving on with great strides. One of the reasons of this move on the part of Russia is our naval victory at Jutland. Germany ought to be attacking Russia towards the North and Riga, but is unable to do this without the help of her fleet. It is thought this fleet, being unable to pass through the Kiel Canal on account of the depth of water required by its newest ships was on its way to the Baltic through the Skagerack to make an attack on Riga, but our victory over it so badly mauled it that [it] is certain that it will [be] useless for offensive purposes for months to come.

Saturday June 17 Russia is still sweeping on and capturing thousands of prisoners. Their total captures since June 6 amount to 166,000 men and officers and enormous war material.

We are having this June a most cold and cheerless time. Temperature is very low. The hay harvest has scarcely commenced. There is an abundance of grass, the great difficulty will be to get labour to harvest it. Women are being much employed in some districts but not very much round here.

Bread has fallen in price this week to 7 ½d per 4lb loaf. This is a direct result of the Government compelling so many ships to carry wheat from Canada and the States. Freights have fallen about 10/- per quarter and English wheat now stands at about 48/- to 49/- with a slow dragging demand. It is quite probable that we [shall] have still lower values as it is quite well known that there was never so much wheat in the world as there is to-day. The difficulty has been to get ships to bring it here.

The optimist view as to the ending of the war continues to grow, and people are eagerly predicting some collapse. The curious thing about this is that in eagerly waiting for some sensational event they fail to realize the greatness of such things as the battle of Jutland, the battle of Verdun and the Russian offensive. These are events of the first magnitude and are having deciding consequences on the war. Some critics look for us to repeat Russia's performance and to break through the lines in France and Belgium and to march in triumph to Berlin. Wait and see.

The growling about the way in which the victory of Jutland was announced has not yet ceased and some sharp and plain speaking will take place when Parliament meets again.

The final calls to the colours of all men between 18 and 41 are now being issued, and all appeals for exemption have to be lodged before June 24.

I do not know if all the Army people manage their business in the same way as it is done at Kettering (which is the centre for North Northants). This week they sent a call to a man who joined six months since and a warrant to arrest a man as a deserter who joined eighteen months since and had been killed in the trenches. Army efficiency ! ? ! Verbum sap

1916 June 19 Monday The Russians on Saturday captured Czernovitz, the capital of the Austrian Duchy of Bukhovina. A place of much importance. They are still steadily doubling the Austrians up and it is possible that we may see a huge debacle of their army yet. Germany is doing what she can to send some assistance but I imagine she has her hands pretty full just now.

The desperate fighting is again in progress at Verdun. The Germans are freely using liquid fire and all other hellish devices.

DAY BY DAY THROUGH THE GREAT WAR

June 20 Tuesday News is reaching us from Germany of the shocking treatment of all prisoners of war there, including and more especially our own men. About a fortnight since a postcard which in some way had escaped the German censor was received by Mr North (of Oundle) from his son Reginald North who is prisoner saying that they had been removed from Germany and were now on Russian territory and that the Germans were half starving them. To-day he has received another card saying that they are not now receiving the parcels of food, which are being sent to them every week from England. These no doubt they are taking for themselves. This is quite what you would expect these German dogs to do.

On the other hand German prisoners are well kept, clothed and fed at all detention camps in this country.

June 21 Wednesday A local tribunal meeting here to-night. Twenty cases were heard and exemptions from 1 to 4 months were given in the difficult cases.

June 22 Thursday The Russian drive still continues especially in the south close to Roumania. After the fall of Czernovitz a part of the army swung back and has got a large number of Austrians pinned up against the Roumanian frontier.

June 23 Friday Verdun fighting still continues. Paris says the "ferocity increases hour by hour". The Germans are now about 4 miles from Verdun. This place is said to be a name only now, as it has been so battered that it is only a mass of ruins.

Saturday June 24 A beautiful bright day for Midsummer day. We are hardly using artificial light at all now. One gets up by daylight and goes to bed by the same. This putting the clock on has been quite accepted as one of the ordinary things of life. The only thing one notices is that the atmosphere is a little chilly in the morning.

It seems quite possible that America may be drawn into this world war even now. Mexico has caused much trouble to the States for the past two years and now Germany is stirring her up to create new trouble. It is quite possible that war may ensue between the States and Mexico. This will please Germany as she thinks the States will have their hands full and so be able to supply us with less war material.

Sunday June 25 Much discontent was expressed by farmers attending Peterborough and Northampton Markets yesterday regarding the Government's proposals as to this year's clip of wool. The Government propose to commandeer the whole clip, to pay 30 per cent higher prices than those existing before Aug 4 1914 (the declaration of war), to pay nothing to the farmer for storing it, and to allow nothing for depreciation. This price is certainly less than it would fetch if it were sold upon the open market. Buyers were quite prepared to pay at least 50/- for it at Kettering when the sale was stopped about three weeks since. Of course many farmers also are not in a position to hold it long as they need the money. Army people are always unreasonable in their proposals, and in many instances have frightfully mismanaged affairs. It is always the same old tale with them . . They never seem to learn anything.

All men who had not joined the Army under the Group system are as from to-day reckoned as having enlisted and are now receiving papers ordering them to join at specified places on certain days. These men still have the right to appeal for exemption to the Local Tribunals, and if an appeal has been lodged (yesterday was the last day for doing this) the Army cannot compel them to join until their appeal has been heard. Here again the muddle in the Army is appalling. As a matter of fact they have to-day at Kettering (which is the centre for this district) 19,000 cases under consideration, and they make the most absurd blunders. Last week they sent a warrant to the police to arrest a man whom they said had failed to join when called up. As a matter of fact, the man had enlisted during the early stages of the war, and had been killed ! ! !

I do not know what will take place after the war, but I am safe in saying that the more the general public become acquainted with this conscription business the less they like it.

We hear nothing in these inland places now about the Zeppelins. We only receive warnings after they have crossed the coast line, and we have had nothing of this for some months now. I saw a friend from Hull this week and am told that there they receive warnings when the Zeps are out at sea. The last they had was about a month since (when there was no moon). It looks as if the means taken to prevent them coming inland had proved effective. The last time they visited Hull <u>5 tons</u> of broken glass was taken away from the Market Place.

THE DIARY OF JOHN COLEMAN BINDER

1916 June 26 The Germans are now within three miles from Verdun. The fighting since Friday is such as [has] probably never been known. The French still say that they can hold it but I am doubtful.

On the Russian side things are much better, especially in the South. Here the Russians have pinned up part of the Austrian Army and are now turning once more south east and climbing the passes of the Carpathians. In the North the Germans have rushed up troops it is said both from the lines in France and also from Italy, and are fighting with much determination.

On our own front to-day's report says that the gun fire has been terrific. This looks like the preliminary to a move if possible.

Tuesday June 27 To-day's report says that the German attacks at Verdun are slackening. It is certain they have been obliged to draw off whole divisions to meet the new menace on their Eastern front. The way in which these Frenchmen fight at Verdun is magnificent. Nothing seems to daunt them, and they are quietly and supremely confident. It is simply marvellous. I think they feel it is the death grip of two peoples rather than that of two armies.

Excellent news comes from Italy this morning. The Italians have regained the initiative and have forced the Austrians back almost to the positions they occupied before their recent advance. This advance had been carefully prepared and at least 400,000 Austrians and enormous quantities of the very heaviest artillery were engaged in it, and it has now quite failed and the Austrians on this front as well as the Russian front are now on the run.

On our own front important fighting is taking place, and General Haig says that our troops pierced the German lines at ten places yesterday and Sunday.

I think the German General Staff and the Kaiser must be thinking rather furiously just now. We are evidently approaching a critical phase in this terrible war.

June 28 Wednesday Yesterday was s quiet day at Verdun, that is comparatively quiet. I expect if any of us could have seen it we should have thought it anything but quiet.

The Germans are making great efforts to retrieve affairs on the Russian front and some very hard fighting in [which] they claim success is going on. But we take very little notice of what is said in Berlin now. It is quite impossible to believe anything they say and their reports are only issued for the purpose of deceiving their own people.

Strong statements were made in the House last night as to the starving of our prisoners in the German camp at Rhuleben. This has been going on for a month or more and our Government has called upon the Germans (through the American Ambassador) either to feed them or release them, threatening if they do not do so to retaliate upon German prisoners here. This course is very hateful to us here, but it seems the only possible plan. I am afraid it will not be of much use, as the German rulers seem utterly callous to any suffering which they may cause either to their own people or to any one else.

1916 June 29 Thursday No very fresh news to-day, except that the intense artillery fire all along our own lines in France continues. I am told by a soldier who has just been home on leave that some very heavy artillery has lately been sent up to the front. Huge monsters such as they have not had before.

The firing of these guns was heard quite plainly yesterday and the previous day in the south and south eastern counties.

The trial of Sir Roger Casement the Irish rebel which has been going on since Monday came to an end this morning. He was found guilty of treason and condemned.

June 30 Friday The Russians have gained another victory in Galicia and have captured 10,000 Austrian prisoners and are still marching onwards.

At Verdun the hand -to -hand fighting continues. On the whole the French maintain their positions but the carnage is simply awful.

DAY BY DAY THROUGH THE GREAT WAR

To-night's report from our front speaks of furious artillery fire and also of raids into the enemy trenches.

July 1 Saturday A day of fate in this great war and one that may mean much as to its duration. About two o'clock this afternoon telegrams were posted announcing that at last the English had been let loose on the German trenches, and that along a line of 20 miles (just north of the Somme (where [we] are linked up with the French) a furious battle was raging. This battle had commenced at 7.30 this morning after a week of violent artillery fire which had rendered the German trenches almost untenable.

A later telegram received about two o'clock in London says that the battle was still in progress and that the first line of German trenches had been quite occupied. The French on our immediate right were also attacking and indeed all along our lines a distance of 90 miles actions were in progress but it is clear that the 20 miles just North of the Somme was the storm centre.

It is generally thought to-day that this is the beginning of the move which has been foreshadowed and talked of so long, but I will reserve my opinion. It may only be that this attack has been decided upon to relieve Verdun and to demonstrate to the Allies that we on our front are doing something and also prove to the enemy that he will have to reckon not with isolated attacks like those of last summer (such as Neuve Chapelle and Hooge) but with huge concerted attacks on each of his fronts.

At any rate there is much anxiety and restlessness to-night throughout the country and we await with much anxiety to-morrow's papers.

July 2 Sunday The Sunday Papers to-day contain only one further brief telegram, which says that we had occupied the first German trenches and were about to attack the second line. We are anxious for more information.

Yesterday the Government announced that no farmer may sell this year's hay or straw crop without permission from the War Office. It looks as if there will be very little hay to sell this year unless we get an alteration in the weather. For seven consecutive days we have had a downpour of rain in the middle of the day, quite enough to soak the hay through and to prevent it being carted.

Monday July [3] This mornings news is quite good and satisfactory. The telegrams and dispatches from Head quarters are quietly confident, and although it is evident we have struck (in conjunction with the French) a very heavy blow at the Germans there is no such boasting as we have had in some papers on other occasions.

The tone is quiet and confident and we feel that along with our Allies we are now going to be on top and that we and not the enemy have the initiative. Reading the accounts of the great battle (which I think will be known as the Battle of the Somme) one cannot but be struck by the careful preparation which had been made on our side. Berlin is, to say the least of it, not jubilant. They recognize that in future the Allies will not strike wild isolated blows, but will carefully co-ordinate their strategies.

Russia still keeps up her victorious march and the Austrian Army is getting very badly mauled. We do not on our side expect to see anything like this at present, but some day we hope to see things moving a bit swifter, but we have patience and all being well victory is certainly coming on our side.

1916 July 4 Tuesday This mornings news is satisfactory. All gains have been held and some further advance has been made. Our casualties have not been published but train loads of wounded are coming through to London, and are being sent to the various hospitals in the country. The first convoy arrived at Charing Cross on Sunday night.

The French made notable advances on our right yesterday and broke quite through the German second lines. They have found some extraordinary fortifications going in some cases thirty feet deep.

To-night's news I do not think is quite so good on our front. The enemy are evidently bringing up fresh troops and the battle is raging furiously. The French report that the pressure at Verdun has been relaxed, so that some good has been done in that direction.

July 5 Wednesday To-day's news is practically of yesterdays. We expect this battle to last for a long time, and we do not expect to drive the enemy back very far at present although the French are advancing more rapidly and their cavalry are said to have been in action.

The 3rd Northants Yeomanry have gone over yesterday at very short notice. These have been trained more as mounted infantry than as cavalry.

July 6 Thursday This great battle is continuing and seems likely to do so. There is a distinctly more hopeful feeling abroad now that the long period of waiting is ended, and it is realized that the Allies have begun to 'squeeze' the enemy.

Train loads of wounded are continually arriving here. To-night 200 came to Duston. The Red Cross work for the wounded still goes on throughout the County and many women are doing great work.

July 7 Friday To-day Sir John Jellicoe's despatch of the Battle of Jutland is published. It is written with remarkable restraint and is conspicuous for rather what it conceals than for what it tells us. These are things which we would very much like to know such as the work of the Zeppelin aeroplanes etc. but we shall have to wait as we cannot afford to give the enemy any information.

This despatch clearly shows that our confidence in the Navy is quite justified, and that they thoroughly beat the Germans. They fought well up to a certain point, but directly they began to receive punishment they [were] all to pieces.

July 8 Saturday Yesterday saw a great renewal of our attack on the Germans, and some terrible fighting in which on the whole the advantage was with us. The French are feeling the benefit of attacks. At Verdun the enemy is relaxing his efforts as he requires all his men to meet us and has no more to throw into the battle there.

Great news comes from Russia to-day. Not content with doubling up the Austrian Army in the South and towards Galicia, the Russians are falling upon the <u>German</u> Armies in the North and have badly mauled them capturing 7000 <u>German</u> prisoners. This pushing of the enemy on all his fronts at the same time must cause him great uneasiness.

The food business in Germany evidently does not improve, and must be a source of much anxiety to them.

To-day has been Speech Day at the School here and much excitement was caused amongst the boys and visitors by the unexpected visit of one of the 'Old Boys' on an aeroplane. He flew from Thetford in Norfolk in about an hour this morning and gave a good exhibition of flying before coming down on the School Cricket Field. He circled round the Church Spire, "looped the loop" etc. etc. He also came over Jesus Church about 5 pm flying very low just before starting for home.

1916 Sunday July [9] A beautiful summer day. Hay making has been very slow this week as we have had frequent thunderstorms.

The rain has done immense good to the corn which has now much improved. Wheat is well in ear. Harvest I think must be late. Wheat has again gone up in value and is now quoted at 52/- to 53/- quite 5/- dearer than it was a fortnight since.

Monday July [10] The fighting along our front died down a little yesterday, but the French made some progress and to-night's news says they are only 1100 yards from Peronne, a most important railway junction.

Our men had a few hand-to-hand [fights] with the Prussian Guard last Friday and made havoc with them. The struggle lasted two hours and finally the Germans gave way, leaving 700 prisoners in our hands and some thousands of dead on the field.

The Russians are still moving forward at a great pace and Berlin this morning seems alarmed. Yesterday they took 7,000 prisoners.

Our casualty lists are very very heavy now. I will this week record the number of <u>officers</u> alone killed

165

and wounded in each day's list, just to show what terrible work it is. To-day 51 killed and 259 wounded and missing.

A curious item of news in to-day's papers. Last week (Wednesday) a German train of 70 waggons all containing dead Germans tied together in bundles of 5 passed through Brussels on its way to Aix-la-Chapelle where they were to be cremated. This bundling them like this well illustrates the utter callousness of the 'Huns'. They may well speak of their men as "cannon fodder".

Yesterday a German submarine arrived at Norfolk Virginia USA. She carried 29 men and 1000 tons of cargo. This apart from all war is a remarkable feat.

July 11 Tuesday Casualty list: Officers killed 33 Wounded 54 Missing 93

Another day's terrible fighting, which in the afternoon was much hindered by a terrific down pour of rain.

The Germans made 5 great attacks to wrest from us a small wood which we had captured from them but all were beaten off with great loss. Details of the fighting on Thursday [?and of] the destruction of the Prussian Guard on Friday say that they lost 75 per cent in killed and wounded.

July 12 Wednesday Officers dead 74 Wounded 113 Missing 32

The above figures need no comment. They reveal how severe the fighting is. The Germans are endeavouring to stem the onrush of the Russians and some great battles are taking place in the West. Austria seems almost to have collapsed.

July 13 Officers dead 93 Wounded 120 Missing 45

A slight lull in the fighting yesterday. Sir Douglas Haig says that the Army has now done what was intended and that preparation will be made for further moves.

It seems to be quite a fact that some of [the] German gunners have been <u>found</u> <u>locked</u> to their guns so as to prevent them getting away and thus compelling them to fight to the very last.

The Prime Minister said in the House to-day there would be no holiday in August. It would have to be postponed until some definite progress had been made. It is quite certain now that we are going to make a big effort to come to some decision before winter. I am doubtful as to the result, but it is evident we shall need every shell and gun we can get. The expenditure of ammunition is incredible.

1916 July 14 Officers dead 98 Wounded 114 Missing 60

So these casualty lists go on day after day. What we are losing in men it is not possible to say, as the actual numbers are not given, but the number of officers is some criterion.

A little further advance on our line yesterday. Some German Howitzers captured and used to fight the enemy.

Later - About 12 o'clock to-day news came through that our Army had attacked in force the second line of German defences at dawn this morning and that a great battle was going on. The latest news to-night says that the battle is still raging.

July 15 Saturday These are wonderful days. Although there is no crowing or anything of that kind there is a quiet confidence that at last the tide has turned and that the Allies at last have the situation in hand.

This morning's news is all to the good. The battle yesterday was bloody and desperate, but the enemy were beaten back and three fortified villages were taken, and the second line of defence was broken. Some of these German dug outs are wonderful places where the officers (not the men) lived in shameless luxury.

The news to-night from Sir Douglas Haig is "All goes well. We have captured 2000 prisoners since yesterday morning and in [some] cases are close up to the 3rd line of the Germans. We have also captured one of [the] Divisional Commanders of the Guards". This is one of the best reports we have had for many a day. Officers dead 104 wounded 313

THE DIARY OF JOHN COLEMAN BINDER

July 16 Sunday People are already saying the war is over. What absurd nonsense. Germany may be hard pressed but is far from beaten yet, and it is absolutely necessary if we are to have a permanent peace that she should be beaten in the field. I quite believe that we could bring her to her knees if we sat still and did no more fighting. She is ruined economically, but she must be ruined in a military sense also, or we shall have a repetition of this war in another year or two.

This has been a terrible week of bloody battles but the nation has made up its mind to bear it. It is recognized on all sides these battles are the only way to bring the war to an end. The loss now is terrible, but it will mean a saving of life in the end. Troops are being sent across in great numbers now, but the constant cry is for guns and ammunition. Wounded soldiers coming back say ' For God's sake send us guns guns guns.' It is evident that only in this way can we drive back the Germans.

The Local Tribunals are still at work dealing with applications for exemption from service. My own impression is that the Army people are not so keen on getting men as they were. I believe they have all the men (and indeed more) than they can use.

What a casualty list of officers this week. As I said I have written them down each day this week and the totals are Killed 447 wounded -- and missing --.

The Northamptonshire regiments have been in the thick of the fighting but do [not] appear to have lost so heavily as some regiments.

What will tomorrow's papers tell us. Sunday is a day now on which patience is needed.

July 17 Monday No fresh news this morning from France except some details of Saturday's great battle. For the first time since 1914 our cavalry got into action. A squadron of Dragoon Guards and some Deccan Horse were acting as flank guards and being much annoyed by German snipers concealed in a field of growing corn charged them completely cutting them up and bringing back 34 prisoners. This must be a welcome change to these cavalrymen, it also shows that a good breach must have been made in the German lines and that the cavalry are ready to act when wanted.

Good news comes from Russia late to-night yesterday they completely routed the Germans in Volkymu, capturing 317 Officers 13,000 men and 54 guns.

The casualty list is a terrible one to-day 228 officers killed 432 wounded and missing.

1916 July 18 Tuesday Hard fighting again yesterday in the Somme district. The breach has been widened and some of our men penetrated to the third German lines.

The news of these victories both on the east and west fronts is gradually getting into Germany and the German Headquarters Staff on Sunday issued a frantic manifesto urging the people to remain calm.

July 19 Wednesday A meeting of the leaders of all classes of Munition and other workers was held in London yesterday. An appeal from Sir D. Haig and the army in France was read, asking the workers to forego all holidays, especially the coming August holidays so that an adequate supply of shells etc. might be produced. It was determined this should be done, consequently there will be no slacking at all this year. As many shells and guns are now being turned out in a week as were turned out in a month last year, and the output is still increasing.

The war is now costing us 6 Millions a day. The Bank rate is raised to 6% this week and money is getting tighter.

The report from the front to-night says some ground has been lost to-day.

July 20 Thursday Wounded men are now arriving in this country in terrible numbers, on Monday 2000 arrived at Cambridge. Of course many of the wounds are not very severe.

The fighting is still going on with great intensity in the Somme district. It is said that our losses are not so heavy as was anticipated.

July 21 Friday To-day completes six months of the great battle at Verdun. The Germans have made no progress there for the last month, indeed they have lost ground. This is a direct result of our move on the Somme.

July 22 Saturday Still the same report of continuous fighting, day and night the great battles continue without cessation. A report last night announced 'a comparative lull' but to-night's report says that it is 'renewed with all its former violence'.

We living here cannot grasp what this means. Letters from men at the front, as few as they are allowed to come through, describe the scenes as they can be described as 'horrible'. In some cases the regiments coming out of the fight have had their clothes so wrecked by blood mud and smoke that they have had to be completely re-fitted.

Sunday July 23 A fine bright July day. The weather has been much better this week and hay harvest has been pushed on with as quickly as the shortage of labour will allow.

Some farms are almost denuded of men. The tenant at Biggin Grange applying to the Local Tribunal here on Thursday said that he only had 3 men and two or three boys (about 13) on a farm of 650 acres.

There were 26 cases applying for exemption on Thursday and we sat from 6.30 to 9.30. They were dealt with according to circumstances. For instance a man running a small business alone was exempted. Men employed in food producing such as vegetable gardeners, bread bakers etc were granted 'conditional exemption', that is they would not be called up so long as they remained in those particular businesses. I am glad to say that we have not had one 'Conscientious Objector' to deal with. This is the most disagreeable work of all. I can quite understand the position of many of them and have great sympathy for them, although I think they are mistaken in many of their ideas.

1916 July 24 Monday The fierce battles continued all day yesterday and the British are storming the third line of German defences. There seems to be no cessation to these attacks and we are warned this morning from Paris that they "may continue for some months". This policy means I take it the wearing down of the enemy and so pinning him down to this western front that he will be unable to resist the attacks from Russia.

Austria goes from bad to worse. Last week the Russians captured 27,000 prisoners and immense supplies. It looks as if Austria is simply giving up. They do not appear to have much fight left in them.

Germany now speaks much more respectfully of our Army. There are now no comments on "Our contemptible little army". They at last realize what they are up against.

July 25 Tuesday Fighting was going on all Sunday night and yesterday for the village of Pozieres. It is regular hand to hand work and the enemy has to be driven out of each house. The losses both on our side and the enemy are very heavy.

There was a short debate last night in the House. The War Minister said the Generals in the field 'were more than satisfied with the work that had been done', that 'we are turning out more guns in a month than the whole army possessed at the beginning of the war' and that 'victory was certain in a few months'. We must wait and see.

July 26 Wednesday The latest news to-night is that Pozieres has been captured.

The Russians won another victory yesterday driving the Austrians before them in all directions.

July 27 Thursday The Russians are making great headway in their campaign in Armenia. To-day they announced they have captured Orizzan and are advancing on a front of 100 miles.

The fight for Pozieres was a great one. Sheer hand to hand work with the best regiments that remain of the Germans but they were routed after a [fierce] fight and the village (a mass of ruins) is in our hand.

July 28 Friday Only heavy artillery work along our fronts to-day. At last we are quite on equal terms with the Germans and a bit more so. The Minister of Munitions said the other day 'that our guns should stand axle to axle from the Somme to the sea if it were necessary'. It is almost incredible the part the Artillery is playing in this great war. It is estimated that since we commenced to move on July 1 our artillery has fired 5,000,000 shells onto the enemies' lines.

Saturday July 29 The Zeppelins came again last night or rather very early this morning. The police received the warning at 11pm and the usual precaution of calling up Special Constables etc. was adopted. A second message about 1 a.m. said they were bomb dropping in Lincolnshire and Norfolk. At 3 am the notice to dismiss was issued as they had cleared off. To-day's report says they dropped about 80 bombs, many of which fell in the sea. No lives were lost. It is quite possible that we shall have more of these raids now. The precautions with regard to lights are as strict as ever. Many other regulations are also in force. My Wife visiting Norwich last week for a few days had to fill up a form of registration and send it to [the] Police Station there. This is [to] check the entry of persons who may be aliens.

Sunday July 30 We have had some very hot days this week and a good part of the hay crop in this district has been secured. What has been carried this week is very good. The earlier stacks have been damaged to some extent by the showery weather. The Government have again requisitioned the entire forage crop and farmers are only allowed to sell to private persons by permit of the authorities. The hot weather has also brought harvest on. Some very forward oats will be cut this week, but I do not think the wheat will be ready until the end of August. Wheat has advanced rapidly in price again, and good samples are now worth 60/- again.

Men are continually being called to join the Army. They are not taken in bulk but a few here and a few there, and so the supply is being kept up. Great numbers of wounded men are to [be seen] in all large centres, and the existing hospital accommodation is being taxed. The Authorities are beginning to requisition Elementary Schools to use as Hospitals. This week they have taken one of the largest in Northampton.

1916 July 31 Monday Some terrible accounts are given in to-days papers of the fighting on our front. The Artillery fire is said to baffle all description. A month ago it was thought it had reached its height but now it has almost doubled. The strain upon the men and officers is terrible. How long can this continue.

The Russians are dealing some real sledge hammer blows on their front. Yesterday and Saturday they drove the Germans before them capturing 32,000 prisoners and 650 officers. Both these battles were near to Lutsk. We are holding the Germans so tight on our side that they find it impossible to rush their men backwards and forwards as they did last year, consequently they are now beginning to feel the weight of the allies on all fronts - they are strictly on their defence.

August 1 Tuesday Another Zeppelin raid last night. They crossed the coast about 8.15 and the first call was received here at 8.35. The danger call was received at 10.55, when the Special Constables were warned. We were on patrol until 3 am but did not hear or see anything of them. It was a very foggy night.

Later. 7 Zeppelins were here. They came into Huntingdonshire. That was the nearest to us

A curious item of news to-day. The American Ambassador in Berlin cables to his government that he has received notice from the German Government that as from to-day no person will be allowed to enter or leave Germany except in cases "of inevitable necessity" What does it mean?

August 2 Wednesday The Russians are trying to make a big coup which if it succeeds will separate the Austrian and German Armies. They are making for Karl a most important [?].

Thursday August 3 Another Zeppelin raid about 1 a.m. this morning, principally in the eastern and South eastern counties. Warnings were received here but nothing was heard or seen. To-nights report says no <u>military</u> damage has been done.

Casement was hanged in Pentonville Prison this morning at 8 o'clock. There is no question that he richly deserved his fate, but whether it was policy to hang him is another matter. A difficult matter to decide. Generally the action of the Government is approved.

August 4 Friday To-day the war enters upon its third year, and meetings are being held throughout the country to express the determination of the people to continue the war to a successful end. In many places religious services are also being held for intercession and thanksgiving but these will be more general on Sunday next.

DAY BY DAY THROUGH THE GREAT WAR

Not much news to-day from our front. The heat is said to [be] intense and the haze much interferes with the flying men and so prevents good observation.

Speaking to-night the Prime Minister said 'The Allied General Staff regard the prospect of Victory as extremely bright'.

Intense fighting has been renewed again at Verdun, and the battle line sways backward and forward, more especially since Wednesday.

August 5 Saturday Evidently a sharp thrust was made by our Army this morning as Sir D. Haig reports at mid-day that 2000 yards of trenches were captured early this morning.

August 6 Sunday Two years ago to-day what a Sunday it was. Rumours and denials. Nothing definite yet all feeling we were moving to the edge of a precipice and that we should be soon going over it. Very few people will ever forget the events of that fateful day, and the two following ones. Personally I can recall every incident as clearly as if it occurred yesterday, but what ages it seems since then, and through what tremendous events we have passed. The declaration of War, the despatch of the Army to France, the mobilization of the Fleet, the savage onslaught of Germany on Belgium, the disastrous retreat from Mons with all its splendid fighting of our Army, and the dramatic stand at the Marne. The Fall of Antwerp, Gallipoli and the Dardanelles like a bad dream with all its horrors. What a beneficent thing it is that the future is hidden from us. If we had known two years ago that all these terrible events were coming we should never have had the courage to face them, but we with God's help have faced them and to-day we are all looking forward with calm confidence to the future.

Well what of the war to-day. Looking across this country and the whole empire I see a people more determined than ever to fight this thing through to the end. Peace. Yes it is true there is a desire and a deep desire for Peace, but only such a Peace which shall make us reasonably certain there shall be no more war like this for many years. This is the fixed and certain resolve of this people of this country and her Allies. Many people profess to see that Peace is beginning to dawn. I do not. At present I see no signs of it. Germany may be beginning to feel the pinch in many directions and probably will feel it very terribly and acutely during the next 12 months, but until she is driven back and has suffered severe defeat in the field I see no hope of a lasting peace.

Much is being said and written just now of the retribution we shall inflict upon the authors of such crimes as the sack of Belgium, the sinking of the Lusitania, the murders of Miss Cavell and Captain Fryatt and all the long list of ghastly abomination these uncivilised heathen have committed, but at present I fail to see where it is coming in, but we shall keep steadily on and some day we may be in such a position that we can even aim at men in higher positions who have been the real cause of this bloody and awful war.

1916 August 7 Monday The Turks made another attempt on Friday and Saturday on the Suez Canal, but met with a severe defeat. To-night's report says we captured 3,500 prisoners and much war material.

To-day is August Bank Holiday and it is a queer mixture. Here all the shops are closed, but in many places they are partly open. All the shoe factories closed on Friday until Tuesday (to-morrow).

August 8 Tuesday The Italians after comparative quiet for a few weeks launched a sudden attack on Saturday against the Austrians and captured 3,600 prisoners. On all sides the enemy is feeling the pressure.

August 9 Wednesday The news from all quarters this morning is good.

On our front continued progress although slow is being maintained. At Verdun (170th day) intense battles are in progress and the French are holding their own. The Russians have struck hard and once more gone through the Austrian line, on another sector they have also driven back the Germans capturing 2,500 prisoners. The Italians are following up their victory with all speed, and our own army in Egypt is pursuing the Turks. Altogether a most enheartening day.

Zeppelins again this morning about 1 a.m. Three people killed somewhere on the East Coast.

August 10 Thursday The Government announces this morning they intend to give all munition workers 4 days holiday in September. This looks as if we had quite surmounted this difficulty.

THE DIARY OF JOHN COLEMAN BINDER

Enormous casualty lists are now appearing in the daily papers. To0day's Times alone contains over 5,500 names of killed and wounded. Of course many of the wounds are comparatively slight, and the men will soon be fit for duty again. What our losses are since July 1 I do not know, but certainly well over 100,000.

1916 August 11 Friday In the South the Russians have captured Stanislav and have driven out the Austrians and the Italians are now in possession of Gorgia. The Austrians fare worse and worse each day. An Army Corps of Turks have gone to help the Austrians. Strange comrades.

August 12 Saturday Good news again from Russia this morning, the enemy is continually falling back, and the Russians are now nearing some of their most important railways.

On our own front there is continual and continuous fighting, but progress is very slow. The German defences are very strong and it is all sheer hand-to-hand fighting.

The Northants Yeomanry is now all together again and is a good fit fighting unit.

Some of the Northants Battalions are at Harrogate, and others at Tring or Halton close to Aylesbury.

August 13 Sunday After three weeks of great heat it is a little cooler to-day, although we have had no rain. I think wheat harvest will commence this week. Wheat has advanced enormously and is now quoted at 63 to 64/- per quarter. It seems to me as if the Americans are squeezing us. They say that great damage to the crops in Canada and the States is the cause of this rise, but one never knows when to believe them. Bread is 9d and 9½d in London.

The Army people are releasing 27,000 men to help farmers gather in the harvest. Some will be employed in this district.

August 14 Monday The Russian news this morning is again good. They are still compelling the enemy to retire.

Our people and the French made a bit of a move forward on Saturday and yesterday.

August 15 Tuesday Sir Douglas Haig reports to-day that 'comparative quiet rules yesterday and to-day on our lines' This does not imply that fighting is not going on. Artillery is always going day and night.

The King has been across to France to look round, and has had a great reception. He came across the Northamptons and had a long conversation with them.

August 16 Wednesday The Russians once more are in the Carpathian Mountains and are looking down on to the great plains of Hungary.

An army order issued to-day says that all boys when they reach the age of 18 years and 8 months must join the Colours, but will not be sent abroad until they are 19. Previous to this they were not <u>compelled</u> to join until they had reached 19.

August 17 Thursday The Austrians are falling back before the Russian advance, but in some sections are putting up strong rear guard actions. The Germans are also doing their best to hold up the Russians and some heavy fighting is in progress. The Russians have captured 390,000 prisoners since they began their forward movement in June.

Some slight movement is [said] to [have] been made at Salonica but I do not think anything serious is intended there at present.

August 18 Friday Sir Douglas Haig reports to-day that in some fighting last night in which the Germans advanced 6 times to the [attack?] they were fairly caught by our machine guns and turned tail and ran. Their losses were terrible.

August 19 Saturday We are still exerting pressure on the Germans and in conjunction with the French are keeping them well at it. Along the Western Front we are holding 121 divisions of German troops not one of which they can transfer to meet the Russian onslaught. It is becoming clearer every day that the plans of

DAY BY DAY THROUGH THE GREAT WAR

the Allies are now well co-ordinated and that instead of the spasmodic blows like Loos and other battles the Germans will have to reckon with steady and relentless pressure on all sides.

1916 August 20 Sunday Last night's despatch says that the enemy are fighting with less vigour than formerly but if this is so they are dealing us some heavy knocks. The list of dead and wounded in the Northants regiment to0day is a very long one, and from private information I hear that the Army people are again pressing for men. They are calling up for re-examination great numbers of men who have been medically rejected, and are passing many of them, in some cases most absurdly, as it is quite certain that some of them are totally unfit for service.

August 21 A fight in the North Sea on Saturday. The Germans came out with a few ships and two of our light Cruisers were sunk whilst looking for them. Two German submarines were also sent under.

Sir Douglas Haig's report of yesterday is distinctly good. All along our line of 10 miles we made an advance and Berlin admits this afternoon that 'they shortened their line according to plan'.. This is quite true, but it is a 'plan' which we have forced upon them.

August 22 Tuesday Good news from the East African campaign this morning. Our forces are gradually rounding up the enemy and before long Germany will not [have] a single colony left. This is the result of our sea-power.

A submarine returning to port this afternoon reports that she has torpedoed and sunk a German battleship. We await confirmation.

August 23 Wednesday A rather surprising bit of news this morning. We are told that Russian troops landed at Salonica on July 30 and Italians on Aug 11. We are not told how many, but not a great number I should imagine. It is more to demonstrate the unity of the Allies I think than for military reasons. It is generally thought that before long we shall see an important move in the Balkans.

Some hint was given in the House to-day that possibly the military age may be raised so as to bring in men over 41.

August 24 Thursday A Zeppelin raid last night. Only one came across, no damage was done . .the bombs falling in the fields. We are told that the enemy is building some super Zeppelins which will be completed in October. They are said to be 750 feet long, 80 feet beam, 15,000 horse power engines, carry 5 tons of explosives and have a flying capacity of 3000 miles. If this is all true we may expect some lively nights this winter.

There will be [no] lamps lighted in the streets here at all this winter. What few were lighted last winter were quite useless as they were blacked out three parts of the way down.

August 25 Friday Zeppelins were over last night again principally in the East and S. East Counties. One came some distance inland. - - people were killed and - - injured.

Some heavy fighting yesterday on the Somme, also at Verdun. It is over seven months now that this Verdun business has been going on, and it is now chiefly the French that are attacking.

There is considerable activity in the Balkans and a good deal of desultory fighting. It is said once more that Roumania is about to join the Allies. I can hardly believe this, we have heard it so often.

August 26 Saturday One of the Zeppelins reached the outskirts of London (Croydon) and did considerable damage.

It is reported from Holland where they were seen in daylight that two of the raiders were the super Zeppelins which I mentioned yesterday.

Sir Douglas Haig reports this afternoon that some desperate fighting took place during the night. His forces are steadily forcing their way to Thiepval. A village of commanding importance in the Somme valley, and which the Germans will make every endeavour to retain.

1916 August 27 Sunday We have broken weather since Thursday and this has retarded harvest work.

THE DIARY OF JOHN COLEMAN BINDER

Barley will be the crop of the year. Wheat is not up to the standard of last year. Most of the crops will be cut by binders as they are standing up well.

Bread has reached the highest price since war began. To-morrow it will be 8 ½ d per quartern. London 9 ½ d. I am much afraid that all kinds of food will be dear during the coming winter. Some people confidently declared that the war would be over. I can see no end in sight at present. The Times Military writer to-day hints that it may extend to 1918. I hope not. We have now reached what we require in arms and ammunition and during the coming winter we shall make every effort to equip the Russians. They are able to raise almost limitless men but lack arms, ammunition and equipment. Unless Germany throws up her hands we shall see some terrible work next year. It is bad enough this year.

August 28 Monday Italy formally declared war on Germany last night. Nominally up to the present she has only been fighting Austria, really she has been fighting Germany as well, and the tension between them has now reached the breaking point.

A Telegram from Berlin via Amsterdam this afternoon says that Roumania has declared war against Austria and Germany. If this is so it must vitally affect the situation in the Balkans. Probably Bulgaria will be conquered, Germany cut off from Turkey and other far reaching consequences. Roumania can at once put into the field 400,000 men, all well equipped and armed.

August 29 Tuesday The report concerning Roumania is fully confirmed and encounters along the Austro-Roumanian frontier have already taken place, war having commenced at 9 p m on Sunday. The news has caused a great sensation throughout the world. Roumania is most cautious and has evidently been waiting to come in on the winning side. Evidently she now regards Germany as beaten. Germany is furious, and threatens dire vengeance upon her. It is one thing to threaten and another thing to perform. A most curious fact in the situation is this. Germany for some months past has been drawing large supplies of corn oil, cattle etc from Roumania and has been paying her in guns and equipment, and now these very guns are turned against Germany. No wonder Germany is furious. She also sees that one of her most vast and ambitious schemes, the founding of an eastern empire in Asia, is doomed to failure, as with a strong and determined power or federation of states in the Balkans her outlet in that direction will be blocked. How and where Roumania will strike is not disclosed, but it is quite certain that the Allies are all well agreed upon certain plans and are working together in one concrete plan.

August 30 Wednesday Events are developing in the Balkans and there are rumours that the Greek King and his party will be forced to abandon their hostility to the Allies and compelled to bow to the will of the people and come in on the side of the Allies. Bulgaria is also said to be wavering and only wanting an opportunity of severing her alliance with Germany.

The weather all along our front has been bad the last few days so that very little has been done.

August 31 Thursday Events are moving this week with startling rapidity. Quite a sensation was caused last night when the news was announced that the Kaiser had dismissed his Chief of Staff Von Falkenhayn and summoned old Hindenberg to his place. The most probable explanation of this is that Falkenhayn has been supporting that wretched Crown Prince at Verdun, and as the Kaiser cannot get rid of him he has made Falkenhayn the scapegoat. Verdun has been and is now a terrible blow to the Germans. The general opinion now is that the Kaiser is trying to save his dynasty, but opinion is daily gaining ground that the whole crew of Hohenzollerns must [be] cleared out. They are the curse of Europe.

A startling rumour reached London early this morning saying that the King of Greece had bolted. Very possibly it is true. He has been getting into a very tight place lately. The greater part of the Greek nation are pro-ally, but the King (who is a Hohenzollern) is pro-[German] and since the Bulgars have invaded Greece matters have gone from bad to worse.

1916 September 1 Friday The news from Greece is very obscure and contradictory this morning. A sort of a semi-revolution against the King has broken [out] at Salonica but has been put down by the Allies forces there. It seems quite certain that the Allies are getting out of patience with all this turning and twisting in Greece for they have sent a fleet of 30 warships to the Piraeus and it is said intend to take action to bring some order.

DAY BY DAY THROUGH THE GREAT WAR

A Russian Army in which are a large number of Serbs is marching across Roumania to attack Bulgaria and to teach her a lesson for her treachery last year in attacking Serbia. (Query how did these Serbians get to Russia?) Possibly they may be Austrian prisoners.

Roumania is pushing on into Hungary and at present has met with no really serious resistance.

September 2 Saturday The Russians have been quite quiet the last few days but this morning comes the news that violent fighting has been resumed on their front and that they have captured 16,000 prisoners on Thursday. These moves are said to be due to the determination of the new German War Minister Hindenberg to force the pace on the Eastern frontier. He is said to have a positive hatred of Russia. It is generally conceded that he is a bull headed fighter, but his powers as a strategist remain to be proved. There is an idea abroad that he may withdraw the German forces in France and Belgium to behind the Meuse in order to shorten their fighting line, and so allow him to use more power in the East. This is a neat way of putting a retreat which may have become a necessity and could only be carried out by Hindenberg who is the idol of the Germans just now.

On our front last night the enemy launched 5 attacks with great violence, but were beaten off in each instance.

September 3 Sunday Surely this has been one of the most dramatic weeks in the war. The declarations of war that have been hurled about are bewildering, and would be comic if the thing were not so ghastly.

On Sunday Italy against Germany, then the same day in comes Roumania, and so on ad infinitum. The bewildering chaos in Greece and the Balkans. One can never tell what extraordinary news may arrive from that quarter. Then the Kaiser's dismissal of his general with all it entails. It really makes one gasp, but through it all runs the clear and certain conviction that everything is now pointing to the defeat of Germany and that the rulers (not the people) of Germany are quite aware of this fact. This does not mean that the end is yet. I do not think it is, but it means that the end is certain.

Zeppelins were raiding again last night. I am not sure if they came within the danger distance of here. We shall have to wait until to-morrow to hear what damage they have done. Electric flash lights have been placed at Corby and the neighbourhood and we can see their rays very plainly. They have also brought some anti-aircraft guns there. I am not quite sure that this is a very wise thing to do as it may cause these Huns to bomb this part of the country. It seems to be generally accepted that we shall be much annoyed by these air ships during the coming dark winter nights.

A aerodrome is being built between Clapton and old Weston so that we shall see a good deal of the flying men before long. Some London firm is doing the work but they are fetching the gravel from here to make the concrete floors.

Harvest makes very slow progress. The weather is so showery. Corn markets are very nervous and jumpy. It is quite possible that Russia may attempt to reach Constantinople and so open the Dardanelles. If she did this it would cause a huge drop in prices as there is plenty of corn both in Russia and Roumania.

Since writing the above a telegram has been received which says that 13 Zeppelins were over last night and that one was brought down near to Enfield.

1916 September 4 Monday There is much rejoicing to-day on account of the destruction of the Zeppelin. She was fairly caught in the beams of the searchlights and on being attacked by aeroplanes burst into flames and fell a burning mass. I have been talking to a man who saw it. He said it was an awful sight and was seen by thousands of people. Much of the frame work was made of wood instead of metal and this helped very much to destroy it.

No material damage was done by these 13 airships. Two people were killed and eleven injured. A fairly expensive game this for the Germans. These trips cost thousands of pounds.

A terribly fierce battle took place on our front and that of the French on Sunday. It is said to have been one of [the] worst in the war, but our soldiers attained every object of their attack. They captured the village Guillement and also part of [Gemely?]. Altogether the French and our men took 6,500 prisoners including a large number of the Prussian Guard and 20 heavy guns.

THE DIARY OF JOHN COLEMAN BINDER

September 5 Tuesday Yesterday the Russian Army gave out an order here for ½ Million yards of cloth. They have also just placed an order at Armstrongs for 2,000 heavy guns. We have reached nearly an adequate equipment for our own army and this winter are going to arm and equip the Russians. They have unlimited numbers of men, but are not able to equip them. I certainly hope to see next year a decisive end to this terrible war.

September 6 Wednesday The fierce fighting on our lines continues almost without ceasing. The Germans admit that we have reached the limit in artillery fire. On all hands it is said that words cannot describe what [it] is like. We are gradually pushing the enemy back. Each day sees a small advance but the price for it is very great.

Thursday September 7 The Russians after a few days interval have made a thrust forward. Their lines are so long stretching as they do from the Gulf of Riga to the Carpathian mountains that [it] is very difficult for them to advance. Yesterday they captured 16,500 prisoners near to Kad[?]

Greece still sits on the fence, but if German news is of any value we may assume that she is coming in on our side.

September 8 Friday The Roumanians yesterday met with a reverse at one point and at another gained a victory.

The Russians drove back the Germans towards Lemberg, which they are now threatening.

Saturday September 9 The fighting on the Somme has slowed down the last two days but there will be a big push again in a few days as the official report announces ' intense artillery fire' and this now always precedes the infantry attack. It is said that many Germans have had all their clothes torn off by tremendous concussion of our exploding shells. Both the Kaiser and old Hindenberg are said to have been along the Somme front this week and the Kaiser has been saying that certain positions <u>must</u> be held. This generally means that they are lost.

The Germans are now raising another War Loan. Some of the better informed amongst them are getting nervous and evidently are beginning to realize that things are going none too well for them, consequently their papers (all under Government control) are imploring the public to invest in this Loan.

September 10 Sunday We have had a fine week since last Sunday and harvest has made good progress but we want another fortnight to complete it. New wheat is just coming on to the market and is selling at about 62/- to 64/- per qr. Flour is very dear. In fact higher than it ever has been since war began. Millers are asking 53/- for ordinary household flour. Other articles are steadily advancing. Meetings are being held in many places to protest against the high price of food. I fail to see much good in this. . We cannot produce nearly all the food we require, and are dependent on the foreigner for much of it. He knows this and is doing his level best to [make] us pay.

There is a huge crop of plums this year but they are of little value as it is quite impossible to get the sugar to make jam. Thousands of tons will never be gathered at all.

We have no Zeppelins since last Sunday morning. The man who brought down the Zep during the last raid has been awarded the Victoria Cross. His name is Robinson of the Flying Corps. He was in the air 3 hours before he got the chance to go for it.

The military are trying to speed up the tribunals so as to get more men. Many amongst the agricultural class have exemption only until October. If they fail to get this renewed there must be a big clear out then. I believe this is a bad policy, as I am sure the ranks of agriculture are quite depleted.

1916 September 11 Monday There is nothing of great importance in to-day's news so far.

To-night's telegrams say that a move has been made at Salonica. Whether this is <u>the</u> move is not yet known. The Bulgarians have been driven out from 4 villages.

A [local] Tribunal Meeting here to-night. Only 7 Cases. Most of these were granted exemption for another month.

DAY BY DAY THROUGH THE GREAT WAR

September 12 Tuesday The French are attacking heavily again to-day according to to-night's advices.

Our own front is quiet.

Russia has joined up with the Roumanians in the Carpathians.

Wednesday September 13 The French attack yesterday and to-day is great. They have captured most important and are astride of the Paris-Bapaume road which ran behind the German defences and which the Germans had been using as one of their main roads.

September 14 Thursday There is an idea getting abroad that the age limit of soldiers will be raised to 45. The War Office deny this but then no one now-a-days believes what the War Office says. They will tell any lie or do any dirty act to meet their own needs.

Evidently the move made by our people at Salonica is not serious as the Army is back again in its original position.

Friday September 15 The Serbian Army is now paying back the Bulgars in their own coin. Re-organised, re-clothed and re-armed, these Serbs outside Salonica and in conjunction with the Italian forces there have the last few days severely punished the Bulgarians, driving them back almost to Monastir.

News of great fighting on our front on the Somme comes to-night. Our troops attacked at dawn this morning and drove all before them, capturing guns and prisoners. Only brief telegrams to-night but more in the morning.

September 16 Saturday Despatches from Sir Douglas Haig last night and during the night fully confirm the account of the fighting yesterday. Our men captured three villages and 3,000 prisoners. These blows of ourselves and the French alternate like sledge hammers on the Germans. First one and then the other, and must be most trying to the enemy. He counter attacks sometimes but this week has had no success whatever. A new weapon of war was tried yesterday and was a great success. They are spoken of as armoured cars.

The Italians also won a good success on their front and the Roumanians are driving the Austrians before them in Transylvania.

This week has been a really good one for the Allies. A steady relentless pressure on the enemy, giving him no rest at all, pressure at all points so preventing him from shifting troops from one theatre to another as he has [been] used to doing. There is a growing feeling of confidence both in this country and abroad in the sure and certain success of the Allies. Slowly but surely we are wearing the enemy down and shall ultimately crush him, if only we can stay it out. I may be wrong but it seems to me it will take a year or two yet to do this.

1916 September 17 Sunday A good fine week for harvest which has made good progress. I think another such week will see most of it gathered in. Some threshing has been done, but the yield is disappointing. I should think the average will not be more than 3 ½ qrs of wheat. The price is about 60 to 62/-

All other necessaries of life are gradually getting dearer. I think the thing that is causing the most talk is the lack of sugar. Although we have [been] fairly well supplied here in many places it is impossible to obtain white sugar. To a large extent this is caused by the decision of the Government only to import ¾ of the quantity that usually comes, and as they have all ships under their own control they are able to enforce this. Their reasons are that the ships are wanted for other purposes and that all the money spent on sugar goes abroad. Thousands of tons of Plums will not be gathered at all this year as there is no sale for them.

September 18 Monday The death of two Oundle men, Afford and Philipson is reported to-day. Both were in the County regiment, and another man Clipston is wounded. The Prime minister's son Raymond Asquith is reported killed to-day.

Friday and Saturday's battle is I think one of the greatest that we have fought in this terrible war, and resulted in a complete defeat of the Germans. They were pushed back from 1 to 2 miles. The use of the armoured cars appears to have quite upset the Germans. They are whining to-day that the use of these is

THE DIARY OF JOHN COLEMAN BINDER

'uncivilised' as if these Huns are any judges of what civilised means.

September 19 Tuesday An agitation respecting the supply of men for the Army is now beginning again. It said that there is a million men who are exempted between 18 and 41. I very much doubt this. The Army people with the assistance of the Police have been trying to round up people they said were absentees from the Army. They have taken possession of the exits at Railway Stations, Theatres etc. and compelled people to produce their Registration Cards or exemption papers, failing this they were arrested. It is quite certain the arrest is illegal, and so strong has been the feeling aroused by these German methods that the Army people have been obliged to drop it. The whole thing is simply ludicrous and absurd. We have given way and done many things in order to secure victory, but English people are not quite ready to adopt the Press Gang again at present.

September 20 Wednesday 24 Hours rain has stopped all fighting in the Somme.

September 21 Thursday The Germans the last few days have been saying that they with the Turks and Bulgarians have won a victory over the Roumanians. The Kaiser says it is 'decisive' and as usual Berlin has been hanging out flags and giving the school children holidays.

The use of the new armoured cars has caused much amusement. Their antics are most comical but without doubt they were of very great use in the last battle as nothing but a direct hit from a very heavy gun could put them out of action. Germany whines they are unfair, inhuman uncivilised etc. etc. They had better try to beat them not whine about them.

September 22 Friday The French are attacking again to-day on their sector on the Somme. News is coming through to-day from Roumania denying that they have suffered any defeat, but saying that a big battle has been in progress. Very little reliance can be placed upon German news.

Saturday September 23 The German victory over the Roumanians is now admitted to be false. The Roumanians stood fast and Mackinson is now in retreat burning the villages as he goes. Another German lie this.

The Allies have captured 60,000 prisoners on the Somme since July 1.

1916 Sunday September 24 An air raid last night. Was called out at 9 p.m. but did not hear or see anything of them. After patrol was dismissed at 3 a.m. this morning. Rumours are going about to-day that 2 Zeppelins were brought down. Wait and [see]. It is probable that search lights and guns will be placed the other side of us at Hemington. Another big gun has been brought to Corby this week.

The substitution of women for men has now reached us even here, and two women letter carriers have come on duty this week.

Harvest is practically finished. Wheat yields badly. Prices firm at about 60 to 62/-.

Later. A telegram received about 4 p.m. to-day confirms the bringing down of two Zeppelins. Fifteen or sixteen were over all down the coast. 28 people were killed and 90 injured. Nottingham appears to have been badly hit.

September 25 Monday The news of yesterday is in to-day's paper with additional details. One Zeppelin was brought down in flames. All her crew were burned to death. The other apparently came to earth through engines going wrong, and is practically intact. Her crew surrendered to the village constable. (How will the Kaiser like that).

Intense artillery fire is going on on the Somme. This as we are now aware is the prelude to another advance.

The Zeppelins are across again to-night. My section of constables is not out. Have not heard where the raiders are. Corby search lights are very active.

September 26 Tuesday The raid was principally in the north east and north midland counties. Last night 29 people were killed and - - injured. It was again 3 a.m. this morning when the constables were dismissed. Some people here say that they heard the bombing. I cannot quite think they did.

DAY BY DAY THROUGH THE GREAT WAR

Insurrection has broken out in Greece and it looks as if the King and his party who are entirely pro-German would have [to] go.

The battle on the Somme was renewed last night and by telegrams received this afternoon we know that an advance is being made. It is said that the British are in Combles a town which the Kaiser said the Germans must hold at all costs.

Very few details of the uninjured captured Zeppelin are available. There is a cordon of soldiers round it and no one is allowed to approach within a quarter of a mile. It is assumed they are trying to repair her so that we may know what she is like and also possibly she may be used by us.

September [26] Wednesday A great victory on the Somme. 4000 prisoners. Combles and Thiepval captured. The enemy fairly and squarely broken and cavalry again in action. France is rejoicing greatly as it is acknowledged this is the heaviest defeat the Germans have received since the battle on the Marne. Germany and Berlin especially is much depressed. We in England are quietly confident. We feel that victory is now assured.

October 1 Sunday I have been unable to write up this diary the last few days as I have had to go to the North of England. Everywhere you see soldiers. The trains are half full of them.

The Zeppelins are over again to-night. Warning was received about 8 p.m.

October 2 Monday The Zeppelins were quite close to us. Not quite over the town but a little to the North. . They or it could be seen quite clearly and the noise made by its engines was like a train crossing a bridge. No bombs were dropped here, but quite a number at Corby. The flash of these was quite visible here and their explosion caused the houses to shake. Corby search lights were playing and the guns were also in action. The search lights soon revealed the position of the raiders and as soon as they were discovered they turned tail and sailed away. All this occurred about 11 to 11.30.

One of the raiders was set on fire and fell to the ground a burning mass close to Potters Bar, near to London. Oundle I should say is about 70 to 80 miles from Potters Bar as the crow flies, yet the collapse of this huge monster was distinctly seen from here by quite a number of people. They describe it as a big ball of fire slowly descending to the earth and the fire changing colour as it did so. Of course the crew were burned to death as usual. At least those who did not jump out and these were dashed to atoms. I wonder they do not use parachutes, it would at least give them a chance. Germany is not fortunate in her air-ships. As far as is known about 32 bombs were dropped in this neighbourhood. One of them did not explode and the police are guarding it until it can be removed.

1916 October 3 Tuesday The Roumanians have crossed the Danube and are attacking the Germans in the rear. Great things are expected of this movement.

All day yesterday a furious battle was going on on our front on the Somme.

October 4 Wednesday The Russians after a week or so of comparative quiet are again beginning to hammer the Germans and it looks as if they intend to try to capture Lemburg.

To-day's report from the Somme says that yesterday our cavalry patrols pushed forward through the war-blasted zone and reached a cultivated country. Of course they did not attempt to do anything, but it shows that the German lines are being broken.

October 5 Thursday Rain and bad weather have put a stop to all operations on the Somme (except artillery fighting).

To-day a huge fleet of about 50 big motors belonging to the Flying Corps passed through here. It is said they were gong to the Aerodrome at Clapton.

October 6 Friday Much fighting is going on around Salonica. The Serbians are driving the Bulgarians out of Serbia, and all the Allies are co-operating in the movement.

Men for the Army are not being got in sufficient numbers. A committee has been sitting in London to consider the matter and to-day they have decided to thoroughly overhaul all Government and munition works where there are a great number of young unmarried men. At last they have seen the folly of taking so many men from agriculture and the Army people have decided that no more men are to be called until Jan 1 next year. Meantime a fresh registration of all farm hands of military age will be made, so as to know exactly what men are left. I quite think that the age will be raised for all men to 45 during this next year.

October 7 Saturday The Roumanians have met with a set back in Transylvania where they had made some progress.

The great Russian move towards Lemberg is being watched with much anxiety. Fighting of a similar character to ours on the Somme is in progress and the battle which has already lasted 4 days is still continuing.

October 8 Sunday There are rumours to-day that the Russians have inflicted a severe defeat on the Germans.

Various peace feelers have been put forward this week, but our War Minister in an interview with an American journalist has knocked them on the head. He said we should brook no interference by any neutral. We were winning and intended to win. No doubt Germany would like peace now she is being hammered, but we did not hear anything about peace at the time we were being hammered and our men were being terribly knocked about. Myself I cannot see any peace in sight at present. All talk is of Germany going to greater lengths of 'frightfulness' in her submarine warfare and her Zeppelins.

The price of all articles steadily increases and roughly speaking prices are double to what they were in pre-war days. All feeding stuffs for stock are especially dear and difficult to obtain. Most flour mills instead of running day and night as they have accustomed to do are only working a day shift of about 14 hours, consequently the output is much reduced. They are obliged to do this as so many men have been taken for the Army and it is impossible to replace them. I am afraid we shall have a hard time during the coming winter. So far the weather has been mild and very little coal has been wanted. Common coal is being retailed at 1/8 per cwt to the poorer classes.

1916 October 9 Monday The Battle of the Somme as it is called has now lasted 100 days and still continues to rage with great violence. To-day's casualty list 5280. This is quite enough to show what is going on. We are constantly assured by all the authorities that all is going well and that we are winning etc. etc. The usual official tale, one sometimes doubts very much what they say. If some real decision is not reached before long, I can see that the Germans will have time in the coming winter to entrench themselves again and all this business will recur again next summer.

Roumania is being hardly pressed but the Allies are advancing from Salonica and are driving back the Dulgarians.

Sensational news comes this evening from America. One or more German submarines have crossed the Atlantic, and were in New York yesterday. To-day they or it, having left within the prescribed time (24 hours) proceeded to sink vessels right and left, and sent 8 or 9 to the bottom. This was technically on the 'High Seas' but really using America as a naval base. What will she say to-morrow.

October 10 Tuesday Another slight advance on our front of about a mile yesterday.

Much excitement has been caused in America by the submarine business. The Presidential election is due on November 4 and the retiring President (Wilson) who is seeking re-election is put in a very tight corner. I suppose it will all end in the usual 'wriggle'.

Yesterday the soldiers exploded one of the bombs which fell near to Kirby Hall during the raid of October 1 but did not go off. We heard it quite plainly here. It made an immense hole about 25 feet across.

Parliament met to-day again and the Government announced they intend to take over all supplies of wheat. If they manage this no better than the supply of sugar we shall soon be in a bad way. I am afraid that the food business is going to be very awkward during this winter. The harvest is by no means a good one, and with the constant sinking of ships must tend to create a very short supply. Harvest prospects in the Argentine from whence we get a lot of wheat during January and February are also very bad. This is owing to drought. The effects of taking so many men from farm work is now being felt. The authorities are constantly urging the farmers etc. to produce more food and more food and on the other hand the Army people are always taking the labour. If the situation were not so serious it would be really comical.

October 12 Thursday I am sorry to say that I have been unable owing to lack of time to write up this diary the last two days. The chief events have been the falling back of the Roumanians from Transylvania and the continued fighting on the Somme.

America as usual has taken the torpedoing of her ships in the usual way. The President "is watching events" as usual and will "take good measures in due time". We have heard this formula so often that we in England look upon it as almost beneath contempt.

Friday October [13] Greece has suddenly come into notoriety again to-day. Yesterday the Allies gave her 12 hours to turn over her fleet to them, and having no option she at once complied. I think they have been far too lenient with her. At any rate she cannot now stab them in the back as they advance from Salonica. The storm centre is in the Balkans again. The Germans aided by Turks are going to make a big effort to crush Roumania. I do hope the Allies will use every effort and strain every nerve to prevent this. I firmly believe that until we join hands from Salonica with Russia and Roumania and thus cut the railway line between Berlin and Constantinople and so bottle up the Germans and Austrians this war will never come to an end.

1916 Saturday October 14 Very little news to-day from the Somme on our side. The French are taking up the running just now, and yesterday advanced some distance capturing Le Transloy.

Northampton has been making a big effort this week to raise £5,000 for the Red Cross. They had a sale of agricultural stock on Wednesday which realized £2,000 and next week will hold a 3 days bazaar by which they hope to complete their effort.

Billets are being arranged this week in Northampton for 20,000 soldiers for the winter. Wellingborough is to have between 4,000 and 5,000.

October 15 Sunday I am told by people who have seen it that country between Kirby and Gretton where the bombs fell in the raid on October 1 is much devastated. Trees shattered. Hedges torn up, but fortunately no damage to houses or people.

A party of Royal Engineers from Chatham last Monday exploded one of the bombs which did not go off when dropped from the Zeppelin. I heard the explosion quite plainly here, but no shock was felt. The Police who were present tell me that it made a hole at least 24 feet across and 10 feet deep.

The Gunners at Corby are much annoyed that they could not have a few shots at the Zeppelin on October 1. They had all their guns in order and were only waiting for lubricants. They say they are quite sure they could have winged it as it was flying so low.

I have heard this week, but I write it down with all reserve, that some officers of the Northants regiment (or who were about to join it) have volunteered to go to Nigeria to train the natives. Not perhaps as combatants but as helpers behind the lines.

October 16 Monday A little better news from Roumania this morning. They are standing fast on the passes and are holding up the enemy.

The French and ourselves took - - prisoners on Saturday on the Somme.

October 17 Tuesday Roumania is being hard pressed . Russia is as far as possible rendering help and Italy also is fighting hard so that the enemy cannot draw any help from any of their fronts.

Yesterday the Allies landed an armed force at Athens and practically assumed control of the country.

1916 October 18 Wednesday Parliament debated last night the question of the supply of food. Some really absurd statements were made by members of the Labour party. These men are continually clamouring for 'more men' more men for the army, and yet cannot appear to see that they are depleting the labour on the land to such an extent that it is going out of cultivation. This year there were 200,000 acres less under corn than in 1915, due chiefly to the lack of labour. The land too is in many cases becoming very foul and does not produce what it should.

October 19 Thursday The news from Roumania to-day is a little better. They are standing fast in the passes and are holding up the enemy.

Much rain is falling on the Somme and military operations are chiefly confined to artillery work.

Greece is fairly quiet according to what we hear but really very little news comes through, the censorship is very strict.

Friday October 20 To-day the sale of 5 per cent Exchequer Bonds comes to an end and a new series bearing interest at 6 per cent is being issued. These will be repayable in three years. The Treasury do not think the time opportune to issue another long dated war loan, and probably prefer to wait until they can float one at a lower rate than 6 per cent. Thirty six Millions has been raised by these Exchequer Bonds this week.

1916 October [21] Saturday The Germans yesterday launched another attack against Roumania further east near to the Black Sea. Late telegrams last night say that the battle is still in progress.

The Serbs the last two days have given the Bulgarians a good shaking and are now well on the way to Monastir.

Much fighting is going on to the north of Salonica. About a month since a friend of mine who is a nurse came over with a hospital ship (the 'Aquitania' of the Cunard line) bringing 5,000 wounded and invalids. Of these 500 were consumption cases. She says the climate there is deadly for this disease and the least disposition towards it very quickly develops. They were chased by German submarines east of Gibraltar.

October [22] Sunday Yesterday and to-day we have had the first touch of winter. Seven degrees of frost yesterday and 9 this morning. This reminds us that woollen clothing is very dear. I am told that it has quite doubled from pre-war prices.

The wheat market continues to advance. The whole situation is very unsettled as the Government have not as yet made any announcement of what they really intend to do. Wheat made 65/- at Peterborough yesterday. Bread will [be] 9d per quartern loaf here tomorrow.

There is much resentment at the way in which the Army people are now dealing with calling up the men. They are appealing against every decision of a Local Tribunal which liberates a man of under 30 from service. That is, which gives him exemption either temporary or conditional. This has caused much indignation, and this week the Northampton Tribunal has threatened to refuse to administer the Act unless there is an alteration in these methods. They say there is a law for the War Office as well as for other people, and that their methods are hose of the 'Star Chamber'. They contend that Tribunals were set up not to act as recruiting officers but to judge impartially between men who are called up and the War Office. Lloyd George is a clever man and has done great service during the last two years but he like all Welshmen is a very excitable personage, and thinks that the office which he fills for the time is the only one in the country, and that upon that office and what it does depends the winning of the victory. When he was Chancellor it was money and money only that was going to do it, when he became Minister of Munitions, it was Munitions alone that could do it, and now that he is War Minister it is men and men only that can accomplish the task. We cannot have all three and before long the country will have clearly to make up its mind what is to be done.

October 23 Monday To-days news good and not good. Fierce fighting again in progress on our Somme front and quite successful. 1500 prisoners are accounted for since Saturday and important positions captured.

The Roumanians are hard pressed in the D----- and have retreated. The danger spot is there.

DAY BY DAY THROUGH THE GREAT WAR

The Austrian Prime Minister was shot dead by a socialist yesterday whilst dining at an Hotel. A political crime without doubt. Austria is [in] a miserable condition as far as we can glean here. No one has been allowed to enter or leave that country for the last month.

October 24 Tuesday The Germans have captured Constanzia, the Roumanian port on the Black Sea, where are enormous flour mills, the largest in the world. This is a real set back but probably they will not be able to over run all Roumania. They have still to get across the Danube.

October 25 Wednesday Yesterday the French made a furious attack at Verdun and recaptured many of the position which the Germans had taken since last February. They inflicted terrible losses on the enemy and took 3,500 prisoners. This is a heavy blow for the Germans.

All men who have turned 41 but have not reached their 42nd birthday are now being called to the colours. This is quite contrary to distinct pledges which had been given by the Government. A sharp debate in the House last night on this subject in which the War Office and especially Lloyd George received some nasty knocks. On this whole subject of recruiting the Government are playing a low down game and are losing the confidence of the better part of the nation. We all know that men are urgently needed but a promise once given should be kept and not repudiated at the first opportunity. If these men are required let the House be asked to sanction their calling up. The War Office are treating their pledges as the Germans treated their treaty with Belgium, as 'Scraps of Paper'.

1916 October 26 Thursday The Roumanian news is not at all good. They are being hardly pressed and are retreating. One does hope that the Allies will do their utmost to prevent the overwhelming of Roumania. They are said to have been forced back across the Danube. The real cause of Germany's attack upon her is that she wants the oil and food which Roumania has. Before leaving Constanzia the Roumanians destroyed all the stores.

October 27 Friday Not much news to-day. The Germans are making furious counter attacks at Verdun to recapture the positions the French have wrested from them, but they meet with no success.

The enemy destroyers coming from Zeebrugge last night attempted to sever our cross channel service with France. A sharp action ensued. The Germans lost two warships (destroyers) and we had an empty transport sunk. It is really remarkable considering what a vital point this is that they have not attempted this before.

A Tribunal Meeting here to-night. There were 24 cases for exemption and we sat from 6.30 to 11. A very large proportion of the men who now come before us are physically unfit and have been passed only for work such as road making, garrison duty etc. etc. and not for the fighting line.

Saturday October 28 Rain has again put a stop to our fighting on the Somme. A letter from one of my nephews from there to-day says the country is again beastly, all Mud.

Sunday October 29 This has been a most trying week in business. All food has increased very much in price and as far as I can judge will continue to do so. Wheat has risen 5/- per quarter and is now quoted at 72/- on rail, and Manitoba wheat is worth about 86/- delivered into country mills. Potatoes have risen to £10 per ton wholesale.

The Germans continue to sink many ships. I hear from millers who were at Mark Lane last Monday that a vessel (a Cunard Liner), which was recorded in the papers as being sunk off Beachy Head, had on board 22,000 qrs of wheat and 9,000 sacks of flour going to London. Millers are asking £14 per ton for Sharps. Barley Meal (or rather Hog Meal) is 27/- per 14 stones. Cheese (Canadian) is 120/- per cwt, Cheddar Cheese 130/- these are wholesale prices. I am afraid we have a hard winter before us. There is no lack of employment as such enormous numbers of men have been taken for the army that principally old men and youths are left.

The Zeppelins have not come this week at all. If this part of the country is any criterion the whole of the east coast must be ablaze at night with search lights. At least six or seven can be seen every night here all within 10 or 12 miles flashing across the sky. They usually show up and then discontinue for a time, and then come on at intervals all night.

To-day there have been a succession of troop trains running through here, taking a division of artillery to their winter quarters at Northampton.

October 30 Monday A little better news from Roumania this morning. They have made a stand in the passes and have taken 2,200 prisoners, but are not out of danger yet.

1916 October 31 Tuesday The enemy are making great havoc just now with their submarines. Every day four or five ships are sunk. I regard this business with great misgiving as I believe it is a most serious menace to us. All kinds of food are constantly increasing in price.

Wednesday November 1 Potatoes to-day are quoted about £11 per ton on rail. This shows a big profit to the grower. Many thousands of acres are still in the ground as owing to the men being taken for the army the farmer has been unable to get them up. Disease is prevalent especially in some districts.

Thursday November 2 Continued wet is stopping all military work on the Somme. Sir Douglas Haig reporting to-day says 'it is a wilderness of mud'.

In front of Salonica our men are having some sharp fighting. Yesterday they cleared three villages of Bulgarians. Monastir is their objective just now.

November 3 Friday The Italians have struck hard on the Calso [?] and yesterday gained a notable victory over the Austrians, capturing 3,200 prisoners. Their objective is Trieste and they are moving towards it through enormous difficulties. The battle is still going on.

November 4 Saturday This morning brings good news both from Roumania and Italy. The Roumanians are steadily holding their own and there is every reason for thinking the worst is over with them. They are not entirely out of danger yet as Germany wants to be revenged on them and is also fighting desperately to secure the oil and corn they own. Much concern has been felt for them here in their struggles and Russia has been urged to send them all the help she can.

The latest effort of Italy will also help them. The Italians announce to-day further success yesterday and have brought up their prisoners to 8,200.

Sunday November 5 I will write down to-day a few impressions of things as they present themselves to me at the moment with regard to affairs in England and our relation to this war. As I have frequently written down in this diary, I have always thought the most serious menace to us would come not from invasion but from want of food, and to-day I am sorry to say it looks as if my forebodings were coming true. There is no doubt we are faced to-day with a serious shortage in wheat. Dealings in this are recorded to-day at 78 to 79/- per qr and flour is practically £3 per sack. Bread is to be sold at 10 ½d per loaf to-morrow and 9 ½d in most parts of the country, and it is predicted that it will be a shilling a loaf before Christmas. Potatoes are scarce and are being retailed at 1 ½d to 2d per lb in London. Here the price is about 1/4 to 1/6 per 14 lb. Of course all meat is very dear and cheese exceptionally so. Colonial cheese is generally retailed at 1/4 per pound and English at 1/6. Lard is 11d per lb on the quay at Liverpool. All wool clothing has roughly doubled in price and boots have sharply advanced. It will be seen by these facts that the situation, if not alarming, is to say the least of it serious. My own opinion is that we shall see a steady getting worse in the matter of food until the war comes to an end. The Labour people are becoming very angry about it, and it may lead (without much reason) to many internal difficulties and perhaps to rioting. I am sure the ordinary Englishman will not be so docile in this matter as the German.

Much of this trouble has been caused by the Army taking so many men from the land. It is simply absurd to leave a farmer with one or two men over 40 and then expect him to produce big crops. The War Office and other departments are in direct conflict over the matter. This is quite well known.

I am quite sure we are faced with hard and bad times this winter and this is also the general opinion. In addition to this one cannot see any prospect of a decisive end to the war. It is true that the morale of the enemy is steadily declining and that we have made some splendid advances since the 1st of July, but the end to all appearance is not yet. I thought at one time that 1917 might see the end of it but now I am doubtful .. It looks as if it were to be a war of exhaustion, and I believe all the nations now engaged in it will be crippled for years. America hugs the 'Almighty Dollar' and is simply rolling in wealth, but this may yet prove her ruin, as it nearly did for us before the war. Life was then simply a mad race for wealth and luxury but thank God this terrible war has knocked some of that nonsense out of us.

I do not wish to be misunderstood. At present is spite of all difficulties there is no dismay or thought of giving way. The general idea of all men and women is for Peace. But they are quite capable of seeing that the time for peace is not yet, and are facing all difficulties with courage and steadfastness.

1916 November 6 Monday The chief news this morning is that Germany has proclaimed Poland a Kingdom under the rule of a Bavarian King. This deceives nobody and is looked upon as mere 'bluff'. The end is not yet.

November 7 Tuesday Scarcely any news this morning. A good deal of interest is taken in the election of the President in USA which takes place to-day. As fat as one can see here the chances are very even, and it seems a toss up as to who will be elected. The retiring President Wilson is the Democrat, Hughes the Republican. I do not think America will interfere in this great war here, although lately two American vessels have been sunk by the Germans. As usual "America will wait. The President is considering the matter and an announcement will shortly be made". This is the usual formula. We know it by heart and it has ceased to excite any interest in this country.

November 8 Wednesday The submarine menace is as great as ever. To-night it is announced that the P&O liner 'Arabia' homeward bound from India with 345 passengers on board was torpedoed in the Mediterranean without the least warning. Fortunately all the passengers escaped in the boats but the report does not say if they all reached the land. Their escape is in no way owing to the mercy of the Huns as they have no compunction in sending innocent women and children to the bottom of the sea, but is due to the precautions taken on all liners coming to or leaving England. During the voyage frequent drills of entering the boats, putting on life belts etc., are carried out by the passengers and when they enter the danger zone no one is allowed to go to bed at night.

We have had no Zeppelins over here since October 1. The awful fate that befell some of them the last two or three times has I think given them a warning of the reception they are likely to meet with here. On the last occasion when one of them was destroyed the captain jumped from the burning wreck and fell to the earth with such terrific force that his body made quite a hole in the earth. Rumour says that the Huns have difficulty in getting the crews to man these vessels as the danger is so great, but I do not give much heed to this statement.

November 9 Thursday To-day being Market day I have come into contact with Millers and Corn Merchants and have been told what is being done behind the scenes with regard to the wheat question. It appears that the Government are seriously considering whether only 'Standard' flour shall be allowed to be manufactured and no white flour at all. Standard flour is what millers know as a 'straight run' flour and contains at least 80 per cent of the sharps and bran. It is contended that by this means the price of bread might be held in check, and possibly reduced from its present price. This 'standard' flour had a boom about 10 years since, and is still made in very limited quantities. The general public do not like it and the bread made from it has only a very limited sale. As it contains all the wheat 'germ' it has a slightly sweet taste. There is also another aspect of this question and that is [the] bearing it will have on sharps which are greatly in use as food for pigs and other stock. The price of these is to-day about £15/12/6 per ton (before the war the price was about £6 per ton) and if this is increased it is quite certain that the quantity of pigs fattened or bred will be greatly reduced, so that we shall lose food in that direction. I do not think the real solution of the food question lies in quack remedies like 'standard flour' but in really more efficient handling of the labour as regards agriculture. As one could foresee the denuding of the land of men has resulted in a decreased production of food, and if this policy is persisted in it will assuredly lead to starvation. A bold and energetic handling of the freight question and every possible increase in wheat and other food production is I think our only hope. The Army people have been warned this last two years what their policy would lead to, but they only ignored or derided the warnings.

THE DIARY OF JOHN COLEMAN BINDER

1916 Friday November 10   After a very exciting contest the result of which was only known definitely to-night the retiring President Wilson has been re-elected in America. Germany is not at all pleased

November 11 Saturday   Hard fighting is going on in Roumania. Russia has sent reinforcements and a Russian General Saharoff is now in command. The enemy has been driven across the Danube, but possession of the one and only bridge is stiffly contested.

A regular aerial battle in the Somme yesterday, 40 of our aeroplanes and about 50 German. As usual we came out top.

November 12 Sunday   A quiet autumn day. The weather has much improved the last few days and some progress has been made with wheat seeding although much remains to be done. Wheat prices have been about stationary this week. The Government commenced to sell foreign wheat through their appointed agents last Thursday. I should not be at all astonished if they were to take over all English wheat as well.

They have fixed the price of hay at £5 to £6 per ton. Straw £3.

Some of the millers are very short of wheat. Mr Springthorpe of Molesworth and Springthorpe of Luffenham told me on Thursday that he had only enough wheat to run his mills that day. It comes to market in such small lots. All they could purchase last week did not amount to 20 qrs. Not enough for one shift.

This week has seen the complete clearing out of the Germans at Verdun. They were driven back to the positions which they occupied last January. Their losses there must have been appalling. The British War Office in a return issued to-day estimates [the] total German losses in killed wounded and missing at 3,749,000.

November 13 Monday Not much news of importance this morning . . but at night we learn that a new onslaught was made by our troops at dawn this morning. A message dispatched at 11 o'clock says that it had been very successful and that prisoners were coming in. We shall get a fuller account to-morrow.

The Serbians won a notable victory over the Bulgarians on Saturday after fighting all day, the Bulgarians gave way completely at dark and fled.

The 'Times' will be raised to 1½d on Monday next. (It has been at 1d) The proprietors say that the extra cost of paper alone is now £70,000 a year. This will give some idea as to [the] way in which everything has gone up in price.

November 14 Tuesday   The attack yesterday morning continued for most of the day and from the meagre telegrams that are to hand seems to have been a big battle. Sir D Haig reports that up to the time of his dispatch 1000 prisoners have come in.

November 15 Wednesday   The battle on Monday turns out to have been a great victory for us. It resulted in the capture of Beaumont Hamel and another village. These two places defied our assault on July 1st and have held out ever since. The Germans said they were impregnable, but our brave men went right through them. Up to this morning 5,000 prisoners are reported.

A most remarkable thing comes from Berlin. For the first time since the war began the German official report admits they have been defeated and acknowledges they have been driven. Of course they [know] the same thing has occurred plenty of times, but this [is] the first time the German Staff has admitted it.

Things do not go well in Roumania. The Germans are making some headway there.

November 16 Thursday   One of the most remarkable days of this great war. From to-day we are to have placed over [us] a 'Food Controller' or Dictator. Such was the announcement made in the House last night. This man whoever he may be will be armed with almost unlimited authority with regard to food and food stuffs. This authority will be given to him under 'The Defence of the Realm Act'. An act which was passed at the beginning of the war, good in some respects, but rotten in many others and which has robbed Englishmen of more liberty than any other act of Parliament passed during the last 200 years.

DAY BY DAY THROUGH THE GREAT WAR

As I said last Thursday, the first thing he will do will be to forbid the milling of white flour, and only allow Standard Flour to be made (already the public are beginning to scramble for the white Flour). He will fix the price of milk, Potatoes etc. and will be able to proceed against any person wasting food in any way. These are only a few of his manifold duties. All I can say about him(whoever may be appointed) is "God help him" for no human being can do what the Government expect him to [be] able [to do], and I have come to this conclusion after carefully reading the proposals. The most disquieting thing about this matter is that one 'reading between the lines' one can see that there is a danger of an absolute shortage of food. This has been brought about by the absurd policy of taking almost every man (of any use) from the farms. I have always protested against this as anyone who has read these notes will see, and last night the Government acknowledged this to be true but laid the blame of having done this upon the wrong shoulders. Instead of clearly acknowledging their error they said it was the local recruiting officers who had been too zealous ! ! ! as if these officers had not received instructions from the Army people to collar every man. Now they are going to return many men both to the farms, to shipbuilding and to steel works.

I do not think this 'Standard Bread' craze is likely to be of much service, as I cannot see where the ultimate gain comes in. 'Standard flour' produces less loaves per sack than white flour, it keeps badly and will draw away the food of the livestock.

1916 November 17 Friday No Food Dictator has been made up to to-night. Several names are mentioned including Lloyd George. I heard a very trite remark to-day re this Food Dictator. It was said that 'either he will be set on a pinnacle in Trafalgar Square or hung on one of the lamp posts there'.

Saturday November 18 First real winter to-day. After three days of bitter east wind we have had a heavy fall of snow.

Roumania news is not good again to-day. They are hardly pressed. The Russians report to-day they have destroyed a Zeppelin.

November 19 Sunday The snow has nearly disappeared this morning. A good breadth of land has been sowed this week, the weather having [been] fine and dry although intensely cold.

Lord French to-day inspects 5000 volunteers of Northamptonshire at Northampton.

Germany is making huge efforts just now and has practically decreed a 'levy en masse'. Possibly it may come to this in England yet. We are prepared to do anything to see this war through.

November 20 Monday Good news from the East this morning. The Serbians and the Allies have re-taken Monastir after a series of battles extending nearly 14 days. The German Bulgarian forces have been driven back and yesterday were in full retreat. The Germans could send no reinforcements to them. It is thought this defeat will have much effect on the Bulgarians as they have now lost the chief object for which they entered the war viz the country around Monastir.

November 21 Tuesday To-day a decree is issued by the Food Dictator fixing the price of Milk at not more than 6' per quart and also saying that all bread made after Jan 1 1917 will have to be made from Standard flour. This applies also to all cakes pastry biscuits etc. No more white flour can be milled in this country after Saturday next so that a month is given to clear up stocks in hand. From what one can gather white flour will still continue to be imported, but most of it will be taken for the Army. I have seen several Millers to-day and they say the new flour instead of being white will be of a yellowish tinge and somewhat darker than the present white flour. They are all experimenting and will endeavour to produce a flour as near as possible to that which we now use, without breaking the regulations. How these regulations are to be enforced goodness only knows. Another army of officials I suppose. Personally I look upon the whole business as a lot of nonsense. In the long run and taking everything into consideration there cannot be any saving and it is causing an upset to the whole milling and baking trade. I believe we are playing at a game which children call "Make believe" and it is being done to give our Allies the impression that we are making sacrifices in this direction.

1916 November 22 Wednesday The Germans are fairly in Roumania, that is the western part of it. This is a real set back to us and must prolong the war, as to some extent it will allow them to get oil and corn if the

THE DIARY OF JOHN COLEMAN BINDER

latter has not been destroyed by the Roumanians as they have retreated.

A warning is issued by the Food Dictator this morning that it is illegal for any person either engaged in trade or a private person to buy white flour now with a view to making use of it after Jan 1 next. How does he think he is going to prevent them doing this.

The old Emperor of Austria died to-day. One rascal less in this world. His death will not influence the course of the war in any way. Austria is now merely a vassal of Germany.

Thursday November 23 Have to-day seen millers who were present at a meeting yesterday convened by the Government in London to confer with them about food stuffs. They gave a gloomy description of the situation. I am afraid it is far more serious than the general public realize. There is only [one] consolation about this and that is the enemy is worse off than we are.

To-day the news comes that the "Britannic" (50,000 tons) the largest vessel in the world, was torpedoed on Monday in the Mediterranean.

November 24 Friday The Food Dictator has placed a severe restriction upon expensive drinks and meals at hotels and restaurants. He met the proprietors yesterday and told them that unless they reduced their menus the Government would do it for them. I think he was right in this case. The luxury and wastefulness at some of these places is scandalous.

Another Hospital ship has been sunk in the Mediterranean yesterday.

November 25 Saturday Roumanian news this morning is bad. At least according to German reports. They claim to have crossed the Danube.

Germany seems to have put the finishing touches to her reputation as barbarians during the last few days. Owing to her want of men she has been raiding Belgium as a slave dealer does Africa and has been transporting thousands of men as slaves to Germany. It seems as if her resources in men were coming to an end.

Sunday November 26 I think this past week has been one of the most eventful ones of the war, not so much from a military point of view as from the fact that food supply has assumed such a prominent place in this country. I can clearly see that it will take all our time and resources to tide over until next harvest. There is a general shortage of food throughout the world (except in Australia). Practically the harvest in North America and Canada is bad. Argentina is holding hers up until she sees what is going to be done in the new harvest due in January and in consequence of these facts we shall be compelled to import the bulk of our food from Australia, an immensely long and costly process. A government paper issued yesterday states that food has increased 78 per cent since war began. This shows how we are steadily going from bad to worse and I am afraid that things will grow worse. I think sometimes that the war will be brought to an end not by fighting but by starvation. So many millions of men all over the world are being used for this war that the output of food is slackening. It is true there are immense supplies in Russia but owing to their being unable to ship them they are useless.

I think people are seeing that we are really at war. It is now assuredly pressing heavily upon us in all ways, and men are feeling severely the continued strain.

Wheat continues about 74/- to 76/- per quarter. Barley made up to 70/- and maize 68/- at Northampton yesterday. These are famous prices.

It is expected that the use of the new war flour will be fairly general next week. Millers are stopping their plant a few days this week to re-adjust it to the new requirements and then will only make the new flour which will be available at the end of the week. Many bakers will have to use it at once as they are quite out of stock.

The nights now are awfully dark. (There is no moon just now.) Last Sunday I think was the darkest night I have ever seen. Several people lost their way even in this small place and quite a number fell down. It is quite a rarity to see any vehicular traffic now at nights.

DAY BY DAY THROUGH THE GREAT WAR

1916 November 27 Monday Grave news from Roumania this morning. The Germans are within 50 miles of Bucharest. The Roumanians are fighting stiffly and to-night the Germans admit they have not taken any guns.

A fleet of Zeppelins are over again to-night.

November 28 Tuesday Things are going badly in Roumania and it looks as if they would suffer disaster.

The Zeppelins paid dearly for their frolic last night. They got inland and dropped bombs but on attempting to get back they were fiercely attacked and 2 were brought down in flames, falling into the sea. One off the Durham coast and the other off the Norfolk Coast. We are certainly 'top dog' now in this warfare.

An aeroplane flying at a very great height to-day dropped bombs on London. Very little damage was done.

November 29 Wednesday No news of importance this morning.

This afternoon it is announced that Sir John Jellicoe has relinquished the command of the Grand Fleet and has gone as first naval Lord at the Admiralty. A good deal of criticism has been levelled at the Admiralty lately and it is felt it required a man of stronger ability than they have there now. Admiral Beatty, the hero of Jutland and - - - - is promoted to the supreme command of the Fleet.

November 30 Thursday Roumanian news is not good to0day. They have not been defeated but are falling back in good order. The enemy are closing in on Bucharest. Very little fighting is going on on the Somme. The weather conditions are very bad, and the country is in an awful state.

Friday December 1 Events are reaching a climax in Greece. An ultimatum has been presented to the King requiring him to hand over certain armaments to the Allies. This expires to-day and possibly there will be trouble. This King is decidedly a pro- German. His wife is the Kaiser's sister. The Allies ought to have removed him long ago, as he has immensely crippled their efforts at the Salonica front.

To-day I have received my first consignment of 'War Flour' from the Millers, and have baked some as a test. It is not much different in appearance to that to which we have been accustomed. It is rather darker in colour, and not quite as light. In fact more like the bread we had 30 or 40 years ago before the 'roller process' was introduced. The use of it will be compulsory after Jan 1 1917 but I think it will [become] fairly general before that date. Possibly this is only the thin end of the wedge, and we may gradually have real brown bread forced upon us.

As one could foresee this different milling has caused a sharp rise in the price of 'offals' which have advanced £ per ton in the last 14 days. Sharps are now £17 per ton (exorbitant) This in turn is causing thousands of immature pigs to be slaughtered and must eventually *cause the price of fat to go up very much.*

1916 December 2 Saturday The German -American financiers in Wall Street are using all their influence to get an armistice between the belligerents and are bringing great pressure upon the American President to make him intervene. They can see that things to say the least of it are not going well for Germany, and would like to bring the war to an end now. This is quite hopeless. The fight is not finished yet. I can see much worse times for us all. The Allies will not be at their maximum strength until next year, and have certainly no thought of giving way until they have used their utmost strength. I do not think I am a 'pessimist' but I really think by the time this awful war is finished neither the enemy or ourselves will be of much use. I think we have some hard and bitter times before us yet.

Sunday December [3rd] Not much news to-day. The second [Zeppelin] last Monday was brought down off Lowestoft. Our airmen have the measure of them now and attack them fearlessly and boldly. I am told they use a phosphorus bullet which clings to the skin of the airship and sets it on fire. Once it has fairly caught it is impossible to put it out. Rumour says the crews of these Zeppelins at once use drugs to stupefy themselves when they find that they are being brought down. Their agony must be awful. The airships once on fire quickly become huge sheets of flame and it is impossible to put them out.

Monday December 4 There was quite a battle at Athens on Friday and Saturday between the King's partisans and the troops of the Allies. An armistice was arranged yesterday and a compromise seems to have been made. This is a mistake. They are not dealing firmly enough with the King. He ought to be removed.

Bloody battles are going on round Bucharest with varying results. At one point the enemy gained a distinct advantage but further south were heavily defeated. The issue is still in doubt.

December 5 Tuesday   It is now certain that the Roumanians have suffered a severe reverse. They are still falling back, but in good order.

The trouble engineered in the Government by Lloyd George, The Times and others has to-day to come to a head. They have made impossible almost any government except one controlled by themselves.

December 12 Sunday   Owing to pressure of work I have been unable to write up these notes since last Tuesday. How remote that seems to-day. We have passed through and are still in most troublous and depressing times.

The Coalition Government has fallen. Mr Asquith has resigned and to-day Lloyd George the Welsh solicitor whom I remember as the most bitterly hated man by the Conservatives, but now their idol, is Prime Minister of England. Whether for better or for worse time alone can prove. One thing is certain. We have lost a man of cool calm and balanced judgement and in his place we have a man of nerves and change. . He has immense driving power and has also a great love of adventure, and I am afraid may be inclined to gamble with such great assets as the Navy and other huge forces which he has at his command. We are promised great things and according to certain people all is now going to be well with us. The reasons which brought things to this crisis are the defeat of the Roumanians (the enemy to-day are in Bucharest) the submarine menace, and the question of man power. There cannot be the slightest doubt that to-day we are in a very bad way. Our gravest peril is I believe the coming shortage of food. To any one like myself who is in contact day after day with the food supply the situation is most disquieting. Food is steadily but surely rising in price, and I think that we may really have to go short of some real necessities of life. The general public do not seem to grasp this fact at all. Perhaps it is as well they do not.

The Army seem determined to sweep in every man that is possible. We have one man in every ten of military age with the colours. Russia has only one man in every 20. The consequences of this are obvious. We shall be in grave danger of economic collapse. Indeed I sometimes think that the war will finish as a struggle in economic force. It will not so much be the fighting as a question of real endurance. Germany has lately adopted the ' levy en masse' and [it] is almost certain this will be adopted in this country. Every man and woman between 17 and 60 will be placed at the disposal of the Government. Several public men have foreshadowed this during this week and Lloyd George is said to be strongly in favour of this. I really think we have almost more upon our shoulders than we can carry.

We have an army of 6 million men. We have an enormous fleet. We are financing not only ourselves, but the Allies also. We have 60% of all our mercantile marine engaged in war service. The rest (numbers of which are sunk daily) are engaged in bringing food to us and to our Allies. We have to build new ships to replace these and also those of the Navy, and above all we have to grow food to help to keep ourselves. This is not my idea only, it is a impression that is daily gaining ground, and I am certain our strength will be taxed to the utmost.

Thoughtful men can see the danger coming and are all very grave and concerned. It is a time of great national peril, and God alone can help us.

We shall have once more a real opposition in Parliament as Mr Asquith has determined to give a cordial help to the new government but will not consent to serve in it. After what we have seen during the last 18 months this is decidedly the best plan. Every discontented fool who had a grievance thought himself entitled to run amok and try to oust the Government instead of trying to help it, and now they have brought it down they are already beginning to whimper and whine.

Events go badly in Greece. There is a terrible welter there. The Allies have not had enough decision. They should have turned the guns of their fleet upon Athens and given the King an hour to clear out.

1916 December 11 Monday   No improvement in the Greek situation. The King threatens to join forces with the Germans and it looks as if they might try to force their way down to him. I know from private sources that troops are being hurried out from France to meet this danger. We could meet the danger in front but when you have these treacherous Greeks ready to stab you in the back it is difficult. The Allies have closely blockaded Greece and a s the country is extremely short of food they may be brought to their senses.

To-day parcels of warm clothing (under) have been sent to all men belonging to Oundle who are at the front. These have been made by the Ladies Red Cross Society here. One hundred and six parcels have been sent, this is not half the men who have gone from here, the remainder are in England and these will not receive parcels.

December 12 Tuesday To-night's telegrams say that in the German Reichstag to-day the Chancellor said that Germany wanted peace and a note had been sent to the Allies saying she was willing to negotiate, but he did not say upon what terms. We look upon this as a mere move in the diplomatic game, and not as a bona fide offer. Possibly she might be glad for peace but solely upon her terms. It is certain there can be no peace at present.

December 13 Wednesday   No definite news of Germany's peace terms is yet to hand. Roumania is still being over run by the Germans. The Army is still intact.

End of Volume Six

THE DIARY OF JOHN COLEMAN BINDER

Volume Seven

14 December 1916 to 28 November 1917

Yet another volume of this diary. I wonder how many more before peace comes.

1916 Thursday December 14 No news of Germany's real proposals has reached London. The reception given to the proposals both in this and other countries is decidedly chilly. It is generally thought that it is a move in the diplomatic game, and that as such it is certain to fail, but still I think we ought to hear what they have to say and then reply as to what our irreducible minimum is.

The peace move has caused unbounded excitement in Berlin. Cheering crowds surged through the streets and it seemed to be thought that the Allies would at once embrace Germany. Not quite so. We Englishmen do not quite so easily forget Belgium, the Lusitania and a hundred other diabolical crimes of the Huns.

Friday December 15 No news from Germany yet of the Peace terms. The note is being sent to us via America.

The Prime Minister is not well so did not appear in the House last night. He is expected to speak on Tuesday next and what he has to say is awaited with much anxiety as he will then define his attitude to the war.

Roumania is still being over run by the Germans.

1916 Saturday December 16 This mornings telegrams announce a great French victory at Verdun. They made a great assault, smashed the enemies' line and captured 7,500 prisoners. That is <u>their</u> reply to peace proposals.

After a long interval things are again moving in Mesopotamia and to-day we read that a decided move towards Kut-el-Amara is being made.

The Food Controller is getting to work either for good or ill (more of the latter than the former I am afraid) and to-day it is announced that Sugar Tickets will be issued before long, also that we are to have meatless days, probably Thursdays. How this is to be worked in private house[s] no one can say. We are also promised that food for stock will be made cheaper. Wait and see. Our real anxiety is the continued sinking of food ships which I think average five or six a day. This morning 9 are reported sunk.

Wheat to-day reached 80/- per quarter at Peterborough market.

Sunday December 17 No news to-day. Yesterday was very foggy all over the country and in consequence of this the women mail van drivers in London were afraid to venture so that to-day we are without London news.

December 17 Fat Stock Show sales have been held this week and some very high prices have been paid. Two fat hogs made £70 the pair at Northampton.

We are being urged by the Government to make the best use of all food and also to prepare to grow the utmost pound next year.

I think if peace does not come next year will be an awful one both for us and the enemy, everything points to the fact that the Allies are going to make a supreme effort and as Germany has still much fight left in her the impact will be horrible.

According to reliable information the real instigator of the Peace proposals is Austria. She is in an awful state internally and starvation is slowly but surely coming to her.

On counting up to-day I found that 335 men have gone from the parish of Oundle-cum-Ashton to the war. This is out of a total population of 2700 men women and children and also the Schools. This will give some idea of how denuded of men England is becoming.

DAY BY DAY THROUGH THE GREAT WAR

1916 December 18 Further news to hand this morning shows that the French gave the Germans an awful hammering on Friday and Saturday at Verdun. They broke quite through the German lines, captured 9,500 prisoners and 80 guns. Berlin admits this disastrous set back but does not publish any details so that the German people are still ignorant of it. The French have been patiently preparing for this for some months and have made 20 miles of new roads so that they could move their heavy guns.

To-day the food regulation forbidding anyone to be served with more than 3 courses for dinner (i.e. between 6.30 and 9pm) and 2 courses for luncheon in any place of public eating comes into force.

No soldier or sailor either officer or private may now spend more than 2/6 upon a lunch, 2/- on a tea and 5/6 on dinner, these prices include tips.

December 19 Tuesday The French victory at Verdun is complete. They captured 11,500 prisoners including 284 officers, 115 Guns and 150 Machine Guns. The enemy counter attacked on Sunday but without any success. This is one of the worst reverses the Germans have had. So well was it planned, organised and carried [out] that the French [loss of life?] was comparatively small.

Wednesday December 20 The Prime Minister's speech last night in the House is to-day the sole topic of conversation. He did not absolutely reject the German offer of peace, but demanded they should declare their terms before anything else could be done. I am not very hopeful about this peace business at present.

The Government are to assume control over the whole of the coal industry, also shipping, and to some extent the land. He asked for a Voluntary enrolment of all persons for War work, and said that if [it] was not forthcoming there would be compulsory enrolment. He did not promise a speedy victory, but said we should either win or go under. These various measures are staggering. It appears to me the authorities think they can manage everybody's business, but their own they cannot.

Thursday December 21 People to-day are more than ever concerned about the Prime Minister's Speech. That is those who have sufficient thought to see to what it may lead. The proposals are so drastic, so novel, and so far reaching in their effects that there is much disposition to await what may be done, but already I see some shadows of coming events. Mr Neville Chamberlain, Mayor of Birmingham, has been appointed Controller of Labour. This is certainly a good choice as he is one of the most able men in this country. But it resolves itself into this: Can one man practically organise and control all the labour in the country. I do not think he can but am content to wait and see.

To-day the new Minister of Agriculture has fixed the price of English wheat for 1917 at 60/- per qr. (To-day's price is 78/- to 80/-) Of course if the war ends the farmer stands to win as it is certain there would be a big drop. If it continues he must lose as wheat will still command higher prices.

December 22 Friday This morning the whole world is startled to hear that Wilson the American President has issued a note to the belligerents asking both sides to state their terms of peace. It has caused much excitement here and the effect may be summed up I think as follows: "We give your proposal a respectful hearing, but will you please mind your own business." Men of all shades of opinion cannot see much hope of a lasting peace at present.

December 23 Saturday There is some disposition to think both here and in America that the President is possessed of some facts which he cannot disclose. It is suggested that he sees that America may be drawn into the war before long and is most anxious to build up a peace before that occurs. If this is not so he has made a blunder and will be blamed very severely both in America and in this country.

1916 December 24 Sunday A fine bright day to-day after a week of snow rain and frost really typical English weather.

Christmas is very quiet in these small country places and indeed throughout the country. No one wishes you "A Merry Xmas". There is little disposition for merriment living as we are under the pall of this awful war and it is generally recognised that this is not the time for much feasting. Please God by another Christmas we may be at peace again.

All Poultry is very dear. Turkeys 1/9 to 2s per lb. Ducks 6s to 10/- each. Scarcely any geese. Pheasants

THE DIARY OF JOHN COLEMAN BINDER

6 to 7/- each. Fowls 9 to 12/- per couple.

Monday December 25 Christmas Day. I quite think the quietest Christmas day that I have ever known. Very very few people have come into the town and so many men being away it is absolutely quiet. Very little festivity or gaiety. Everybody's thoughts are away with the men in France, Salonika, Egypt Mesopotamia, East Africa, and with the Sailors of the Grand Fleet guarding our own shores. Shall we have peace by next Christmas. Time alone can prove.

Sunday December 31 Since last Monday I have not had any opportunity of writing up these notes as I have been away from home in the North on business, but nothing of real and special importance has occurred. Events along our fronts in France and Salonica are quiet. The Germans are still pushing on in Roumania, but in Egypt there has been some sharp fighting and we have badly mauled the Turco-Germans.

Various Peace Notes are flying about from different countries. These do not appear to advance the prospect of Peace and very little interest in them is taken in this country as we feel there cannot be any peace at present especially in view of the arrogant terms of the German Note.

Now that Christmas is over we are expecting our new Government will announce many and drastic changes either for better or worse. The greatest change at present announced is regarding Railway travelling. All fares will be increased 50 per cent and hundreds of trains will [be] withdrawn. Hitherto we have had 12 passenger trains through here each day. These will be reduced to 6 and similar reductions are taking place all over the country. This will give some little idea as to what will be done. It is hoped by these means to release more men for service, to consume less coal, gas etc, to keep the railways more clear for the transport of munitions, men and war material, and also of food etc. No one grumbles at this as it [is] quite felt we must be prepared to make many and heavy sacrifices during the coming year

Great changes are indicated in the Drink Trade. What form they will take is not yet disclosed, but the evil of this ghastly business is so marked and flagrant that the Government will be compelled to take action. The waste involved in food alone is so appalling that something must be done.

1917 January 1 A New Year. Shall we see the close of this dreadful war. Nobody knows. So many men, so many opinions. I think myself that at any rate the climax <u>must</u> come this year. Which will hold out the longest our money or Germany's men.

The Allies answer to the German Peace note is published to-day. They all say No. There can be no Peace upon your terms.

January 7 All this week the chief topic has been the German desire for peace. She has blustered and swaggered very much on receiving the Allies answer and has threatened us with unheard of 'frightfulness' but this has made no difference to us. The Allies demand is still the same: Restitution Reparations and Guarantees for the future.

If reports from neutral countries can be credited, the situation in Germany has lately become much worse. One cannot say they are starving but clearly there is not sufficient food to go round, and on the showing of their own food Organiser their system of distribution has broken down. They had hoped to get a huge booty from Roumania. Their real object there was food not conquest, but so thoroughly had the Roumanians (acting on the demands of the Allies) destroyed the stores of corn, oil and cattle, that really the enemy obtained but a very small quantity. Our blockade by sea is also being tightened up.

The impression is gaining ground that peace will come this year. Possibly it may (I think myself it will) but it is of no use to prophesy unless you know.

The food organisation for increasing the supply of home grown food is getting to work, and various schemes are being put forward. It appears that the work will be chiefly carried out by County War Committees who will really be responsible for seeing that the land in each county is made to produce its utmost.

Speaking on Friday one of the Agricultural Commissioners said that "we had been silly fools in trying to get every man into the army." Every one in the county knows that, yet these fools in London at the War

Office have been utterly unable to see it and now we are suffering from their pig-headedness. They are now talking of using German prisoners and also of returning men to [the] land from the Army.

I hear that Government propose to forbid Millers from sending flour above a certain distance from their own mills. Each miller will be given a zone in which he will be allowed to sell flour but not outside it. This is to be done to save freight, but one can see great complications.

It is generally thought the Government are about to deal with the Drink Traffic in a drastic way, either by leasing it or by buying it outright and putting it under national control. Certainly something will be done. In consequence of this the Barley trade is very nervous and unsettled.

1917 January 11 A great day this. The New War Loan is launched to-day at a big meeting in the City. It has been well boomed and probably will be a huge success. It will have to be so or as we are told with little ceremony there will be a forced loan. I think its attractive terms will ensure it a great reception. Four per cent free of income tax or 5% liable to tax and the Government agree to see that it does not depreciate. They will do this by means of a sinking fund.

It is hoped that the total sum (including conversions of the two old loans and other borrowings together with new subscriptions will reach 2,000 Millions. This is beyond human power to grasp. It looks to me as if this struggle will resolve itself into a battle between our money and German man-power.

Various 'Peace Notes' have been flying about the last few days. To a request from the American President the Allies have stated their terms generally. Restitution and reparation to Belgium, Serbia, Roumania and Montenegro. The complete kicking out of Europe of Turkey and a free passage of Russia to the Sea. Also a rectifying of the French Frontier as regards Alsace Lorraine. Germany has received these terms with a howl of rage. They differ as far as they possibly can from her terms and unless there are concessions peace at present is impossible. I do not think the Allies are very desirous of Peace at the present juncture for I think they firmly believe they are now in a position to deliver a smashing blow during the spring and early summer.

In domestic concerns things are moving rapidly, especially as regards food. A new bread order which comes into operation on Jan 29 compels the miller to retain an extra 6 per cent of offals in the flour thus making an output of 81 per cent of flour instead of 76% which we had since December.

The order of December has made so little difference either in the colour or appearance of the loaf that most people were quite unaware that any change had been made. The new order also <u>allows</u> 5 per cent of Barley Rice or Maize to be added to the wheat.

The feeding of wheat to stock and poultry is forbidden (except damaged wheat or screenings).

Great changes are also made as to cultivation of land. If a farm is not adequately tilled the State will assume possession (temporarily) of it and all buildings connected with [it] and work it themselves.

No sugar is to be used for icing biscuits, cakes or anything of the kind and it is hinted that the use of starch may be forbidden.

These are some of the new provisions and it will be seen how quickly we are moving. They have all been received with tolerance, as people are willing to accept them if it means a shortening of the war, but certainly they have not received them with enthusiasm.

It is very easy to make all these restrictions and orders but I see very grave difficulty in enforcing them. Take for instance the cultivation of land, the oversight of this is to be left to local War Councils and what body of farmers will go and tell one of their number that his farm is badly cultivated. Unless the offence is flagrant and notorious the answer they will get is 'Look at your own land'.

Military matters move very slowly just now. The weather is simply abominable both here and in France, Snow Sleet Frost and Rain. This puts a stop to nearly all operations. Tens of thousands of men from the front are now coming home for a few days leave.

Monday January 15 The Germans are frantic with rage either real or assumed at the Allies reply to their peace proposals. They are to-day threatening us with dire vengeance and to hear them talk one would think they could wipe us all out. The "All-highest "Kaiser as they love to call him has issued a most bombastic manifesto on these same lines. All this makes very little impression here. People only laugh at him. The reply meets with the approval of all neutrals.

Tuesday January 16   A new order is issued concerning flour and other articles. Millers after Jan 29th will be compelled to leave an extra 5 per cent of sharps in the Flour making 81%obtained from the wheat. This will probably make a reddish brown loaf. They may also add another 5 per cent of barley oats rice or maize to the flour but I do not think this will be generally done. The use of this new flour will be compulsory by bakers (and all the public) on and after March 12. The first change which took place on Jan 1 is so slight that it was not generally noticed by the consumer. It is quite probable that the next step will be a still further brown bread. In fact wheat meal bread, with only a very little of the bran taken out.

There can be no question that the food business in this county is a serious one, far more so than the public generally are aware of and is causing serious anxiety to all connected with it. And yet future generations will find it difficult to believe in the face of all this that to-day the Army people have issued orders calling up 30,000 of the skilled labourers who are left on the land and suggesting that men who have been rejected (that is the unfit) mostly clerks, sedentary workers etc. etc. should be substituted for these skilled men. The situation would be comic if it were not so serious.

75 German prisoners have been allotted as a start for farm work in each county. These will have a guard of 35 men. Probably they will work in gangs.

Friday January 20   A tremendous explosion to-day at Munition work at Silvertown, London. The casualties are estimated at --- and enormous damage has been done to property. It is said to have shaken half London.

Sunday January 21   Very little move on all the fronts this week. The weather conditions both here and on the Continent are atrocious. Bitter east wind and sleet, making all movement almost impossible.

Well authenticated reports from Germany disclose serious food trouble there. Far more so than with us. Fats are almost unprocurable at any price. The very rich manage to do fairly [well] as they can pay fabulous prices but the poor are very hard hit. A war of starvation between us and the enemy. Which can hold out the longer.

There is really no lack of anything here. Living is much simpler with most people as it must be when food has advanced 87 per cent since August 1914.

1917 January 23 Tuesday   To-day an order is issued by the Army calling up all boys as they reach the age of 18. Hitherto the age has been 18 years and 8 months. It is estimated that 250,000 boys attain this age every year in this county.

January 24 Wednesday   A sharp naval action is reported this morning between 10 English and 12 German patrol boats. These Germans were coming out of Zeebrugge to escape the ice. One of them was sunk and the others severely mauled.

The weather in Germany is very severe. Ten people have been frozen to death. One of the disabled German boats had to put [into] Uminden for safety and it was found the men killed in action were frozen to the decks and axes had to be used to get them away.

Sunday January 28   Very little news the last few days. A small German raiding ship was off the Suffolk coast on Thursday night for about ten minutes but was soon off after firing a few shots. No damage was done.

We have had a bitterly cold week. Hard black frost from the east. The men in the trenches are suffering much and many are getting frozen feet.

DAY BY DAY THROUGH THE GREAT WAR

Food is gradually getting dearer and on the average has increased nearly 90 per cent since August 1914. The following are some of the local retail prices:

Bread is 9 ½ d per lb

Best joints of Beef, Mutton and Pork 1/ 4d to 1/6d

Potatoes 1/6d to 1/9d per 14 lb

Apples 4d to 6d per lb (bad crop last year)

Milk 5d quart (most places 6d)

Cheese (Canadian) 1/4d to 1/6d

Butter 2/- Eggs 2 ½d each (these are a little cheaper)

Oatmeal 4 ½ d (used to be 2d to 2 ½ d)

Flour 3/4d per 14lb

Coal 1/8d to 1/10d per cwt (the price to-day in Paris is 10/- per cwt)

The only article which you cannot get in full supply is sugar. This is still retailed at 5 ½ d to 6d per lb but the supply is limited. It is said we are to have sugar tickets. I cannot think they would be a success.

This week the Government have announced that after April 1st the output of beer will have to be reduced by 30 per cent. This will make a reduction of 50 per cent from pre-war days.

They also demand this week that all foreign securities held in this country shall be placed at their disposal. They will be prepared to buy them at the price they are quoted on Change on the day of purchase. This will be a serious loss to many people as they have depreciated a good deal from their original value.

January 29 Monday Very little news to-day except the usual account of trench raids etc. from our lines in France. Men coming home on leave (usually about 6 to 7 days) say the ground is covered with snow and that the shells ricochet like india rubber balls.

1917 January 31 Wednesday Germany is 'at it' again. This morning she declares she will sink all hospital ships (belonging to the Allies) at sight. She says that these have been used to carry guns and war material. This is an infamous lie as she is quite aware and is told so by the Allies to-day. They invite her to stop and examine all hospital ships (as she has a right to do) and then say if she can find any of the kind on board.

February 1 Thursday Four people were charged at Derby to-day with conspiring to kill the Premier and other ministers. I do not think there is much in it.

February 2 Friday Another amazing manifesto from Germany. She announces that her submarines will sink at sight all and any ship approaching the allied countries except that she will graciously allow America to send one vessel a week to Falmouth on due notice being given to her.

This notice was only sent to America late yesterday and already judging from the press reports it has caused an overwhelming outburst. The whole country appears to be clamouring for war against Germany. Of course the President has had no time to consider the situation, so to-day there is nothing official, but it is reported the US navy has received certain orders.

We in this country quite realize the object of this. The Huns are determined to starve us out. The danger is realized and while there is no panic there is much uneasiness. As I have said many times in these notes some of us have foreseen this danger for many months and have protested against the War Office denuding the farms of labour to the extent they have done. The extent to which they have done this is almost incredible. They seemed to imagine that the war was to be won by getting every man into khaki. A stupendous mistake and folly. Now these people are beginning to climb down and to realize that it is an economic war we are fighting.

Saturday February 3 No official signs from America. All other neutrals are awaiting her decision and the eyes of the whole world are turned to her. The chance of her joining the Allies is eagerly discussed on all sides. I do not think her practical aid could be much but her moral support would be an enormous factor. She would probably seize all merchant vessels which have been lying for safety in America's harbours since Aug 1914. This would be the best help she could render to us.

To-day the Food Controller (Lord Devonport) asks everybody to ration themselves and supplies the following formula: 4lb Bread 2 ½ lb Meat ¾ lb sugar for each person. This I think may be considered a very fair allowance. He says if this is not done voluntarily it will be made compulsory.

I can see that we may have to endure many things yet although this has not come as a surprise to anyone who has been in touch with the food business for the last two years. It is quite possible and feasible that we may yet adopt Communal Food Kitchens which would probably save 30 per cent of our food.

February 4 Sunday A snowy wintry day. We have had winter now almost since November. The Sunday Papers this morning announce the German Ambassador in America has been handed his Passports and requested to leave. This looks like war. We await to-morrows papers most anxiously.

The past week has been one of the most dramatic of the war. Somehow one feels rightly or wrongly that the climax is coming and coming swiftly. I am afraid we have much bloody fighting to encounter yet. Both sides are grimly preparing in France. Thrusting here and feeling there to discover the weak spots.

February 5 Monday America has given the German Ambassador his passports and also withdrawn her own Ambassador from Berlin.

The President made an historic speech to the Senate on Saturday and firmly restated his position.

I think that America (like ourselves) does not want to fight but may be compelled to do so. Everywhere the probability of war discussed.

A large American liner was sunk off the Scilly Islands on Saturday at noon.

A wireless message from Berlin this afternoon says that Germany is trying to negotiate with America.

1917 Tuesday February 6 No further action from America to-day

Wednesday February 7 Events continue much as yesterday. America is making every preparation for war.

Germany has given her a nasty slap in the face by declining to allow Slaid (the American Ambassador) to leave Berlin until Bernstoff, the German Ambassador, has left America. This has caused a terrific uproar in the States.

Ships are being sunk every day off our coasts, both English and neutrals. Fourteen are posted to-day.

Thursday February 8 The terrible ship sinking goes on. Yesterday a liner was sunk without the least warning, over 100 of the crew and passengers were drownded.

The severest frost this morning we have had for 25 years. 30 degrees were registered here and at Market Harboro 36. This is a terribly trying winter.

Friday February 8 The American Ambassador is now to leave Germany but the conviction is growing that war is inevitable.

We gained a notable success on the Somme yesterday by clearing the Huns out of the village of Grandecourt.

Saturday February 10 The Americans have determined to send one of their liners across under just ordinary conditions (except that she will be fully armed) but not marked in any way to distinguish her as ordered by Germany and thus defying the Huns. We await the result with some interest.

February 11 Sunday Although the American situation has occupied a good deal of our attention this past week, I think the chief and foremost place has been given to the submarine menace and its effect upon our food supply. The requests made by the Food Controller to ration ourselves are receiving attention and are welcomed in some quarters but I do not think the bulk of the nation yet apprehend the seriousness of the situation and will not do so until the restrictions are made compulsory. Then and only then will they learn to retrench.

Food of all kinds grows daily in value. Many housewives are setting their wits to work to find substitutes for Bread and Flour. It should be explained that the ration is really a _flour ration_ of 3lb per head per week. This would make about 4lb of Bread, but if it were all consumed in that form nothing would remain for puddings or cakes.

The amount may be sufficient for some people but it is undoubtedly a starvation allowance for others. A man at work on the land can easily dispose of his share in two days. I think the voluntary part is only a feeler - I quite think it will be made compulsory at a very early date.

It is generally acknowledged on all sides that we are reaching the climax of the war. Germany has made her last throw (a desperate gambler) on this submarine business and has staked her all upon it. I think she has quite calculated what she hopes to gain by it, but then her calculations have gone wrong many times in this terrible war and may do so again. She hopes in the first place to cut our food supply and starve us before the terrible campaign which will open very shortly, and in the second place she is trying to force America into the war, so that when peace comes America may be able to take part in the negotiations as one of the belligerents, and by this means to modify the terms which may be imposed by the Allies.

I think as I have always thought that this food business is our most vulnerable spot and quite realize that that we may yet have to endure great privations.

It is also quite on the cards that we may yet see another naval battle or battles. The condition of Germany is getting bad and may cause her to do desperate things yet.

Cheese is now being retailed in most places at 1/6 per lb. Lard 1/2 Bacon 1/3 to 1/9 to 2/- Potatoes 1/9 to 2/- Bread goes to 10d in London tomorrow. Oatmeal 4d to 4½ d per lb (doubled since war). These prices will give some indication of how events are going.

1917 February 12 Monday Eight vessels reported sunk this morning. We are assured that effective means are being taken to combat this danger. One knows that this is a small proportion of the shipping coming each day to this country, but at the same time over 60% of our total shipping is engaged on necessary war transport it leaves only 40 per cent for all other purposes.

A sharp action on the Western front on Saturday. We took 220 German prisoners.

February 13 Tuesday As bearing on the shortage of labour I saw a remarkable sight to-day. The North Pytchley (Woodland) Hounds were out for exercise and the Whips (one man and one boy) were mounted on bicycles. Enough to make old huntsmen turn in their graves.

Another incident also shows how serious the times are. Tenant farmers have just been given (by the Food Controller) the _right_ to kill pheasants. "What even in the breeding season" exclaimed a horrified country Member in the House last night "Yes" retorted the Food Controller "if they are eating food suitable for human beings". This bird has hitherto always been regarded as sacred by the country gentleman.

February 14 Wednesday A reassuring statement was made last night by the Government as to submarines. They declare that they have the situation well in hand and the measures taken are proving successful but we are warned that we may expect to endure further sacrifices both in food and other things.

A extraordinary campaign on behalf of the War Loan is being conducted all over the country. The lists close on Friday. It looks as if it would [be] a great success.

War Saving Associations have now been formed in nearly every town and village in the country and in nearly all schools, factories and workshops. The money is collected in many places by house-to-house collection. Children also carry it to school. This money is invested in War Saving Certificates costing 15/6 each which in 5 years will have grown to £! Each, but should the money be wanted by a depositor they can get their certificates cashed at any post Office with the interest due on them.

THE DIARY OF JOHN COLEMAN BINDER

Thursday February 15 The papers publish this morning an account of an (alleged) interview with Sir Douglas Haig, in which he is made to say that we are certain of victory this year and shall completely smash the Germans. This kind of talk does not commend itself to us at all. We will do the business first and then talk about it.

Friday February 16 America still holds back although Press reports say that war is regarded as inevitable.

The frost after nearly six weeks has practically broken up to-day and we have had rain.

   All agricultural work is much in arrears.

February 16 Saturday The Germans seem yesterday to have opened the 1917 campaign by a violent attack on the French in Champagne. They met some little success but not much.

February 18 Sunday Yesterday and to-day enormous movements of railway material are taking place. Passenger traffic yesterday was only about half its usual quantity. This material is being shipped to France for use behind the lines where many railways are being made. Many thousands of plate-layers have been at work there during the winter and now the frost has gone great efforts are being made to complete the work. Thousands more are going.   180 alone from Northampton to-morrow.

   We seem now to be living in a theatre and any day may now see the rise of the curtain and disclose to us the tremendous clash of arms which we all know must ensue during the next few months. I do not think the war can endure beyond this year, the strain is too great.

   The War Loan closed yesterday amidst many memorable scenes. The Bankers have in many places been 'snowed under'. Gold has in hundreds of cases been produced from most unlikely places. In many cases it must have been hoarded for many many years. (Some of it bears the dates of early Victorian years). Old and young, rich and poor have all subscribed to this loan. . The total amount is expected to be announced to-morrow. In this small place nearly £4,000 has been placed through the Post Office. This is quite apart from subscriptions through the Banks and other channels.

1917 Monday February 19 There was sharp fighting on the Somme yesterday and Saturday. Our men made notable progress, drove back the enemy a mile and captured 800 prisoners. These landed at Southampton this morning.

The total war loan subscription is announced to-day £700,000,000. . An enormous sum.

Tuesday February 20 All kinds of provisions are advanced rapidly in price, owing to this submarine menace and the market for all foodstuffs is very much excited.

Wednesday February 21 The Army people are now calling up men in every direction especially those who are A1 men, that is - fit for the first line.

February 22 Thursday A long speech last night by the First Admiralty Lord, explaining the submarine war affairs. He said that during -   -   -   - tons of shipping had been sunk, but at the same time nearly 11,000 ships had entered and left our ports. At the same time he quite ignored the large number of neutral ships which are being scared off the seas.

February 23 Friday A long and elaborate statement by the Premier in the House to-day on the food and other questions. He announced that the import of many articles including Tea (otherwise than Imperial), Coffee, Cocoa, Apples, Dried Fruits, canned Salmon would be totally prohibited. That there would be a further restriction on many other articles including paper. This will mean that we shall [see] another reduction in the size of our daily papers. It is quite obvious that we are now approaching a difficult and trying time in this terrible struggle and that we may [be] called upon to put up with many things we have not done before. Beer is to be reduced to ten million barrels per year. This is a great reduction and brewers say that it will all be sold at 1/- per pint. The clearest and [soundest] men demand that it should not be brewed at all, but that all the materials of which it is formed should be used for food, but this Government, all powerful as it is supposed to be, I am convinced dare not tackle the drink business. It is simply scandalous.

Saturday February 24 Yesterday's proposals are on the whole being well received but I will wait to see the effect when they actually touch the general public.

Respecting the voluntary food rations mentioned some time ago, it is quite certain that some people are trying to comply with them, but that taken as a whole they are not a success, especially as regards bread.

Sunday February 25 The absurd struggle for men between the Government departments still continues and has even increased this week. I believe that Mr Prothero the Minister of Agriculture may be driven to resign as it is clear from his speeches that his position is far from an [agreeable] one. Ploughing has been started again this week but everything is very backward.

February 26 Monday The Food Controller announces this morning that stocks of Flour and wheat are the lowest on record and permission is given to include beans in the admixtures which may be used with wheat.

The Chancellor announces that the total sum of <u>new</u> money subscribed to the War is over a thousand millions. Enormous !

The Germans in France on Saturday retired for a distance of 3 miles and abandoned two strongly fortified villages Serre and Meranport. I think they have some object in this.

To-night it is announced that at last we have captured Kut in Mesopotamia. This is after weary months of fighting. Goodness only knows of what value it will be to us now we have got it. The men who are fighting in that outlandish place would be far better employed in producing food in this country.

A German Gun boat bombarded Margate and Broadstairs about 11.30 last night. One woman and a child were killed and two children injured. The whole affair did not last more than ten minutes.

1917 Tuesday February 27 The food Controller issues an order to-day forbidding the sale of bread which has been baked less than 12 hours. This will make it awkward for bakers. They will have one day's supply and distribute it the next.

Seven Dutch steamers were torpedoed on Saturday in the Channel. Three sunk and the others were towed into port. This business has made an immense stir in Holland, but I am afraid they are helpless.

A Cunard liner, 18,000 tons, was sunk off the Irish Coast yesterday. About 18 or twenty passengers are missing.

Wednesday February 28 The German retreat still continues in France. We do not know quite what to make of it. Probably they are retiring to what they think a more advantageous position.

There is a call to-day for 10,000 women for the Army! These will go to France to act as store keepers, clerks etc etc.

Thursday March 1 Still the Germans are falling back on the Somme battlefield . . . It is conjectured to-day that they do not mean to make any big offensive on this front this year but are going to make a push on the eastern front. <u>We</u> shall have something to say about that. Preparations are being made all over this county to receive the wounded. To-day it was agreed to receive about 20 into the Workhouse here when necessary.

The Turks are in full retreat on the Tigris and are now 30 miles beyond Kut. Our cavalry are in rapid pursuit of them. They have abandoned enormous stores and guns.

Friday March 2 It seems impossible to doubt that America is slowly heading for war. Events are forcing her in that direction and I believe will continue to force her until she has to come in. To-day she publishes the details of intrigues by which Germany with her usual clumsy methods hoped to induce Mexico to invade the States. This with the sinking of the Cunard Liner 'Laconia' (18,000 tons) and the loss of American lives thereon has apparently roused the entire American nation. I think that if they have any grit at all they will be compelled to fight even if it is only to defend their own interests.

Saturday March 3 At last the German retreat has stayed and yesterday they attempted by counter attacks to stop our advance. It is surmised that they have withdrawn so as to try to prevent our people seizing

THE DIARY OF JOHN COLEMAN BINDER

Cambrai which is the German principal railway centre. At any rate it looks as if we were on the eve of stupendous events. Everybody is watching with the greatest anxiety for the next moves. I think it must mean both to us and the enemy an enormous sacrifice of life.

March 4 Sunday At yesterday's meeting of Congress the president had granted to him full powers to take whatever steps he considered advisable to protect American interests.

To-day is published a long list of occupations in which any employer is forbidden to engage any fresh man between the ages of 18 and 61 except such man has been discharged from the Army. These constant new regulations and orders are causing very very great inconvenience and loss but they are being accepted loyally as it is hoped by these means to bring the war to a successful end, but woe betide the authors of them if these various orders do not effect this. People will be furious. There is really much fussing, fadding and interfering by men who have no adequate knowledge of the matters with which they are dealing.

Farm work has made fair progress this week. Weather much better, but work is still much in arrear.

The new bread which we are now just beginning to use, is close and dark and personally I do not like it as well as pre-war bread, but we shall have to accept it. I believe that this is an absolute necessity.

Fats of all kinds are becoming scarce. Lard is retailed at ¼ per lb, Cheese 1/6 to 1/8, English Cheese at Dorchester realized 182/- per cwt at the Cheese fair this week.

1917 Tuesday March 6 To-day it is announced that voluntary enlistment for National Service (between 18 and 61) will close on March 31. I suppose that after that date there will be compulsion if the requisite numbers are not forthcoming. I do not propose myself to enrol as I consider my present work both public and private is of quite as much importance as to any to which I might be sent at 25/- per week.

Thursday March 8 Very little has been done on the West front the past few days. We are having very bitter winter weather again, and similar conditions prevail there. Air fights in great numbers are taking place and it seems as if the Germans were making an effort to obtain the mastery of the air which they quite lost last year. I hear to-day that 200 or 300 German prisoners are coming to Corby to work in the ironstone pits there.

Friday March 9 To-day the Government takes over the control of all fats, oils etc. As I predicted 12 months since, fats are becoming very scarce and dear.

To-night it is rumoured that our cavalry is in Bagdad. Cui bono?

Saturday March 10 To-day we have had real winter again. A perfect blizzard in the west with one of the worst storms of this long and dreary winter. Seeding must be hindered again.

Sunday March 11 To-day we have been baking bread, in order that it may be stale for tomorrow. On and after that date no bread will be allowed to be sold unless it is 12 hours or more old. We have had to bake to-day, Sunday, but after this week shall be able to manage so that Saturday's bread will be sold on Monday and Monday's on Tuesday and so on.

This food question is engaging the attention of nearly everybody. I hope and trust that there will be sufficient to go round, but again yesterday we were warned that imports must again be much reduced.

The real opening of this year's campaign on all fronts still hangs fire. The tension and suspense is great. The public is getting 'nervy' and 'jumpy'. Germany the last few days is apparently more confident. This is on account of her submarine business and she is beginning to talk about indemnities again.

All men under 31 who have certificates of exemption from the army are to-day notified that they will be revised and that they will have to appeal to the Tribunals again. There are about 18 in this town.

Wednesday March 14 Much fighting is going on around Bapaume and the Huns are being driven from the ridge. This is said to be the last position in which they will be able to make much use of trenches.

The rout of the Turks at Bagdad is complete. They are in full retreat. This capture of Bagdad has caused much dismay in Germany as it means that their pet scheme of a Berlin -Bagdad railway is knocked on the head.

1917 Thursday March 15   Momentous news from Russia is being published in London to-night. The news here is very vague.

Friday March 16   The news from Russia is epoch making but not altogether unexpected by people here who have carefully watched what has been going on there. Practically all news from Russia has been suspended since last Friday, but to-day the veil is lifted and we see a drama of world wide importance. A revolution has been put through. The Duma or Parliament is supreme. The Czar has abdicated or been deposed (it is not very clear at this moment which). A regency appointed, and to some extent order has been re-established. The thought that instantly occurs to each and all is this - What influence will this have on the War. Opinion in all countries both enemy and ally agrees that the war offensive on the allies part will now be pushed with more vigour and determination. Russia is a strange country and at least 100 years behind us, and so it is difficult to judge her by Western standards. It is abundantly clear that the Reactionary Party in Russia is quite pro- German and has all through been aiding her as far as it could and thus paralysing the conduct of affairs. At last events were driven to a head and it became a question which was to rule, Parliament or the Bureaucrats (with whom the Czar, through the influence of the Czarina, was identified). The Reactionaries have lost and to-day Russia stands forward as a self-governing people. Surely a stupendous event and one which we living so closely to can scarcely estimate. Revolutions however have a knack of spreading and this occurrence must give the Kaiser some occasion to think.

Saturday March 17   The latest news tonight says that the Czar is on his way to the Crimea as a prisoner under military escort. The Army strongly supported the Parliament and this made the Revolution complete.

Good news from France to-night. Our men captured Bapaume this morning and once more the enemy are falling back. One does not quite know [what] to think of this continual retreat. Germany is credited with having great reserves in the interior. What does she intend to do with them.

Sunday March 18   Wheat reached 92/- at Lincoln yesterday, and last night the Leader of the House of Commons said the War Cabinet attached more importance to the production of food than of taking every man into the Army. What idiots and fools and what a belated confession. Every man living in the country has known for the last 18 months that we were going headlong to this position, and in spite of all their repeated warnings our wise rulers ! ! ! refused to listen to any reason. Food I am convinced is still going to be the determining factor in this war. A shortage of food almost everywhere, and prices continually advancing. To-day the average price of food is 92 per cent more than in 1914.

It seems to me that National Service is a failure. All men (except a few idle ones) are working at their full capacity and strength and to take them from one occupation to put them into another is ridiculous. But I fear this wise Government of ours will endeavour to do it by compulsion. This is Prussian rule with a vengeance. Men growl deeply about this continual compulsion and to a close observer the signs of the times are ominous.

Monday March 19   Great news from France this morning. The enemy has retreated many miles along the Ancu front. Has abandoned 60 towns and villages and is being sharply pressed by the English and French cavalry. The Germans say this is a 'strategic ' retreat. If so they are moving much faster than they anticipated. In many cases they are burning the villages and poisoning the water. All this is quite in keeping with their usual practices. A more blackguardly nation has never existed on this earth.

It is quite certain they will fight again. One wonders when they will elect to do so, but fight they will and must.

A naval scrap occurred during last night off the Kentish coast. We lost a destroyer. What damage the enemy suffered is not stated.

Zeppelins also made their appearance again last Friday after being quiet since the 1st of October last. Some bombs were dropped on Kent but no damage at all was done.

1917 Tuesday March 20   Affairs seem to be settling down in Russia, but all danger is not yet passed.

THE DIARY OF JOHN COLEMAN BINDER

The enemy still falls back in France and during the last few days has retreated from 1,000 square miles of French territory.

Wednesday March 21 There are some signs that the Germans are again going to make a stand. The pursuit is slackening, but cavalry skirmishes continue.

Once again America is approaching war. Indeed to-day is stated from New York that a state of war 'virtually' exists between the States and Germany. This last phase has been brought about by the sinking of two American ships either on Saturday or Sunday and the drowning of a number of their crews.

March 22 Thursday There are rumours again to-day that Germany will ask for peace. I do not think so at present. It is fairly certain that rioting is taking place in many German towns.

Letters coming here from men at the front say that the condition of the country now being abandoned by the Germans is almost indescribable. Dead horses are lying about literally in thousands. They are poisoning the wells with human excreta and similar abominations. From one town they have carried off 50 young women to act as 'servants'.

Friday March 23 A long debate in the Commons to-day on the food situation. It is becoming very clear that as I pointed out as long since as last November, we are in for a very bad time between now and next July. Food is becoming scarce although at the present moment there is no actual scarcity except potatoes, and these are in many towns and villages quite unobtainable. The price as fixed by government is 1½ d per lb retail, otherwise I believe they would be sold at 6d or 8d per lb, and strict measures have to be taken to see they are not sold at more than 1½d. I think it is only now slowly dawning upon many people that we are short of food. I can say that never in all my life have I known the demand for bread to be so great. This is accounted for by the cold weather (we have real winter again this week - snow, frost and hail), by the dearth of potatoes, and also by so much of the winter green food being killed by the frost. Bread goes to a 1/- the 4lb loaf on Monday and I cannot think it will remain there. The present general price in this district is 10d. Wheat to-day at Stamford is reported at 90/- per quarter. This I think is exceptional, the average price I should imagine is about 87/- or 88/-. Flour is 62/- per 20 stones. It is gradually becoming much darker but nothing at all to find fault with at present.

Saturday March 24 The Germans are making more of a stand to-day. I am very suspicious of this retreating business. I believe they intend to make a big push on some other front and should not be surprised if Italy is selected. Italy has enough men but I am afraid she is not over well supplied with munitions.

Russia seems to be settling down again but news from there is very fragmentary and disjointed. From all accounts it appears that the Ex Empress has been the cause of most of the trouble. She is a German and has as usual been acting the German role of spy and traitor. She is now a prisoner. We here had hoped much from Russia this year. Perhaps it may yet come.

Sunday March 25 A milder warmer day to-day. We have had a real winter week. Frost and blinding snow at intervals with cutting winds. Vegetation is very backward. Fruit trees even apricots show no signs of bud at present.

The topic in which every one is just now concerned is food. Shall we have enough is being asked by every one almost. I am doubtful.

Sensational Rumours as to the German Fleet coming out are current to-day. All men on leave have been called up again by telegram, and the railways are in full working order.

1917 Thursday March 29 I have not had time to write up this diary since Sunday. Work increases so much and every spare minute is devoted to digging and planting my own garden. It is quite impossible to get a man to help and it is imperative that it should be done, as if the war should continue through next winter we shall be in a worse plight than ever. All of us millers bakers etc can see that we shall have a most critical time to tide over between now and July.

The Germans are still slowly falling back, hard pressed by ourselves and the French. Ours are chiefly cavalry skirmishes, but the French are fighting some stiff battles between St Quentin and Laon.

DAY BY DAY THROUGH THE GREAT WAR

Friday March 30 A Hospital ship torpedoed is announced to-day. Fortunately she had no wounded on board.

Saturday March 31 Continued fighting on western front in France. From what one can gather we are closely following up the retreating enemy. Much more quickly than at first seemed possible. Bridges and roads are being repaired in a wonderful way and our horsemen are constantly attacking the enemies' rear guard. To-day they have driven him out of three villages.

Sunday April 1 What a day for the 1st April. After a very sharp frost we have had a fall of about 3 inches of snow. Fortunately it is rapidly thawing this afternoon. The first snow we had this winter fell early in November about the 9th, so it will be seen what a long trying severe winter we have had. Pneumonia of a virulent type has been very prevalent and many deaths have occurred.

The food business continues to engage the greater part of the thoughts of those who are compelled to remain at home. At present food is not actually scarce but many articles are difficult to obtain by the retailer and as much as six or seven weeks sometimes elapse before they are delivered. The most serious part of the business is that Millers have now reached the same position. They cannot go on to the market and buy foreign wheat, but have to put their names on to a waiting list and then take their turn.

The Government this week introduced a bill into the House for the re-examination of all rejected men, but it met with such a hostile reception that they have had to accept an amendment by which all men engaged in farm work prior to March 1915 are exempted from its scope.

   Bread continues to become darker and not nearly as palatable as formerly.

All eyes are now turned to America where momentous events are expected to occur this week. Congress meets on Monday and it is assumed The President will announce that 'a state of war' exists and will ask for powers to deal with the situation.

Our English Army working its way into Palestine has badly defeated the Turks this week, capturing their general and 1000 prisoners.

April 2 Monday The Army people are now applying to the Tribunals to get the certificates of exempted men revised, and a lot of these cases came up at the Rural Tribunal held here to-day. In many instances the exemption was renewed but probably the military will appeal against some of these and they will have to come before the County Tribunal at Peterborough.

April 3 America's Congress met last night but reports of its doings will not be available until late to-night.

The Germans are still on the run backwards, hard pressed by our men. Letters received here from men and officers say the destruction and havoc these savages have left behind them is utterly beyond description. They have even destroyed very carefully all fruit trees and every thing of the kind. They have set fire to each house separately and the officers have carried away most of the young girls and women to act as 'servants'. Our men are furious, and very little quarter is being given to the enemy. Very few prisoners are taken.

1917 April 4 Wednesday Great and momentous news from America to-day. At last after many delays and setbacks she finds herself obliged to come into this world conflict. The President's Message to Congress is one of the finest speeches I have ever read. He declares he is forced into this war not so much to defend themselves as for the sake of humanity and civilisation which as he truly says is now hanging in the balance. He says that they will [use] all their power and might to back the Allies. Their quarrel is not with the German people but with their rulers (I do not agree with them in this respect. I had the same idea when this war commenced, but now I am forced to the conclusion that the people are equally guilty with the rulers.) What practical part America will take remains to be seen. I think their chief assistance will be financial and food. Their army is quite insignificant as armies go now. Food we must have and again I say, as many times before, food is our chief concern in this country. Food is our greatest menace and peril. There are at present lying in American harbours 98 vessels, interned since August 1914. Their total tonnage is 620,000 tons. They will need some repair and doing up but should prove of great value in replacing ships that are being sunk (31 last week alone).

THE DIARY OF JOHN COLEMAN BINDER

I can only think and hope that this adhesion of America to our cause will and must materially shorten the war, especially as it seems probable that other South American countries will also declare against the Huns.

Thursday April 5   To-day we are told the Army must have 500,000 more men before July.   I wish they would pay more attention to the Navy. There is distinct uneasiness about this branch of our forces. Not with the officers and men but with some of the chief commands.

It is foreshadowed to-day that the Army age may be raised to 45.

The Americans have seized the interned German vessels and are already at work on them.

Tuesday April 6   Good Friday The ground covered with snow this morning and very cold. The snow soon disappeared and bright sunshine came. I never remember such a continuous cold spring. Not a bud or a leaf to be seen at present and farmers are seriously disquieted at the absence of grass. The ice this morning was quite a quarter of one inch thick.

Saturday April 7   The Russians and English have joined hands in Central Asia and Persia and are moving the Turks rapidly before them.

I hear to-day (on fairly good authority) that we are to have bread Tickets before long. The demand for cereals and bread is enormous. Oatmeal has risen from about £18 per ton before the war to £44 and Oats have again advanced 5/- per qr on the week.

The bread we are now eating is decidedly dark and there are some but not many complaints about it. I find it much better two days old than when new. Potatoes are almost unobtainable although I have quite enough to last through the season.

Sunday April 8   Easter Sunday (Summer time commenced at 2 a.m. to-day with ice more than a quarter inch thick. This year this change is accepted almost without comment. Other events are so tremendous and of such vast importance that this is quite a trivial affair.)

This morning's telegrams say that the Germans in America are doing some damage but I imagine the Americans are quite capable of dealing with anything of that kind.

There have been tremendous air-battles yesterday and Friday in France. We have lost 29 machines and the Germans 36. It looks as if this means something more serious in the way of fighting.

Easter Monday April 9   Great news from the front came from Sir Douglas Haig this afternoon. He made a determined and big attack on the Germans this morning at 5.30 on the line between Arras and Lens and especially the Vimy Ridge which dominates the road to Douai and Cambrai. This has been the scene of terrible fighting the last two years and hitherto the enemy have held it in spite of all our efforts but to-day it seems as if they must be driven back. The battle is still going on. We anxiously await to-morrow's papers.

1917 Tuesday April 10   The report issued at 11 last night is good. Over a front of 12 Miles we cleared 3 miles deep and many prisoners have been captured. The Germans apparently were taken by surprise and suffered terribly from the deadly artillery fire. One whole brigade with its commander surrendered. To-night's telegrams give a total of 12,000 prisoners   240 officers and 150 guns, many of them of heavy calibre.

Wednesday April 11   America proposes to raise a loan of a thousand million pounds 600,000,000 of which will be lent to the Allies at 3½ per cent. This will greatly ease the money situation in this country.

Heavy fighting was going on yesterday all day and seemed to be spreading northward along the lines. A distinct advance was made towards Cambrai, a most important German position.

Thursday April 12   Some fighting yesterday but they out there have had very heavy snow showers as we have had here. The big battle on Monday and Tuesday was under the command of generals Allenby and Horne. The latter is a Northamptonshire man and resides at East Haddon. He commanded that part of the Army which captured the famous Vimy Ridge, a German stronghold which has defied all the efforts of the Allies for the last 2 years.

DAY BY DAY THROUGH THE GREAT WAR

Friday April 13 The fighting was renewed yesterday with increased vigour and the enemy is being pushed back. He fights well in some places but in others simply gives out without much trouble. Our artillery fire is said to be marvellous. The German positions are simply knocked out of all knowledge. So deadly was this fire that for four days before this battle of Arras began the Germans were unable to get any food up to their front lines. Another big move is reported late to-night.

Saturday April 14 Yesterday the weather was better in France and a push was made towards Lens a place of much importance to the enemy as it is the centre of the French coal fields and has been of enormous value to him during the last two years. Our brave men are now within 3 miles of it on 3 sides. Up to to-night our capture of prisoners this week is 13,000 men, 300 officers and over 250 guns. This cannot fail to have some effect in Germany if they are allowed to hear it, but we are not sure that they will do so.

A tremendous munition factory explosion in America yesterday - 200 lives were lost. This is no doubt the work of German spies. America is having a taste of what we have had here, but I think she will be more prompt to deal with it than we have been. Germans are dealt with far too leniently in this country, and I have no hesitation in saying that prisoners here are fed quite as well as I am and certainly their hours of labour are far less than mine.

Sunday April 15 I will write a few lines again to-day about the food business here, as next to the great battles it is the one thing that demands our closest attention. That we are in a very tight place as regards food especially wheat cannot be denied, and that this danger must increase the next five months is certain. I do not want to be misunderstood. No one goes short of food, but we are living from hand to mouth and there are no reserves of grain here. It seems almost impossible to get the great mass of the people to realize this and to take the necessary steps to meet the danger. This week the Government have forbidden the sale of maize except to millers and they will be obliged to mix it with wheat and also to make separate maize products such as maize flakes, maize meal and maize semolina. This is not a step that would be taken if we were not in grave danger, as it is well known that too much maize, oatmeal etc is not good for human beings and to-day I am told by the doctors here that numbers of people are already complaining of rashes and skin trouble. This is the natural consequence of eating this kind of food, except that it is counteracted by green vegetables but these scarcely are to be had to-day having all been killed by the terrible winter we have had. This winter has not left us yet. All through this week we have had snow and biting winds, in fact real winter. It is recorded we have not had such a spring since 1797. All this combines to make us very anxious as to our food. Yesterday the Board of Agriculture issued a notice urging that farmers should dispose as quickly as possible of one sixth of their livestock as it might become impossible to find food for the great quantities we now have in this country, far in excess of what we have ever had and yet they are making tremendous prices. Store beasts at the market here on Thursday made £40 each and upwards. A very speculative business I imagine. Beef is selling at 1/6 per lb, Mutton 1/5 and 1/6 Pork 1/4 to 1/6.

THE DIARY OF JOHN COLEMAN BINDER

1917 Monday April 16 Great news from France to-night. This morning the French Armies attacked all along the line from Soissons to Rheims, German positions of enormous strength which the enemy have held since the Battle of the Marne in 1914 and according to to-nights report are doing as well as our men did a week since.

April 17 Tuesday The fighting yesterday and during last night was of most desperate character but the French made considerable headway and captured 6,000 prisoners. On our part things are comparatively quiet after the heavy fighting of the last week.

Wednesday April 18 The French continue to press forward in many places and the Germans do not appear to [be] able to resist their impetuous attacks.

Terrible stories of last week's bloody battles are now coming through. The Germans made a desperate effort to recover part of the Vimy Ridge, and for 3 hours were in possession of one village, but our men attacked again, drove them up against their own barbed wire and shot 1500 of them, and these crack fighters of the Prussian Guard.

Thursday April 19 Yesterday an order fixing the price of wheat at about 87/-, 76/- for Barley and 55/- for oats was issued. It seems to have quite upset all the markets as it was certain to do as the drop is a heavy one.

Millers yesterday received an order telling them to clearly state on each sack of flour the various proportion of grain etc used in its manufacture.

Friday April 20 The furious battles on the French front continue without cessation. Up to to-night the French had captured 19,000 prisoners and immense quantities of guns and materiel.

Saturday April 21 Power was given to the Food Controller yesterday to take over any workshop or factory used for producing food and to still make the owner work it. By another order the use of wheat, rice or rye was absolutely confined to human food. We are told that we must each consume 2oz of bread less than we have been used to and then possibly we may scrape through. I am quite certain the position is an extremely serious one and will call for our utmost self control and endurance. It seems to me that if the war does not collapse through famine before next August or September it may last for some time longer. By that time America will have built hundreds of wooden vessels and has pledged herself to send food only to the Allies. Neutrals will scarcely receive any. The late American Ambassador at Berlin who is now back again in USA yesterday warned his people that the war was likely to be a long one.

Sunday April 22 Germany continues to sink our hospital ships and in consequence of this huge hospitals will be built on the continent so as to prevent the wounded being brought over. Last night the government issued a proclamation calling up for service all doctors of military age that is from 18 to 41. These have hitherto been exempt, but I take it will now be required to staff these new hospitals.

Monday April 23 This morning the Food Controller announces that on this day week he will assume control of all flour mills in the country. What he intends to do remains to be seen, but I fail to see how he is [to] make bricks without straw or in other words flour without grain.

A very smart little naval action took place off Dover about 12.30 yesterday morning. Five German destroyers attempted a raid but were rounded up by two of our patrols. Two at least of the enemy were sunk, and [it] is doubtful if another of them got back to Zeebrugge. The affair only lasted about 10 minutes and reflects much credit on our seamen.

The great battles on our front were resumed again this morning. Telegraphing at noon   Sir Douglas Haig said that he attacked the enemy at day break and that the battle had gone well.

1917 April 25 Wednesday What is said to be some of the most terrible fighting during the war has been taking place on our front near to Arras during the last two days. The Germans know this to be the most important position they have and have been making every possible effort to hold us up.

April 26 Thursday A most depressing day to-day. The returns issued this morning disclose that 62 vessels were sunk by submarines last week. This is double the number of any previous week and has caused much anxiety and disquietude to the people. In addition to this the Food Controller speaking last night in the House of Lords made the gravest and most decisive speech and warning that we have heard as regards food supply. He said that it was imperative that food should be curtailed and that we were bordering upon actual want, and that if consumption did not decrease during the next six weeks or two months he would ration us. He had already made arrangements to set up the necessary machinery for so doing. The obvious retort to this and the one most sane people are saying to-day is "If this is necessary why not do it now instead of two months hence". There is no question but that there is much muddle and confusion lack of co-ordination and jealousy between different departments in this heaven born government of Lloyd George's. I will only mention one instance but it is quite typical of what is being done. Two months since we were being advised and begged to all keep pigs and poultry, even to keep them in our back yards. To-day in less than two months we are told on the authority of the same department there are a great too many pigs and poultry and that we shall have to kill them. This sort of thing is causing the ordinary man to say "These fellows in London are fools. I know what to do much better than they can tell me. I shall just do as I like." There is much truth in this.

Friday April 27 Yesterday's disclosures have made a profound impression on the people and have brought home to them the seriousness of the situation far more than the continued talk talk talk of the men in Parliament.

The man in the street is beginning to see that the food problem is the problem that most concerns us. I do not lay claim to more than ordinary foresight, but if the reader of this diary will take the trouble to refer to what I wrote 12 or 18 months since, he will find that it was quite clear even then to some of us that food was going to be our weak point. I deprecated the wholesale clearing of labour from the land, and I say emphatically that the present Premier Lloyd George is personally and directly responsible for this. During the time he was War Minister he made it his one object to get every man into the army, and we are reaping the consequences of that disastrous policy to-day.

Fortunately the coming in of America has saved us from financial disaster, which was also a direct consequence of the same policy, but she is not able to save us from famine. That is a grim word.

April 28 Saturday The deadly fighting on our front was resumed this morning after a day or two of comparative quiet. We are assured that all is going well, but our progress is slow. At the present moment the whole brunt of the fighting is upon us. France made a big effort last week but is now almost quiet. Russia with her internal affairs is also now out of the running. Italy is doing nothing. So you who come after us can scarcely realize what a tight corner we are in to-day.

April 29 Sunday This has been quite a fine and dry week and much field work has been done. The land owing to the great frosts of the winter works well and makes a much better seed bed than last year. Women are being employed on the land in much greater numbers than heretofore. Potatoes are being grown very largely. I am glad to say that I have finished planting this week. The seed came direct from Scotland.

Ramsgate was badly shelled for 10 minutes on Friday morning about 1 a.m. Two people were killed and a number wounded.

1917 April 30 Monday The fighting yesterday was chiefly in the air. The aerial combats are very deadly. It is a frequent occurrence for us to lose 10 or 12 machines a day and the Germans quite as many or more.

It was admitted by the Government to-day that the submarine danger is growing. Arrangements are being made to work the rationing business through Local Authorities but at present no instructions have been issued. When I say that it would require 130,000,000 tickets per week it will be seen what a tremendous business it will be.

Tuesday May 1 A real warm summer's day. Fierce fighting on the Salonica front the last two or three days. That is going to be a tough business for the Allies I can see.

Wednesday May 2 I was on Special Constable duty last night. This is only for about an hour, just to see that all the lights are well shaded in case of a Zeppelin raid, but I think that we have done with Zeppelins. They are one of the decided failures of the war. So far as offensive war goes they have been of service to the German Fleet as scouts and that is all that can be said for them.

THE DIARY OF JOHN COLEMAN BINDER

Awfully bloody fighting yesterday and to-day east of Arras. We are now fairly locked in a real death struggle with the Germans, and the battles are terrific. It is estimated that 2,000,000 men are now engaged in this awful and bloody work on this front in France. Is it worth it ? A curious question to ask, yet one that must be answered. Personally I think it is worth it. One can see that unless we win this bloody war civilisation is doomed, for to allow the German to come out top would mean a relapse into barbarism.

Thursday May 3 The weekly returns issued to-day show a loss of 59 vessels sunk. There is much real dissatisfaction with the Admiralty (not with the Fleet) over this business. The problem is a most difficult one, but yet one which I think can and must be solved. There is no question that we are supreme on land but are confronted with this menace of want owing to the sinking of ships. Of course, the whole business of this wholesale destruction of food is real foul action of the wretched Huns. It is not as if they captured the food and used it for some good purpose. They simply sink it and that is an end of it.

Friday May 4 The casualty lists now are awful. Nearly every day over a hundred officers reported killed, and losses in the ranks are equally great in proportion.

A fierce attack on the enemy was launched just before dawn yesterday morning, and continued most of the day. When I say that some of the positions were lost and re-captured seven or eight times it will be seen how deadly the fighting now is.

May 5 Saturday We are getting very little help from Russia now. It is said that all the best German men are up against us and that the older men are upon the Russian front.

May 6 Sunday We have had a real fine hot week of summer weather but yesterday there was a decided fall in the temperature. To-day is warmer again. Vegetation has made much progress but rain is wanted.

The chief topic and concern with all people who are at home is the food business. Shall we hold out for food until harvest. I have no doubt we shall but we shall have to be very sparing and careful. To-day a Proclamation by the King enjoining strict economy in the use of all cereals and asking for a reduction in the consumption of Bread by one quarter was read in all Churches and Chapels and will also be read on the three following Sundays. There is much talk about rationing and food tickets but the Authorities do not appear to have made up their minds as to whether this will be necessary or not. Apparently they are going to set up the machinery in readiness so that it may be brought into action if and when required, but we are told this may not be necessary before July. This week many of the Hounds of the Fitzwilliam pack at Milton have been killed in order to save food. No oats are now allowed to be given to horses and there are many similar restrictions. It will be seen from this how serious the situation is. Vegetables of all kinds are extremely scarce owing to the severe winter and spring. Barley is not now allowed to be milled by itself but must be used with wheat to make flour. The bread we now get is decidedly dark but not at all bad, considering how we are fixed. There are a few grumblers but they are few and far between, and receive no sympathy from the general public.

1917 May 7 Monday Yesterday the French made a great attack on the Germans on their front on the heights of the Aisne and won a great success , capturing the village of Cloume and taking up to tonight 8,100 prisoners. Thus the Allies keep hammering the Huns, but our losses are terrible - nearly 5,000 names killed and wounded in to day's list.

Bombs were dropped by an aeroplane this morning on NE London. One man was killed and several wounded.

Tuesday May 8 Great quantities of Hay are being sent away from this district to the Army. It is being baled up by men of the Army Service Corps, who use a steam press, and is being put on rail at Oundle station. We had a very big hay crop last year, but there is very little left of it now. The price paid by the Government is from £5 10s to £6 per ton and they find all labour.

May 9 Wednesday A general statement by the Food Controller was made yesterday. He hopes with great care and economy we may scrape through until harvest but meantime is getting machinery in order for food tickets should they have to be issued. At present no instructions have been received by Local Authorities as to this.

DAY BY DAY THROUGH THE GREAT WAR

There was desperate fighting on our line round Fresnoy village yesterday. After holding it for several days (it is a most important place) the Germans regained it but tonight's news says it is again in our possession.

May 10 Thursday The Gas and Flame warfare has been very much in evidence the last few days and nights. The men in many instances throwing away their weapons and endeavouring to tear off each others masks. This of course means death to one who loses their helmet and mask as these gases are most deadly.

May 11 Friday Much uneasiness has been caused the last few days by the way in which events in Russia are moving. The country is in such a state of chaos that it seems impossible to expect much help from them this year and some of the extreme sections are said to be willing to conclude a separate peace with Germany, but advices yesterday and to-day are more reassuring and it is possible that the danger has been overcome, but as I said it does not [seem] probable they will do much until their internal affairs are more in order.

A secret session of the House was held last night. Men for the Army and the submarine menace were the chief topics. As usual Lloyd George was optimistic and declared that next year we should be able to produce all the food we required. This is sheer nonsense. Besides what about the next 4 months of this present year?

May 12 Saturday This morning voluntary enlistment of men up to 50 is announced. This I think is only a preliminary to compulsion of this class of men. America is moving but moving very slowly and it must be months before she can do anything effectual in the way of man power.

May 13 Sunday The King's Proclamation as to economy in the use of cereals is being read again to-day in all Churches and Chapels. Horses are being put upon rations and no horse is to receive more than 10lb of oats or the equivalent in other corn per day. No corn at all is to be fed to pleasure horses. This morning's news says that Sir D. Haig again attacked heavily yesterday.

May 14 Monday A Zeppelin was brought down and destroyed in the North Sea this morning by one of our war ships. These Zeppelins seem almost to have dropped out of the war. One scarcely hears them mentioned now, and no serious raid has been attempted by the Germans since last October. All precautions both as to lighting and other things are still carried out and the special constables still go on duty each night.

1917 Tuesday May 15 There are serious labour troubles going on amongst some of the munition workers in this country. Some thousands of them are out on strike, and this must entail serious consequences on the army in the field. The reasons for this striking business are too long and complicated to explain here, but the chief one I think is the admission of unskilled men and women into the engineering shops. It has been found that much of the work which was said to require skilled labour can easily be done by these women and unskilled men, after they have had a few weeks training.

Wednesday May 16 Very little news to-day. America is getting ready but the preparations will take months and I do not expect to see any effective fighting force this side of the Atlantic for another 12 months.

Thursday May 17 We are told this morning that an American Flotilla has arrived in British waters and is now co-operating with our own navy. They are said to be very smart and their ships well found in every respect. This is an historic event and I believe is the first occasion upon which England and America has fought side by side.

Friday May 18 General Haig reports to-day that he has captured the whole of the village of Ballecourt, around which awful fighting has raged for the last three weeks. It is said to be a most important point in the German lines and they have struggled to keep it, hurling thousands upon thousands of men into the attack, but they were beaten and decisively beaten. What does the Kaiser think of our Contemptible little Army now? Vide Aug 1914

Much unrest exists in the labour world to-day. Tonight the Government have arrested seven men charged with delaying war work. A dangerous policy this, trying to drive discontent underground. Say what you like, there is much distrust amongst labour of the present Government, controlled as it is by Lords Milner and Curzon. The former nothing more than a Prussian bred and born, and entirely eaten up with Prussian ideals. He has never been able to divest himself of these ideas, and his whole tone and policy is absolutely at variance with democracy.

May 19 Saturday This week's returns show a decided drop in the number of ships sunk by submarines – 26 only are posted as missing. One swallow does not make summer, but we are hopeful that the means taken by the Admiralty are proving successful. It is said they are using some new devices but this may only be rumour.

May 20 Sunday A beautiful growing May day. On Thursday the drought which had lasted for nearly a month broke and we had heavy rain for 6 hours. And Friday and Saturday we have also had showers. The change is marvellous. The earth heated by the great heat we have had has responded and all vegetation is bounding forward. It is a late season. At present there is no 'May' on the hedges, Gooseberries are just forming, Strawberries are coming into flower, and the Apples, Plums and Pears are a picture. All old vegetables are very very scarce. The boys of the School here were yesterday buying potatoes (old) to send away to their friends. There is only a limited quantity here but in most towns they are not to be had at any price.

May 21 Monday Good news from Russia is arriving here. After passing through some very stormy times she seems to have evolved one or two really strong and determined men. Germany during the past ten days has had great hopes of detaching her from the Allies and concluding a separate peace, but these men have fully realized the danger of this course, and it seems to have been prevented. They also have recognised the danger of allowing the Army to get the upper hand, and in a manifesto the report of which has reached us to-day, say that iron discipline must take the place of anarchy in the Army. Things are distinctly more hopeful there and we may perhaps see some decisive measures adopted instead of the vacillation which has prevailed during the last few months.

America has decided to send an Army Corps of 20,000 men at once, (that is as soon as they can get shipping) and hopes to have half a million men ready in September.

The fighting on our front is very desperate and is of a hand to hand description. I saw a letter to-day which has escaped the censor. The writer, an Oundle boy, describes how they fought with rifles, grenades, the butts of their rifles, bayonets and even with their fists. He says that out of a thousand of them who were ordered to attack only 80 were uninjured.

From returns published to-day it is computed that 7,000,000 men have already been killed in this awful business and that the total killed, wounded etc amounts to 47 millions and yet it is going on with increasing fury. The Labour Member of the War Cabinet (Arthur Henderson) speaking yesterday aid that in spite of three years of unparalleled exertion he could hold out no hope of an early termination of fighting. What a prospect.

1917 Tuesday May 22 The Italians yesterday and Sunday launched their spring campaign and dealt a heavy blow at the Austrians. To-nights news says that they have taken 3,000 prisoners including nearly 200 officers. They were much helped by British Guns and gunners who had gone to help them.

Wednesday May 23 The labour troubles have eased somewhat and most of the men have now returned to work. There are considerable faults on both sides and the Government are not at all free from blame. They are trying too much of the Prussian method of driving discontent under the surface and the result is we are having these constantly recurring labour troubles.

May 24 Thursday After nearly 7 months of quiet we had a Zeppelin raid last night. I was wakened at 20 minutes to one this morning and told to get my sections of constables on duty at once as the second warning had been received at 12.30. (The first came at 12.20 . Which meant the enemy were over the coast). I at once did so. It was raining in torrents and so dark that I had to feel my way to some of the houses. After being on duty for about 2 hours the message came 'All Clear' and we were allowed to return home. We did not hear or see anything of them. This afternoon I learn that the nearest point they came to us was Thetford but very little damage was done and only one person killed.

DAY BY DAY THROUGH THE GREAT WAR

Friday May 25 The submarine situation is distinctly more hopeful. Returns published to-day show that only 26 vessels were sunk this week, and various hints and suggestions, made by men in a position to know, disclosed that effective means had been found to combat this danger. To-day these are confirmed by the Premier in the House. He said he hoped that we had passed the critical point and that we had the business now well in hand. I hope we have, as it is a very serious one as regards our food.

A terrible raid took place this evening in broad daylight (between 5 and 6 o'clock) by 16 enemy aeroplanes over the south eastern counties. One town suffered terribly. We shall hear more in the morning but one can only wonder how this big fleet was allowed to come over like this.

A meeting was held here last night to form a detachment of the Volunteer Training Corps. About 25 joined at the end and it is hoped more will do so later on.

May 26 Seventy-six persons including 15 women and 29 children were killed in the raid last evening. There will be a great outcry about this. Evidently there must be serious blame resting on some person or persons.

There is great news from the Italian front this morning. They have quite broken through part of the Austrian defences near the sea. Have taken 7,000 prisoners and are making a great bid for Trieste. British warships gave them much help by shelling the enemy from the sea.

I attended a prolonged Tribunal meeting last evening lasting from 7.15 to 10.30. Very few really fit men are now left in civil life.

Two Oundle men have been reported killed this week.

1917 May 27 Sunday Whit Sunday. No holiday and very very quiet. Yesterday the Government announced that very shortly they intend to fix the price of Bread. They may do what they like but it is quite certain that if the consumer does not pay the whole cost of a loaf when he buys it he will have to pay for it in another way, that is by taxation. We may be able to fix wheat prices here, but obviously it is quite impossible to fix them in the world markets, and if we want grain we shall have to pay the price for it.

There is quite a lull on our own front this week in France. Various American Ambulance Units are arriving in this country and are going into training. Russian news is a little more hopeful this week, but things seem much out of gear there. Discipline is very lax, both in their Army and Navy.

Monday May 28 Whit Monday A hot sunny day. Scarcely any news to-day except details of the raid on Friday.

Tuesday May 29 Italy is doing great things. She is fighting splendidly helped by ten batteries of heavy British guns and is now only 10 miles from Trieste. Much credit is due to us for this. It is pretty well known that the Germans had intended to smash them up this year but the French and ourselves have mauled them so badly in the West that they have been obliged to send their reserves against us instead of against Italy.

Wednesday May 30 Russia is a source of much anxiety to us. Evidently she is causing much uneasiness to the Allies. Henderson a member of the war Cabinet here has gone on a mission to Russia to try and pull things together.

May 31 Thursday Not much news from our front this last few days except the usual Artillery hammering.

Men are now being called up very rapidly to the army, and almost every man who has two legs to stand on is being passed for general service.

To-day has been Red Cross day here. A sale by auction of Farm Stock, old implements and general produce, all of which has been given, was held on the Cattle market in the morning and a Jumble Sale &c in the Victoria Hall this afternoon. The amount realized is £1300, not bad this for an agricultural district, but there is no question about farmers making money. They are simply coining it with the present price of all produce.

Friday June 1 Twelve months to-day since Jutland Battle The Germans received a lesson that day. Never since then have they ventured on a fair and open sea fight. All this bloody submarine business .. which is after all a most cowardly method of war. Sinking hospital ships, killing women and children, destroying food, but one has given up even trying to understand German mentality. It is quite incomprehensible to any ordinary civilised person.

Saturday June 2 The first Food Controller (Lord Devonport) has resigned. This is not to be wondered at. Of all the difficult tasks in the war, I think his is the most difficult. The Labour Party are shrieking for one of their own party to be appointed to office. I hope not. They are too much obsessed with their own view of things, and do not seem capable of taking a wide survey. I do not think they have a man capable of filling this position.

Sunday June 3 A list published this week shows that since the war commenced about 38 or 39 Oundle men have been killed or died of wounds or are missing. How many have been wounded I cannot say. This is a heavy toll for a small place like this. Multiply it by all the towns and villages in the Kingdom and you will then see how dreadfully this war is draining the very life blood of England. And yet we can see no end .. Do we intend to see it through. I think if a poll of the country could be taken to-day the answer would be decisively Yes.

June 4 Monday America this morning promises to send 50,000 men very shortly and to increase the number to 250,000 early in September. I think it is becoming evident that unless the unexpected happens we shall have this war another winter.

The Russian news is no better – all seems chaos and confusion with very little hope of any real help from that quarter. There is also much real unrest in this country, perhaps more apparent than real. We have many difficulties. Many of these arise I think from the fact that the present Parliament is stale and worn out, but a general Election at the present is impossible.

1917 June 5 Tuesday The Germans came over again to-night about 5.30 with a squadron of air machines. They were over Essex and the Medway. Some damage was done but only 2 men killed, 27 wounded.

Early this morning our airmen raided Ostend and Zeebrugge and drove out the German destroyer flotilla which lies there. Our warships were lying outside watching for them. They sunk one and badly crippled some of the others. No captures are made now. They are all sent to the bottom.

Wednesday June 6 News was received here to-day that amongst the killed in the Medway raid last evening was a young man named Smith. He lived close to me and had joined a labour battalion of the Army about three months since.

Thursday June 7 To-day all eyes are again directed to Ypres a name that has been very familiar to us all since war began, for round it have been fought some of the bloodiest and most desperate battles of the war. A telegram published this morning from General Haig announces that at three o'clock this morning a tremendous attack was launched on the German position on what is known as the Ridge of Messines. One has been expecting something of the kind would occur there for the Germans spoke of terrific gunfire there. This ridge has defied all our efforts for nearly two years but to-night's telegrams say that the battle is entirely in our favour and that we hold complete possession of it and now look down upon the plains of Flanders. The battle was fought upon a front of 9 miles and commenced with what is probably the greatest explosion the world has ever known. . For over 12 months our men had mined the position and at 3.10 am this morning 600 tons of explosives were fired. The report was clearly heard in the south east of England. .The result of it was awful. Thousands of Germans were literally blown to atoms and our men had comparatively little fighting to do early in the day, but this afternoon and evening hard fighting has been going on.

The air raiders returning from the Medway on Tuesday were caught by aeroplanes from the North Sea Fleet and received a very smart lesson. Ten were destroyed and two others were brought down.

DAY BY DAY THROUGH THE GREAT WAR

Aeroplanes are becoming a very familiar sight to us now, and we see a good many go over us. They make a very droning humming sound. This is very faint when they are flying at great heights.

Tuesday June 8 We captured 6,500 prisoners yesterday 130 officers and 20 guns. The Kaiser said last week that our offensive was at an end. This is the answer to that boast.

To-day General Pershing the U.S.A. Commander in chief arrived at Liverpool with his staff. He said troops were following him quickly.

Saturday June 9 To-day F. Smith who was killed in Medway raid was buried here.

Sunday June 10 The delightful office of Food Controller is vacant. Lord Davenport resigned early in the week and Lloyd George seems to find much difficulty in getting anyone to take it on. This can scarcely be wondered at. It is a thankless task. The noisy [?] set of men amongst Co-operatives, Labour men and Socialists seem to expect that we can have war like this upon our hands and that things should be quite normal. I fancy they have some hard lessons to learn yet. They are now clamouring for one of their own party to be appointed to this office. A most fatal thing if it is allowed. For the present we seem to have overcome the food difficulty. By concentrating all their efforts upon cereals the shipping people seem to have accumulated sufficient reserves in this county to carry well over harvest. The submarines have been scotched and it appears to be hopeless for Germany to try to starve us out. Germany is also well in sight of their harvest although from trustworthy reports it does not seem that it will be a very heavy one. This chiefly owing to lack of fertilizers and labour. I think the same thing will apply to us here. The arable land is getting very foul, and it does not appear we can expect a heavy yield of corn.

One does not know what is in store for us but according to my own judgement it seems that this war will last well into next year.

The talk about rationing with Bread, Sugar and other tickets has been dropped for the present. The coolest heads amongst us can see that it would make worse of things instead of better.

1917 Monday June 11 The Battle of the Messines Ridge has made a great impression on the world. The whole affair was so well planned and carried out with the utmost precision. The Germans of course try to belittle it, but with very little success. The value of the German Mark declined sharply on neutral exchanges on Friday and Saturday. This shows what effect it has had.

June 12 Tuesday News reached London this afternoon that the King of Greece had at last been compelled by the Allies to abdicate. They ought to have done this 12 months since. He is a most treacherous rascal. He is succeeded by one of his sons. Possibly now we may see some move at Salonica.

June 13 A terrible air raid on London this morning by about 15 Aeroplanes. It occurred about 11.45. Bombs fell principally on the East end. One or two on Liverpool Street station. 104 people (a good part women and children) were killed and 243 wounded. It is reported from there that it was most difficult to see these aeroplanes. They were at a very great height and painted. One report says they did not appear to be larger than butterflies. Aeroplanes are becoming very common in this country, even in country places they do not now cause much comment. We have had 5 or 6 over here this week.

Thursday June 14 The German official telegrams of this morning claim that yesterday they bombed the "fort" of London. This is to hide their callousness. Of course they know that London is not fortified. A strong demand for retaliatory measures against German towns is gaining ground in the country and I think the Government will be obliged to comply. We cannot wage war in kid gloves with an enemy like Germany. One cannot understand their mentality at all, and Englishmen have long ceased to try to do so, and most of us now look upon them as real savages, but unfortunately they have been able to bring science to aid their savage and bloody ways.

Friday June 15 The first case in this district in which the War Food Committee has compelled to a man to leave his holding on account of bad cultivation has taken place to-day at Glapthorne. The holding is on the road from Glapthorne to Benefield, is 97 acres mostly arable and has been badly neglected for the last two years. The landlord acting under pressure from the Government has resumed possession of it without any compensation and will now cultivate it.

THE DIARY OF JOHN COLEMAN BINDER

Saturday June 16 A new Food Controller is announced this morning, Lord Rhondda, a Welsh Colliery owner. A man of much business capacity but little acquainted I imagine with food conditions. The food situation is a little easier but meat is as dear as ever and other essentials continue to rise in price.

The Northamptonshire regiment was engaged at Messines and has suffered heavy casualties. I am not sure which battalions have been engaged but think it must be the 1st or second. The Germans have fallen back the last few days all along that front and since the battle we look down upon them instead of they upon us. The mining which destroyed the ridge of Messines was a really splendid piece of work by English and Australian miners and took 12 months to prepare.

Zeppelins were over to-night. Specials out 11 to 3 [?]

1917 Sunday June 17 We have had a very very hot week and rain is much needed. The wheat crop has much improved, and looks well. Barley Oats Potatoes etc require rain. I think we shall have a fairly early harvest. Hay cutting has begun in many places.

I heard yesterday that German aeroplanes made another attempt on London on Friday but were foiled by our men.

At last the Irish business seems likely to be settled. A convention is to meet within the next week or two in Dublin to come to some agreement on the question. It has been set up by the Government and is quite representative of all parties in Ireland and is quite non-political although political parties will be included. On Friday all prisoners who took part in the late rebellion were released. A really wise act. If we can only get peace and contentment in Ireland it will add much to our resources and fighting power.

The detachment of Volunteers formed here a month ago now numbers 65 or 70. They drill 2 hours in the evening three times a week and 2 hours on Sunday afternoon.

A telegram this morning says that one of the zeppelins was brought down in flames in Kent at 3.30 this morning. It was first winged by guns and then finished off by airmen. As engines of war these Zeppelins are a complete failure. They are only useful as scouts to the navy. The Aeroplane is a much more dangerous affair, and I think will play a much larger part in future wars.

Thursday June 21 There has been scarcely any news this week. I hear from Margate that aeroplanes have been over most days this week, but have been kept in check by our aviators. America last week allocated £120,000,000 for their air service, so they intend to send huge quantities over to the Western front.

News is a little more hopeful from Russia the last few days.

Friday June 22 Great fighting on the French front yesterday and to-day about Laon but little change in positions.

We have had a series of terrific storms during last Sunday and Monday. I do not remember seeing a more violent one than that which broke over us about 7 pm last Sunday. A good deal of damage was done to the crops.

After much agitation and continual fighting our precious War Office has been beaten on the question of taking labour from the Land and in future no man is to be taken without the consent of the County Agricultural Committee. If a man receives his papers calling upon him to join up he is at once to report the fact to this Committee and they will decide if he can be spared.

One of the most painful and shameful debates that I ever remember took place on Thursday in the House on the question of calling up for re-examination men who had been rejected as unfit. Many of these men - notoriously unfit- have been passed by Medical Boards as fit for General Service. The whole affair had become a crying public scandal. After much twisting turning evasion and shuffling the leader of the House, clearly seeing that the Government were likely to be defeated, promised a Committee to enquire into the charges. I simply do not believe a word of what they say. The War Office is the ruling power in this country to-day and unless the Democracy take measures to counteract this our position will be as bad as the Russian one. Militarism is becoming rampant and is sitting on the safety valve. There is much discontent and distrust amongst all classes, and the situation is a dangerous one.

DAY BY DAY THROUGH THE GREAT WAR

Monday June 25 Minor actions only are now taking place in France. An advance is being made towards Lens. It is computed the Army has lost 300,000 men since April. The Russian business has upset all our calculations. I quite think that if they could have carried through a vigorous offensive we might have seen an end of the war this year, but at present they seem quite powerless.

1917 Wednesday June 27 Big gun fire was distinctly audible here to-day. I heard it from about 11 am to 2 pm. I cannot say what it was, whether practice on the east coast or an air raid or possibly guns at Zeebrugge, but it was quite distinct.

Later The sound of the guns came from where gun practice as going on.

Thursday To-day a huge flotilla of American vessels convoyed by their war ships arrived off the French coast and at once proceeded to disembark the vanguard of the American Army. What their numbers were or where they landed we are not told but they are only a forerunner of what is to follow. We are under no illusions here as to America or American help. It is quite certain she has made up her mind to put all her strength into this business, but [it] is equally certain that even the beginning of her help cannot be felt before 1918, but at the same time it is a most historic event. For the first time America is sending troops to Europe and thus recognises that she feels herself unable any longer to keep out of world politics. Plenty of European troops have gone to America, but now the situation is reversed.

Friday June 29 General Haig's news to-day is that he is slowly encircling Lens and the Germans are falling back.. There is stiff fighting going on (as there always is). The French are being heavily attacked by the enemy and are only holding their own. It is quite evident the French are awaiting the American Forces, and as I said yesterday these will not be available in great numbers this year.

Saturday June 30 The situation in Greece has changed with marvellous rapidity since the King was toppled off his throne and the new man put on. M. Venzelos, the great Greek statesman is again Prime Minister and to-day Greece is at war with Germany or will be so within the next 24 hours. This will relieve the Salonika Army of a great nightmare as they were always afraid of being attacked in the rear by that most treacherous rascal the last King.

Sunday July1 Lloyd George made an important speech at Glasgow on Friday as to our war aims. He emphasized what has been obvious to us all for some time, viz that peace i.e. a stable and lasting peace can only come with a democratic and released Germany, and that there can be no real peace so long as the Hohenzollerns are paramount there. Of course he did not name them, but everybody knows what he means. I am afraid this is 'crying for the moon' at present, although from what can be gathered, the Germans themselves are dimly beginning to see this.

The Food Controller has begun to issue various Orders. A great many of these Orders are evaded, and it would pass the wit of any man to remember half of them. Food is not at all scarce in spite of the enemy's submarines and has not increased much in price the last 6 or eight weeks. There are many complaints about the bread. It varies very much with flour which one gets from different mills, but where the extreme dilutions and extractions are carried out the result is that the bread is <u>bad</u>. There is no question as to this, and the public is beginning to complain. I think that some relaxation of the Orders will have to be allowed.

July 2 The Russians have at last made a move and in Galicia have attacked the enemy in force. Fighting commenced yesterday morning and to-night's telegrams say that it was severe. At least that is what Germany says, the Russian report is not to hand at present.

July 4 Wednesday Russia's report of the great battles of Sunday and Monday is now to hand. She has captured 18,000 prisoners and 60 guns. These tidings have given immense satisfaction here as they indicate that Russia has in some little degree recovered herself and that the attempts of Germany to conclude a separate peace with her have failed.

July5 Thursday Some of the bloodiest fighting in the whole war has been taking place in France the last two days. The Germans have made desperate attempts to re-capture the ground which the French won from them earlier in the year but without success. Their attempts which cost them thousands of men have failed, but the French have also lost heavily.

THE DIARY OF JOHN COLEMAN BINDER

Friday July 6 Very little news from our own armies the last few days. Men on leave say that another great offensive is preparing and will [be] launched during this month. This may be only surmise. Meantime things continue to grow steadily worse in this country. Many articles which we are accustomed to get are unprocurable or if you do get them you have to wait months for them. Men are steadily being called up for service and the standard in the various classes is I am convinced much lower. That is a man who as formerly passed for duty at home in class B2 is now passed as an A1 man that is fit for general service. There is also a strong undercurrent about peace, but this is ruthlessly suppressed by the Government. Personally I can see nothing at present to justify a real permanent peace. I cannot see that Germany is really beaten, and until this is so I imagine the war will continue. It is a bad time for us here. We are being ruled by 3 or 4 men who issue the edicts (many of them simply unreasonable) as they were issued in Russia and we have no redress. The present House of Commons has lost all its authority and has simply become a tool of these men. This week they do appear to have made an attempt to reassert it in some degree by using that old weapon of theirs – control of the purse and have demanded that they shall be more fully consulted before these huge sums are spent. But what is to be expected when we have men like Lords Milner and Curzon at the helm. The former man, a German bred and born and imbued with the traditions and ideas of the Prussian Junker.

Saturday July 7 Rumours reached us to-day about 12 of a terrible aeroplane raid which had taken place in London between 9 and 10 this morning. Scarcely any authentic news has come through all day and consequently the rumours are flying about in all directions. I think there is more excitement and uneasiness in the place than I have seen since war was declared. Tonight's telegrams are very vague.

Sunday July 8 The news in this mornings papers is not at all full. The Government say that only 30 people were killed but we are getting to doubt these tales told by the authorities and which they try to palm off upon us as true. No mention is made of what damage was done. Perhaps there may be more details in tomorrow's papers.

Monday July 9 A few more details this morning. The death roll is 54. This is 54 too many. A wave of intense anger has swept over the country during the last 48 hours at the way in which the enemy were allowed to leisurely come and bombard London. I think it will scarcely be credited by the next generation that although nearly two hours warning of the raid was given none of our machines was up in the air to meet them. There will certainly be a row in the House to-night about it.

Tuesday July 10 The Government adopted a very lame course last night. To avoid meeting the nation in the open they held a secret session of the House and thus tried to smooth matters over. According to official reports they said the Army must stand fast etc.etc. This thing we have heard hundreds of times. Probably they must but it is the clear duty of those responsible to see that the nation is also equally protected. Strict enough measures are not taken with those who are responsible. If they are not competent they ought to be cashiered.

Russia is doing remarkably well. {Some} of her armies are making swift progress and Germany it is clear is becoming alarmed. They quite thought she was paralysed for the year. Austria is making frantic efforts to induce Germany to come to peace as she can well see that unless this is done it is quite possible that her ramshackle empire may collapse. Great fighting is going on in Galicia.

Wednesday July 11 General Haig reports intense artillery work on the Belgian lines close to Ostend. He does not say any more this morning but the firing must have been very heavy as it was clearly heard in London.

The Russian news is good again this morning. The Austrian army is being driven in quickly and cavalry are in pursuit. A wedge has been driven in between the German and Austrian armies. The prisoners captured on Monday and Tuesday are 10,000 and 30 guns. Germany is very much upset by this Russian offensive.

Thursday Late last night reports of the Belgian Coast fighting came to hand. After intense artillery fire the enemy rushed the trenches and drove our men in. Haig acknowledges this but does not confirm or deny the claim of the enemy that they took 1200 of our men prisoners.

1917 Friday July 13 Fierce debates yesterday and to-day in the House over the Mesopotamia business.

DAY BY DAY THROUGH THE GREAT WAR

The Government have muddled the whole affair and have come out of it with much lowered prestige.

Russia is still moving on and is now threatening Lemburg the city about which we heard so much 2 years ago. Austria appears to be unable to stem the advance and is calling loudly for re-enforcements.

Saturday July 14 All Northamptonshire to-day is glorying in the splendid behaviour of the Northants regiment at the affair on the Belgian coast on Tuesday. They one and all fought like heroes and deeds of some of them read like romances. A considerable number of them were cut off by the breaking of bridges across the Yser and I am afraid have fallen into the enemies' hands. When last seen the officers were standing back to back calmly using their revolvers. The whole country is intensely proud of them. With them were the King's Royal Rifles.

To-night the Food Controller issued a ukase forbidding any person to buy or sell any corn of the 1917 crop without a permit. This means that I shall have to apply as I and my people before me have been corndealers for nearly 80 years.

July 15 Sunday There have been momentous events taking place in Germany during this week. At last the Germans seem to be seeing a little light and stirred up by the Russian revolution have begun to demand a clear and definite share in the Government of the country, not a sham one like they now have. Evidently this has alarmed the Kaiser, and he has been tearing about here, there and everywhere. Austria also has been urging peace. Both Austria and Germany are clearly alarmed at the revival of Russian fighting power. They did not expect it and this coupled with the virtual failure of the submarines against us has caused much heart burning in Germany The people there have been told the submarines would bring us to our knees in 8 months' but now they see this is hopeless. American intervention has also added to this feeling. Probably the offensive last Monday was due more to political than military reasons. It was felt in Germany that they must have a '<u>victory</u>' to reassure the people.

July 16 Monday The German Chancellor, Bethman Hollweg has been compelled to resign. The forces against him were too strong. The reactionaries led by that wicked Crown Prince and old Hindenberg overthrew him. However this is a matter for Germany to settle. No one here is very sorry. This is the man who taunted us three years ago for fighting for 'A scrap of paper' and said the Germans would 'hack their way through'. He is to-day a sadder and a wiser man (as most of us are). His successor is a mere Prussian bureaucrat of the reactionary type. How long will he stand.

The King has been in France for a fortnight and has been inspecting the various battlefields. One of the biggest air battles took place yesterday over our lines. We lost 9 machines – the Germans 30.

A Committee of parents and old boys of the School (here) has been formed and will meet in the Grocers Hall, London on Friday to decide what steps shall be taken to erect a memorial to the old boys who have fallen in the War. At present these number 95.

Tuesday July 17 There have been some dreadful fighting in Champagne on the French lines yesterday and to-day. The enemy seems determined to make an impression here, but even Berlin admits they have not succeeded. The carnage has been dreadful.

Wednesday July 18 Events on our own lines continue very quiet beyond the ordinary fighting which of course continues day and night without ceasing. Men home from the front say that there is very much being done in anticipation of another move. When and in what direction they do not know but from what one can judge it looks as if the move would be towards Belgium.

1917 Thursday July 19 The Russian news is again bad. The country seems torn by factions and no one party seems able to take supreme command. The fighting on their fronts is very variable. In some places the armies fight like heroes, in others they retire without fighting. This complicates matters very much and causes much dismay in this country.

There has been a reshuffling of the Government here, and the War Cabinet has grown to seven members. How bitterly Asquith was attacked when he had 5. We see many strange things now-a-days but nothing stranger or more sinister than the attempt of the reactionaries led by Lloyd George to rule this country without

THE DIARY OF JOHN COLEMAN BINDER

Parliament. I write emphatically that it is a most disastrous thing, this attempt to rule by bureaucrats and has signally failed. I am confident that if we could have a General Election the whole thing would go down like a house of cards. Give us a party system of Government - it is much better than this sort of thing.

Friday July 20 The new German Chancellor spoke for the first time yesterday but in quite the approved style of his predecessor. They were winning etc .etc. and if they only continued the submarine war we should be brought to our knees. We were being starved - but of this I can see no evidence. There is not much indication of any desire for peace in his speech.

There has been much grumbling about the war bread in this country and certainly in many places it has been abominable. Pressure has been brought upon the Government to relax the restrictions and to return to a larger percentage of wheat, but they absolutely refuse to do this. Amongst millers and bakers it is well known that there has now been accumulated a good wheat reserve here, but I am afraid from what I hear it is not all of good keeping quality. Our own harvest will not be a really good one. I think potatoes will be the crop of the year. I never saw them look better.

July 21 Saturday To-day we have the casualty list of the Officers who fell at that terrible 'Battle of the Dunes' on the Belgian coast on July 10. Twenty two are dead (or missing) These all belonged to the 1st battalion of the Northants the old 48th regiment. Of the number of men who have gone under at present we have no information but it must be terribly heavy. It was a most scandalous affair. These brave men were left on a sandy dune unable to dig themselves in and exposed to all the concentrated devilries of modern war – gas bombs   flame sprayers from six in the morning until the evening. They could not retreat as the Yser was behind them, and two small bridges over it were destroyed early in the day. Finally the Germans rushed them with three successive waves of picked troops and it is supposed they perished almost to a man. The whole affair has caused much indignation in Northamptonshire. The men fought like heroes which they were and this episode must rank as one of the bloodiest in this awful and bloody war. The authorities seem determined to hush it up and conceal it as much as they can, and one has to receive even what they do let us know with much suspicion.

July 22 Sunday The Food Controller announced last night that Bread would be reduced to 9d the 4lb loaf in Sept. In London it is 1/- to 1/1. The general price is 11d to 11½d. Here it is 10d. He also said that he proposed to sell sugar through the Town Councils and other Local Councils. We await the proposals with much curiosity.

An air raid took place over Harwich and Felixstowe early this morning. Evidently the enemy intended to again raid London but were met and fought over Essex. Eleven people were killed.

It was decided on Friday to erect a Chapel here as a memorial to the old Oundle School boys who have fallen in the war. It will not be undertaken until the war is over. The Grocers' Company will [bear] the cost of the main building and the parents and old boys the cost of the Choir and Sanctuary. It is estimated it will cost altogether £20,000.

1917 Monday July 23 Ominous rumours come from Russia to-night. It is said there is mutiny amongst the troops at the front.

Tuesday July 24 There has been some terrible fighting on the French front the last two days. It commenced on Sunday morning and lasted without ceasing for 36 hours. It is a second Verdun. The Germans were attacking but have not gained anything. Both sides have suffered horribly. It is estimated the Germans have had 120,000 casualties.

Wednesday July 25   The Russian news is very grave this morning. They are in retreat in the centre of their line in Galicia and the Germans claim they are following hard after. They are doing better on the extreme north and south, and have made some progress. There is almost anarchy in Petrograd.

The Army Medical Service for examining men for the Army has at last received its death blow. Their system and methods had become such a glaring scandal that the Government were compelled by public opinion to appoint a Committee to enquire into their doings. Thousands of men absolutely unfit were passed into the Army as fit for active service. Scores of these men have died within a few weeks and it was stated that at least a hundred thousand were discharged after having cost £100 or £150 to train. The whole business of recruiting together with the medical examination is to be turned over to civilians with I hope better methods and results.

July 26 Thursday The Russian retreat in the centre continues and it is difficult to stop the dry rot which has set in amongst some of their troops. This Russian debacle has entirely upset the whole campaign of this year. If they had been able to carry out their part of the programme I quite think the end would now have been in sight, but this is hopeless now. Another dreary winter's war is before us, I believe, with all its horrors and savagery.

Terrible artillery battles are reported by our own people to-day. Another attack is being prepared.

The weekly return of ships sunk to-day shows that 15 have gone down. From this it is quite clear that the submarine is still active, and although it has been scotched we cannot afford to disregard it. The Prime Minister said the other day that our food supply for the winter was safe. I sincerely hope it is but we shall have to be very very careful. I can already see a tendency to waste or misuse the potato crop of this year. At the present moment there is a glut of them and prices have fallen to about 90/- to 100/- per ton wholesale. Great quantities are being used in the place of bread. The quality of this article at the present moment leaves much to be desired. The corn (wheat, barley, beans oats maize) from which the flour is made is old and stale. In consequence of this the bread quickly develops a musty taste. I think this will be remedied after harvest. Harvest is now commencing in the South of England.

Friday July 27 To-day Lord Rhondda the new food man explained his proposals in the House of Lords. His chief aim will be to cheapen bread and meat and a more equitable distribution of sugar. He proposes to do this through Local Committees (to be formed by all Local Authorities). All I can say is this. These local Committees will have a most invidious task. I am thinking it will [be] rather worse than the work of the Tribunals. The Local Committees will have to see that all Orders issued by the Food Controller are carried out (what an army of officials this will require) and also many other duties. They will issue tickets for every household the head of which applies for them. These tickets are to [be] taken to any grocer which the householder may select and he will have to keep a register of all applications and in his turn apply to the Wholesale houses for supplies – but how are these people to send them if they are not there as Lord Rhondda somewhat naively suggests they may not always be. Another point he quietly ignored when announcing the high cost of living, and that is the inflation of the currency of this country. As regards this we in this country are living in a fools paradise, and 90 per cent of the people cannot see we are burning the candle at both ends and in the middle also. The amount of money (paper) is enormous, and people imagine that it is real and tangible. What fools and idiots. They will have a rude awakening some day, either before the war ends or when it is over.

July 28 Saturday The Russians are still retreating but the news to-day is a little more hopeful. They appear to be stiffening a little. The German Emperor is said to be in Galicia watching this show. I notice that he is sure to be anywhere when things are going well with his army, but when events are against them he is not at all in evidence.

Prisoners continue to escape from the camps. Two Germans got away from Corby last Saturday but were recaptured at London yesterday. Very rarely do they get away altogether.

Sunday July 29 The School Boys here are going down to-morrow but some are remaining to continue munition work which is still carried on in the workshops. Many of the older ones who are 18 are going straight into the Army or Navy.

July 30 Monday The tremendous artillery conflict around Nieuport Ypres &c in Belgium still continues. It is acknowledged both in German dispatches and our own to be the greatest artillery battle in this great war. All along the Kentish coast and also in Holland the roar of the guns is practically continuous. The air fighting is also being waged with great vigour, 61 German machines were destroyed yesterday and Saturday. We lost 16. Amongst the missing pilots is a young fellow named Curtis whose father is a seed merchant here. Possibly he may be a prisoner.

THE DIARY OF JOHN COLEMAN BINDER

Tuesday July 31 This morning at 3.50 a great attack on the German front at Ypres was launched by Sir D. Haig. It covered 12 miles in length and the French continued the battle to the North as far as the Coast. It appears to have been quite successful and the telegrams to-night say that all the objects have been attained. Query what are these objects ? It seems as if we get a tremendous battle about every two months and then we slide back again into the old monotonous trench war. 3,500 prisoners are reported up to to-night.

August 1 Wednesday Not many details of the battle at Ypres are to hand except that 47 bridges were thrown across the Yser, and that the Germans seem to have been quite outclassed. The Prussian Guard was there but could not stand against our men.

August 2 Thursday Wet weather has set in in Flanders and has much hindered the fighting.

August 12 Sunday. I have been away for 3 days for a holiday to Norwich so have been unable to write up this diary, not that there has really been much to chronicle as the wet has caused terrible mud at the front and until Friday very little took place but on that day a very hot skirmish took place near Ypres and it looks as if the battle would continue there as soon as fine weather comes.

We have had a fortnight of real bad weather, drenching showers and continual thunderstorms. I fear much damage has been done to the corn crops. In coming back from Norwich last Tuesday, I noticed the corn was much 'laid' in the fens especially between Ely and March. The floods also were out at the former city. The land is now very very wet and it will be a long harvest I am afraid.

Last Monday was Bank Holiday and was more of a holiday than we have had since war began. The strain has been so great that it had become a necessity to have a break. There were no public events but people went to the various holiday resorts in quite pre-war style. Many of them have been earning enormous wages and were glad to have an opportunity to spend the money.

We are to have sugar tickets and the carrying out of the scheme will be in hands of the local authorities. Steps are being taken to organize it but it will not come into operation until Dec 30. I think possibly it may result in a more equal distribution of sugar but I cannot see the supply will be better.

1917 August 13 There is much talk of Peace the last few days but at present I can see no hope of it. The Pope (prompted by Austria probably) has made certain proposals, but they do [not] seem acceptable to us.

Germany is just now striving to overrun the rest of Roumania and so capture what corn there is there. The Roumanians are fighting well but are slowly retiring.

August 15 Wednesday To-day about 4,000 Americans marched through London on their way to France. They had landed at Liverpool.

A great battle commenced at daybreak this morning near Lens and at mid-day General Haig reports that his men had carried the first line of trenches.

August 16 Thursday The Canadians were the chief troops in yesterday's battle. They captured the famous hill '70' which gave our men so much trouble at the battle of Loos.

To-day the Food Controller has fixed the price of cereals for the crop that is just being reaped. Wheat is 73/6 per 18st. Barley 63/9. Oats 44/- with a slight increase from Jan next. I hear to-day that the price of flour at the Mill door is likely to be 44/3 per 20 stones. This is a drop of about 17/- per sack from the price we now pay. Of course flour cannot be made [sentence unfinished]

August 17 Friday Fierce battles continue on our front. To-day at day break an attack was launched against Lens and news at midday said our men were on the outer suburbs. This Lens position is exceptionally strong as it is a mining centre and the slag and refuse heaps make it an ideal place to defend, but a good move forward was made and the village of Largemart was captured.

The Peace proposals issued by the Pope have fallen decidedly flat and seem already to have been forgotten. It is generally assumed they were prompted by Germany via Austria.

August 18 Saturday Events seem to be shaping a little better in Roumania. The Russo Roumanians are pulling themselves together and are offering a better resistance.

August 19 Sunday We in this district have had another very bad week for harvest. The climax was reached I think last Wednesday when we had a series of thunderstorms with drenching rain lasting all day. Thursday and Friday were a little better and some progress was made, but the ground is saturated and the self binders run with difficulty. I am sure a considerable quantity will have to be cut by hand.

The Local Authorities are now appointing their Food Control Committees. These will consist of 12 Members one member at least a labour man and also one woman. The immediate duties of these committees will be to make preparations to issue sugar cards. This scheme will take 4 months to get into working order, and is too complex to write down here. Other important duties concerning food will also be entrusted to these committees and I shall hope to give further details as these develop. Their duties certainly will be very varied and also very delicate, but in spite of this I think they may be helpful in the present position of affairs. That is if the Ministry of Food will listen to the opinion of men who have been concerned with the distribution of food for many years and so have the whole business at their finger ends. It is to be hoped that it will succeed better than the National Labour Service. This has been a complete fiasco and failure and one of the greatest mistakes in our war business. It is now practically dead, but efforts are being made to transfer its affairs to other departments. These departments offices etc etc continue to increase at an appalling rate, and their cost is enormous. As I have indicated before we are governed by a regular bureaucracy and an army of officials who issue their ukases (which have all the effect of laws) under the sanction of the Defence of the Realm Act. Probably the most iniquitous act and the one most subversive of personal liberty ever passed in the history of this country.

August 20 Monday Italy and France are both striking hard. The French at Verdun and the Italians towards Trieste. Hard fighting is also going on by us towards Lens and so the terrible war continues. Week in week out without cessation. One wonders how long this bloodshed and agony is to continue.

1917 August 21 Tuesday Early this morning one of the rare occurrences of the war took place. A real hand to hand fight in the open. The Canadians were advancing towards Lens and the Germans had planned a counter attack at the same moment. They met outside the trenches and a terrific combat ensued for about half an hour. Although the Germans were in close heavy formation and the Canadians only in skirmishing order they held them and forced them back into their trenches which they then captured.

August 22 Wednesday Our old friends the Zeppelins paid us a visit last night. They appeared off the mouth of Humber about 10.30 but were speedily driven off. About 8 o'clock this morning a squadron of enemy aircraft on their way to attack London were sighted off Margate and Dover. The Huns dropped their bombs killing 13 people in Dover and then an air battle ensued. Eight of them were destroyed and the rest got back to Zeebrugge.

The Italians have made a great show this week. They have captured 13,000 prisoners and 32 guns.

August 23 Thursday The weather has again broken and we have had some tremendous rain storms again to-day. The fierce battles continue on all fronts.

August 24 Friday Fierce fighting still continues all yesterday and to-day. The Germans admit that they have had to 'retire' –a very convenient way of admitting defeat.

August 25 Saturday Up to to-day the Italians have captured 21,000 prisoners and a large number of guns. The French also have forced back the enemy at Verdun to the position in which they were in May 1916. That wicked Crown Prince has received a good thrashing, unfortunately it is his soldiers who pay the price, not himself. One wishes that he could be wiped out.

August 26 Sunday This week has I think seen as much and indeed probably more fighting than any week during the war. France, Italy and ourselves have all been dealing heavy blows. Our only regret is that Russia although holding the enemy up has not been able to assume the offensive. I think that could she have done so we might now be hoping to see the end. The brunt of the fighting on our front has been near to Lens and the Canadians have been the chief actors. They have done well and are gradually fighting their way into the city.

THE DIARY OF JOHN COLEMAN BINDER

The local food control Committees are now seeking 'Executive Officers' as they are called to carry out their duties. Northampton offers £200 a year, Wellingborough £150 and so on. By this it will be seen what a huge army of officials we are still creating. It is officials here, officials there, and officials everywhere.

August 27 Monday The rain it raineth every day. The outlook in this direction is fast becoming serious. A good breadth of corn has been cut but there it stands in the fields. It rained all last night and after a fairly drying day the rain is now pouring down in sheets.

The Italians on Saturday continued their drive of the Austrians, captured Monte Santo and caused the enemy to retreat for 5 miles. They also made great captures of men and materiel.

Sunday September 2 There has not been much fighting the last week excepting on the Italian front, the weather has been so terribly wet both here and in France and Belgium. The Italians are making good progress and are causing the Austrians to retire. Russia still remains in a bad plight and continues to cause the Allies much anxiety. Anarchy chaos and confusion. Some regiments retreating without fighting, others fighting well but left without support – such is the condition of Russia to-day. If she had been what we expected, probably we should [have] been now in sight of the end of this ghastly war.

The chief events here have been the issue by the Food Controller (or shall I say Dictator) of several orders or decrees relating to food and its distribution. He proposes to reduce the wholesale price of meat as from tomorrow. All meat is to be sold by dead weight.

Beef 8/6, Mutton 8/6, Pork 9/6 per 8lbs. This will entail the weighing of all animals at market and a certain percentage allowance for the offal. There is to be a most complicated system of control by these Local Food Committees over the Butcher. They will fix the retail price of all the different cuts of meat and the butcher will be compelled to exhibit this in his shop window. The profit must not exceed 2½d per lb or 20% whichever is the less. The local committee will verify his books every 14 days to enforce this. Of all the silliest childish schemes we have had since war began I think this is the most childish. I say this deliberately and I sincerely hope and think it will be a miserable failure, as it deserves to be. The responsibility for a great deal of the present high price of food rests entirely upon the Government. They started by paying huge wages to the Munition Workers and others they employ, and in consequence of this these people have enormous wages to spend and compete furiously for everything that comes along. Mere boys are earning anything from two to three pounds per week and it is no uncommon thing for one family to be taking home £20 per week. Yet these are the very people who are screaming about the high price of food, and the Government are continually throwing them sops in the way of reducing price of food by artificial means. There are too many people interested in this bloody warfare to wish it to come to an end. I do not mean the rich contractor altogether but also everybody concerned in it. They say 'Let the bloody war continue. We are having a good time.' This is quite true, and if we had an election to day they would vote for it to continue. Many of them really think very little about the men who are doing the fighting and whom the grateful nation pay a shilling a day.

1917 September 3 Monday A great improvement in the weather yesterday and to-day, and corn carting commenced again this afternoon.

The Germans are making a dead set at Riga and apparently hope to strike a blow at Petrograd. The dry rot still continues in the Russian Army and to-night's telegrams announce that they have abandoned Riga and are falling back. This is a very nasty blow for us all. Everyone laments this failure of Russia and thinks that had she been strong and true the war would have finished this autumn but there is no hope of that now. I cannot see why Japanese troops should not be brought on to the Eastern front (via Siberia) to help the Russians but there seems to be a great dislike to the 'Yellow Men' although we ourselves are using thousands of black men as labourers in France.

Tuesday September 4 Last night the Germans raided the South East Coast and Thames estuary by aeroplanes. It as a beautiful bright moonlight night, not much damage was caused to civilians but two bombs fell on naval barracks at Chatham killing 107 men and injuring many more.

DAY BY DAY THROUGH THE GREAT WAR

Wednesday September 5 Another air raid last night. The planes reached London and were in evidence at least two hours. Much damage was done, about 16 people killed and a large number wounded. These enemy aeroplanes never come far inland and at present we are quite free from their attacks. Zeppelins have almost been forgotten.

Thursday September 6 Not much news to-day. Flanders at present is a sea of mud enveloped in a white fog. Much damage to the enemy has been done by our aeroplanes at night. Last night they raided Bruges.

Friday September 7 The Italians continue to strike heavy at the Austrians and up to to-day have captured 50,000 prisoners since August 9. Austria wants peace badly.

Saturday September 8 The Food Controller's order fixing the price of meat has now been in force since last Monday. As far as one can judge it has not been a success. Confusion has become more confounded. In very few instances have the scheduled prices appeared in any shop. As a matter of fact the prices we have paid here (although high) are lower than the prices fixed by the Controller. At market the prices certainly show no reduction.

The Government are now commandeering a fixed quota of fat beast from every district each week (in this district 10). These are bought by their agent (generally an auctioneer) at the fixed price of 74/- per cwt. They are taken to the Railway station, weighed and sent to Islington for slaughter and then go into cold storage for army use. They may be commandeered at any market (or any farm) and after they have been taken are sold off by auction in the usual way. The consequence is that there is not the usual supply and prices continue to harden. I think the Food Controller will be beaten in the end. There is so much evasion of his orders. They are so complicated that no one man can understand. He (the Controller) wise in his generation has deputed the enforcement of these orders to Local Food Committees who will have to bear all odium that attaches to them.

1917 Sunday 9 September Before next Saturday every shopkeeper who wishes to sell sugar must make an application to the Local Food Committee to be allowed to do so. If he does not get this permit (it cannot very well be refused) he will not be allowed to sell sugar after October 1.

Harvest is going on well. Many farmers are carting to-day. I hear some good reports of the yield of wheat, as much as 7 qrs to the acre in one instance at Tansor. I should think the average will be 4½ qrs. This is much better than last year.

September 10 Monday Telegrams from Russia this morning disclose how great is the anarchy and confusion prevailing there. All access to Petrograd has been stopped and   martial law proclaimed. According to to-night's news civil war has commenced.

September 11 Tuesday Yesterday's telegrams announcing civil war were premature. No actual fighting appears to have taken place. The Allies are making great efforts to prevent this.

Wednesday September 12 Very little news of fighting to-day. The ground in Flanders is said to be a regular swamp. A soldier home from the front to-day described to me the situation out there as 'blasted hell'. Horror upon horror accumulates. How long will it last. No-one can say.

Thursday September 13 Red Cross day here to-day. A great effort is being made throughout the County to raise £15,000 during this month for the Red Cross. I think it is probable that more than this will be raised. A real Old English Fair is to be held on the Market Square at Northampton on September 27 and 28. Also a sale of Antiques which are being given by well known people.

Friday September 14 Forms of application are being distributed by the postmen to every house this week. I received mine to-day. They are quite simple. The information asked for is the names and occupations of each person in the house. The age if under 18. These forms are returned through the post to each Local Food Committee who will issue sugar tickets for each household in due course.

September 15 Saturday The Russian revolt or civil war seems to be weakening and, according to what can be gleaned, Kerensky the foremost man in this great revolution appears to be getting the upper hand. Much as we deplore this collapse of Russia we cannot disguise from ourselves the fact that, had not the revolution taken place, it is certain the Czar and his German advisers would have concluded a separate peace with Germany and then we on the western front would have had to face the whole weight of the enemy's offensive. As it is the Germans are compelled to keep large numbers of men there even if the Russians do not fight very much. Austria also is bound to do the same. Besides this there are 750,000 Austrian prisoners in Russia who would have been liberated to fight us.

Sunday September 16 We return to Greenwich time at 3 am tomorrow Monday morning so shall have to put the clock back before going to bed to-night. As far as one can judge this 'summer time' will become a permanent institution in this country.

Tomorrow we begin to sell the 9d loaf as it is called and flour at 2/6 per stone. As I have said before bread cannot be made to sell at this price under present circumstances. It will be carried out by the Government paying to each miller a bonus of about 18/- on each sack of flour he makes. The miller will then have to sell his flour at a corresponding reduction to the baker. As the whole of the mills are under Government control this will not be difficult. The usual price of flour is about 61/- to 62/- at the mill. All railway carriage and cartage has to be paid in addition to this by the baker (even if the miller delivers it by road). The price tomorrow will be 44/3 at the mill showing a reduction of about 17/6 per sack. I regard the whole business as a bribe to the working classes to keep them quiet. It puts one in mind of the Roman 'Panem et Circenses'. Of course the deficit will have to be made up out of the taxes. What this deficit will be cannot at present be accurately stated but it is generally estimated at about one million of money per week. We have had to make a return of all flour we had in stock last night at the close of business and send it to the Local Food Office. Each miller whose flour we have will be obliged to allow us the difference between the 61/- we have paid and the 44/3. He in his turn will get it refunded by the Exchequer. All flour is supposed to be alike, but in practice it varies much. Country millers are much handicapped and cannot produce nearly as good flour as the mills which are situated at the Ports. This is accounted for by the larger proportion of foreign wheats which the latter receive, especially on the western coast. I have lately been buying from the Mersey Ports.

1917 September 17 Monday We wake again to the steady relentless pressure of this grim and bloody {war}. A fact that is never absent from all our thoughts day and night.

The news to-day is that Russia has proclaimed herself a Republic and that the revolt is dying out and civil war has been averted. The Russian armies seem to be pulling themselves together a little. Stubborn fighting is going on around Riga.

Tuesday September 18 General Haig has spoken of 'intense gunfire' the last few days. We know now that this indicates preparation for another battle. Probably it is now close at hand.

Wednesday September 19 Much 'peace talk' is going on in Germany and the abandoning of Belgium is being advocated by some of the papers. This retention of Belgium by Germany is one of the foremost obstacles to peace. So long as she is there and refuses to deliver it up there can be no peace. The rulers of this country are continually saying that Germany must evacuate Belgium and give her recompense. Why are they not more honest and declare that <u>we</u> cannot allow Germany to retain Belgium on account of the menace it would be if she were paramount there. But this [is] only one specimen of the chicanery and double dealing of official diplomacy. One gets absolutely sick of it all, and distrusts all official statements put forward by the Government.

Thursday September 20 Telegrams about midday announce that the expected battle commenced this morning about 5.15, and that good progress had been made. It is said the German fortified positions in Belgium extend to a depth of 4 or 5 miles. I am rather doubtful if ever 'the breaking through' we are promised will take place, and the war become a mobile offensive. We are told it will but at present it does not seem probable. At any rate cavalry are being rapidly trained as infantry. Swords, spurs and lances are obsolete. Guns guns guns have taken their places. It is only guns we hear of.

Tonight's telegrams say that all we wanted by the offensive this morning has been acquired and that 2,000 prisoners were captured.

DAY BY DAY THROUGH THE GREAT WAR

Friday September 21 Yesterday was 'calling up day ' in America and 600,000 men joined the colours. America has now nearly 2 million of men under arms.

Saturday September 22 The government are again embarking on an economy campaign. If the situation were not so tragic it would afford materials for a comic opera. Last Monday they launched the 9d loaf scheme. As a natural consequence, owing to the reduction in price the consumption has much increased. (I can vouch for this in my own business). To-day they are imploring us to eat less. What folly. People say 'Bread must be more plentiful or you could not lower the price.' Ninety per cent of the people do not grasp the fact that it is being paid for by other means. . I consider this lowering of the bread to 9d (although the profit given to me as a baker is much better than when we sold it at 10d) as one of the greatest mistakes we have made. It is absolutely opposed to all the laws of political economy.

1917 September 23 Sunday A real wet day to-day, but Harvest is nearly finished. There is very little corn left in the fields. Potatoes are being lifted, there is a certain quantity of disease, but really a very heavy crop of potatoes.

September 24 Monday Very little news this morning except that Germany is again engineering her peace proposals which no-one in this country takes seriously. We feel there can be no real peace until the enemy (or we) are really beaten either by fighting or starvation. Of this there is no sign at present in this country although many things are very dear and difficult to obtain.

Tuesday September 25 The enemy raided London last night coming over with a regular fleet of aeroplanes two of which reached London and by dropping bombs killed 15 people and wounded 70 more. There was a quite pitched aerial battle all day along the S E coast. Two enemy planes were destroyed. The old Zeps also paid a visit to the Yorks and Lincolnshire coasts. This I think was more of a feint than a serious business as they are quite aware how helpless these huge things are. The alarm was given here about 9 pm but nothing was seen or heard of them. I think Lynn was the nearest place to us to which they came. The Specials were out all night, but it was not my night out so escaped the business. I am told by friends in London that the gun fire there was terrific and no doubt this helped to defeat the Huns.

Tonight General Haig reports that he again attacked at 5.30 this morning and that all has gone well.

Wednesday September 26 Yesterdays battle east of Ypres was a very hot one, but we came out top. Took 1600 prisoners and advanced quite a mile on strongly fortified front. The enemy are now erecting small concrete structures (hundreds of them) holding about 40 men, armed with machine guns. Our men call them 'Pill Boxes' and it was against these that they had to fight. There is much satisfaction to know that we are capable of dealing with this new warfare. Another air raid in London tonight.

Thursday September 27 To-day the older school children are being taken by their teachers to gather blackberries to convert into jam for Army use. This is being organised throughout Northants Beds and Bucks and it is hoped that at least 500 tons will be gathered. From this district they are being sent to Wisbech where there are several jam factories. To-day about a ton was despatched.

Friday September 28 The nights are now quite moon light and the Germans take advantage of this to come over. London is again raided tonight.

Saturday September 29 A big effort is now being made in the County to raise money for the Red Cross. A great fair was held yesterday and Thursday on the Market Square at Northampton which it was hoped £5000 would be raised but much more than this has been done. At first 15,000 was the amount aimed at for the whole but I think at least twice that will be raised.

Sunday September 30 No London letters this morning. Another raid there last night, but at present have heard no particulars.

Monday October 1 Twelve people were killed in the London raid and 39 injured last evening about 6.45 to 8. The moon is full just now, and we may be sure the enemy will take every advantage of it.

Tuesday October 2 Another London raid last night. Zeppelins were also over on the east and north east coast. Bombs are said to have been heard here about 12 o'clock , but they were very indistinct. Special

THE DIARY OF JOHN COLEMAN BINDER

Constables were called at 12.30 but the air ships did not come here and the 'All clear' signal was received at 2.15. I was not out. The greater part of the people do not know anything about these alarms until the morning, but if anyone is showing the smallest light a constable at once orders it to be put out.

1917 Wednesday October 3 Much damage and havoc was caused by the raids and Londoners are getting very impatient with the Government and are demanding that German towns shall be bombed as a retaliation. I think that this demand will have to be conceded, much as it is disliked by a large section of the people here, but it is quite certain that the Germans will respect nothing but brute force and the only way to cope with them is to meet them with their own weapons. One knows that their object in these raids on women and children is to wear us down and to create 'war weariness' but this is the last thing they will do. It only creates a more determined spirit and a readiness to endure much more than we have done. They also hope to draw away some of our airmen and machines from the Western front where they feel and know that we are superior to them. The colossal dimensions to which this air war has grown are almost incredible. America announces to-day that she has ordered and is rapidly completing 20,000 machines.

Thursday October 4 Telegrams this afternoon announce that General Haig attacked again east of Ypres at 6 o'clock this morning and that 'all is going well'.

October 5 Friday Yesterday was a remarkable and splendid day for our soldiers in Flanders, and will mark one of the most decisive and terrible battles in this awful and bloody war. I think it will be known as the Battle of Broodsemde. The object of the terrible fighting we have had in the last great 'pushes' has been to obtain possession of the last line of low lying ridges looking down into Belgium. To obtain these and to force the Germans off them into the low lying plains and at the same time to make it impossible for the enemy to retain his hold on the coast of Belgium from Ostend to Zeebrugge from whence he chiefly directs his submarine and air attacks.

The enemy had determined to attack us at 7 am and was mustering his divisions at 6 am when they were caught by terrific gun fire and infantry attacks launched by our people. The enemy was hammered according to all accounts as he has never been hammered before and his casualties in slain are enormous. Two of his divisions (including one of Guards) were completely broken, and tonight's telegrams say that nearly 5,000 prisoners are in our hands. Try as he may, he cannot stand many blows like this. I think it is only in this way we can bring the war to an end and secure a lasting peace. Germany wants peace and wants it badly. For the last fortnight she has been prompting the Pope to send up kites to see which way the wind blows, but the Allies are obdurate and are determined that Prussian militarism must be crushed once and for all. I wonder if Germany will hang on until the power of America becomes effective. Sometimes I think she will not.

Saturday October 6 To-day is the last day for sending in applications for sugar tickets. Hundreds of thousands have been filled up improperly and great confusion must ensue. About 17,000,000 application forms have been issued.

Sunday October 7 Great success has attended the efforts for the Red Cross throughout the County during the last fortnight. It is estimated that nearly £40,000 has been raised.

The Food Controller has not succeeded in his efforts to limit the price of meat. As far as 'dead meat' is concerned it is practicable to keep a fixed price, but when animals are sold by open competition at Market this has been found to be impossible. The only way to ensure that the price should not be exceeded would be to weigh every animal that comes into the market, [and] sell it at its live weight allowing so much for offal, but there is no time to do this, consequently meat is making as high a price as ever. There is an absolute shortage of Pork and it is very difficult to obtain any. Many butchers are not killing pigs and bacon is at famine prices, ordinary American is being retailed at 1/8 to 2/- per lb and the best English up to 2/8 and 2/10. Pigs sold in the open market make about 20/- per 14lb.

Monday October 8 To-day I sold 6 pigs for £96, probably about 1/6 per stone.

1917 Tuesday October 9 To-day Haig made another blow at the Germans. He gives them very little rest,

DAY BY DAY THROUGH THE GREAT WAR

he says to-night that all he wanted was gained but the mud and water in Flanders are terrible. Men to-day have been wading through water well up to the middle and simply covered with mud, caked from head to foot with it. The battle this morning extended farther north and the French and Belgians who are holding the line from our left up to the sea were engaged in it and fought their way up to the edge of the great forest of Houlthurst.

Wednesday October 10 The farmers have compelled the Food Controller to give way on the price of meat and instead of bringing the price of beef to 60/- per cwt in January as he proposed he has now decided that the price of 65/- shall rule up to July1 1918.

Butter by auction sold yesterday at Thrapston market at 2/10 per lb in spite of the Food Controller's order that the price shall not exceed 2/4. This will show how little his orders are really enforced. Occasionally there is a prosecution here and there but I venture to say that these orders are more honoured in the breach than in the observance.

Thursday October 11 Michaelmas Day. Farm work makes slow progress the weather is wet and we are getting much rain. Progress is being made with the pulling up of new ground, but seeding is slow. About 1600 steam tractors are at work and it is estimated about 6,000 will be available in January. These are at work from light to dark, Sundays included.

October 12 Friday Another bloody day in Flanders. Haig again attacked at day break and advanced his line somewhat but blinding rain came on and he does not appear to have advanced very far. . For the present it seems it is his intention to capture the village of Passchendaele, a place of great strategic value, and thus to force the Germans off the Belgian coast.

October 13 Saturday There are rumours to-day that Japan may send an army on to the eastern front to stiffen the Russians. If this is so they would come via the trans- Siberian railway, a task of immense difficulty as for a greater part of its length it is only a single line. In addition to this there would be the transport of the trains across the Baikal Lake.

Sunday October 14 The rival leaders here and in Germany have this week reminded me much of two cocks crowing defiance to each other from their own dung hills. The German Foreign Secretary on Wednesday declared that matters with regard to Belgium might be arranged but on no account would they make any concession as regards Alsace and Lorraine.

Lloyd George and Asquith retorted on Thursday that we should force them to do so, and that we should wage war until this was done even though our resources were strained to the utmost. We must remember that none of these men are actually fighting and that ultimately they may be compelled by forces over which they have no control to assume a different attitude. I mean by the menace of famine. . This is a distinct danger which I believe really threatens the world and may do much to bring the war to an end. It will demand the utmost exertion, calm judgement and real statesmanship to restore the equilibrium of the food supply of the world, even if war were to cease to-day. We have a hundred millions of men either directly or indirectly concerned in this terrible war and not only not producing food but actually <u>destroying</u> what the limited number who are left are producing, 14 large vessels were sunk this week coming to England, but I do not think the German U boats will ever starve us out.

Monday October 15 The Russian news this morning is unwelcome. Germany is attacking in the Baltic and under cover of her navy has landed a force on Ocsel Island at the mouth of the Gulf of Finland. The Russian navy apparently was unable to prevent this. Russia has been most unfortunate the last 6 months.

Tuesday October 16 Friday's battle in Flanders did not have much result. The rain came on and rendered effective artillery fire impossible. Unless weather conditions alter it hardly seems possible that we shall be able to force the Germans off the Belgian coast this year.

1917 Wednesday October 17 Russia fares badly. The enemy have overrun the whole of Ocsel Island and have taken 5,000 prisoners.

Thursday October 18 Reports tonight say that the Russians are evacuating Petrograd and falling back on

THE DIARY OF JOHN COLEMAN BINDER

Moscow. The naval fighting continues in the Baltic without any decisive result. It does not seem possible for us to render any real help as Holland and Denmark are to say the least of it not friendly to us, or are compelled to appear so by German pressure.

Friday October 19 The Germans attacked us tonight with a strong fleet of Zeppelins. Probably 8 or 9 also with aeroplanes. The police here received warning about 6-30 that they were crossing but took no action until 8 o'clock when they received the 'Stand-by' warning. I was at a meeting but it being my turn to summon my section of constables was fetched by the Inspector and ordered to at once summon them to duty. As I was doing this about 8.20 to 8.30 I heard the sound of a Zeppelin approaching from the north-north east, but could not locate it, apparently it turned on its course and went north. I think that it was about 3 or 4 miles away when I heard [it]. About 10 minutes later I heard the report of 4 Bombs exploding at intervals of about 5 seconds but could not see the flashes. After getting my section of constables on duty I was ordered on patrol duty and about nine o'clock heard bombs dropped much nearer to us (did not see them) on the north. These caused many of the doors and windows here to vibrate. On reporting shortly after to the Police Station I heard that they had been dropped close to Easton-on-the-Hill, the constable there having 'phoned in to this effect. They did no damage. Was out on patrol until 12.30 but did not hear anything more except an aeroplane which from its flight we took to be one of ours from the aerodrome at Wittering. This aerodrome (a large one) at Wittering was probably the objective of the enemy but they were several miles away from it. After being on duty until 1.50 we received the welcome news (from London) 'all clear' and as old Pepys says 'So home to bed'. It was a very fine quiet night, plenty of stars but very cold and foggy about midnight.

Saturday October 20 Very little news this morning about the raid except that the enemy were over the midland eastern and n. e. counties. We shall hear more during the day.

Petrograd is in grave danger and the Russian government is moving to Moscow. Later. I hear that 3 persons were killed at Northampton. The total reported casualties up to 3 pm are 27 killed and 53 injured. Telegrams tonight say that 3 Zeppelins were caught by the French on their return and brought down. This is not a bad haul and will give the enemy cause to think. My previous opinion that these Zeppelins are a military failure is confirmed by this last raid. They are not nearly as effective as aeroplanes, but as we are now raiding German towns we may expect they will continue to pester us. Five bombs were dropped in a field close to Holme (about 8 miles away). Later: several more Zeppelins were brought down.

Sunday October 21 An airship sailed over us yesterday about 1 o'clock. This is the first we have really seen here. The shape of a huge fish (a chub) and a beautiful silvery gray colour. It came up from the south and went north.

Food Control does not seem to make much progress. Confusion is worse confounded. There is a distinct shortage of butter, bacon, sugar, margarine and many other things. We are not starving but feel the inconvenience of all this.

The rout of the Zeppelins took place over France. This is disclosed by short telegrams to-day.

Monday October 22 The full story of the disastrous rout of the Zeppelin fleet is told in this morning's papers. They were kept at a very great height (16,000 to 18,000 feet) by our airmen and at that altitude a violent northerly gale was blowing although there was little wind nearer the earth. This forced them southwards. It is also surmised that they stopped their engines and they became frozen and unable to be used. In this helpless condition they drifted over to France and were espied soon after daybreak. The French airmen and gunners took up the pursuit and as they had now descended some distance they were quite able to deal with them. They were chased about all over France during Saturday and six certainly, possibly seven, were captured or destroyed. One came down quite intact and the whole crew quickly surrendered. Others were burnt or blown to pieces and the seventh is supposed finally to have plunged into the Mediterranean. So ends Germany's great aerial invasion. There is much wailing and gnashing of teeth in that country and much rejoicing in this. This little trip cost Germany at least 1¼ Millions.

1917 Tuesday October 23 The Germans at present are held up in Northern Russia and do not appear to get much further, but there are reports to-day that they are attacking strongly in Italy.

DAY BY DAY THROUGH THE GREAT WAR

Wednesday October 24 Tonights telegrams say that a terrific fight is going on on the Aisne opposite to Laon. The French army attacked at daybreak after much artillery bombardment.

Attacks are also being made in Flanders but the country is all rain and mud.

October 25 Thursday The French victory on the Aisne is complete. They captured all they set out to do, took 160 guns and over 8,000 prisoners, besides much other booty. It is estimated the total German losses were 26,000. . The French now look down upon the Laon plain and thus see all the enemy's moves.

October 26 Friday There is ominous news from Italy. The Germans owing to the weakness of the Russians have withdrawn large numbers of men and are throwing them against the Italians. They claim to have captured 30,000 prisoners.

October 27 Saturday The Italian business grows worse. It seems pretty well certain that Italy has had a bad mauling. Their losses tonight are estimated at 60, to 80 thousand men. Apparently they were able to cope with the Austrians but the Germans were too much for them. There is a considerable number of our own soldiers out there helping the Italians and drafts are constantly being sent. This week an Oundle airman (Ashworth) has been ordered out there, and on his way out was joined by at least 20 more flying men.

Sunday October 28 I think we have felt the pressure of war more this last week than at any time before. At every turn we are confronted by some aspect of the war. The food business is gradually becoming worse. At present there is no restriction on bread, but it is very very difficult in fact impossible to obtain adequate supplies of bacon butter tea margarine sugar and paraffin. Today an order is entirely forbidding the use of horses for pleasure. Petrol is also exceedingly scarce, and constables are now directed that they may stop any motor car which is apparently being used for pleasure and demand their business. If they find it is only pleasure then they will be fined. Some fines inflicted for contravening the various orders are very heavy. This week a farmer in Bedfordshire was fined £3,750 for selling potatoes at a higher price than the regulation one.

The submarine war against us continues without cessation and the average number of ships over 1600 tons sunk each week is about 14 to 16. This does not include neutral vessels.

October 29 Monday Disastrous news from Italy this morning. Aided by a new poison gas and assisted by heavy reinforcements drawn from the Russian frontier the enemy made a surprise attack on the Italians and completely staggered them. They claim to have taken 100,000 prisoners and over 1,000 guns. This is the worst reverse the Allies have had and has caused much misgiving here in England, so much the more because it was unexpected. Of course aid will have to be sent from here and France but it <u>must</u> prolong the war. The Italians are said to be retreating in good order.

October 30 Tuesday A smart attack this morning by Sir D.Haig in Flanders but I take it of not very great importance. From what men tell me who are home on leave it is next to impossible to do much more this year. The mud is the enemy and defies all description.

October 31 The Italians are still retreating but in good order it is said. We are told they make no appeal for help either to us or France but said they were ready to meet the blow. This is what we are told but one becomes very chary of accepting official statements now-a-days. Some of them are so obviously 'faked' that no-one believes them.

1917 November 1 Thursday The enemies' flying men made seven attempts to raid London last night but only once did about three machines get through. The battle raged for about 4 hours. Eight people were killed and 21 injured. It was a beautiful moonlight night and perfectly calm.

November 2 Friday Rather more cheerful news from Italy this afternoon. The retreat has been stayed, and the Italians are consolidating themselves on the Tagliamento. There are rumours of a naval action to-day in the North Sea.

Saturday November 3 The naval action turns out to be a 'scrap' in the Cattegat. Our patrols caught the enemy outside their defences and a smart little action took place. One German light cruiser and 10 patrol boats were sunk. We escaped without damage.

THE DIARY OF JOHN COLEMAN BINDER

A scare to-day. All soldiers on leave were ordered by telegram to rejoin at once.

November 4 Sunday A beautiful autumn day. Bright sunshine after a week of fog. Wheat seeding is going on well, but labour is scarce, and the ground is getting very foul. Women are being employed in increasing numbers on the land but they are only a poor substitute at the best. Potatoes are an abundant crop and this very fact has created a comical situation. The Government in the Spring in order to secure as large a crop as possible fixed the price of this autumn crop at £6 to £6.10 per ton, not lower or higher, now there is such an abundant yield that many farmers would be glad to sell at half that price, but others are opposed to any reductions as they contend they ploughed up pasture land on the assurance that the price would not be below £6. This all comes of interfering with the natural law of supply and demand. You stop a hole here and the result is a much larger one is made somewhere else.

Bread is much better in quality since harvest, now that we have a better wheat supply and maize is not so plentiful. More barley is being used as a mixture. Maize is getting very very scarce and is worth 90/- to 95/- per quarter.

Monday November 5 The news from Italy is disastrous. After attempting to make a stand on the river Tagliamento they have been compelled to withdraw again and are now falling back. The Germans to-day claims they have taken another 20,000 prisoners. Public opinion here is strongly demanding that effective aid must be given to the Italians and to-night it is announced that Lloyd George together with a military staff is in Italy and that allied troops are being rushed into Italy. From what one can gather from a very confused situation it is certain that much of this debacle has been brought about by German intrigue in one of the Italian Armies and that they have proved treacherous. Germany is claiming all the credit for this defeat but it is principally Austrians who have been doing the work.

Tuesday November 6 Good news from Palestine to-day. General Allenby has captured Beersheba and it looks as if he would soon turn the formidable stronghold of Gaza. We have heard very little from his part of the war since March when we were quite held up by the Turks at Gaza. The 4th Northants are in this fighting there, and were badly mauled on that occasion.

Wednesday November 7 The Government have had to deal with the potato business. Growers are to be allowed to sell at prices below £6 per ton, but sellers of not less than 4 tons per month will have the difference between their sale price and the £6 made up by a government subvention. What folly. This subsidizing business is one of the most absurd things in the whole war. It is clearly shown by returns that since Bread has been reduced to 9d by subvention the consumption has increased by 5 per cent. I can bear this out from my own observation and knowledge.

Thursday November 8 Startling news from Russia tonight. Another revolution. Revolution and counter revolution follow swiftly in that country. All seems chaos and confusion. I quite think Russia will never be able to strike another effective blow for the Allies. Her condition is terrible, but at the same time she ought to have our sympathy and help, for in the success of her revolution lies the hope of all democratic government in the future.

1917 November 9 Friday Great news from Palestine. Gaza has been captured and the Turks are in retreat pursued by the English, who are now within 35 miles of Jerusalem. The British Government announce to-day that they are quite prepared to reinstate the Jews as a nation in Palestine. Events move at a marvellous speed in these days.

November 10 Saturday Fierce fighting all along the Ridge in Flanders. There at least the Germans have met more than their match. When they meet the English soldier they are done, and in spite of frantic appeals and proclamations are gradually being forced backwards.

November 11 Sunday Sitting down to write to-day I can only say that the past 10 days have been some of the gloomiest and most depressing since the retreat from Mons in 1914. The huge battle line sways backwards and forwards. I can see this bitter struggle prolonged, possibly for a year or two, with all its bloodshed anguish and death, but looking calmly round I can only say that in my judgement England is as determined as ever to fight on. I think if it were not for America the outlook would indeed be grave and ominous, but from every source both private and public we receive good tidings of their intention to back us with their last man and dollar. The strain of the war continues to increase here and we are now feeling its consequences in all and every direction. Business is carried out with increasing difficulty and goods of all kinds are difficult to obtain. For instance for a whole week it has not been possible to buy oil for lighting purposes here and as this is the general illuminant amongst the poor and also in all the villages it has caused much discomfort. Candles are being used as far as possible in place of it.

Sunday November 18 I regret that I have been unable to write up this diary daily this past week so will endeavour to write down to-day some impressions of current events during this period.

It has been a remarkable week as indeed all time is now remarkable but I think the chief event apart from the actual fighting has been the speech delivered by Lloyd George on Tuesday night in Paris on his way back from Italy where he and other Premiers had been to confer with the Italians. A speech which if it had been delivered in this country and by any other man would have certainly led [to] his being prosecuted under the Defence of the Realm decrees (acts I do not call them). A more disheartening speech I am confident has not been made since war began, and it has caused much dismay and anger in this country. He charged us [as] a nation in one word as being 'slackers' and not having done our duty and as being responsible for all the disasters of the war, and many other things in a similar strain. He had not a good word to say for us, and what shall we say to him, who has been an autocratic dictator during the last 12 months and has had such powers entrusted to himself and his war cabinet as have never been given to any other man or men during the history of this country. Naturally there has gone up from the enemy a shout of triumph and there is corresponding depression here. At once steps were taken to call him to book and the outcome is that he will have to 'face the music' in the Commons tomorrow Monday night. As a direct consequence of this speech the French Ministry fell the next day and signs are not wanting which point to a similar downfall of the Ministry here. Indeed some of the most influential papers are calling for his dismissal.

After a week's hard fighting the situation in Italy is to say the least of it no worse. The Italians reinforced by French and British (some of whom have crossed the Alps in deep snow) are holding their own and making a much better stand, although there is still a distinct menace to Venice.

A much brighter sphere is Palestine where General Allenby's army has been dealing the Turks a series of heavy blows, fighting in the good old style, quite free from trenches, and rounding up the Turks towards Jerusalem. Allenby is now about 20 miles from that city, but there will [be] much hard fighting as the Turks are being reinforced by Germans and may yet make a determined stand.

The food question tends daily to become more complex and involved. The Food Dictator issues a fresh order on some subject almost daily and one cannot keep pace with his decrees. In many cases people run the risk of fines and disregard them and in other cases they are disregarded from sheer ignorance.

The Government are providing 1,000 motor tractors for ploughing (especially grassland and seeds). I saw one at work at Oundle Lodge farm on Wednesday but cannot say I was much impressed with it. The weight is very great and presses the land very much. It is also very cumbersome and cannot plough the headlands but as horses are very scarce and it is imperative we should get more land under corn growing I expect we shall have to do the best we can with them.

Monday November 19 The political situation to-day is uppermost but tonight's debate in the house has cleared the air. Lloyd George made a great speech, achieved a great triumph and --answered the ridiculous speech of Lloyd George in Paris. He did this in one sentence, he acknowledged he made the Paris speech in order to frighten us, a sort of bogie affair. What childish business – Lloyd George is a great man but he lets his head lose itself.

Tuesday November 20 Italy is still holding out well. The German advance has been stayed but there is still much danger and a distinct menace to Venice. Allied troops are being hurried into Italy and are stiffening the Italian forces. Incidentally from cards and letters one hears this from Oundle men when writing home.

Wednesday November 21 War news of a sensational character is to hand this afternoon.   A short telegram from Haig late last night reported that he had attacked yesterday and that considerable progress had been made. That was all. This afternoons news tells of an amazing feat of arms and of a real great victory. With the utmost secrecy he and his subordinate Sir Julyan Bing in command of the 3rd Army had planned an attack on the German lines at their almost strongest point viz just opposite to Cambrai which is farther south than the scenes of all the fighting lately. With much secrecy they collected a huge fleet of 'Tanks' and early yesterday morning, just as day was breaking, they launched this fleet against the German lines without any bombardment at all. It was a tremendous success. The tanks simply walked through miles of barbed wire and 'dug-outs'. The Germans were completely taken by surprise, and our men poured through the breach, six miles long, thus made, liberated a dozen or so French villages and advanced their own lines about five miles. The Germans surrendered in shoals. How many we shall probably learn tomorrow. This is a most welcome victory after the depressing days of this month.

November 22 The importance of the victory is maintained to-day. 9,000 prisoners and 100 guns were taken. The ground was firm and dry and the Tanks appear to have enjoyed themselves immensely, careering round and causing the Germans to shout 'Kamerade' in great numbers.

Friday November 23 The Russians disaster is getting worse and worse. Anarchy and confusion. Confusion and anarchy. Civil war. Russia at this moment seems hopeless. I wonder if she will ever be able to strike again during this war. I am doubtful.

Saturday November 24 Italy is still holding on well and although it is not possible to say that danger is past things are decidedly more hopeful there.

The Food business continues to engage our most serious attention. As I predicted, things are growing gradually worse, and I am convinced will continue to do so. There is no lack of bread and flour, but there is a very pronounced shortage in fats of all kinds. Butter margarine lard etc are very scarce and in the larger towns almost impossible to obtain. In towns of any size queues of women may be seen waiting outside to buy if possible a small quantity of these articles and it is quite a common thing to see a shop closed with a notice outside 'No tea, no butter, no margarine'. Paraffin for burning is almost unobtainable. Matches are exceedingly scarce and many other things are difficult to get. I almost think it would have been better to have let affairs run their normal course. This week the Government have had to acknowledge the Sugar Tickets a failure, and this before the scheme has come into working. They have scrapped the whole system and instead of households having tickets each and every individual will be compelled to have them and this after months of preparation. The whole thing is maddening to those who are concerned with the working of it, and now we are told that it is almost certain that we shall [have] food tickets for everything, but it is really difficult to believe what is told us. Lloyd George said on Monday the submarine menace was over   (5 German submarines were sunk last Saturday). On Tuesday he announced in view of the grave situation drastic food restrictions would be imperative, and the Food Man did the same. What are we to believe. Having been connected with food stuffs for the last 40 years I am quite certain that it is quite impossible to carry out any system of compulsory rationing. It would require three parts of the nation to watch the other part and even then the regulations would be avoided. However we must hope for the best.

1917 Monday November 25 The Italian Line still holds in spite of the enormous pressure of the enemy to break it and every day renders it more unlikely that they will be able to do so. Fierce fighting still continues especially round Asiago.

I forgot to mention that on Friday the bells were rung in London on account of the Cambrai victory. This is the first time since war began. I do not think they were rung in other places.

Tuesday November 26 The accounts of the victory at Cambrai read like fairy tales. The cavalry got through the gap and had the time of their lives. One detachment captured a whole battery of German guns, sabreing the artillery men as they stood. The enemy appear to be rushing up men to stem the tide and it is very evident there will be stiff fighting there. The coveted point is Bourlon Wood which dominates the country for several miles, and by holding this we make Cambrai of little use to the enemy.

DAY BY DAY THROUGH THE GREAT WAR

Wednesday November 27 To-day we are informed that the whole of the sugar cards as issued are to be scrapped and that each person will have to be supplied with an individual sugar card by the retailer. This will mean taking a census of the people. Nothing less. What is the object. It cannot be necessary for this purpose alone. I imagine it is to form a basis of the food supply altogether. It will mean the issue of about 40 million application forms. Their return, and then the issue of the same number of tickets. This is a very unjust burden to a class of men who are very much depleted of labour.

Thursday November 28 The total amount of the money raised in the Town and County of Northants during the last effort which extended from September 1 to October 31 was £31,000. This is about double of what was hoped for.

A very largely attended meeting was held at the Victoria Hall this afternoon at 3 o'clock to urge upon farmers the urgent necessity and obligation to produce all the food they possibly can. It was organized by the County War Agricultural Committee. The figures of total numbers of British ships sunk by submarines are issued each Thursday. To-days figures are ominous. Fourteen large ships are down. The largest number in any week since April. This does not look as if we had overcome the menace. I really think we shall yet feel the pinch of hunger.

END OF VOLUME SEVEN

THE DIARY OF JOHN COLEMAN BINDER
Volume Eight
November 30 1917 - July 14 1918

1917 November 30 Friday Yet another book. This book in pre-war days cost 1/- To-day I paid 2/6 for it. This is a sample of the huge rise in the price of everything. To-night's news from Cambrai reports a fierce battle is going on.

December 1 Saturday This morning's news from Cambrai clearly tells of a critical situation although it is very guarded. Last night the largest convoy of wounded which has been received at Northampton arrived there 125 men.

To-night's news is a little better. It says the enemy obtained a little gain in Bourlon Wood yesterday but was driven out again. The Germans say they took 4,000 prisoners. Probably this is not true.

December 2 Sunday A bitterly cold day but fine. Haig's telegram shows much better results. He denies that the Germans obtained anything like what they claimed to have done, although they attacked with 5 Divisions. They were beaten off but without any doubt it is a terribly bloody affair. Prisoners were taken who said they had been on the Russian front two days before.

Russia has gone from bad to worse during this week and to-day her envoys and the enemy are meeting to see if they cannot agree to an armistice. It will mean terrible work for us if they do conclude peace as there [are] 125 enemy divisions on the Russian front, and these will largely be brought to bear upon us.

December 3 Monday An armistice has been arranged with Germany by Russia and already we see one result. Her armies are being rapidly shifted on to the Western and Italian fronts. Germany evidently hopes to give us a 'knock-out' blow before America can help us much.

A telegram to-night announces that another desperate and bloody battle is in progress on the Cambrai front.

Tuesday December 4 So far the Italians have been able to stem the German Austrian onslaught. They have been stiffened by British and French divisions but I am very doubtful if their line will hold. Haig's report to-night as to the Cambrai battle is very obscure.

Wednesday December 5 The battle at Cambrai has died down, but one cannot say it was a success for us, or even for the enemy. He certainly did not achieve what he intended to do and we were obliged to yield some ground. It is estimated the enemy have had 200,000 men put out of action on the Cambrai sector since last Thursday. This will show what a terrific fight it has been.

Thursday December 6 Haig announces this morning that he has withdrawn (without molestation) from Bourlon Wood. It was found to be untenable owing to the fact the Germans were able to attack it on 3 sides.

Yesterday Wilson the American president made one of the clearest and most reasonable speeches on the war that we have had for some months. He clearly defined what we are fighting for and also the methods by which we hope to attain our objects. This man is a real Statesman and much as I regret to say it, it is to him and not to our present Government that I look to for guidance in this hour of peril. I am afraid that the Government here has largely lost the confidence of the country. Lloyd George is a 'driver' but lacks 'balance'. He is a Welshman and as such is far too emotional. He told us last week that we had 'got' the submarine menace. To-day's figures disclose the fact that 16 large vessels were sent down last week. What can we think or believe.

A stiff air battle over London this morning from about 2 to 5. Moon in last quarter and so fairly light. The enemy came in three squadrons, but only two planes got through the defences. 25 people were killed.

1917 December 7 Friday A West African Liner, the Mpapa, homeward bound, submarined yesterday. Eighty passengers and crew sunk. What ghastly work. Such things as this steel our nerves and make us determined to hold out and fight to the very last man.

DAY BY DAY THROUGH THE GREAT WAR

December 8 Saturday To-day we are taking the first steps to scrap the first issue of Sugar cards which are now to be superseded by individual cards. The real reason is to obtain a detailed account of the whole population with a view to set up 'rationing' for food of every kind. This food business is going to be the hardest thing we have to tackle. Germany has had to fight it for two years but now it is coming home to us. Shall we stand the strain as well as she has done. Time will prove. Hungry people are difficult to deal with and I see serious trouble ahead if we get starved.

Sunday December 9 I think this last week has been one of the worst of the whole war, and we are passing through a real black phase of it. Things seem to be going very much against us (except in Palestine) and it will need all our courage and tenacity to pull through. There was much 'Peace' talk current in London yesterday but much as we all want peace and would welcome it, it is impossible to consider peace at the present juncture. No, in spite of all drawbacks and discouragements we must still fight on and keep steadfastly in mind what we are fighting for. This is nothing less than the saving of civilisation. If Germany comes top then goodbye to all hope of making life worth living in this world. I would rather see the whole planet blown out of existence at once.

December 10 Monday An announcement made this afternoon in the House has moved the whole nation, and this is that Jerusalem was yesterday captured by Allenby. By its capture German prestige has received a fatal blow in the East and it has also rendered much more secure our Eastern Empire. There was no fighting in the City but by skilful tactics Allenby compelled the Turks to retreat and thus the City passed into his hands without damage. Great care was taken to respect the Holy Places. The Jews in this country are immensely elated and foreshadow a return to their own country.

December 11 Tuesday Civil war and anarchy in Russia. This is the ghastly business there. Scarcely any reliable or authentic news. Meantime we can do nothing but look on. Germany is withdrawing her troops from that front and only leaving old men and boys to hold up the enemy. Her best fighting men are coming west and we are once more confronted with a situation of dire peril.

Wednesday December 12 Haig announces to-day that the whole western front is ablaze with intense artillery fire. A precursor this of renewed attacks. No dying down of the fighting this winter I think. Meantime we are confronted by the Army with new demands for men, men, men, and various proposals are being made to secure this end. Conditions of life are daily becoming more hard, and fresh demands are constantly being made upon our patience and resources.

Certain kinds of food are becoming scarce, more especially fats. Early in the New year we (the retailers) will only be able to obtain bacon, lard etc. from the Government, and I have to-day spent several hours in getting out the necessary returns so that I may obtain my quota.

Sugar tickets are being distributed by all grocers this week and after December 30 no sugar can be obtained without these tickets. Each person is registered with a grocer and can only obtain his ½ lb per week from that particular shop.

The Meat trade is going from bad to worse and many butchers say they will close down after Christmas unless some alteration is made by the Government.

Thursday December 13 Hard fighting to-day round about Polygon Wood (not far from Cambrai) and also in the Italian mountains. At present the Austro-Germans have been held up in the mountains and have been able to debouch into the plains.

Friday December 14 Meetings are being held all through the country to impress upon the people the necessity of the economy of food, and thus try to stave off the rationing of food. Such a meeting was held here to-day.

Speaking to-night the First Lord of the Admiralty said we had not conquered the submarine menace (Lloyd George said last week we had). We had only checked it and our most vital necessity was men and women for ship building in order to cope with it and to bring food.

Saturday December 15 Not much news to-day, except the announcement that railway travelling at

THE DIARY OF JOHN COLEMAN BINDER

Christmas will be much restricted. The School boys here went down yesterday in order to avoid this. The difficulties of feeding them during the term have been very great and I am afraid these difficulties will be greater next term.

December 16 Sunday   No news of any importance to-day.

December 23 Sunday   I have not had time to write this diary since Sunday last, so will to-day give a short account of the week's doings. The distribution and collection of the Sugar Cards has occupied much of my time and has caused an enormous amount of work. They come into operation on December 30 and every person will be then entitled to receive ½lb of Sugar per week, if it is available, but I can see many loopholes and also difficulties.

We have received this week many grave warnings as to our food supply and various schemes are being organised in the larger towns to make a more equal distribution, especially of Margarine, Butter and Lard. These are the three chief articles of which there is a great scarcity. Although there is an equal scarcity here we do not see the queues standing for hours to get food as they do in larger cities, but I am thinking that much of it is due to the desire for advertisement on the part of the large multiple shops. They have received warning that unless they adopt different methods their stocks will be commandeered and distributed by the Government. There is no lack of bread etc or potatoes. Meat is decidedly scarce and we are [to have] one meatless day per week commencing with the new Year. On that day no meat of <u>any</u> description will be allowed to be sold, but almost certainly the public will evade it by buying more another day. This whole food business bristles with enormous difficulties and I am certain can never be satisfactorily controlled.

The other chief topic has been the re-iterated demand of the authorities for more men, more men. Of course, the collapse of Russia (who has concluded an armistice with Germany and who is also locked in civil war) and the reverses in Italy, have changed the situation, and it looks as if we shall have to bear the burden. The full proposals are not yet made known but [will] evidently be most drastic. Lloyd George made a speech in the House on Thursday and in quite a different key to his last one. A great deal more sober, and much less froth. I think he can see we are in a tight place.

A convoy of 14 ships crossing from Scotland to Norway was sunk on December 12th by enemy vessels. This was not told to us until Monday and naturally caused much indignation. An enquiry is being held and perhaps may show good cause but the public resent this very much.

1917 December 24 Monday   An armistice was concluded yesterday between Russia and Germany and amongst its provisions is that Germany shall not bring men from the Russian frontier on the western to fight us. How childish the Russians are. These men have already been transferred and are up against us, in fact some of them have been taken prisoners.

Three of our destroyers were sunk off the Dutch coast on Saturday either by mines or submarines, 118 men and 12 officers were lost. Evidently the enemy are testing our lines on the front, a determined thrust was made near to Ypres to-day, but was repulsed.

Tuesday December 25   Christmas Day. How unlike the traditional Christmas. No merriment, very little extra in the way of food and very little railway travelling. There are few Plum Puddings or Mince Pies this year. Only those who made them very early have been able to get the necessary fruit. To-day there is absolutely none to be had. Of dried fruit of all descriptions the market is quite bare. Green fruit is also extremely dear. Oranges 6d and 7d each (I have not seen one this season) and other things in proportion. The usual Christmas beef is to a very large extent conspicuous by its absence. There is a fair amount of meat but as a rule it is below the ordinary everyday quality. Instead of Goose or Turkey (which now cost from 2/- to 2/8 per lb) we have had Beef for dinner and it was a really prime meat but this is the exception. Rabbits are making from 2/- to 2/6 each Hares 8/- to 9/-. We are not starving, but we are now feeling the pinch and unless the submarine menace is broken we shall get steadily worse.

It has been a really beautiful day. Bright sunshine and frost, but a bitterly cold wind with occasional snow flights.

DAY BY DAY THROUGH THE GREAT WAR

Wednesday December 26   A rather sensational piece of news this morning. Admiral Jellicoe has resigned as first Lord of the Admiralty and has been kicked upstairs to the House of Lords. I think this foreshadows a bolder naval policy. There has been much criticism of the Admiralty and its doings during the last few months.

To-day inquiries are being made here for accommodation for about forty German prisoners who will be hired out to farmers to assist in agricultural work.

December 27 Thursday   Snow has fallen heavily in France and all fighting is at a standstill. Meanwhile we continue to advance in Palestine. How far do we intend to go there.

December 28 Friday   Scarcely any news to-day. Australia by Referendum has decided by a considerable majority against Conscription. I do not think this means any war weariness, but it means that Australia is exceedingly short of labour and cannot see her way to release any great quantity of men. Canada has just as decidedly voted for Conscription.

December 29 Saturday   Snow has fallen heavily in Italy and has put a stop to the fighting to a large extent there. The Italians have pulled themselves together since they have been stiffened by English and French re-inforcements and have made a splendid stand, but the situation there is still very critical.

December 30 Sunday   There has been much peace talk during this week. Germany is evidently using her proposals to Russia as a feeler to all the Allies but at present these are quite unacceptable to us as she refrains from all mention of reparation and restitution to Belgium and other small countries, and until she does this I think the war will continue.

The Government are about to make further demands upon the Labour of the country and this week the Labour Congress meeting in London emphatically calls upon them to declare what we are really fighting for and what our aims are.

1917 December 31 Monday   Allenby's Army continues to advance steadily in Palestine. On Christmas day the Turks made a great effort to re-capture Jerusalem but after a battle lasting 26 hours they were heavily repulsed losing 1,000 dead, many prisoners and a huge amount of war material.

So closes the year 1917. A year which has brought us some advance, and also much disappointment. We had hoped when the Year opened that the War would have been ended by its close, but this has proved to be a false hope. The central reason has been the collapse of Russia. If she had only been able to play her part I quite believe that the end would have been in sight to-day. But this is not so, although from what one can gather the peace negotiations are nearing a collapse, and it is quite possible that Russia may do us some good yet. Her collapse has been to some extent relieved by the adhesion of America but it [may] be months before she intervenes with any great weight.

1918 January 1 Tuesday   A bitterly cold day. Sharp frost and 'flurries' of snow. So opens the New year. Will it bring us Peace. This is the hope and wish of every one of us. That is if the Peace be satisfactory to us. Germany is ready for Peace to-day on her own terms, but we cannot accept these.

January 5 Saturday   Very little fighting on the West Front the last few days. The whole area is frost bound and under snow. Some sharp fighting in Italy where weather conditions are better. The Allied line there continues to hold and the Austro-Germans are kept at bay.

January 6 Sunday   A National Day of Intercession and Prayer. Wonderful to relate all Public Houses are closed throughout the day. Will the Liquor trade survive. This Liquor Trade has only been 'scotched' not killed and I think after the war unless it is carefully handled will be a greater menace than ever.

The Food question continues to engage most of our attention and thought. That [it] is growing worse I think cannot be doubted. This is inevitable so long as we continue to have ships sunk as we are doing. Eighteen are all posted this week besides neutrals. Both the quality and quantity of many articles of food are becoming very much restricted. All imported food such as cheese butter bacon lard margarine are getting quite scarce. These are all under Government control and they are only giving them out in very much reduced quantities. They are supposed to allocate a certain amount to the trade each month, but last month they did not [release] any cheese to us at all. I believe they had not got it for us after feeding the Army and our Allies. One thing we may congratulate ourselves upon and that is that the Army and Navy are being well fed, really much better than civilians. Men home on leave say that food is plentiful with them and of really good quality.

The real shortage this week has been in Beef. Roughly I should say it is 75 per cent short and many people to-day will have to do without their Sunday joint. In many places butchers have been closed more than half the week. Friday and yesterday the Butchers here were asking their customers to do with as little as they possibly could. I have a shrewd suspicion that much of this shortage is only temporary and is being caused by farmers holding back their cattle. Under an order which came into force this week they cannot sell cattle privately but are compelled to take them to the nearest market where they are graded into 4 classes by a Committee consisting of Auctioneers, Butchers and farmers. Each of these classes is sold [at] a fixed price live weight. Each Butcher has to state his requirements to this Committee and if there is not sufficient to meet their needs they have [so] much given to each of them. This only came into operation on Tuesday and I think many farmers are holding back their beasts to see how it works. The Food Controller hints that if they do so he will commandeer them and sell them as he may require.

Of course we cannot expect the full supply of meat to which we have been accustomed. So many millions of tons were imported, and now this is largely cut off.

You will wonder how all this affects us as a nation. Well there is a certain amount of grumbling especially in the larger towns and, I am afraid, a spirit is being created there which may cause us to cry out for peace, but in these smaller places the situation is being faced calmly and there is a disposition to accept the inevitable, to tighten our belts and make up our minds to bear it, especially if it will bring us a satisfactory peace.

I think it is fairly certain we shall have Food Tickets for many things during the next few months. April is generally expected to be the month when they will commence.

In many large towns the Food Committees have commandeered the Margarine supply this week and have distributed it to all the shop[s] in proportion, thus avoiding the queues. On Friday 4½ tons was so distributed in Northampton. It is also purposed to start Communal Kitchens in the large cities. This perhaps may help a little.

1918 Monday January 7 Saturday will mark a decisive day in the War. Lloyd George speaking to the Labour Party then made a speech or rather if I may so say 'uttered a document' which cannot fail to have a great influence on the question of Peace. He spoke soberly, without any 'gas' (which he often uses) and evidently had been in conference with all parties in this country and also the Allied Governments. He clearly stated what we were fighting for, and evidently it is the minimum terms which we shall accept. President Wilson also endorsed his statement in a similar speech to-day. His most debatable point to my mind is the question of Alsace Lorraine. Here he pledged the Allies to stand by France 'to the death' in her demand for the retrocession of these provinces. I think if this demand is persisted in it will mean some more years of war if we can bear the strain.

Sunday January 13 So far as fighting goes the week has been an uneventful one. Winter has gripped the whole of Western Europe (20 degrees of frost on Wednesday) and this has caused practically a cessation of all active fighting. The Huns torpedoed a hospital ship on Monday on its way up the Bristol Channel. All the poor wounded fellows on board were saved and landed at Cardiff after undergoing terrible suffering. These are the kind of events that madden us and nerve us to continue this bloody war.

Judging calmly I think the food question is still causing us the greatest anxiety. It would be difficult to point to any real change in a day but we are slowly but surely getting worse. Meat has been the chief trouble this week although the supply is somewhat better than it was last week ,that is throughout the county. There was a fair supply here at Market on Thursday, but no beef was allowed to be bought locally. As the butchers had secured a supply the previous Thursday, it was all binded and sent to other districts where the need was obvious. After yesterday no butcher will be allowed to kill more than 50 per cent of his killings during last October and an Oundle Butcher has a notice in his window to-day saying that he has obtained a supply of venison which will be on sale on Wednesday next at prices from 7d to 10d per lb according to the cut. It has met with a ready sale. I myself have ordered some. The price of rabbits has this week been fixed at 1/9 each without the skin, 2/- with it on. Most butchers throughout the country are closing 2 days a week, in some places 3 days.

In reply to enquiry in Liverpool I yesterday received advices saying there are no Hams Bacon or Lard on sale there, and they cannot say when there will be. People are economising in a really wonderful way, some because they have made up their minds to do so and many others because they simply cannot get the food. Matches are extremely scarce and probably if there was not a fixed price (½d per box) would be sold at fabulous prices.

1918 Monday Jan 14 Of fighting there is very little in France just now. The weather conditions are very bad but as soon as they improve it is generally expected the Germans are going to try their luck in a big blow.

To-night the Government introduced their new proposals for what they call Man power (but what I call Conscription) into the House. They always wrap things up very nicely and always carefully avoid the word conscription. They propose to take another 425,000 men for the army and an equal number for other labour. They admit there are nearly 6½ millions of men already taken and this will bring it up to 8 millions and yet Lloyd George taunted us in October for being a nation of slackers. However he has had a little more sense drilled into him since then.

January 15 Tuesday Interned men are returning from Germany after being there for 3 years (some of them). One a Mr Kirkby of Elton (a schoolmaster) reports that food is still to be bought in Germany if you have money enough but it is very dear. He thinks the German Autocracy will never ask for Peace as they are fighting for their very existence as a ruling class.

Wednesday January 16 We woke this morning to a real white world. The snow commencing to fall about eight o'clock last evening had reached a depth of 10 inches.

Yarmouth was shelled this evening either by submarine or cruiser. Six people were killed.

Thursday Jan 17 The Russo-German negotiations for Peace seem to have reached a deadlock, what the next turn there will be God only knows.

Friday January 18 Some trouble is threatened in Scotland by workers on the Clyde concerning the new conscription business. They threaten to 'down tools' on Jan 30 unless an armistice is called and peace negotiations are begun. I do not think much will come of this threat, but there can be no question that the majority of people are getting very wearied with the constant strain and struggle.

To-day the School Boys return here after their Christmas Holidays. The influx of about 600 people into a small place like this will make most serious demands upon the food supply and there will be much difficulty in finding food for them. Indeed I should not be surprised to know that if the war continues that it will compel them to break up the School.

Saturday January 19 Replying to a Trades Union Deputation to-day the Prime Minister said "We must go on or go under." That is about true, but it is this constant 'going on' which concerns us. If we could only see some little light events would be more cheerful.

Sunday January 20 On account of weather conditions very little agricultural work has been done this week. Meat is in very short supply. The Butchers here only have half their normal supply. They now close on Mondays and Wednesdays and are quite sold out early on Saturday. Cheese Bacon Lard Margarine are extremely scarce. Bread is a full supply but we are warned that it will be much darker, also that it will be practically impossible to get food for pigs. The Food Controller speaking yesterday said probably the use of wheat flour in cakes pastry and biscuits would be forbidden. The weekly list of Ships sunk is lighter this week, only 6 are down

There is said to have been another revolt at Kiel by German sailors, but it is difficult to find out the truth.

I hear on reliable authority that our men at the Front are getting very restive on account of the difficulty their wives and children at home find in getting food. Soldiers coming home here on furlough (they get 14 days now) tell me there is no lack of the best food out there and are surprised to find the conditions existing here.

1918 Sunday January 27 During the past week there has been very little fighting, as it is impossible to move much over the sodden ground in France and Belgium, but if there has been no fighting, the pressure at home continues to increase. The food business accentuates itself every week and I think will eventually cause the Governments of all the countries to conclude peace.

It appears to me that the questions of War or Peace are gradually being taken out of the hands of the Politicians by irresistible pressure from the Peoples, who are both here and on the Continent absolutely sick of this bloody and disastrous war. These men either here or in Germany will only go as far as they are pushed and now they are feeling the pressure from behind and finding there is a greater authority than themselves. Hunger is a sharp thorn and will goad men into extreme courses and it is evident that an extremely restive spirit is rising. Austria is probably the worst and very important events have taken place there. Strikes and rioting, and even here in this country it takes the authorities all their time to smooth over matters by making concessions regarding food. I do not think the end is yet. We shall probably see much bloody work this summer or spring and tens of thousands of valuable lives will be sacrificed, but above all this one can discern this spirit of the people to which I have referred.

The Military Service Bill is now law and we are to have 450,000 more men called up.

One very important piece of news is that the 'Golbin' and the 'Breslau' two German ships which were in the Mediterranean when war was declared and which by the supineness of Admiral Frankidge were allowed to escape to Constantinople have this week been destroyed. They came down the Dardanelles early last Sunday morning to attack some of our Monitors and were smartly attacked by some of our destroyers. After a fierce scrap in which we lost one monitor and one destroyer the Breslau was sunk and the 'Golbin' bolted, struck a mine, and had to be beached in the Narrows where [she] has since been a continual target of our airmen. Thus ends the career of these notorious warships. The allowing of them to get to Constantinople was I think probably the most disastrous step to us of the whole war. Turkey was 'sitting on the fence' and their arrival decided her to come down on the enemy's side, thus entailing the Gallipoli campaign and all its horrors. To this day this episode has never been satisfactorily cleared up.

We are looking forward with some anxiety to the offensive which the enemy threatens to make during the next two months. As to where and what it will do there is much speculation. One theory is that Paris is their objective, another that Calais and the Channel ports is what they most covet. American troops are coming across in large numbers and it may be that owing to the large amount of ships required for this purpose that we are so short of food.

There are a great number of Americans at Easton on the Hill (Stamford) training as airmen. The Aerodrome there is an enormous one and is said to be the largest we have in England. We see many 'Planes' from it and also others going about.

Monday January 28 A great air raid on London to-night. A beautiful bright moonlight night. German aircraft came over about 7 and a prolonged battle ensued, some of them got through the defences not much material damage was done but there was a terrible loss of life. One bomb dropped on a 'Shelter' which proved to be anything but a 'Shelter'. Casualties are reported at 47 killed and 167 injured. This is probably much below the real thing. The public does not rely much on what [it] is told by the authorities.

January 29 Tuesday Another raid on London to-night but only one enemy craft got through. Three people were killed. In last night's fight one of the German planes was brought down in flames in Essex. The three men in it were burned to ashes.

1918 January 30 Wednesday During yesterday and Monday the Italians gained a success. In conjunction with British and French troops they drove back the Austro-Germans and captured 1500 prisoners.

The Turks announce that the 'Golben' has been re-floated and towed back to Constantinople.

DAY BY DAY THROUGH THE GREAT WAR

January 31 Thursday At a meeting of the Board of Guardians here to-day it was decided to agree to a request from the County War Committee to provide accommodation in the Union Workhouse for 40 German prisoners. They will occupy one entire wing of the House, and the inmates (old men) will have to be removed to another neighbouring workhouse. These German prisoners are all agricultural labourers. They will [be] under the charge of 10 soldiers as guards. They will bring Army horses and ploughs with them (these will be housed in stables in Black Pot Lane) and will undertake to do work for any farmer who makes application. This work is the breaking up of pasture land for corn growing. The War Committee will charge the farmer so much per acre, so that really he will have very little to do actually with the prisoners. They will go out each morning and return at night.

Friday February 1 Since Wednesday all the German frontiers have been rigidly closed, but it is generally well known that there is much internal trouble there. Strikes have broken out in consequence of the wretched food conditions and it is said that in Berlin alone 400,000 men are out. It is difficult to appraise these demonstrations at their real value and meaning but one cannot help thinking that a crisis is actually coming.

Saturday February 2 Very little news from Germany to-day. Telegrams from Amsterdam say that fighting is taking place in Berlin streets between the police and soldiers and the strikers. There is scarcely any news from our own fighting fronts this week.

Sunday February 3 Events seem to have moved this week very swiftly, not so much in actual fighting but in economic conditions. The labour conditions in Germany are causing much unrest and a deep determination to bring on peace. The Military oligarchy there is fighting for its life and will not yield without a bitter and desperate struggle.

In this country we are steadily getting worse and food conditions are causing much unrest and bitterness. We are to be rationed in all the chief articles of food in March, but I am thinking great events may occur before that time, the spirit of revolution breaking out in Russia seems to be permeating the whole of the peoples engaged in this war. Forces have been unloosed which threaten to sweep away many established ideas. The Rulers in all these countries seem to stand powerless and unable to grapple with this flood and it seems very probable that unless they can formulate some better conditions they will be swept off their feet by this flood.

In Russia the conditions are really awful. I have said very little about them because it is most difficult to get reliable news, but there is revolution, anarchy, civil war, famine and pestilence, and these threaten to spread to other countries. These are indeed dark and dreadful days. God only knows what the end will be. Some of the working classes here are getting very restive, chiefly on account of food and this last Conscription Bill. Parliament is worn out and now that we have had a new Reform Bill and women may vote I hope that an election will not be long delayed.

Monday February 4 Much wet the last few days and agricultural work is getting very greatly in arrears.

Tuesday February 5 To-night the Americans had their first real taste of war. One of their transports the Tuxana of the Cunard Line (13,000) bringing over nearly 3,000 men was torpedoed off the Irish Coast. She kept afloat 4 hours and fortunately all were saved except 166.

1918 Wednesday February 6 Last night the reform Bill which very largely increases the male electorate and also gives all women over 30 the vote received the Royal Assent. A veritable Revolution, but it has excited very little comment and I venture to think would have taken years to pass except for the reason we are at war.

It is generally thought there will be a General Election this next summer. I am very glad to think that all the Pollings will now be held on one day instead of being spread over three weeks.

Thursday February 7 The weekly submarine toll shows that 14 large ships and 5 smaller ones have been sunk this week.

To-day the first prosecutions on the food business in this district took place at the Police Court here. A man from Kings Cliffe was fined £2 for having an excessive amount of food in his house and a grocer from

THE DIARY OF JOHN COLEMAN BINDER

Nassington £5 for selling articles at more than the fixed prices.

People are getting afraid of having their houses searched, and this week I have had goods returned to me by people who were afraid they would be found to have more than they should have.

A lot of this business is simply bosh and is only intended to throw dust in our eyes and to justify the existence of a huge army of officials. In fact one of the persons who returned me goods was the Executive Officer who had to do with the prosecution to-day. Verbum sap.

Saturday February 9 A whole host of orders and regulations as to rationing of meat which will come into force in London and the Home Counties is issued this morning by the Food Controller. Each person will receive 4 coupons value 5d each which will allow him to buy about 20 ounces of meat per week. Not more than three may be spent in butchers meat, the remainder will go to buy bacon, rabbit or poultry. These regulations it is pretty certain will be extended to the whole country.

Sunday February 10 This week we have had very dark bread, in fact the darkest since war began. We are told that wheat is getting scarce (I am doubtful) and in consequence the millers are being ordered to take 90 per cent of flour out of the wheat and also to increase the mixture of Barley. I cannot say the result is very pleasing. I do not like it at all, but suppose we shall have to put up with it. From all accounts German Bread is much worse than ours.

The Strikes in Germany have quite collapsed this week. Really what has taken place is very difficult to learn but it is fairly certain the Military Party there were alarmed and used drastic measures to suppress the outbreak. Court Martials were set up and heavy penalties dealt out.

Monday February 11 Germany reports that Peace was concluded with Russia on Saturday at 2 am. Time alone can prove if this is true. I do not think that there is any authority in Russia stable enough to conclude a peace. All there is anarchy and confusion.

Thursday February 14 The Food Controller continues to issue regulations in shoals. Some of them upon the most trivial and useless subjects.

Friday February 15 There has been much raiding along the Western Front the last few days. Airmen are also very busy. Reports from Paris say the clash will not be long delayed.

The Government here has had a bad time. It seems to have quite lost the confidence of the House, but no one wishes to change it when we are so near to a General Election which will almost certainly come in August or September.

Telegrams to-night report that the enemy raided the Dover Flotilla this morning and sank seven small vessels but bolted back to Zeebrugge before they could be brought to action. This Zeebrugge is a real nest of hornets and causes much annoyance to us.

1918 Saturday February 16 Very little news to-day

Sunday February 17 The German Prisoners have not at present arrived here, as the old men inmates of the Union have not been removed. The Authorities at Thrapston have agreed to take them "if they can find food enough". This last sentence will give some idea as to our present conditions. We are getting very short of essential articles. It is generally conceded that the whole country will be put on rations in April or May. Meat at the present is almost the worst article. Butchers here close their shop at mid-day on Monday until Thursday and by Friday night or Saturday mid-day they have quite sold out. A few German Prisoners have arrived at the old Parsonage at Winwick and are doing farm work in that district.

A London raid last night. No letters (London) this morning. There is a moon again so expect the enemy will come.

Monday February 18 The enemy did raid London again last night and also again to-night.

Sunday February 24 There is not much news of fighting except raiding this week. Of this air business there has been a great deal. Each side is endeavouring to get accurate knowledge of the others movements.

DAY BY DAY THROUGH THE GREAT WAR

We are still awaiting the great offensive of the Germans.

Food rationing has been the chief topic this week. We are to be rationed here for Margarine early next month. The system will be the same as that of Sugar Cards and each person will be entitled to 4 oz per week. We are also to be rationed here for Meat by March 25. This system will be similar to the London one. When it comes into operation I will explain it more fully.

Russia is sinking into a terrible state. Germany has again declared war on them and is advancing toward Petrograd. The whole country is in a wretched state.

Sunday March 3 Another week of comparative quiet except on Friday when the Germans attempted to cross the Yser but were driven back.

The chief interest now centres in food. Many prosecutions are taking place for hoarding food and tradesmen are also being prosecuted for charging more than the fixed price. Many kinds of food are getting very difficult to obtain. To-day we have not a pound of cheese of any kind in our warehouse, and very little bacon. Our butcher sent us two pounds of meat yesterday and this will be our total supply of butcher's meat until next Saturday. About a pound per head per week. The Sugar distribution works fairly well so far. Every person gets 8 oz per week but it is very difficult to make it enough. Many people have given up using it in tea.

The men's ward in the Workhouse here was cleared on Tuesday. Fifteen old men have gone temporarily to Thrapston. The army took possession on Wednesday. The Guard arrived on Friday and about 40 German prisoners are expected on Monday.

There are continued talks about peace. I am afraid nothing will come of them at present.

America is not doing as well as we had hoped. Under the strain of war and a terrible winter her railways are in a state of chaos and the food we had hoped to secure is still unshipped. This is adding to our anxieties and it looks as if we should have a tight time during the next 6 months. No 'offal' is being taken out of wheat now when it is ground except 8 per cent of bran, and 10 to 20 percent of barley is being added. In consequence of this our bread is very dark and I cannot say it is at all agreeable. Most butchers shops are closed half the week.

Sunday March 10 Another week of waiting for the promised great battles in France. Much air fighting, on Thursday 18 German machines were destroyed. And on the same day the Germans made a heavy attack near Ypres. They suffered heavily and obtained a very small gain which was quickly wrested from them in a few hours. The same night an air raid took place on London. The night was moonless but it is surmised the airmen were able to see their way by a brilliant display of Aurora. Two machines got over London and killed eleven people and injured 46 others. Many people are rather sceptical about the German offensive this summer. They contend that she will be content to hold up the line and behind that to work her will in other ways. Mean time she seems to be carving up Russia just as she pleases. A treaty lopping off from Russia an area equal to Austria and Germany combined was signed last Sunday. One feels that such a treaty can never stand, but Germany having once acquired these provinces it will be hard to make her return them.

Here we go steadily on. I do not think I am a pessimist but decidedly I do not like the trend of events. Things are at a very low ebb. Food is scarce, and difficult to obtain, and the military outlook is not very hopeful. Every day we are spending six and a half millions in this wasteful way, to say nothing of tens of thousands of lives, and of the end there is no sign. It seems possible that the war may continue for years unless the People of this and every other warring country can get rid of their present rulers and substitute for them men who are inclined to bring the war to an end.

Huge efforts are being made to raise money for carrying on the war by the sale of War Bonds. Last week it was Northamptonshire's turn and £1,500,000 was raised, but what is that, it does not amount to the sum we spend upon war in one day.

Much grass land has been ploughed up this winter and is now being seeded, chiefly with oats. Wheat is looking well this spring, much better than last year. We are now having very dark bread. The flour is wheat ground just as it is (only 5 per cent of the husk being taken out) with the addition of 10 to 20 per cent of barley. The result is we are now getting an almost black bread. After having real white bread I cannot say the change is at all pleasant, but there is less quarrelling about it than I anticipated.

Food for all farm animals is getting very scarce, and what food there is of a decidedly inferior character. It has no fattening qualities and it is most difficult to bring stock to maturity, especially pigs. They grow but do not fatten. In consequence of this dearth of food thousands of immature pigs have been slaughtered, also sows, and as usual our wise men in London who imagine they and they alone know the needs of the country are waking up to the havoc they have caused by their interference and are trying to devise all kinds of silly remedies. They were warned as to what would happen, but were too conceited and ignorant to take advice from people who knew better than they did.

1918 Sunday March 17 Another week of comparative quiet on the Western front. Germany does not appear to relish the prospective attack, although she has now massed 190 divisions in France and Belgium. Some people are saying that it will never come off.

Men are being called up to the colours as fast as they can get them, but the supply of first class men under 40 is very low. Of the 12 men who were before us at the Local Tribunal last Monday evening only two were 'A' men – the residue were quite unfit for the Army.

The German prisoners of war arrived yesterday Saturday at 1.48 and were marched via Station Road and New Road to their barracks, that is the Workhouse, half of which has been placed at the disposal of the military. I did not see them myself, but am told they were quite a mixed lot. Some young, some old, and dejected. They came from Eastcote Camp near to Towcester, and will commence work tomorrow, Monday morning. The guard chiefly old soldiers consists of about 20 men. These and also the prisoners are fed from a central depot at Northampton.

The zeppelins have been over again this week, not in this district but in Yorkshire and Durham. They did not accomplish much. This is the first time they have ventured since last October when they received a tremendous thrashing.

The Volunteer Training Corps of Northamptonshire and other counties were inspected by Lord French at Bedford last Sunday. The Oundle Platoon about 70 strong was picked up by special train about nine and arrived home again at 5.30. Altogether 7,000 men were on parade.

Railway conditions are growing steadily worse and we on this branch line are now threatened with the loss of two more trains during the day. If this is carried out, there will be no train to Northampton between 7 in the morning and 4 in the afternoon, and no train to Peterboro between 9 and 4. For some time past we have only had one goods train each way per day. This causes very great inconvenience.

1918 Monday March 18 Air fighting is increasing in violence at the front in France and Belgium but so far our men are in marked superiority. Reports from both sides also tell of increased gun fire.

The American and English governments appear likely to seize all Dutch shipping to prevent them falling into the hands of Germany. Every nerve is now being strained here and in the States to increase the output of ships. Much blame attaches to the English War cabinet for their mishandling of this affair and yet it is one of our most vital points

Tuesday March 19 Some heavy fighting in Belgium yesterday. Raiding and counter raiding but evidently not the real attack.

An air ship sailed over us to-day. Aeroplanes have become very familiar and scarcely cause any comment but at present air ships are few and far between.

Wednesday March 20 The German prisoners here are all now at work and so far they have won good opinions of those who are employing them.

I saw some going to Barnwell Mills to-day where they are at work spreading artificial manure.

DAY BY DAY THROUGH THE GREAT WAR

Thursday March 21 At last the Great Offensive promised by the Germans on the Western Front has come. Telegraphy at 10 o'clock this morning Haig reports that the enemy attacked on a 50 mile front in enormous strength at 5.30 this morning and that a terrible battle is in progress.

To-night's report says the battle extends from Arras to Cambrai. No mention is made of any attack on the French. These are days of tense anxiety. We all feel that this must be the climax of this awful and bloody war. We recognise that it will take all our strength and men to hold up. God give us the strength to do so.

There was a sharp naval action off Dunkirk early this morning about 4 am. Four German ships were sunk but none of ours.

Friday March 22 Reports to-day indicate the battle yesterday was intense and to-days are of the same description. The enemy are flinging their men in in masses and the carnage is beyond all description. Evidently they hope to break through by sheer weight of numbers.

Saturday March 23 Haig's report this morning is not at all re-assuring. Evidently he is hard pressed at some points. At others he is well holding his own.

An ominous telegram about noon to-day. The enemy have broken through near to St Quentin. Haig says our men are retiring in good order to the second line of trenches. The enemy claim to have captured 25,000 prisoners and 350 guns.

Sunday March 24 A day of brilliant sunshine as indeed every day has been this week. So quiet and calm, and yet we know that within 250 miles of us the greatest battle the world has ever seen is being fought. The suspense of it is dreadful. Scarcely any news except a few short telegrams in the London Sunday Papers. It is said shells are being dropped into Paris from long distance artillery.

Later A telegram posted shortly after seven says the Germans claim to have taken 50,000 prisoners and 600 guns. The British Official telegram at 5 o'clock does not admit this. One wonders what tomorrow's papers will reveal.

1918 Sunday March 31 Owing to business pressure I have been unable to write up this diary since last Sunday. It has been a week of continued bloody battles day and night which have continued without ceasing since last Thursday week and still continue.

A week of constant anxiety and scarcely knowing from hour to hour what would come next, but still at all times believing that eventually we shall hold through. I think I may say that never since August 1914 have we gone through such times as this week and there is a feeling that the pressure in some slight degree has relaxed but that it is still most critical.

The German plan is now perfectly clear. Striking with almost incredible numbers of men and guns they endeavour to separate the English and French Armies, to capture Paris, roll up the British and capture the Channel Ports Calais etc. In this so far they have not succeeded. There seems to be a feeling that this is the supreme hour of the war. It may be the supreme hour but I do not think it is the final hour. I believe it is the turning point. If we flinch and go down now, we shall never pull ourselves up again. We well know this and to-day there is no voice of discord raised. Every man and woman I believe realizes what is at stake and is prepared to do and suffer anything. Our losses are dreadful, we have never been told what they are but they are very very great as we all know. The Germans are equally hard hit. Coming on in their usual close formation they were mowed down like corn but other divisions were thrown into the terrible furnace. My God, what an awful responsibility for the men who were responsible for this. I hope they will be blasted for ever. At any rate this cannot be laid at our door. By a curious coincidence there has been published this week the secret journal of the German Ambassador in London in the year 1912 – 1914. He explicitly declares that England did not want war, that Sir Edward Grey did all in his power to avert it, but that Germany and Germany alone (not Austria) was determined to fight. Well upon these men must be fixed the guilt.

Sunday April 7 Another week of tense existence. There was a comparative lull on the front from Sunday until Thursday but on that day fighting re-commenced with doubled ferocity if that were possible, and the battle line has been swaying ever since. Here a small gain, there a loss, but on the whole no great gain on either side. It is true the enemy is a little nearer to Amiens which at present seems to be their objective. They hope to capture .. a most important railway centre and thus hamper our connection with the French. At present, that is on Friday night, they were about 8 miles away. The casualties are appalling. It is computed the Germans have lost 350,000 men. We are not told what our losses are. I do not believe the Government dare announce them. They are discreetly silent, for they know very well that if the naked facts were put before us, the outcry would be tremendous. Wounded men are arriving in this country by the thousand, one might say tens of thousands. There is a growing feeling that the disaster has been due to much incompetence on the part of some one in high command, indeed one General, Gough, has been suspended, and an inquiry is to take place. (Shutting the stable door after the horse is stolen).

America has behaved exceedingly well. Their Secretary of War is in this country and it has been agreed that American troops instead of waiting to form an army of their own shall at once be brigaded with English and French, and thus help to stiffen the line.

As usual, the Government have lost their head. Directly any reverse comes along they immediately begin to squeal for more men, and this week they intend to rush a Bill through giving them power to call up every man to the age of 50. There is a kind of panic amongst these army men and they appear to be incapable of forming a cool and reasoned judgement. It is obvious that by the time these fresh troops are trained there will [be] a million of Americans over here, if they will find ships to bring them. Ships and food are far more important to us than new levies, who after all will be of very little use. What use is a man of 50 for soldiering. The fact is this country is drained of effective soldiers and America has at least ten millions of men of good military age. This new proposal I think will cause far more distress than any previous step we have had to take. I can certainly see it will mean the break-up of business in every direction. Things are growing steadily worse every day in business and the last straw will break the camel's back.

1918 April 14 Sunday Another week of terrible strain, and anxiety, culminating yesterday in the report the Germans were only 40 miles from Calais and that our communications had been cut and the whole of one of our armies was 'in the air'. There was a little relief last night when it was announced that that the Germans were being held. This new danger is much farther north than the fighting last week and has occurred in an attack which the enemy launched on Tuesday near to Armentieres. Most deadly struggles have been going on ever since. The gravity of the situation is disclosed by a proclamation which Haig issued to his armies on Tuesday in which he told them that we were fighting 'with our backs to the wall' and that no man must yield a foot of ground. These are indeed ominous words and have caused much dismay at home.

In addition to this comes the new Conscription Bill enabling the authorities to call up all men to the age of 50 and in certain counts to 56. The country has been profoundly moved and distressed by this and I have never seen so much gloom and depression since war commenced. For the first time all Clergymen and Ministers are included and they will be called up with the others. Another provision is that all men up to 25 will be called up, no exemption of any kind being allowed; also all men in class A between 18 and 40. This will show what a state we are all in, although I think much of it is panic on the part of the Government. There is a shrewd suspicion that they having made such an awful mess of it are in reality 'riding for a fall'. Probably we who are now alive will never know the real state of the case. In the face of all this there is no recrimination and the nation is keeping its head determined that it will do its part in supporting the men who are so gallantly fighting for us.

Businesses will be closed down in all directions. I myself shall have three men taken which will only leave me with one boy of 14 and there are numberless cases like this..

The Zeppelins raided us again on Friday night. I was sitting reading about 11 o'clock when I heard a terrific explosion which caused the window and doors to 'chatter'. On going out of doors I could hear the Zeppelins but could not see them. They were passing away in a north westerly direction. I went to the police station and reported for duty but was told they had quite enough men warned (my section was not on

DAY BY DAY THROUGH THE GREAT WAR

duty that night) so home to bed as old Pepys said. Personally I did not hear any more of them, but was told in the morning that there were four of them. They went into the west midlands and returned back again about 2.30 a little to the south of us.

The bomb which shook us fell near to Nassington, into a wheat field opposite the Cemetery on the road to Yarwell and made a cavity 15 feet in diameter.

April 21 Sunday Another most critical and depressing week, that is up to Friday. A week of great rainfall (the floods are out) and leaden skies. This combined with critical days in France has depressed us all. Early on in the week under tremendous assaults our men had to fall back in the fighting in the sector around Ypres. It is here that the most severe struggles have taken place during the last 14 days, the enemy having relinquished his onslaught on the Somme towards Amiens, although it is generally accepted that this will be renewed at no distant date. In this Ypres section fierce and bloody battles have occurred every and all day and all night without ceasing. They seem to have culminated in a tremendous struggle at Givenchy on Thursday when the enemy was definitely held and received a bad mauling, but mark this – we do not deceive ourselves we know that the danger is not past and that any moment may bring the tidings of renewed battles.

The Military service Bill is now law and the first step will be to grade all men between 40 and 50 in medical class. No man will be called up until he has been medically classified, probably those between 40 and 46 will first be called. What the consequence will be it is impossible to say. These are the men who have been generally relied on to carry on the business of the country more especially since the younger men have been called up.

Tribunals as we know them at present are to be abolished. In future they will be nominated by the Government. This is a most retrograde step as the Tribunals on the whole have worked well and have made a buffer between the Army and Civilian life. This has not at all satisfied the Government and they want these independent bodies replaced by nominees of their own. There is deep resentment at this. There is not the least doubt that the present Government would be ejected from office to-morrow if it were not for the dangerous and difficult fix we are in. They promised so much when they assumed power and candidly no set of men ever received such consideration and support, and yet I think few have ever made such disastrous mistakes. To-day they are trying to conscript Ireland and she retaliates this week by issuing what is really a declaration of war. Men are being drafted into Ireland by the tens of thousands in order to hold them down. If Home Rule had been put into effect when it was passed, Ireland by this time would have been contented and would have passed conscription for herself.

This week we have had our first real experience of rationing (apart from Sugar). Meat of <u>all kinds</u> is now rationed, as is butter and margarine. At present each person is entitled to 1/3d worth of Butcher's Meat and about 4 ounces of Bacon without bone and 5 ounces with. 4oz of Butter or Margarine is the ration. Probably Tea and Cheese will be rationed next and preparations are being made to ration Bread.

1918 Sunday April 28 This week all the Empire has been ringing with the deeds of the Navy. Zeebrugge and Ostend since they were captured by the Germans have been formed into bases for their submarines and as such have proved to be a great annoyance and danger to us. On Monday night an expedition of our Navy (all men who had volunteered for this service) raided these places. It was a most desperate enterprise, but nevertheless completely successful, especially at Zeebrugge. A most bloody fight lasted for nearly 90 minutes. This was carried out by a storming party who had landed on the Mole. As the fight was going on three obsolete cruisers, filled with cement, were sunk at the entrance of Bruges canal, completely blocking it. The Germans seem to have been quite taken by surprise and have [been] trying to explain away their defeat but without any success. It was a most brilliant [feat] and one worthy of the old Nelson days.

Furious fighting still continues in France especially opposite Amiens where on Thursday we scored a complete success over the Germans. The County regiment (Northants) were quite in the thick of the fighting there.

On Friday the enemy had their turn and captured Mount Kemmel near to Ypres. This was held by the French who fought to the last man. Yesterday affairs were quieter but I do not expect they will remain so for long.

THE DIARY OF JOHN COLEMAN BINDER

Increased taxation was unfolded by the Chancellor in his Budget speech on Tuesday. Letters increased from 1d to 1½d, income tax 6/- in the £. Tobacco raised to 8d. Sugar 7d. Loaf sugar 7 ½ d and a tax on luxuries. A committee will be set up to decide what these are. On the whole the taxation has been received without much grumbling. Nearly 900 millions was raised by taxes last year, and this year it will be more.

Sunday May 5 Following his advantage on Friday the enemy tried on Monday to break through towards Ypres and without doubt was badly mauled and defeated. He did not gain a foot of ground and is said to have lost heavily. Since then there has been quite a lull, except for our fighting.

The Army are calling up men now with all speed. The 40-50 men have not yet been summoned but a Proclamation is daily expected summoning them to the Colours.

This week we are only to receive 10d worth of Butchers Meat, but we shall get an increase of bacon. Great quantities of this have arrived and each person can now buy if they wish about 1lb each per week. This probably will continue for a month and will then be reduced. In the country districts there is now a lot of farmer's butter and margarine is also abundant. Bread is very indifferent now; quite dark brown, not exactly black. I think this bread is the thing I miss most. After having been accustomed to white bread I do not find the present bread at all palatable. I hope it will be better before long as the millers are now receiving a fair quantity of imported white flour to mix with their own and this should make it much better.

If we can rely on reports from Austria, the storm clouds seem to be gathering there and ominous events are foreshadowed. One cannot doubt that Austria is feeling the strain very severely and would be glad to make peace.

1918 Sunday May 12 A good deal of severe fighting this week especially in the air but no really great battles. The enemy are said to be planning another big move. This is according to Lloyd George who seemed to me to be in a very hysterical mood in the House on Thursday night.

Large numbers of wounded continue to arrive in the country and it is very probable that much larger accommodation will have to be provided for them. This week the Bishop's Palace at Peterborough has been inspected with a view to turning it into a Hospital and it is most probable it will be accepted.

The Military Service Act passed a few weeks since is now being put into operation. Yesterday a proclamation was posted, calling up men of 44 to 46. All these men will be medically examined and will also have a right of appeal to a Tribunal. This latter much to the annoyance of the Military who had hoped to scoop up the whole lot without any such safeguard, but the country would not stand it and the Army was compelled to give way. There are about 100 men in Oundle who are affected by this Act. That is men of 40 to 51. I imagine we shall have some difficult work when their appeals come before the Tribunal.

About midnight on Thursday the Navy made another dash at Ostend and succeeded in sinking the old 'Vindictor' full of concrete near to the harbour entrance. According to all accounts although the entrance has been made very difficult it has not been quite blocked. There was a good deal of 'gunning' but it was not such a bloody affair as Zeebrugge. We seem gradually to be getting the best of the submarine. This blocking of Ostend and Zeebrugge and the mining of a great part of the North Sea has made their work very difficult. Also the Allies have nearly reached the goal at which they have so long aimed. That is to build as much new tonnage as the enemy sinks, and the April returns show the building and sinking now closely approximate.

May 19 Sunday Another week has gone by and at present the battles in the big way have not been renewed, but signs are not wanting that the lull will not last much longer.

There have been some remarkable debates in the House on a letter which the Austrian Emperor sent 12 months since to the French President containing an offer of Peace terms. The British Government say it was a trap and offered no adequate basis for negotiations. After reading the whole affair I thoroughly disagree and contend that the whole business was shockingly mismanaged by the Allies. The fact is this old M. Clemenceau the French Premier is a regular old fire-eater and is determined to force us to fight for driving back the Germans entirely across the Rhine to the position they were in 1814. This is clearly impossible and the sooner he is disabused of this notion the better it will be. If I am any judge of the people of this country I do not think they are going to slaughter all the best of their men for a preposterous idea like that. If France wants this restitution of territory let her fight for it herself. <u>That</u> is not [the] idea with which we went into the war, and if we are overridden by France this bloody and devastating war may last for years. We have it now in the Government's own admission that we lost 50,000 prisoners in the terrible battles in March – April when there is no doubt we were within an ace of a most awful disaster. Where the blame lies cannot be said just now but it is a significant fact that no inquiry has ever been made and that although General Gough the commander of the 5th Army has been superseded he is still walking about London a free man.

1918 Sunday May 26 A very quiet week, scarcely any fighting at all. Various rumours are afloat as to the reasons why the Germans are delaying the renewal of their offensive, such as peace missions etc.etc. but I think all these may be dismissed, and it is fairly certain they will have another try when it suits their purpose. In the meantime America is hurrying over troops and by the end of this week will have half a million men in France, but I am afraid many of them are not very seasoned men.

Last Sunday night London had a bad air raid, nearly 250 killed and wounded and on Wednesday the enemy with the ferocity of hell hounds attacked a group of hospitals behind our lines, and bombed them for some time. No deed I think has caused more horror in this country, and it has caused us all to harden our hearts against these fiends.

There has been no beef in the town this week, as there were no bullocks at market. The authorities sent down some frozen sides which had been <u>five years</u> in cold storage. The butchers refused to have anything to do with these, and at once returned them. Mutton is plentiful and there is any amount of bacon, chiefly American.

Harvest prospects are not so good as they were two months ago. Wire-worm has made terrible havoc with crops on the newly ploughed pasture land, and has almost ruined them. Of course it is too late now to sow again with corn and other catch crops must be used.

June 2 Sunday The quiet interval came to an end last Monday morning at 3.30 when the enemy attacked with tremendous force between Soissons and Rheims and we have had a bloody and continuous battle day and night ever since and one that has gone to a large extent against us. By the help of great forces the enemy has caused our lines (which are still intact) to fall back to the Marne so that to-day we are as in 1914. This time it is the French who were not able to stem the torrent and our men were compelled to keep in line with them. It appears we had four divisions in this part defending Rheims. This was not generally known in this country until the battle had been in progress a day or two. It was rumoured late on Friday that the enemy had taken Rheims but there is no confirmation of this. The Germans are now about 47 miles from Paris but the French seem confident that they cannot get much further. Opinion here is not so sure. At any rate it has been a week of great and deep anxiety. This morning the prospect is slightly better. Soissons which had fallen into the enemies' hands has been re-captured after terrible fight. Indeed all the fighting through the week has been of a most appalling description. Real hand-to-hand business. It seems probable that we have lost about 30,000 prisoners and about 300 guns. It is difficult to ascertain what really is the view the country takes of these repeated reverses. The military censorship over all the newspapers is exceedingly strict, and there is a deep suspicion that we are being 'humbugged' by the Government. Only a week since we had Lloyd George shouting at Edinburgh that all was well and yet within seven days we are back again on the Marne. To say the least of it the country is becoming very sceptical about these continued shoutings. It is a foregone conclusion that we shall see the recruiting conscription exercised with ruthless severity again in this county. Yesterday it was announced that the Army or the national Service under which name they now try to disguise themselves intend to take 36,000 men from the farms before June 11. Each county will have to furnish its share and there is no doubt other industries will have the same call made upon them. The men in civil life are rapidly decreasing. Each week sees a considerable diminution in their numbers. Boys in the secondary schools immediately they reach 18 receive their calling up notices and have to leave and join the army. The pressure is becoming almost unbearable. Our great reliance at this moment is in America, whose reserve of manpower is enormous and is being mobilised as fast as possible but it will scarcely be available to a large extent this year, meantime we shall have to bear the brunt. Much of our present distress has been caused by the withdrawal of Russia and I say it without fear of contradiction that had the Russians been handled by the Government of this country with more sympathy and tact they would have still been an effective fighting force, and we should not have been in our present difficulties. But no. The Russian revolution has always been hated by the aristocracy of this country and is hated still.

1918 June 9 A very mixed week. There was great and terrible fighting and slaughter until Tuesday when the enemy were again definitely held. After an unsuccessful attempt to cross the Marne they swung round and headed for Paris, but Foch having brought up his reserves was able to stem the torrent and there has only been minor affairs since. We are clearly aware that this calm will not continue long and it is quite possible the next thrust may carry Paris. These are indeed troublous and trying times. Meantime America is hurrying men and arms across. Americans early this week were engaged very sharply on the Marne and according to all accounts gave a very good account of themselves. America herself has had a sharp touch of War. Last Sunday German U-boats appeared off the American coast and sunk about 18,000 tons of shipping, and caused the loss of about 350 lives.

Meantime we here in England are feeling more and more the stress of war, especially now these men of 42 – 50 are being called up. To-morrow evening we have a Tribunal Meeting when several men of this class, mostly owners of businesses are appealing for exemption. A most disagreeable and invidious task, to sit in judgment upon ones fellow townsmen. I shall do my best to give such men as these what exemption I possibly can.

The aviators are much in evidence just now with us. About ten days since one crashed down near to the Union Chapel, and yesterday another who was starting from the School Playing Fields failed to gather way and after narrowly escaping collision with the houses on the Glapthorne Road came down crash in the gardens at the back of the houses in Rock Road. Fortunately in neither case were the pilots killed although they both had narrow escapes. Both of them were old Oundle School Boys.

This week being unable to find men to mould up potatoes for me in the Garden, I have been employing two German prisoners from the Depot at the Workhouse. They started at 7 a.m. each morning and worked until 4 p.m. with only about 15 minutes for dinner. Their work for the day was then finished and they returned to the Depot. They worked very well and I was quite satisfied with what they did. They were in charge of one soldier (English) as guard and I paid [ ] per day each for them. Payment being made to the County Agricultural War Committee. There are 40 of these prisoners now here and one may see them going to work in groups each morning about 7 a.m. They do no work on Sundays. It is quite impossible to get any labour apart from these prisoners.

Sunday June 16 Another week or at least four days of hot fighting. On Monday morning the Germans again made a determined attack down the valley of the Oise towards Paris. The battle continued until Thursday night. Very little advance was made on either side but a frightful lot of men were killed on both sides. The English were not so much concerned in this affair as the French were holding this sector. Yesterday and to-day so far things are quieter but we know it will not continue long.

The fit men (or those who are graded as fit) between 40 and 50 are now being called up rapidly and many have left this week. Yesterday a Proclamation was posted warning men up to 51. This is as far as the Army can go at present until they receive fresh powers from Parliament. I quite expect they will ask for these shortly, and will call up men to 55. My turn will then come as I am now 55.

I think we are now at the most critical period of the war and much must depend upon what occurs during the next few weeks say until the end of August. If we can hold the enemy until then we may see some relief, but it is a terribly anxious time. This week my last and sixth man has to join up and we have had to substitute boys and a woman for them. We have only one man left. He is 37 years old and Grade 2. If he is called up part of the business must certainly be closed down as it is utterly impossible to obtain further help.

We continue to see a good many Americans. They are dressed in Khaki but wear quite a distinctive hat. A kind of soft 'Billy Cock' pinched in on four sides. A sort of typical 'Uncle Sam' affair. Their clothes seem of very good quality and they are well set robust men. There are quite a lot of them at the aerodrome at Wittering and Easton and it is quite a cosmopolitan sort of affair there, Colonials of all kinds, Americans, Japs, Chinese, Portuguese and Indians. The place has grown tremendously and aircraft are so common with us now that they cause little or no comment.

We are having a very dry summer, not very hot. Crops are fairly good, except fruit and this except a few soft fruits, currants etc. is a distribution failure. Jam it is certain will be very very scarce next winter, and already we are told that it will be rationed.

On Wednesday Mr Brassey of Apethorpe MP for this division of Northants announced that he had given 913 acres of land in the parishes of Glapthorne, Southwick and Apethorpe to the Government for the purpose of making a forest. I do not think it will be planted at present unless German prisoners are employed in the work as labour is impossible to get.

1918 June 23 Sunday Attention this week has been turned to the Italian front where the Austrians have made a tremendous attack upon the allied lines but have gained very little. In fact it may be written down as a failure. Austria is in a bad way and I do not think would have made this attack unless Germany had compelled her to do so. Events seem to be moving to a crisis in Austria, chiefly caused by lack of food and by internal troubles. If the Allies handle Austria rightly I think it might be possible to detach her from Germany. It is quite certain she is sick of the war and would be heartily glad to be out of it.

The Germans made a determined effort on Monday evening to capture Rheims but were unable to do so.

The Northants Agricultural War Committee have failed or at least have had the very greatest difficulty in finding their quota of 500 men from the farms to help make up the 35,000 called up by the Army. There was a conference in London on Friday between the Army, the Board of Agriculture and the War Agricultural Committees but it failed most decidedly to reach any agreement and at present there is a deadlock. The fact is our manpower is nearly drained, and if many more men are taken the most serious consequences must ensue.

Sunday June 30 The Austrians have suffered a severe defeat and are back again across the Plave. The Italians mauled them very badly. They are said to have lost 180,000 killed, wounded and prisoners, so ends at any rate for a time the much vaunted Austrian offensive. The Italians have avenged their disasters of last autumn.

Meantime events continue very quiet on [the] Western front. Germany does not seem inclined to renew the battle for the moment although Lloyd George in the House on Monday said that tremendous events were likely to occur in a few hours on the Western front. The German Secretary of Foreign Affairs has raised a furious storm in Germany this week by declaring some of the truth. He said Germany could not hope to win a decisive victory and much more of the same kind.

Some of the older men i.e. above 45 are now being given an opportunity of going to land work instead of joining up. That is if they make application before July 6. We are having very dry weather and field and garden produce is suffering very much. The fruit crop is practically a failure. Gooseberries for the less than 5lb quantities are retailed up to 8d per lb. Strawberries have been taken by the Government from the large growers for making jam. No person is allowed to sell them except on Saturday and then not before 8 am, the retail price on that day is 9d per lb.

1918 Sunday July 7 A very very quiet week. Except that on Thursday the Australians and Americans made a smart attack and captured about 1500 prisoners. This kind of thing worries the enemy who at present are very quiet. Various reasons are adduced for this lull, but the one generally accepted is that the Austrian defeat has upset their plans very much.

America continues to make much progress in her war preparations and to-day it is announced that she has now over a million men in France. These thanks to our own and her navy have been brought across with only the loss of about 200 men. The enemy must rave when he considers how impotent he is to prevent this.

THE DIARY OF JOHN COLEMAN BINDER

Meantime the pressure on England to secure recruits is extreme. There has been a regular battle between the Army and the Agricultural people, and it was bluntly admitted in the House on Thursday that the Army were to have their way and that in consequence of this the harvest might be in serious danger. What a gamble! We well know that the waste of man power in the Army is almost beyond belief. One and sometimes two servants for every officer and yet here they are drawing away skilled workers from the fields to carry on this wicked waste. During a short railway journey this week I had never seen so little labour at work in the fields.

The new system of rationing comes into operation next Sunday. Every person will have a small book containing coupons for Meat, Bacon, Sugar, Lard and Tea. It involves an enormous amount of labour and I myself in a small way of business took over 700 coupons last week for Bacon alone. This coupon business acts as a check on the consumer but I can say that there is very little check on the retailer, it is quite easy to evade the restrictions which the authorities think they are imposing.

July 14 A very quiet week. Both Germans and English are down with influenza which greatly retards them. This is all to our good as it gives more time for the Americans * * *

Here entries in this book end abruptly, even though there are many more pages left.

END OF VOLUME EIGHT

DAY BY DAY THROUGH THE GREAT WAR
Volume Nine
August 4 - November 12 1918

1918 Sunday August 4   It is more than three weeks since I was able to write some short notes in this diary, but tremendous events have taken place during this time. About July 16 the Germans made a great attack on the front of Soissons - Rheims. They were held on the wings but succeeded in penetrating in the centre, and came on down to the Marne which they crossed in somewhat restricted numbers and penetrated almost to Elsernay. Their object was to reach Paris, but so sure were they of the success of this offensive and despising our Allies and ourselves they left their flanks without much protection. Taking advantage of this General Foch ordered a counter attack and striking from Soissons to Chateau Thierry severely defeated them. The troops principally employed on that side were French and Americans. On the opposite side of the salient the British and French and Italians were fighting. The Germans were as it were caught in a vice which began to close on them. They soon began to retreat and their forces across the Marne, after being in what they described as 'Hell' for four days, recrossed the Marne under terrible gunfire. Most fierce and bloody fighting has continued almost every day since. The Germans are being driven back but are putting up a good fight. They are able to withdraw most of their heavy guns (about 500 have ben taken) and according as times go have not lost a great number of prisoners probably about 30,000. They have not met a disaster but have suffered a very severe defeat.

In a great many well-informed quarters this defeat is looked upon as the turning and decisive event of the war. Germany has had her chance this summer and that chance is not likely to occur again. America is now pouring in troops at the rate of 250,000 to 300,000 per month and soon will have two millions of men this side of the water. These are not war weary men, but the very pick of the American nation. Men of 21 to 30 and as such capable of great things. We have been through a very tight place, and it is only by God's help that we are through it. It is quite obvious that the men we are now sending are not a patch on the men two years ago. They are boys of 18 and men of 40, and as such are not capable of such exertions as the 20 & 30 men.

To-day comes the news that the enemy are still falling back and that the French and British are in Soissons. Where the enemy will elect to stand remains to be proved. He has done an immense amount of destruction in his retreat. Burned and destroyed villages and hacked everything to pieces he possibly could, but has also had to abandon enormous quantities of his own supplies ammunition etc.

To-day is the commencement of the 5th year of this awful war, and a special service of Intercession is being held throughout the whole Empire for Peace and Victory. I can see no peace in sight yet. Germany I think will fight until she is beaten and certainly she is not that yet. America will be the deciding factor unless Russia is pulled together again. Awful chaos still rules there. The ex-Czar murdered by --, the German Ambassador assassinated in Petersburg, and now another German Governor in the Ukraine, blown to pieces by the Russians.

These events pass so quickly that one is almost bewildered by them.

1918 Sunday August 10th Great events have taken place this week. The battle on the Southern Front seemed practically to have died down by Tuesday. The Germans received a very nasty blow and lost nearly 30,000 prisoners besides being driven back a long distance. Suddenly on Thursday morning at daybreak the English and French on the Western front attacked the enemy. Evidently he was completely taken by surprise and had no idea of what was about to take place. Both French and English went rapidly forward on a twenty-mile front killing a tremendous lot of the enemy and capturing up to last night 24,000 prisoners and over 300 guns. This mornings telegrams say the advance still continues. This is the second disastrous defeat the enemy have suffered within three weeks, and in consequence of it they are beginning to talk in a very different way. On the other hand we are correspondingly elated and now think to say the least of it that we have turned the corner. It is still recognised that we may still have a long and weary road to travel before the end comes, but humanly speaking it seems victory is sure. How long it will be before the German people see that the game is up we cannot say. America continues to pour in men arms and munitions and it is estimated by October will have two millions of men over here and another million under training in the States.

Strong efforts are being made by all the Allies to pull Russia together, and this week our allied force has landed at Archangel and also at Vladivostock to form a nucleus for the Russians to gather to. Germany is getting alarmed and sees that eventually Russia may again become a fighting factor in the war.

At home here we continue plodding on our way. Harvest is now in full swing. Crops are excellent and generally above the average. Very little hand labour will be required as there is scarcely any 'laid' corn. The weather so far is very fine and we are looking forward to a real good harvest. The only difficulty will be labour. The Government have skimmed the land almost to the last man that could be got but now this week have had to recognise that very few more men can be taken if we are to have the crops gathered in.

There is a good deal of anxiety about coal for the coming winter. At the present moment it is almost impossible to buy coal for domestic purposes in any quantity. Miners have been taken from the pits in ever increasing numbers. The Allied countries are all clamouring for us to send them coal, and there is an enormous demand for all purposes in this country. Altogether the outlook is decidedly disquieting in this direction.

1918 August 18 Sunday Another week of good fortune for us. A week of severe and ghastly fighting, but it has gone in our favour and against the enemy. The advance east of Amiens has slackened down but it still continues. Germany and German newspapers have been compelled to admit they have been badly knocked about and there appears to be very little danger of their attempting a big offensive again this year. Nearly 50,000 prisoners have been taken and these are now pouring into England. The German army and navy people are beginning to squabble. The army says the navy ought to have stopped the Americans coming and the navy says the army ought to have beaten them when they did come.

It is quite on the cards that the German Navy may have to revise its tactics. They thought the submarine would bring us down, but it is now generally conceded that this submarine is a nuisance which causes us much loss, but it is beyond its power to starve us out. Consequently it is possible the German army men may demand that their navy shall initiate a more vigorous policy and come out to attack. The general public seem to have lost all fear of the Germans and this year the East Coast towns are all crowded with visitors. This has not taken place since 1914.

We have had a glorious week of real harvest weather. No rain but not too hot and harvesting is going on most favourably. Wheat is easily the best crop of the year. All crops stand up well and easily cut by self-binders. Some farmers are using petrol motors drawing two reapers which of course do an enormous amount of labour compared with the horse drawn machines. German prisoners are being largely employed. I see them go out to work each morning about seven and return at five, only about half an hour at midday. No Sunday work is being done. These prisoners look extremely well and evidently are not overworked. They are also well fed, quite as well as we are.

Fruit continues to be very scarce. Plums are being sold locally from 1/- to 2/- per pound. Apples are also very dear. Pears are conspicuous by their absence.

1918 August 25 Sunday The Allies have been hammering the enemy all the week. First at one Place then at another, giving him no rest and causing him in every instance to fall back. The whole western front is now in a blaze with fighting, that is except the Belgian part. The initiative has clearly passed into our hands and Fritz is compelled to do very much as we want him. It is surmised he will fall back to his old positions of last winter and elect to make a stand there, but the Allies may have something to say to this. There are still two months in which operations are feasible if the weather continues, and if events develop during the next two months as they have done since the middle of July, vast changes may take place. However I cannot see Germany beaten this summer much as I desire it. Much will have to happen before Peace is possible. There can be no Peace with the German High Command as it now is. Much as we all want it, it is clearly recognised by all (except a small Peace at any price party) that to have peace under present conditions would simply be laying the foundations for another war at no distant date.

There can be no cessation of war until Germany either gives up or is forced to give up Belgium without any reservation whatever. I believe this to be the opinion of nearly every person in this country. There are also many other awkward questions that will come along, such as Alsace- Lorraine also the German Colonies which have passed into our hands. Our own people abroad seem determined that these colonies shall never be handed back to Germany What will be done time alone can prove.

Harvest has made amazing progress this week. Nearly all the grain is cut and a considerable breadth has been carted. Wheat is a magnificent crop, but I am afraid we shall still have to have it mixed with barley for bread. The bread is not bad, but one does long for the white bread of pre-war days. Jam is to be rationed out to the civilians this year. The allowance will probably be 4oz per head per week. Syrup or treacle is also to be rationed.

The anxiety about coal has not diminished this week. Probably the railway trains will be very much reduced in number in October. Travel is very uncomfortable even now. Trains are not numerous and they are simply crowded with passengers. If you go on the main trunk lines it is quite possible you may have to stand for an hour or two if you are giong any distance, as there is not nearly sufficient accommodation. If the number of trains is much reduced, railway travelling must become almost unbearable.

Sunday September 1 A week of amazing progress on the battle lines. Germans retreating after hot fighting at some points and without much resistance at others. Speculation is rife as to their intentions. Where they intend to make a real stand. At any rate they are falling and being driven back day by day now. The latest news from the front says that even in Belgium they are giving way and that Mount Kemmel, a position which it cost the enemy thousands of lives to gain has now been wrested from him at a comparatively small cost. Signs are not wanting that the enemy is feeling the strain, and as usual he is beginning to talk a great deal about Peace. We have heard of this kind of thing before. When things go badly he usually cries out and says that Peace is good etc. etc. but we have learned to discount all this.

We have now about 100 (hundred) German prisoners in the neighbourhood. Sixty are housed at the Union. Twenty at Elton and twenty at Winwick and twenty move about in one gang to [various] centres as they are wanted. They appear to be very well contented with their lot, and may be seen going to and from their work accompanied only by a farm hand, sometimes a boy.

Farmers have finished harvest in some cases and have already commenced ploughing again. Motor tractors are being much used, but are somewhat dangerous especially the American ones. Last Monday Mr Hankins of Biggin Grange was ploughing with one when it caught in some hard ground, turned a complete somersault and killed him instantly. There is not sufficient weight on the front wheels in fact they are very light altogether for this heavy land.

Great efforts are being made to collect the blackberry crop and the price has been fixed at 3d per lb to the pickers. Nearly all of the crop is to be requisitioned for Jam.

It is estimated that since General Foch assumed the offensive on July 15-16 the Allies have taken nearly 200,000 prisoners.

1918 Sunday September 8 Another wonderful week. Hard and terrible fighting it is true, but forward forward without a real check. On Monday came a most wonderful victory. Haig's men broke right through the German lines not unexpectedly but [at] a point the enemy were prepared for them, having no less than eight men to each yard of line. General Horne [?] of East Haddon, a Northants man, was in command and a real defeat was inflicted on the Germans. Ten Thousand prisoners were captured and the enemy's line was turned, since then he has been retreating day after day, and is now back again on his original ground from whence he made his great push in March. Where he will try to stand is not yet seen. This will rest as much as with the Allies as with himself. He is being hustled day by day. To-day is the English the next day the French and then again the Americans, but these have not taken such a prominent part lately, as their Armies are now being formed on their own, and in command of their own officers. Where Foch will determine they shall strike remains to be seen, but it is evident the enemy is dreading their blow. Signs are

THE DIARY OF JOHN COLEMAN BINDER

not wanting that the truth is beginning to dawn even in Germany, and they are coming to recognise facts. Here in this country there is no great rejoicing. We are thankful for the great success of the last month, but we are all aware that it has been bought at a great loss of life, and all are longing for the time when the end shall come. This does not mean that our purpose is less resolute than it has ever been. I think England's determination to see this thing through to the end is greater than ever it was. America continues to pour in men day after day, scarcely a day passes but several ships arrive at Liverpool (in spite of all the German submarines) laden with American soldiers. Some of them finish their training in England, others are taken across to the Channel the same day. Many of their airmen come to Kettering and Easton for training. These aerodromes are really awful places. On an average there are eight or nine men killed every week there through accidents.

We have had a real break in the weather and little corn has been carted since Tuesday. Wednesday and Thursday were real wet days, and nearly 1¼ inches of rain fell. This was very welcome as the land was really parched, and the pastures and roots were very badly in need of it, but we should now be glad to see a fortnight's fine weather, so that harvest could be finished. Friends coming up from Lowestoft via Ely tell me that there are hundreds of acres still to cart in the Fens.

Advertisements or notices are appearing every day in all the chief newspapers warning the public to economise fuel. These are inserted by the Government and they are trying to justify themselves in the eyes of the people for their senseless proceeding in denuding the pits of labour. They contend that it was necessary in view of the German onslaught in March but this is traversed by men who are able to judge, who say that we had ample men to meet all emergencies. One can only hope that it may not be a severe winter.

Sunday September 15 We are still hammering the Germans although now that they are back again on the line of march they are making a stiffer fight. Events up to Thursday were slow, but on that morning at daybreak the Americans who are now a separate army

(but under the supreme command of Foch as all the Armies are in France) struck the Germans at St Mihul. There has been a most pronounced bulge or salient as it is called for over two years. The Americans wiped it out by attacking on two sides and captured nearly 20,000 prisoners. The French again attacked at dawn yesterday but up to to-day not much news has come through.

Terrible news continues to arrive from Russia. The reports are very brief and difficult to estimate at their real worth. Petrograd appears to be in flames and civil war accompanied by thousands of executions is raging. A sensational report to-day says the ex-Empress and her children are murdered but this is not confirmed.

We had had a most stormy week and much rain has fallen , delaying completion of the harvest.

Tonight a telegram announces that Austria is asking for Peace.

1918 Sunday September 22 The chief event apart from continued and heavy fighting has been the Austrian Peace proposal. The terms she proposes backed by Germany are quite unacceptable, so much so that America rejected them in twenty minutes. I think there can be no Peace until the enemy is defeated, It is a fight to a finish this time. We cannot make peace whilst the Huns do such wretched deeds as they do. Last Sunday they torpedoed without warning the outward bound South African liner the "Galway Castle" conveying about 1000 people to Africa, principally women and children. One hundred and 24 were drowned and it was only by the splendid work that all did not share this fate. This is the kind of thing that makes us determined to carry on the war until Germany goes under.

Americans continue to arrive in continually increasing numbers. This week they had a Registration day in America and registered over 13 Millions of men capable of bearing arms. These will be called up as required. Nearly all men who are really fit in England are soldiers or are doing work in some way. Since America is sending such vast numbers, the strain here has been relaxed and easier conditions prevail. A new list of men in protected trades has been issued this week and has modified the calling -up notices very much. Of course all boys who reach the age of 18 still have to join the army at once.

DAY BY DAY THROUGH THE GREAT WAR

We find it very difficult to get coal and at present I have not been able to secure more than a quarter of our usual winter supply.

Yesterday news arrived that fighting had re-commenced in Palestine and that Allenby had given the Turks a severe defeat. Operations have also taken place on the Salonica front this week, while the French and Serbians have been whacking the Bulgarians. These minor operations do not count much . The real decisive place is in France.

Sunday September 29 Events have moved during this week with dramatic swiftness. Allenby's victory over the Turks has been complete and has completely cleared the Turks out of Palestine after centuries of bloody misrule. The whole affair was exceedingly well planned and carried out. After the infantry had broken through the English, Australian and Indian cavalry took up the running and cut off the enemies' retreat, 50,000 prisoners, enormous stores and 300 guns were taken. To-day thanks are being offered in all Churches for the deliverance of the Holy Land from the rule of the Turk.

On the Salonica front the Allies have completely routed the Bulgarians, who are in full retreat, so great has been the Allied success that it has quite demoralized the Bulgarians and on Friday afternoon the news came that they had asked for an Armistice. The Germans are furious and are uttering all manner of threats against them for doing this. Up to a late hour last night no armistice had been granted and furious fighting was still going on.

In France also the enemy have been very badly knocked about both by our own men and the Americans. Yesterday morning we were close to Cambrai and the Americans were advancing from the South in the Argonne.

I think this is really the best week we have had since war began and it gives one hope that the war has to some extent been shortened, but we do not think the end is yet.

At Home events have not been so satisfactory. There is much trouble with Labour and there is much unrest. A good deal I quite believe is engineered by German gold.

Sunday October 6 Another week of tremendous events. Such happenings as nobody dreamed of during the dark days of March and April.

On Monday Bulgaria capitulated without any reservations. An armistice was signed as she is now quite out of the war and with her go Germany's hopes of a great Middle Europe empire. Turkey is also confidently hoped to be ready to give in as she is now cut off from communication with Germany except by the Black Sea. Austria it is also known is only waiting her opportunity to throw up the sponge. These are great and tremendous changes but events of far greater import are happening in France. Germany is being beaten there. Of this there can be no doubt. She has met defeat daily there during this week. Some awful and bloody fighting has taken place there during this week, especially by our own men at Cambrai on Wednesday but she has had decidedly the worst of it, and what is more, knows it. Her armies are withdrawing or preparing to withdraw in all directions. They have already abandoned Lens, and yesterday's report says they were preparing to leave Ostend and Zeebrugge. In fact they are being out-generalled and out-manoeuvred. In some places they are still fighting with the utmost fierceness and doubtless will continue to do so as the German Higher Command is fighting for its life. When will the end come? Not yet I think, but many think differently and say it will be all over by Christmas. Please God it may. One is so stunned by these tremendous events that are occurring daily that we cannot realize them. No sooner is one battle over than another begins. In fact it is one long bloody fight. We are all glad and thankful that events have taken this turn, but whoever reads this do not imagine that there is any shouting of 'Victory' or other signs of losing our heads. We are thankful and truly thankful but also remember at what a tremendous sacrifice and cost these victories are being won, and can only hope that the generations which come after us may be able to realize what we have had to go through.

What will the end be. One cannot say. There are signs that the War may before it ends break up the German Empire and leave the Kaiser King of Prussia only even if he retains that. Kings have an awkward knack of tumbling off their thrones in these days. One has done so this week. (Ferdinand of Bulgaria).

THE DIARY OF JOHN COLEMAN BINDER

He and Constantine of Greece are two of the greatest rascals living. Both ought to [be] shot out of hand. Mean treacherous scoundrels both of them.

A telegram this afternoon says that on Friday evening the new German Chancellor sent a note to President Wilson asking him to arrange an Armistice so that Peace terms might be discussed. Naturally there is much excitement all through England, but no-one seems very enthusiastic about Peace. Wilson will certainly consult all the Allies and then return his answer. What will it be.

We hear to-day of a terrific battle near to Cambrai in which our own men are the chief actors.

1918 Monday October 7 Yesterday was a most smashing defeat for the Germans. The British Army drove them back after a terrible battle. They were completely defeated and we captured 12,000 prisoners and 300 Guns. Germany may well want Peace. It is obvious she cannot stand many blows like this. Reports coming through neutral countries say that Berlin was much excited when they heard that their Chancellor had asked for an Armistice. I think that at last the truth is beginning to dawn even upon their thick skulls, and they are beginning to realize that the end cannot be far off. Up to to-night Wilson's reply to their request has not been published. My impressions of yesterday are confirmed to-day. No one is very eager for Peace at this moment unless the enemy quite throws up the sponge. We all feel (except a few extraordinary people) that we have gone too far to allow affairs to settle down quite so easily, and that unless Germany surrenders, fighting will continue until she does. Meantime as her Armies retreat they are doing most abominable deeds. Burning ravaging destroying in every possible way. This kind of thing done in cold blood is only hardening our hearts and the feeling is most bitter against her.

Tuesday October 8 Wilson's reply to-day. Very simple, decisive and clear. He asks Max. Do you speak for the German People, or only for your own Ruling Caste. In the latter case I cannot listen and secondly, before we can even mention an armistice you and your allies must clear out of all invaded territories (that is France Belgium, Serbia, Montenegro, Russia and Albania and Italy). And then we will begin to talk about an Armistice as a preliminary to a discussion of Peace. Until you go all of you bag and baggage we shall fight you without mercy. This is plain straight talking and as such commands the assent of us all.

Meantime our armies are acting instead of speaking and the whole front from the Belgian coast to Verdun is literally alive with fighting. Everywhere the enemy is being hammered and driven losing thousands of prisoners and guns.

1918 Wednesday October 9 Wilson's Note was handed to the Swiss Ambassador at Washington yesterday.

Thursday October 10 Wilson's reply has been received in Berlin to-day. Meantime events are moving swiftly. Rumour says that the Kaiser has abdicated. I think this cannot be true, but we know that his position is not at all secure and that he is now endeavouring to save his dynasty from being turned out of Germany.

Friday October 11 The whole country this morning is moved with horror. Yesterday the cross channel Irish steam boat was torpedoed just outside Kingstown Harbour. One torpedo struck her and whilst she was helpless these hell hounds of Germans fired another at her. Nearly 700 passengers and crew were drownded and yet these fiends come and ask us for Peace. I venture to say that no act since the sinking of the Lusitania has inflamed this country to such a degree as this one has done.

Yesterday we entered Cambrai and the vaunted 'Hindenburg Line' is completely smashed.

Saturday October 12 It is rumoured this afternoon that Germany has climbed down and has agreed to come to Wilson's terms. But up to six o'clock tonight we have not received the Official telegram to confirm this.

Sunday October 13 Yesterday's rumour is confirmed. At 12.30 this morning the official news was published in London and as soon as the office was open at 9 a.m. it was posted up here. What will it mean and what does it mean. Personally I am not glad. I do not think Germany is beaten, and never will be until we carry the war into her own country and give them a taste of what real war is. Her Fleet is intact or nearly so, for since she received such a dressing down at Jutland Bank it has never kept outside her harbours long enough to offer a chance of fighting. It means I believe that Germany is in a bad way and that the more sane of her rulers hope to pull her out of the hole by a sort of compromise for they clearly see that the longer she goes on the worse will the end be for her.

What the consequences will be in that wretched country when they see their defeated army trailing home from France, Belgium, Russia and Turkey no one can say. And no-one can imagine what the future has in store for us. The nation is too grimly in earnest to be fooled with in the way of allowing Germany to escape scot free. She and her rulers were the sole cause of this war, and as such she must pay the penalty. I do not see much desire for revenge, but only that justice shall be done, and that the men however high in position who have caused all this wanton horror bloodshed and destruction of the last four years shall be brought to judgement and punished, Unless this is done, the people of this country will force their leaders to fight until it is done. The possibilities opened up by the chance of a return to Peace are such that we cannot realize them and to-day I think we are all stunned and want time to re-adjust ourselves to the changed conditions.

1918 Monday October 14 A curious world this morning. Some people imagined yesterday that Peace had come and in more than one Church Te Deums were sung. Nothing of the sort and people of saner and cooler judgement could see that the end was not yet. Germany imagined that we should fall on her neck and kiss her and all would be well, and consequently went mad with joy. In this country the news was received with coldness and we could see that Germany was not beaten, and that the proposals were quite capable of being turned very much to our own disadvantage: consequently we await Wilson's answer with intense eagerness.

Meantime what the soldiers think of the proposal is shown by the fact that at dawn this morning English French and Belgians delivered a smashing attack in Flanders and are driving the enemy before them.

The general feeling is that we cannot trust Germany and that she must give guarantees. She has dealt too much in the past with "Scraps of Paper" for us to be taken in again.

Friday October 15 In every position the Hun is giving way and being forced back. In many cases he is leaving a trail of devastation and horror behind him, but he is being driven back into his own country and when he is there then we shall be able to deal with him. Rumours of all kinds are innumerable.

Wednesday October 16 To-day Wilson has spoken to Germany in stern measured words and has addressed her in such language that I am sure has never been used by one country since the days of Napoleon. He tells her that her blackguardism must cease on sea and land, that she and her allies must clear out of every invaded counry (they are being cleared out rapidly whether they will or not) and that she must give guarantees as to her promisess. His words are those of a true Statesman. I regard him to-day as the first Statesman in the world. His reply has met with the wholehearted support of all civilised nations whether they are in the fighting or whether they are neutrals. There is no room for evasion and Germany must now make up her mind. Meantime Americans are steadily coming over at the rate of 300,000 per month. In consequence of this the pressure for men is much reduced here.

Thursday October 17 Every day the enemy gives way. Yesterday they were forced out of Ostend and are rapidly leaving the whole Belgian Coast. Six months ago they were going to capture Calais and Boulogne they said and to invade us here. Further south they to-day have been forced out of Lens and indeed all along the line they are going. If we can believe reports from Rotterdam, Berne and other countries their internal condition is becoming almost unbearable and it is possible that anything may happen. It is persistently rumoured to-day that the Kaiser has abdicated.

Friday October 18 To-day the Belgians are vigorously pursuing the defeated Germans. Do not misunderstand. The Germans are defeated but they are not a broken demoralized army all along their line. In some places where their best men [are] they resist with vigour and Haig is having some bloody work near to Le Cateau. In other sectors they fall back rapidly and their morale is exceedingly low.

No confirmation of the Kaiser's abdication is to hand.

Saturday October 19 French cavalry are reported to-day to be in Bruges and Belgians are closing in upon Zeebrugge. A force of nearly 20,000 Germans is being cooped up near to the Dutch frontier which it is most probable they will cross.

THE DIARY OF JOHN COLEMAN BINDER

Up to a late hour to-night no reply has been made by Germany to Wilson's terms.

There is so much to write about in these days that it is difficult to take notice of all, but Serbia is being rapidly cleared of the enemy. Albania also and Herzogovina is being wrested from the Austrians. In Palestine Allenby is going forward and has occupied Damascus.

1918 Sunday October 20 I will turn to-day for a minute or two to ordinary things at home. The Food Authorities continue to muddle along making confusion ten times worse by their silly methods. This week they have issued a notice saying tht all fat swine should be killed by Christmas as after that date there will be no food for them. Result : pigs 8 weeks old are being sold in local markets @ 2/6 to 4/- each.

After various promises contradictions orders and notices followed by demands they have apparently made up their minds to ration us with jam, syrup etc. Vast quantities of blackberries have [been] gathered by the children of the Elementary Schools in the country and from Oundle and district alone six and a half tons had been sent away up to Friday last to the jam factories. Apples and pears are almost unobtainable and if it had not been for blackberries we should not have had much fruit this Autumn. The children have been paid 3d per pound for gathering them.

On Thursday we had the first close sight of an Air ship. It was a very clear calm day and she came up from the South, very low down, in fact so low that we could see the men in the car. Although it was a calm day and no wind, I noticed she rocked very much. I think they are quite of no use as engines of war. Aeroplanes are much more effective and I look for an enormous increase of them when Peace comes again.

The Government are sending travelling Cinematograph Shows through the country to give the people some idea (in the country places) what the war is like. The van was here last night and gave an exhibition in the Market Place at 7o'clock to a great crowd of people. It lasted about 2 hours and the screen was fixed on to the house next to Bramston House.

Sunday October 26 A week of tremendous interest. A week of terrible battles around Valenciennes and the Scheldt, also in the South where the Americans are attacking. Meantime replies and counter replies have been exchanged between Berlin and Wilson and we see gradually Berlin and the Kaiser being forced backwards. What a sight. The man in the black coat gradually destroying the man in ' Shining Armour' as he delights to call himself. On Tuesday Berlin professed to have accepted all Wilson's demands. On Thursday he replied and stated he would hand on their plea for an Armistice to the other Allies, that is England, France etc., but warned them that such conditions would be imposed that they would make it impossible for Germany to continue the war. These conditions would be framed by the Generals in the Field, and if I am any judge, will be such that Germany will not accept at the present moment. Ultimately she will have to accept them, but unless she is in a much worse condition than we are aware of, she will not do so now. What about her Fleet. It is practically intact and it is generally assumed that she would have to hand it over to the Allies. I do not think for one moment she will do so.

The Belgian coast is quite cleared of the Germans, and already Belgium is beginning to re-organise itself. Austria is visibly going to pieces before our eyes. Day by day her different peoples are proclaiming themselves separate states. Rumour to-day says the Emperor has abdicated, at any rate he has fled from Vienna.

A tremendous battle was opened by Haig on Wednesday and has continued without intermission since. The fighting is just north and south of Valenciennes. This mornings report says that up to last night we had captured 30,000 prisoners and 150 guns. It is estimated that since July Germany has lost a quarter of her Artillery.

At present the Coal business has not caused us much trouble. Up to the present we have been able to do without fires except in the evening. I expect there will be a pinch when the real cold weather comes along.

A telegram to-night announces that Germany has agreed to Wilson's terms and that the Prime Minister Balfour together with naval and military men are leaving for Paris to-night to arrange terms for an armistice.

DAY BY DAY THROUGH THE GREAT WAR

1918 Monday October 27 A great battle has been raging to-day and yesterday on the Italian front. The Italians stiffened by a British and French Army have launched a big attack and so far are making great progress. Probably the Austrians knowing the utterly helpless state of their country at home will not fight with much heart..

Events are moving in Germany. Ludendorff the real organiser of the German Army has resigned. It was he who planned their great advance in March last and now it has resulted in such dire disaster he has had to go.

Great news also from Turkey to-day. She has given in, acknowledged herself beaten and asks for Peace. Thus goes another of Germany's dupes. First Bulgaria, now Turkey and it cannot be many days or perhaps hours before Austria takes the same course.

Tuesday October 28 Austria to-day asks for an Armistice and seeks terms from Italy. Now Germany is alone. How long will she hold out. She publishes very little news to the world but it is clear from reports received from neutral countries that she is fast hastening tremendous events. Abdication rumours have been again revived.

Sunday November 3 Surely this has been one of the greatest if not the greatest week in the whole war. A week of such tremendous events that it is impossible to realize them. One thing can be said with confidence, and that is that the end for which we have longed and prayed is in sight and such an end one could scarcely have dared to hope for. Such an end that seemed last March and April to be utterly impossible. Then Germany was carrying all before her and was telling the world what she was going to do and what her terms of Peace would be. To-day she is beaten and she is aware of it. Deserted by all her allies, she is at her last resource and the end is certain; it may come now or be delayed a few weeks, but it will come; but what an end it is. One can scarcely dare to think about it. The whole of Europe is in the melting pot. Russia in the throes of a revolution compared with which the French Revolution was child's play. Austria collapsed. Her Emperor has abdicated and is a fugitive. The same spirit of revolution is awakening there as in Russia. Count Tisza, one of her chief men and certainly one of the leaders who caused this dreadful war, was on Thursday sought out in his house by three soldiers who shot him dead. The greatest fears are expressed that Germany may follow the same course and that anarchy may gain the upper hand. What a welter, and above and over all hangs the grim spectre of famine. Russia we know is already in its grip and Austria also. Travellers coming from Russia (they can only get out with the greatest difficulty) say that potatoes are a shilling each and milk 10/- per pint. Neutral countries are not in a much better condition. The mind reels when it attempts to gather in these conditions. The future is indeed fraught with enormous possibilities and we can only grope our steps one at a time. It will need the clearest heads and coolest brains to keep civilisation from going under. I look to Wilson to-day as the real leader of the world. A clear level-headed strong man. But what of the men who have brought all this terrible suffering especially the hideous men in Germany. There is a great and growing demand, in this and all civilised countries, that they shall be punished, and there will be deep disappointment if this is not done. If they had observed the ordinary usages of war, we could have forgiven them but they are amongst the most incarnate devils who ever lived upon this earth. I say this deliberately.

Armistice terms with Turkey, published on Thursday, are rigorous but just. She at once demobilises her Army, liberates all our prisoners (we return hers), gives us free access through the Dardanelles to the Baltic Sea [?Black Sea]. We occupy all her forts including Constantinople. What fleet she has is to be turned over to us.

1918 November 4 Monday The Armistice with Austria is concluded and comes into effect at 3 o'clock to-day. So goes another of Germany's supporters. Austria is completely smashed. Since the allied armies commenced their great attack on her a fortnight since, they have captured 300,000 prisoners, over a thousand guns and immense booty. She is broken up as an Empire and the rule of the Hapsburgs ceases. We have no pity for them. They have been one of the curses of Europe, especially of late years, and were one of the instigators of this war.

THE DIARY OF JOHN COLEMAN BINDER

By this armistice she concedes us everything, and if Germany does not give way she will be attacked through Austria. Steps are already being taken to do this.

Having concluded their talkings about Armistice terms with Germany the Prime Minister and his advisers returned to England to-day. Nothing as to their nature is disclosed but Germany is told that if she wishes to know what they are she must apply to Foch in the usual manner - that is with a White Flag.

This morning English, French and Americans launched another huge attack on the enemy from the sea to Verdun and are hammering them without mercy.

November 5 Tuesday Wilson sends a note to Germany to-day telling them if they want to know Armistice Terms Foch will tell them what they are.

We captured 10,000 prisoners yesterday. The French 8,000 and the Americans some 2,000. The enemy dies hard but he is being punished without ceasing and is being driven back day by day.

Wednesday November 6 Germany announces that she has appointed envoys to see Foch and that they will at once leave to cross the lines. Meantime there are ominous rumours of revolution in Germany and the Kaiser is difficult to find.

Thursday November 7 The German Fleet have mutinied and have seized their vessels at Kiel. Soldiers sent to quell the outbreak only joined hands with them. Sensational rumours that Armistice terms have been signed are current in London to-day and have been wired here. I hardly think this is true. The enemy are in rapid retreat and the Allies are following them up. There is only a strip of France about 100 miles long and 15 to 20 wide now in their possession.

Friday November 8 Foch receives the German envoys who came across through Belgium. Excitement is increasing here and all through the world as to the result.

Saturday November 9 Surely a marvellous day and one for which we have waited, fought and prayed for over four years.

The Kaiser has abdicated.

Such is the official telegram circulated between 5 and six this evening. This mornings news disclosed a terrible and appalling state of affairs in Germany. Revolution has spread to Hamburg and all the sea ports and also many places inland. Their new Chancellor Prince Max of Baden has resigned after saying that Germany can fight no longer. And the Socialists in Germany called upon the Kaiser to resign within 24 hours, otherwise there would be further trouble. Evidently he has had to submit. So he goes for the present but I think the world will demand that he be brought to justice and tried together with many of his advisers for their crimes. What a hell he must be living in to-night. He and his cursed system have as nearly as possible brought civilisation to an end, and he must be held directly responsible for the awful and bloody crimes of this war. Belgium to wit.

What will come next? Foch announces the envoys have returned to their lines, and that they must either accept the armistice terms by 11 o'clock on Monday

Bavaria to-day has proclaimed a Republic and her King is gone. Kings are cheap in Europe to-day - we think nothing of hearing that one or two have been hustled off their thrones.

1918 Sunday November 10 As may be imagined this is a day of suspense. A telegram posted this morning says there will [be] news this afternoon.

Meantime you will wonder how we are taking all these momentous happenings. Quite calmly, I can assure you, but with a deep sense of gratitude to God that we seem to be nearing the end of this four years of dreadful bloodshed. It has been a time of endurance and trial for us all, but I think that thanks to God we have borne it like Englishmen.

No news to-day. Only a promise that there will be some tomorrow.

1918.
Monday
Nov 11. At last !!! After four years and three months of the most bloody and awful warfare which has ever occurred in the history of the world. Peace has come again.

Everybody was in a state of suppressed excitement this morning and the continual greeting was "Any news?" About 11-30 a telegram which had been despatched from London at   and received here at   was posted up in Markham's window. It was as follows.

Armistice signed at five o'clock this morning. Fighting ceases on all fronts at eleven. Official.

England and the allied countries have gone almost wild to-day, and great rejoicing is all taking place everywhere.

At Last!!

THE DIARY OF JOHN COLEMAN BINDER

Monday November 11 At last ! ! ! After four years and three months of the most bloody and awful warfare which has ever occurred in the history of the world, Peace has come again.

Everybody was in a state of suppressed excitement this morning and the continual greeting was "Any news?". About 11.30 a telegram which had been dispatched from London at ----and received here at ----- was posted up in Markham's window - it was as follows:

Armistice signed at five o'clock this morning.

Fighting ceases on all fronts at eleven. Official.

England and the allied countries have gone almost wild to-day and great rejoicings are taking place everywhere. Words cannot express the feelings of us all. Everybody seems to feel that a tremendous load has been lifted from them and that they are free to breathe again. No-one who has not lived through these dark days can conceive what it has been like, and I sincerely hope that no generation will go through it again. I think the Commons and Lords quite interpreted the feelings of the people this morning. After they had received the news they immediately adjourned and went over to St Margarets for a service of thanksgiving and I believe this is what we all feel.

But what an end it is. Revolution like a hurricane has swept through Germany and Austria, and there is not a king or reigning monarch left there. They are all gone. I hope that Anarchy may not ensue. The Kaiser is in Holland where he arrived at 7.30 yesterday morning in a motor car. What will become of him.

Already to-day we are beginning to feel the effects of peace. The Church Clock, which has been silent from sunset to sunrise on account of air raids, will strike again during the night, and lighting will be resumed in the streets, although only a few lamps will be lit on account of coal shortage, and we shall not be obliged to darken our windows to-night as we have done for three years every night. These new regulations were issued this afternoon.

1918 Tuesday November 12 The Armistice Terms are published this morning. They are stupendous. Alsace Lorraine to be given up. All prisoners to be at once returned here. We to retain their prisoners. The Germans to at once return to their own country and to retire 6 miles beyohd the Rhine. The Allies will advance up to this, and certain crossings over the River and certain territory the other side. 5,000 Locomotives 130,000 railway waggons, 3000 Guns 2000 aircraft and innumerable war material to be given up.

The enemy to hand over to us a greater part of their Navy including all submarines, and many other conditions, but I have written the principal ones. These show how completely Germany has collapsed. Her soldiers fought well until the last week or so, but the civil population had lost all hope, and this brought the debacle. Food was getting very short and there was no hope of more coming. These facts are clearly broughtout by the appeal of Germany to America and the Allies to find them food. They had come to the end of their tether, and this has been brought about by the British Navy. I have not the slightest hesitation in saying that it is upon our Navy that we built all this superstructure of war, and a firm foundation it has been. So long as those grim grey spectres lay up in the North Sea, we knew that we were safe, and what is more Germany knew it also. Slowly surely but almost imperceptibly and certainly silently she has for the last four years been throttling our enemies. We now know that about ten days since the Germans ordered their Fleet to come out and fight but the sailors mutinied and declined to come. Everything was ready and a tremendous conflict was hourly expected but it did not come off.

At this point the diary ends, and nothing further is written in the book.

Unveiling of the War Memorial, 14th November 1920.

Oundle School Memorial Chapel 1922, in memory
of Old Oundelians who died in the Great War.

THE DIARY OF JOHN COLEMAN BINDER

Names of the men in the Royal Navy and H.M. Army who died in the Great War

Royal Navy
Lieut. A.E.G. Coombs A.B. Seaman J.E.F. Boulter

H.M. Army

Colonel	E.P. Smith	Private	F.E. Garrett
Lt-Col.	G.A. Tryon	"	M.W. Gurton
Major	M.J. Miskin	"	H.B. Hancock
Captain	F.C. Norbury	"	J. Hill
"	H.E. Williamson	"	W. Johnson
Lieut.	R.B. Sanderson	"	G. Lacey
2nd Lt.	H.N. Curtis	"	T.J. Leverett
"	B. Lees	Gunner	R. Lilleker
"	D.W. McMichael	Private	C. Mancktelow
"	P. Munds	"	J. Mears
"	J.H.M. Smith	"	F. Peacock
Sergt.	J.E. Crawley	"	A. Phillipson
"	J. Hunter	"	F. Phillipson
"	B.L. Siddons	"	F.H. Preston
Corpl.	T.L. Cooper	Gunner	J.T. Pridmore
"	B.F. Loakes	Private	F.O. Rollerson
"	A.E. Smith	"	J. Roughton
"	W. Stafford	"	R.B. Seaton
L-Corpl	W. Craythorne	"	J.W. Sexton
"	H. Malsbury	"	W.E. Sharpe
"	H.G.M. Markham	"	C. Sharpe
"	A. Page	"	W. Sharpe
Private	G.E. Afford	"	F. Smith
"	R. Barrett	Gunner	G.E. Smith
"	I. Bell	Private	A.J.S. Smith
"	A.F. Bennett	Gunner	T.E. Smith
Gunner	C.J. Bennett	Private	C. Stretton
Private	T.G. Chaplin	"	P.J. Stretton
"	S.J.T. Cooper	"	S. Swan
"	E. Cottingham	"	S.H. Taylor
"	F.H. Cullop	"	H. Titman
"	P.E. Cullop	"	C.L. Vear
"	T.P. Ellis	"	F. Whistlecroft

DAY BY DAY THROUGH THE GREAT WAR

John Coleman Binder kept this diary for posterity, telling how the Great War affected life in Oundle. Belgian Refugees, recruitment, Zeppelin raids, the use of aeroplanes, paper money, and the news from telegrams and newspapers arriving in the town were all recorded.

He followed the debates in Parliament with interest, and was often critical of Government regulations. He is aware of the anxieties of those whose husbands and sons were reported missing, and the growing list of men killed.

As a Grocer, Baker and Corndealer he was concerned with food shortages, rising prices and rationing. He worried about the frequent sinking of ships and the call-up of farm workers.

He served as a Special Constable, out at night to check that no lights were showing during air raid warnings. He was on the local tribunal deciding on appeals for exemption from military service.

The nine volumes of his diary show hopes and fears rising and falling as the months go by and still the war rages on, until at long last the end comes, and he lays down his pen with great relief and rejoicing.